THE COMPLETE
ENCYCLOPEDIA *of*
DOGS

ESTHER J. J. VERHOEF-VERHALLEN

CHARTWELL
BOOKS, INC.

© 2001 Rebo International b.v., Lisse, The Netherlands

Text: Esther J. J. Verhoef-Verhallen
Photographs: Furry Tails/Esther J. J. Verhoef-Verhallen
Layout: Studio Imago, Amersfoort, The Netherlands
Cover design: Atelje Villa, Ljubljana, Slovenia
Translation: Marion Drolsbach and Rosemary Mitchell-Schuitvoerder
for Bookpros UK
Proofreading: Jarmila Pešková Škraňáková

This edition published in 2005 by
CHARTWELL BOOKS, INC.
A division of BOOK SALES, INC.
114 Northfield Avenue
Edison, New Jersey 08837
USA

ISBN-13: 978 0 7858 1999 8
ISBN-10: 0 7858 1999 1

Printed in Slovenia.

Contents

Foreword

When I began to compile The Jumbo Dog Encyclopedia I was thinking of dog breeders with broad interests as well as people looking for a breed of dog to suit their lifestyle. Regards characteristics I have not only consulted previous publications on breeds, breed standards, the experiences of various owners and breeders and the information available from breed societies, but I have also included my personal experiences of the relevant breeds and the impressions they made on me. It was my foremost intention to represent the breeds most naturally and objectively, in words as well as in pictures. That is why, whenever possible, I took photographs of different breeds, ages, colors and sexes.

Many four-footed photo models had such unique personalities that I will never forget them. It became clear to me that characters are largely associated with breeds, but nevertheless each dog has its own individual character, formed not only by its genes, but most certainly also by its experiences.

The entire project would not have been possible without the kind cooperation of hundreds of owners whose dogs you see in the photographs. I would like to thank all those people who have enabled me to do this work for their enthusiasm, their faith in the outcome and particularly their commitment. I also wish to thank people behind the scenes, such as the inspectors and members of breed societies and dog schools.

Here you see the final result of an intensive period of studying dog breeding. I hope that you, the reader, will find what you hoped to discover in this publication, if not more.

Esther J.J. Verhoef-Verhallen

History and development

Hundreds of dog breeds

The strong ties between man and dog go back thousands of years. With the possible exception of a few African breeds, the dog has evolved from the wolf to the domesticated animal we know today, in a variety of shapes and sizes. The differences between breeds can be so great that it is hard to believe they belong to one and the same family, *Canis familiaris* or the domestic dog. We cannot separate breed development from the cultural and historical history of mankind. Dogs have always served man, and their characteristics and appearance have always been geared up to their function. In our modern society where the dog is predominantly a companion, we care a great deal about the appearance of a pedigree dog. Appearance used to be far less important, although even then dogs with a particular type of coat, color or build could actually cope better with the job they were meant to do. Consequently it is not surprising that dogs doing similar jobs in the same region began to

We encounter dogs throughout the world; this one is in a Bedouin village on the edge of the Sahara.

So different and yet the same species: *Canis familiaris.*

6

Two Am. Staffs with a friendly gaze

The Basenji is
an African breed

look alike. Maybe this justifies the existence of hundreds of breeds spread all over the world with their own unique characteristics.

Various backgrounds

Prior to the discovery of the rifle, men would take so called 'long' dogs with them on their hunts, swift sighthounds, who could capture the prey for their masters. These dogs were well-known and loved in Ancient Egypt. We know that pharaoh Tutankhamen among others owned such a dog, probably a jackal crossbreed, who lived at court and joined the hunt for gazelles. For a very long time sighthounds were popular as hounds dogs, not only in the Middle-East but also in Europe. When the rifle appeared, other breeds emerged with their own unique features which made them very useful to man. By selecting desirable characteristics, gradually breeds evolved that were specialized in pointing game (pointers and setters), breeds that could chase foxes and badgers from their burrows (terriers) and breeds that could drive out game (spaniels) or who could retrieve after they had been shot (retrievers). Hounds, regardless of their qualities, represent the highest number in the current stock of pedigree dogs.

Of course, there is not only a variety of hunting dogs but there are also dogs with other specialist qualities. Best known are the sheepdogs, which can be divided into a category of breeds that guarded their flocks independently against predators and thieves and a category of breeds that assisted the farmer herding and driving cattle. Next we created yard dogs: guard dogs who watched over the farmer, his family, the yard and house. We also know about a smaller category of war dogs: big dogs with a solid, heavy build who were used in Roman days to fight in battles and to perform in shows in the arenas. Much later we began to see dogs with a compact build, particularly in nineteenth century England, but also in Europe and Japan, who were bred to participate in dog fights among other things. One minor group among recognized

Bracco Italianos

Afghan

breeds is the sled dogs; they are solely selected for speed, stamina and strength. They were extremely important in the snow covered Arctic regions before the snow scooter. We should not forget a category known as companion dogs for as long as we can remember. These 'luxury dogs' are portrayed in old paintings, always beside an upper class (South) European lady. Not all these 'luxury' dogs would enjoy a long and happy life on a velvet settee; it is thought that several naked dogs were not taken to bed by the Incas as hot water bottles, but that they were also used as sacrificial animals.

A companion since early times:
the cheerful Bolognese

Today's dogs

The dog has served us well in the past millenniums, and in such varied and sometimes extraordinary ways. In numerous breeds character and physical appearance have been achieved by selective breeding of animals who were best suited for their functions both mentally and physically. Their build, coats, working aptitude and even the color of their coats will tell the expert what kind of work they used to do and the kind of climate they were accustomed to. Their existence is inextricably bound up with our lifestyle through the ages. In our western society many dogs no longer perform their original functions.

A young Bordeaux

The rifle has taken over from the formidable jaws and speed of the hound, fences contain flocks of sheep and cow herds, alarms and police protect our properties and the arrival of snow scooters has replaced the jobs of sled dogs. Only a very small number of working dog breeds still carry out their original function, mainly in countries and regions where the modern way of life has not yet penetrated. And of course a number of breeds that have been 'retrained'; apparently their qualities cannot be rivaled by any of our advanced machinery. Just think of guide dogs, avalanche search dogs, signal guide dogs, drug sniffer dogs and police dogs. In proportion to the total dog

Once kept as a fighting dog, yet Staffordshire Bull Terrier's have been affectionate family pets for almost 100 years

Skye Terrier

population the number of working dogs is relatively small.

Most pedigree dogs have adapted extremely well to being domestic pets. However, many of them have not lost their original working aptitude embedded deeply in their genes; we

German Quail Dog

cannot just eradicate centuries of genes in a couple of decades. A group of dog lovers want to give these dogs a chance to use their qualities. Therefore, we may see greyhounds ready to take off on the racing tracks and the courses, there are organized dog hunts and sheep dogs can show off their skills at sheep dog trials.

Not all breeds have retained their original characteristics and aptitudes. For instance, the savage war and fighter dogs of past times have changed character due to the selective breeding of today, that most of them are now known to be docile and reliable. They have taken on the role of companions and take part in dog shows. Their counterparts who are used for their original functions today are represented by a small number of breeds.

Natural and adopted characteristics

If this encyclopedia is meant to help you make up your mind before buying a pedigree dog, you need to consider that all presented breeds have their own specific characteristics, which might or might not suit your family circumstances and way of life. You might be attracted to the visually delightful appearance of a sled dog. You then need to know that there is a personality attached to that beautiful appearance that cannot be manipulated by training. For instance, a Border Terrier kept as a family dog might disappear down an underground burrow while on a walk in the woods; a Beagle will not be able to resist the temptation of following an interesting scent and an average Golden Retriever, controlled by its genes, loves to run around with something in its mouth. In this encyclopedia we have mentioned the original function appertaining to each breed and we also discuss the individual needs of the breeds and their typical characters.

Bracco Italiano

Grand Basset Griffon Vendéen

External characteristics

Breed standards

Specially trained experts judge appearance and movements of pedigree dogs at dog shows according to the official breed standard. The official breed standard is the same for all countries who are members of the FCI (Fédération Cynologique Internationale). Members of the FCI will find that the breed standard is set by the pedigree society of the country where the pedigree originates from or by the country that has taken this job on itself: the patron country. The Afghan Hound for instance originates from Afghanistan but it is England, its patron country, that issues the breed standard.

Bull-mastiff

English Toy Spaniel or King Charles Spaniel

The standard gives detailed descriptions of what the most beautiful specimen imaginable of a breed should look like. Dog breeders aim to breed dogs that fulfil these requirements or desires to the highest standard. Breed standards are important to you, too, when you intend to breed with your new pet, or if you wish to embark on a show career. However, the amount of detail in the breed standard varies from breed to breed; some allow a variety of interpretations while others discuss all (external) characteristics of the breed in great

Borzois

representation of the original breed standard. Breeders, exhibitors and anyone who is interested and might benefit from a precise, detailed description can request the official breed standard from the appropriate breed society.

depth. Particularly the latter tend to be riddled with specific terminology that will raise many questions if you are not an insider. The intention of this encyclopedia is to provide a shortened and simplified description of various standards, so that people who are unfamiliar or ignorant of the matter will have a good idea. It is not only useful for dog breeders to be acquainted with the desired features of a breed, but it also means that someone who is hoping to select a puppy at a breeder's is better prepared. The descriptions you will find under the heading Features are not an exact

Bergamasco

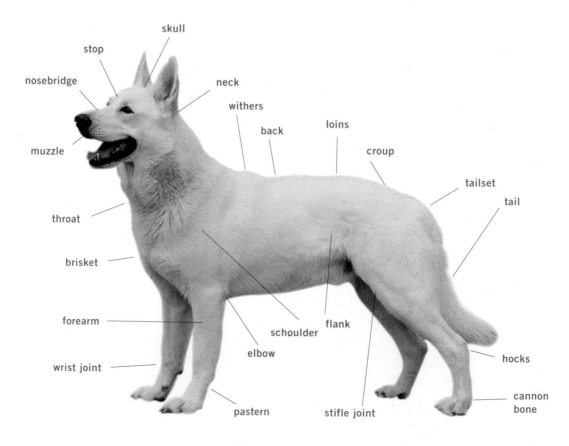

Buying a pedigree dog

Considering that the dog of your choice may be part of your family for more than ten years, will be around every day and consequently will influence your daily activities considerably, you should not take the purchase lightly. If you are not sure of the type of breed you wish to buy, then it might be a good idea to put your wishes down on paper. Which characteristics are you looking for in your new member of the family? And which would you rather avoid? How much time do you have available to exercise your dog and groom it? How important is it that your dog can get on well with other pets, dogs, children and visitors? On the other hand, you should be honest and decide what you can offer the dog yourself. Although we have

Czechoslovakian Wolf Dog engaged in its
favorite pastime of digging.

discussed the characters and social behavior, degrees of exercise required and aptitude to work of all breeds, it is good to know that these descriptions apply to the well socialized, carefully bred, 'average' sample of the breed. Each breed has different family lines, and dogs from different lines could, within reason, differ in some respects, both in external and internal characteristics. If you wish to take your dog out hunting, it is best to contact a breeder who concentrates on blooded breeds. Your chance to purchase a suitable hound will be greater than if you fall for a puppy who only has winners of beauty contests among its parents and ancestors. And vice versa. Although the one does not automatically exclude the other, and there are breeders who specialize in a combination of beauty and working aptitude, it is wise to investigate in advance the breed you are

Beagles like to be out of doors and on the move
and need an active owner.

interested in. Even if features such as working aptitude and such do not appear to be of interest to you, it should not be regarded a waste of time to ask a number of people who are acquainted with the breed to inform you. For instance, the coat structures can vary within the same breed, which affects the amount of grooming required. Their temperaments will vary, too, and of course health is a matter of concern. Nearly every breed has its hereditary problems and it is possible, moreover necessary, to have the breeding animals tested. Do ask for information beforehand so that you will not fall prey to an irresponsible breeder. If possible, contact the breed society that looks after the interests of your preferred breed.

Working dog and family pet: the popular and versatile German Shepherd.

When you join the breed society you will generally receive the members magazine several times a year, which will contain invaluable information. And do visit and talk to a number of breeders and dog lovers. Try to visit various dog shows, club matches or working dog competitions and try to obtain a picture of the various types of characteristics within the breed. Sometimes it will mean that you need to look beyond the borders of your state or country. For instance a breed that hardly occurs in the Netherlands may be quite popular in France, and vice versa. Particularly if you are considering breeding, exhibiting or working, it might be worth your

You can speak to owners and breeders of your chosen breed at shows or club competitions.

Choosing the right puppy for you is not easy; these English Setter pups are all just that little bit different.

Scottish Collie

might be cheaper, the difference in purchase price might be converted into a loss within a matter of months when you receive veterinary bills as your puppy appears to be suffering from a chronic illness. When you have taken the trouble to find out which breed suits you best, please buy a puppy from a reliable breeder; a puppy that has received the care and understanding from its breeder so that it has been given all it needs to grow into a healthy and pretty dog, with features and character typical for its breed.

while to visit dog shows and breeders further afield. Whatever you do, think about it carefully and never buy a dog from these unauthorized dog breeders or dealers, in shops or in markets. These are places where you will not find out much or anything at all about health, appearance or character of parents or ancestors of the puppies and nothing at all about how the young dogs have spent their crucial impressionable age which affects the development of their personality. Even though a puppy

Saarloos Wolfhound

Coton de Tuléar

Using this encyclopedia

Lay-out

For this book we have decided to adopt the categorization used by the FCI (Fédération Cynologique Internationale). This umbrella organization sets the tone in more than eighty countries. The majority of European, Asian and South-American dog breeding countries are members of the FCI. A number of other countries, such as the USA, Canada and Great Britain have their own categorization, while a number of FCI countries have occasionally made exceptions. It is possible that you might not find a breed in the category where you would expect to find it. If you need to know to which category your dog belongs, please contact the society that deals with your breed.

The FCI recognizes nearly 350 breeds and varieties and you will find most of them in this encyclopedia. You will also read descriptions

Icelandic Dog

of a number of breeds that have not been recognized by the FCI. However, they have become so popular that we feel they should be included in this publication.

Australian Shepherd Dog

A stable living environment with positive experiences
is important for character development.

Sloughis

Descriptions of breeds

You will find a technical description of
a particular breed under the heading Features.
Each pedigree will give you a general description
of build, height and if possible weight, type of coat
and length, and color(s) which are recognized for
that particular breed. The breed standard is taken
as a guideline. The heading Temperament explains the characteristics that are typical for the
breed in question. These characteristics are
subdivided into Character and Social Behavior.
You will read about the
general characteristics
such as disposition,
watchfulness and
will-to-please. If you
would like to know if
the breed you have
chosen gets on well

Great Dane

American Cocker
Spaniel

This Borzoi clearly enjoys competing in agility trials

Behavior. The descriptions under temperament are based on the desirable features which are often listed in the breed standard, with additional information given by breeders and owners of this particular breed. And we should not exclude the personal interpretation of the author. Each dog is and will be a unique individual. Characteristics with other dogs, cats and pets, children, visitors and strangers, please turn to the heading Social

Shiba Inu

Bouvier

Dutch Partridge Dog

18

Épagneul Bleu de Picardie

are partly inherited, while the other part is formed by external circumstances which are difficult to define. For instance a dog of a sociable breed, bottle-fed in isolation from other dogs will be socially damaged for life. Impressions and experiences acquired by a dog in its younger or later years, can either reinforce its inherent features or create the opposite and weaken them. Therefore you cannot assume that any Golden Retriever you meet in the street will be a very

Kelpie

Tibetan Mastiff

sociable, friendly, balanced and self-assured dog. If the dog descends from a typical pedigree line of a certain breed, has been raised by the breeder under normal conditions and there has been a good process of socializing and training by its owner, it will certainly exhibit the desired characteristics.

Under the heading General Care you will learn about the grooming requirements required for a particular breed (Care Required), guidelines and hints regards training (Training), the amount and kind of physical exercise this breed will need (Exercise) and finally Uses. The latter will tell you which types of sports or other means of exercise are most suitable for the breed, in terms of its characteristics and build.

Sheepdogs and Cattledogs (except Swiss Cattledogs)

SECTION 1   Sheepdogs

SCHIPPERKE

COUNTRY OF ORIGIN	BELGIUM
ORIGINAL FUNCTION	VERMIN DESTROXER AND FARM WATCHDOG

APPEARANCE

BODY

The Schipperke has a short and stocky body, a broad chest and a fairly raised belly. The back is level but the fur creates an appearance of sloping down towards the croup. The legs have fine bones and small, round feet. In some countries where docking is permissible, the tail is usually docked short.

HEAD

The Schipperke's head might look like that of

A Schipperke puppy

a fox. The eyes are oval shaped and have a lively and alert expression. Its small ears are triangular and erect. Schipperkes have a scissors bite.

SHOULDER HEIGHT

The body of this particular breed is 10–12 in (25–30 cm) high.

WEIGHT

Varies from 6$^{1}/_{2}$–17$^{1}/_{2}$ lb (3–8 kg). Dogs are considerably heavier than bitches.

Schipperke male dog

COAT

A straight, close, very springy, harsh coat. Longer fur round the neck gives it its manes and the hindquarters also have longer fur, known as culottes. Fur on the head, the ears and at the front of its legs is very short.

COLORS

The most common color of this breed is plain black, and it always has a black forenose and dark brown eyes. In non-FCI countries other plain colors are also recognized, although they are fairly uncommon.

TEMPERAMENT

CHARACTER

Dogs of this species are agile, alert, self-confident and lively. They are extremely intelligent and shrewd. They are hardy, tenacious, indefatigable and not squeamish. Their thick and harsh coats mean they can cope well with all kinds of weather.

The Schipperke has a compact build.

They are very adaptable; this dog will feel at home both on a farm and in an apartment. Schipperkes are brave and watchful by nature and will resolutely guard yard, house and grounds with a loud bark when they meet two-legged or four-footed intruders. Schipperkes are considered to be fairly "yard bound', so they do not tend to explore the world beyond your yard or grounds provided they are kept busy. They are devoted to their owners and members of the family. The breed is praised for its unfailing loyalty.

SOCIAL BEHAVIOR

This farm dog usually gets on extremely well with members of the family and pets. The Schipperke needs to be introduced to small pets as a puppy, including cats, because otherwise it will have a tendency to chase them. Once a Schipperke is used to them and knows that its owner does not approve of chasing, it will behave. Most of them are naturally quite tolerant to children. When strangers visit, the Schipperke will initially observe from a distance: they have their likes and dislikes. Most Schipperkes can usually get on well with other dogs, but they will not be bullied.

Schipperke

GENERAL CARE

GROOMING

The coat needs fairly little care. Grooming once a week is usually adequate. During the molting season loose dead hair can be removed from the undercoat with a teasel brush.

TRAINING

As they are extremely intelligent and keen to learn, training this breed should not usually be a problem. However, this expressive little dog is fond of its shrill bark. If you are surrounded by neighbors you will need to spend considerable time training this dog to control its bark.

EXERCISE

The Schipperke is a bundle of dynamite and needs a lot of exercise to be happy. In addition to its daily walk you will need to let this dog run and play off-leash. Most Schipperkes love to retrieve. If you have a spacious yard it will be happy to run around, satisfying most of its desire to let off steam.

USES

This farm dog can be extremely useful on a farm chasing and killing vermin and announcing visitors. As a family dog in an active family this dog will perform well, too. In various types of dog sports like obedience-training, flyball and agility classes the Schipperke will not do badly at all. Many associations will have equipment suitable for smaller breeds of dogs.

Schipperkes

DETAILS

Schipperkes usually grow to a good old age.
The name "Schipperke" can cause some confusion. It is often thought that this breed used to be kept on ships. Although these dogs might be seen on (inland) barges, it is more likely that the name is derived from the Belgian "Scheperke" which means "shepherd dog".

CARDIGAN WELSH CORGI

COUNTRY OF ORIGIN	WALES
ORIGINAL AND CURRENT FUNCTION	CATTLE DROVER

APPEARANCE

BODY

The fox-like expression of the Cardigan Welsh Corgi needs to be obvious. Its body length including tail should be at least $35^{1}/_{2}$ in (90 cm). The chest is fairly wide and its breastbone is clearly visible. The forechest is pronounced and the ribs are well rounded. The tail is set low, close-coupled to the topline. It is quite long, well feathered and nearly touching the ground. The short legs are sturdy and well angulated with round, fairly big feet. The neck is muscular, well developed and changes gradually into sloping shoulders.

HEAD

The skull is quite wide and flat between the ears and narrows towards the eyes. The muzzle's proportion to the skull is 3:5. Its erect ears are com-

Cardigan Welsh Corgi, black brindle

paratively big and far back. The eyes are set apart. The dog appears watchful and sharp-eyed. Cardigan Welsh Corgis have a scissors bite.

SHOULDER HEIGHT

Ideally this should be 12 in (31 cm).

WEIGHT

Dogs vary between $33^{1}/_{2}$–$39^{1}/_{2}$ lb (15–18 kg). Bitches are a bit lighter.

Cardigan Welsh Corgi

COAT

Short or fairly short hair makes a protective weather-resistant coat.

COLOR

All colors are recognized but white should not cover more than 30 % of its body surface. Common colors among Cardigans are brindle, black and white, beige and blue merle. All Cardigans have brown eyes except for blue merles who may have light blue to silver colored eyes, called glass eyes.

TEMPERAMENT

CHARACTER

This breed is highly intelligent. The dogs have a fairly quiet temperament, are devoted to their owners and family and they make excellent watchdogs without barking their heads off. This breed is noted for being hardy and brave and showing great adaptability.

Cardigan Welsh Corgi bitch

SOCIAL BEHAVIOR

Provided this dog is introduced to cats and other pets appropriately there should not be any problems mixing together.

In comparison with other breeds these dogs tend to be rather dominant. They get on well with children, but in return children should respect this dog.

Cardigan Welsh Corgis

TRAINING

The Cardigan is keen to learn and because of its intelligence and natural "will to please" training should not be a problem. They tend to respond well to voice inflection which means you generally do not need to resort to corporal punishment.

EXERCISE

This breed has always produced working dogs and they are used to running about in the open. The weather is not likely to bother them. Take a Cardigan on regular long, varied walks, but do not overdo it during the growing stage. It is best not to allow the dog to climb stairs before it has turned one, or tire itself too much. If a Cardigan does not

GENERAL CARE

GROOMING

The Cardigan Welsh Corgi needs little grooming. A good groom once a week should be adequate. Daily brushing is essential during the molt season. Because of its relatively long back it is advisable to prevent a Cardigan Welsh Corgi from becoming overweight.

Blue merle Cardigan Welsh Corgi

get much exercise it will generally adapt itself to circumstances.

USES

Not only do they make good family dogs but they are not bad at dog sports either. Agility skills and flyball are usually quite popular and Cardigans have been known to work as avalanche search dogs.

Blue merle Cardigan Welsh Corgi

Cardigan Welsh Corgi

PEMBROKE WELSH CORGI

COUNTRY OF ORIGIN	WALES
ORIGINAL AND	
CURRENT FUNCTION	CATTLE DROVER

APPEARANCE

BODY

The Pembroke Welsh Corgi is a low-stationed, sturdy dog with an intelligent expression. Their body

Pembroke Welsh Corgi

length is average and they have a well rounded ribcage, a level topline, a deep wide chest that needs to be quite deep between the forelegs. Pembroke Welsh Corgis might be born with a complete tail, without an (obvious) tail or with a shortened tail. In some countries where it is permitted, the tail is usually docked. The short legs are very strong, heavy boned and preferable as straight as possible. The elbows are close to the body and the feet are oval with strong pads. The neck is fairly long. The head is shaped like that of a fox.

HEAD

The skull is quite wide and flat between the eyes. The stop is moderate. The muzzle's proportion to the skull is 3:5. The muzzle is slightly tapered. The ears are average and are carried erect. An imaginary line from the tip of the nose through the eye should pass entirely or nearly through the tip of the ear. The eyes are round and medium-sized. The dogs have a scissors bite.

SHOULDER HEIGHT

Should be between $9^3/_4$–$12^1/_4$ in (25–31 cm).

Pembroke Welsh Corgi

WEIGHT

Dogs weigh $19^3/_4$–$22^1/_2$ lb (9–10 kg) and bitches $17^1/_2$–$22^1/_2$ lb (8–10 kg).

COAT

Weather-resistant, fairly long and tight.

COLORS

The four different colors or color combinations are red, beige (sable), roe and black and tan. There may be some white on chest, legs and neck. At shows white on the head – for instance a blaze – is permitted but an overabundance of white is not appreciated.

TEMPERAMENT

CHARACTER

This breed is energetic and intelligent. They are devoted to owners and members of the family. Pembrokes are hardy and not perturbed by bad weather. They are quick to notice what goes on around them and will bark as soon as they detect anything unusual. They also make excellent watchdogs but their high level of self-confidence tends to border on recklessness. Most Pembroke Welsh Corgis are happy to stay in their backyards.

SOCIAL BEHAVIOR

It is important to socialize them early with cats and other pets. Usually they get on well with children, but the Pembroke will not allow bullying. They tend to be watchful when they

Pembroke Welsh Corgi male dog

Pembroke Welsh Corgis

meet strangers but they will not be over-suspicious. They can be rather dominant towards their own kind.

GENERAL CARE

GROOMING

The Pembroke's coat requires very little grooming; give it a good brush once a week to remove any dead and loose hair. During the molt season you will need to groom the dog once a day. Mind that you do not overfeed the dog; apart from obesity being unhealthy for any dog it would cause too much pressure on the Pembroke with its low-legged build.

Pembroke Welsh Corgi puppy

TRAINING

Pembrokes are not difficult to train because of their intelligence and alertness, and their willingness to please. They usually respond well to an inflection of the voice.

EXERCISE

This energetic dog needs a chance to burn off its energy. A short walk three times a day will not satisfy. It will, however, love ball games and similar activities. This breed is quite happy to stay in the backyard as they are not inclined to explore beyond their boundaries on their own. When they are off-leash they prefer not to move too far away from their owners.

USES

Pembrokes are sharp and like to work. Combined with their "will to please" it means that agility skills are very suitable for this breed.

Pembroke Welsh Corgi

GOS D'ATURA CATALÀ

COUNTRY OF ORIGIN	SPAIN
ORIGINAL FUNCTION	SHEEPDOG AND WATCHDOG

APPEARANCE

BODY

The Gos d'Atura Català is a muscular dog with an angular build. Its back is level and the croup slopes down a little. Its tail is set low, and hangs down reaching beyond the hocks. The chest is wide and the ribs are well rounded. The sturdy legs are well hocked and parallel to each other. The muscular neck is quite short and strong.

Gos d'Atura Català

HEAD

The dog's skull is slightly longer than its muzzle and has a pronounced occiput. Its long triangular and hairy ears are set high. They are pendent close to its head. This breed may have a scissors as well as a level bite.

SHOULDER HEIGHT

Dogs may vary between $18^{1}/_{2}$–$21^{3}/_{4}$ in (47–55 cm) and bitches between $17^{3}/_{4}$–$20^{3}/_{4}$ in (45–53 cm).

COAT

The Gos d'Atura Català has a long smooth or slightly wavy coat with hairy ears and tail and quite a hairy mustache and eyebrows.

Gos d'Atura

COLORS

They range from brownish to gray. Very small white markings on chest and toes are acceptable, contrary to white toenails. The eyes are hazel.

TEMPERAMENT

CHARACTER

The Gos d'Atura Català is a lively and yet sober working dog, eager to learn, highly intelligent and courageous. They are watchful and maybe a bit reserved towards people they do not know. They are indefatigable workers but for the rest they are quiet and fairly relaxed.

SOCIAL BEHAVIOR

This particular dog gets on extremely well with other pets, provided they have socialized at an early age. Their background as a sheepdog seldom causes problems with cattle and their contact with

Gos d'Atura Català

children is generally superb. They tend to be reserved in their response to strangers; new visitors will be observed from a distance. Dogs can occasionally be dominant towards other dogs.

GENERAL CARE

GROOMING

The Gos d'Atura Català needs to look rough and ready, an image that will be lost if the dog is groomed meticulously. Do, however check its coat regularly with a coarse comb, particularly where its hair tends to become entangled. This dog does not molt evenly; in general its forequarters shed first followed by the hindquarters.

TRAINING

This type of dog likes to learn and does so relatively quickly, but its owner needs to be the boss who is obviously in control. They dislike having to repeat the same exercises, so provide change as well as challenge to keep their attention.

EXERCISE

This sheepdog, sometimes called Catalonian Sheepdog, needs plenty of exercise and likes being outside. Nevertheless the dog will readily adjust to circumstances if it misses a walk. If it is given plenty of exercise it will also feel happy in a city.

Gos d'Atura

Gos d'Atura Català

USES

Various types of dog sports, such as obedience and agility skills and flyball are perfectly suitable. Even training the dog to be an avalanche search dog is possible.

SCHAPENDOES	
COUNTRY OF ORIGIN	THE NETHERLANDS
ORIGINAL FUNCTION	SHEEPDOG

Schapendoes

APPEARANCE

BODY

The Schapendoes is a sheepdog with a regular, proportional build, though a bit longer than tall, with a deep chest and a moderate tuck up. The topline is arched where it reaches the strong muscular loins. The legs have straight and light bones. The feet are quite big and they have a broad oval shape. Its tail is long and hairy. It is carried hanging downward at rest and should never be carried stiff over back.

HEAD

Carried high with a flat skull and a moderate stop. The forenose is slightly shorter than the skull. The small, hanging ears are set fairly high, covered with long hair and they are twitchy. The big eyes are round with an open and honest expression. The Schapendoes has a scissors bite.

SHOULDER HEIGHT

Dogs vary between 17–19$^1/_2$ in (43–50 cm) and bitches between 16–18 in (40–47 cm).

WEIGHT

Approximately 33 lb (15 kg).

Gos d'Atura Català

Schapendoes

COAT

The Schapendoes has a double, long haired coat. The outer layer is long, dry-textured, and wavy, while the inner layer is thick and soft. The coat needs to be at least $2^3/_4$ in (7 cm) long.

COLORS

All are permissible but blue-gray to black is generally the most popular color. The eyes are brown.

TEMPERAMENT

CHARACTER

The Schapendoes is a friendly, attentive and high-spirited dog. They are cunning, eager to learn, but also a little stubborn. They can be courageous when needed and will bark if they sense danger.

SOCIAL BEHAVIOR

This type of animal is sociable by nature. In general they like other dogs, pets and cattle, and of course children. They are loyal to the family, but when the owner is away they do not mind strangers and are neither suspicious nor aloof.

Schapendoes

GENERAL CARE

GROOMING

A Schapendoes is not meant to look highly groomed but it is necessary to groom the coat once a week with a coarse comb. If this is not kept up,

Schapendoes

you will have to cut the tangles out of its coat. Because its hair covers the eyes you may not notice dirt and irritation in the eyes. Please check daily. Cleaning inside the ears needs to be done regularly. An overabundance of hair should be trimmed. Long hairs between the pads of the feet are typical for this breed and should not be cut, however hairs growing underneath the feet tend to pick up little stones, blades of grass, etc. Please cut them.

TRAINING

The Schapendoes is ready and quick to learn, but if you

Schapendoes

Schapendoes

give them a chance, they will play tricks on their owners. The owner therefore, needs to be consistent. Vary skill training with play – particularly at an early stage – so that the dog continues to enjoy it.

EXERCISE

This type of dog is not very demanding as far as physical exercise is concerned, but they do need a chance to let off steam. If they can run about they will be peaceful indoors. They love ball games and retrieving as well as running and playing off-leash in the woods. They are not likely to wander out of sight.

Schapendoes

USES

The Schapendoes will feel happy in a sporty family and be a good companion. It will enjoy dog sports such as flyball, agility skills and obedience classes.

POLSKI OWCZAREK NIZINNY	
COUNTRY OF ORIGIN	POLAND
ORIGINAL FUNCTION	SHEEPDOG FOR HERDING AS WELL AS GUARDING THE FLOCK

APPEARANCE

BODY

The body of the Polski Owczarek Nizinny, Nizinny for short, is slightly longer than tall. The top is level and ends in a short croup which slopes down slightly. This type of dog has a deep chest which should not be too wide and there is a slight tuck up. They have straight legs and oval shaped feet. The tail is either docked in countries where this is permissible or naturally short. The neck is set quite low and is not throaty.

HEAD

Not too big but with a pronounced stop. The muzzle and skull usually have the same length. The nose bridge is straight and the skull is slightly arched. The nose is quite big. Its ears are moderately big and set on high. They are carried hanging against the head. The eyes are oval and have a lively expression. The Nizinny has a scissors or level bite.

Polski Owczarek Nizinny

SHOULDER HEIGHT

Dogs tend to be $17^3/_4$–$19^3/_4$ in (45–50 cm) high and bitches are $16^1/_2$–$18^1/_2$ in (42–47 cm).

WEIGHT

Dogs are 44 lb (20 kg) and bitches around $39^3/_4$ lb (18 kg).

COAT

This breed features rough, long and coarse hairs, with a thick and soft underlayer.

COLORS

All are permissible, but white with gray or black and plain gray are most common. The nails and preferably the nose as well should be dark.

TEMPERAMENT

CHARACTER

The Polski Owczarek Nizinny is generally an obedient dog. They are alert to what is happening around them and make excellent watchdogs. Although this breed is known to be lively a Nizinny will usually be peaceful indoors. They are affectionate to their owners and extremely loyal, but they can also demonstrate a hint of independence; they are not submissive. They also have a good memory and their intelligence is above average.

Polski Owczarek Nizinny

SOCIAL BEHAVIOR

This dog will get on well with children provided the children are fair-minded and do not treat the dog as a toy. Sociability between dogs and other animals is generally good. If they meet strangers they will stand back a while. They are not everybody's friends; their owners come first.

red by hair. Check the eyes regularly for both dirt and irritation. Also clean inside the ear frequently, and do not forget the hairs between the pads of the feet.

TRAINING

Training this breed is not difficult. They are intelligent, like to work and learn quickly on the job. Even so their training needs to be extremely varied, as this dog particularly dislikes repetition.

Polski Owczarek Nizinny's are also known simply as a Nizinny or Pon.

EXERCISE

Originally the Polski Owczarek Nizinny was a working dog, bred for herding and guarding cattle on the great plains of Poland. It still is every inch a sheepdog, not made for an uneventful life. You will need to stimulate their minds with a variety of impressions. They would prefer to be in action. They will not shy away from ball games and love running and romping off-leash.

USES

This breed is ideally suitable for active, varied types of dog sports. They love agility skills and flyball and they will perform well in competitions.

GENERAL CARE

GROOMING

The coat deserves a good brush once a week and should then be combed to prevent tangles. The eyes are always cove-

Polski Owczarek
Nizinny

PYRENEAN SHEEPDOG

COUNTRY OF ORIGIN	FRANCE
ORIGINAL FUNCTION	ALL-ROUND SHEEPDOG

APPEARANCE

BODY

The Pyrenean Sheepdog has a fairly long back with definite withers, slightly rounded loins and a short, sloping croup. The chest is fairly shallow. The tail set low can be long and hooked, naturally short or docked (in countries where this is permissible). The legs are straight, although the hocks of the hind legs are slightly cow-hocked. Dew claws may occur on the hind legs; the shape of the feet tends to be oval. The neck is long and muscular.

HEAD

The skull does not have a visible stop. The muzzle is straight and fairly short. Its fairly short ears are set high. If they have not been docked they hang downward. Pyrenean sheepdogs have a scissors bite.

SHOULDER HEIGHT

For bitches this may be around 15–18 in (38–46 cm) and for dogs $15^3/_4$–$31^1/_2$ in (40–80 cm). Differences of $^3/_4$ in (2 cm) more or less are accepted in outstanding pedigree dogs.

Three different colored Pyrenean Sheepdogs

COAT

The coat of Pyrenean Sheepdogs is either luxuriously long or half long and can be smooth or a little wavy. On its hindquarters the hair tends to be longer and fuller. Most dogs of this breed have eyebrows, a beard and a mustache. There are also Pyrenean Sheepdogs Dogs with a smooth haired muzzle.

Pyrenean Sheepdog

This variety is not very common and is known as face rase, and is usually rather long-legged.

COLORS

Vary from red in various shades, with or without black hairs in the coat to almost black, and gray patches (blue merle/harlequin), with or without white markings. The dogs have black eyelids and expressive, orange colored eyes. Black and white dogs as well as harlequin dogs may have (partly) blue eyes. The nose is always black.

TEMPERAMENT

CHARACTER

It is easy to recognize this breed by its hardy, yet restrained nature, its will-to-please and above all intelligence and inventiveness. Pyrenean Sheepdogs are not at all squeamish. They are lively, agile and active. A Pyrenean Sheepdog is alert to what is happening around it and makes an excellent watchdog. Its sense of smell is very keen.

SOCIAL BEHAVIOR

Pyrenean Sheepdogs get on well with all members

of the family, but they tend to become a one-person-dog. They like children provided the kids respect the dog. A dog that has been socialized well with other pets will reward you by being exemplary. Some dogs may appear to be a little domineering regards other dogs, particularly concerning members of the same breed. Towards strangers Pyrenean Sheepdogs tend to be rather reserved.

Pyrenean Sheepdog

GENERAL CARE

GROOMING

Pyrenean Sheepdog

The Pyrenean Sheepdog needs relatively little grooming. In appearance it needs to be authentic and rugged. Its coat is such that a quarter of an hour of grooming and combing a week should be ample. If necessary pluck a surplus of hair out of the ear passage by hand. The beard will need to be washed from time to time, or cleaned otherwise.

TRAINING

This breed needs a firm hand and consistent training, although it should not be too severe. They are intelligent, will understand quickly and they are generally keen to please their owners. Their level of intelligence requires a great deal of variety during their training. Nothing would discourage this dog more than monotonous training.

EXERCISE

This dog is not suitable for people who cannot be bothered. A Pyrenean Sheepdog that has to stay in its basket all day and is only taken for a walk round the block three times daily could become quite difficult to manage. Allow your dog to let of steam each day by playing, running off-leash, by means of sports or working. This breed comes into its own in a sports-minded family.

USES

Pyrenean Sheepdogs are extremely well suited working as rescue dogs. this breed scores highly in sports such as flyball and agility-skills.

Pyrenean Sheepdog

Pyrenean Sheepdog

Australian Shepherd

APPEARANCE

BODY

The Australian Shepherd's body is slightly longer than tall. It has a level topline and the croup slopes a little downward. The tail can be naturally short or docked in countries where this is permissible. The chest is deep and it has a slight tuck up. The sturdy legs are straight and well angulated. Its compact feet are oval. The strong and muscular neck is slightly rounded.

Blue merle male Australian Shepherd

HEAD

It is strong and has a flat or slightly rounded skull, almost as long as its muzzle. The Australian Shepherd has a clear, but not a very pronounced stop. The ears are triangular and medium-sized. They are set high and are carried hanging down. It has clear almond-shaped and rather slanting eyes. Australian Shepherds have a scissors or level bite.

SHOULDER HEIGHT

The dogs range from $19^3/_4$–$22^3/_4$ in (50–58 cm) and bitches $17^3/_4$–$20^3/_4$ in (45–53 cm).

COAT

This breed has a weather-resistant semi-long coat. The fur can be straight or slightly wavy. The undercoat is dense and the thickness depends on climate and season. Typically it has a ruff that shows up well in dogs.

COLORS

Sometimes the Australian Shepherds are called Aussies and their colorings can be blue merle, red merle, plain black or brown (red) with or without white and tan markings. White coloring should not run beyond the withers. The eyes may be brown, amber or blue and combinations of these colors could be possible, too. (Partly) blue eyes are most prevalent in merle colored dogs.

TEMPERAMENT

CHARACTER

Australian Shepherds are extremely intelligent, shrewd dogs who are keen to learn. They are watchful and alert, but tend to bark only when there is danger. They are very loyal and attached to owners and families. At work these active dogs are hardy and inexhaustible.

Blue merle Australian Shepherd

Blue merle Australian Shepherd

TRAINING

The Australian Shepherd is easy to train. It learns quickly and eagerly, but definitely requires variety and lots of activity. If an Australian Shepherd is never asked to do something for its owner, it will look for things to do. Very often these are less desirable activities.

EXERCISE

If condemned to three obligatory outings a day, the Australian Shepherd may behave very tediously in the home. It is an energetic dog who needs something to do like a short but intensive quarter of an hour where it has to use both mind and body. Perhaps the best home for it is with sporty people, who like spending time doing things with their dogs.

Three-color Australian Shepherd

USES

This versatile breed can apply itself to many types of dog sports and is well liked at many kinds of games. Flyball, agility skills training, but also obedience competitions are ideally suited for this type of dog.

SOCIAL BEHAVIOR

This dog is naturally sociable and gets on well with both dogs and pets. It will generally like children, although it is important to socialize them while young. They can be a bit shy with strangers; good socialization will prevent this characteristic from becoming exaggerated. Whatever the case, its own family will come first. It is not a dog that gets on well with everyone.

Brown Australian Shepherd

GENERAL CARE

GROOMING

Weekly grooming is generally adequate to keep the coat in good trim. During molt the undercoat sheds heavily and the fur needs to be groomed daily. It is preferable to use a coarse metal comb.

DETAILS

The name of the breed implies it originates from Australia, but the breed has been developed in the USA.

Blue merle Australian
Shepherd puppy

AUSTRALIAN KELPIE

COUNTRY OF ORIGIN	**AUSTRALIA**
ORIGINAL AND	
CURRENT FUNCTION	**SHEEPDOG**

APPEARANCE

BODY

The Australian Kelpie has an angular body with a level topline and strong loins. The groin is low and slopes downward slightly. The tail is set low and the end curves upward. It is always carried below the topline. The chest is deep, but not wide. The legs are well angulated with round and closed feet. The neck is moderately long and slightly arched with a tight and close fitting skin.

Australian Kelpie

HEAD

It should resemble the head of a fox. The skull is slightly rounded and slopes downward to a definite stop. The back of the nose bridge is straight. The muzzle is a little shorter than the skull. The ears set on low are medium-sized. They are wide at the bottom and end in a point. Their edges tend to curve inwards. The eyes are almond-shaped and have a lively expression. Kelpies have a scissors bite.

Australian Kelpie

SHOULDER HEIGHT

Dogs range from 18–20 in (46–51 cm) and bitches from 17–19 in (43–48 cm).

COAT

Kelpies have a double and weather-resistant coat. The top layer is short and harsh and the under-layer is dense. Fur on stomach, trousers, tail and collar is longer.

COLORS

Accepted colorings are black, chocolate-brown, red, black and tan, red and tan, fawn and smoky blue.

TEMPERAMENT

CHARACTER

This breed, currently uncommon, is agile and hard working. Kelpies are extremely intelligent and shrewd. They are affectionate and loyal to

Australian Kelpie

The Australian Kelpie is extraordinarily intelligent.

important, however, that you give the dog a job to do because any Kelpie that is never asked to do a job for its owner, will get terribly bored and might get into mischief.

EXERCISE

Kelpies need lots of it to be happy. If you have a good rapport with your dog and it is kept busy, you need not fear that it will go off on its own or wander too far from you during a walk off-leash in the woods.

USES

Originally this breed typically herded sheep. A dog needs a lot of stamina to keep this up and

Australian Kelpie

should be agile. Apart from herding sheep, which still is a daily occupation for many of them, this breed is ideally suited for sports such as agility skills and flyball. This dog is not likely to let you down, from a recreational as well as from a competitive point of view.

their owners and their families and very obedient. An average Kelpie is stable and well balanced. They are alert to what is happening around them and will bark if they sense danger.

SOCIAL BEHAVIOR

Australian Kelpies mix well with other dogs. Once socialized they will get on with cats and other pets. Their attitude towards children is good, too. They are rather shy to strangers.

GENERAL CARE

GROOMING

Australian Kelpies need relatively little grooming. The coat should be combed through from time to time. During the molt a sheepdog's rake might be useful. Keep claws short.

TRAINING

Its highly praised intelligence and amazing will-to-please makes this dog fairly easy to train. It is

Kelpies ears are pointed.

PUMI

COUNTRY OF ORIGIN	HUNGARY
ORIGINAL FUNCTION	SHEPHERD DOG, WATCHDOG AND VERMIN DESTROYER

Pumi male

APPEARANCE

BODY

A Pumi is a medium-sized, angular dog. Its withers stand out and its topline slopes downward. The belly slopes upward. The tail is set on high and is carried in a curl. If the dog is born with a blunt tail, it is acceptable. In countries where this is permissible a docked tail will also be allowed. The neck has an average length and is set on high.

HEAD

Fairly elongated with a straight nose bridge and a very faint stop. The medium-sized ears are set high on the head. They are erect and the tips turn over. The eyes slant a little. Pumis have a scissors bite.

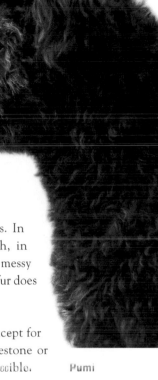

SHOULDER HEIGHT

Ranges from $13^3/_4$–$17^1/_4$ in (35–44 cm).

COAT

Its hair is semi-long and grows in wisps. In some parts the coat is short and rough, in other parts long and tangled. Its rather messy appearance is typical for this breed. The fur does not felt.

COLORS

Pumis may have all kinds of colorings except for patchy coats. Mostly the colors are limestone or gray. Black, white and reddish are also possible. The eyes are dark brown.

Pumi

TEMPERAMENT

CHARACTER

This type of breed produces very active dogs that are observant and high-spirited. During their work they are indefatigable. Pumis are very intelligent and quite capable of learning new commands within a very short time. They do not spare themselves, they are courageous (sometimes over-courageous) and they are keen watchdogs. They like barking.

SOCIAL BEHAVIOR

Pumis do not like everyone. They tend to attach themselves to one person and are shy and wary of strangers. In the company of other dogs they may show dominant tendencies. Potentially they get

Pumi

Pumis are alert to what happens in their territory

on excellently with (small) live-stock, although it is wise to socialize them. They are always ready to chase rodents, rabbits and cats; another reason to help a puppy get used to these animals. If older children respect them, Pumis are good dogs to live with.

GENERAL CARE

GROOMING

Its coat will need grooming from time to time. It is best to hand-pluck excessive hair from the ear passage. Usually the Pumi needs to be clipped and groomed for a show, but not excessively.

TRAINING

Pumis are not difficult to train. This breed is intelligent enough to understand what you want it to do and eager to learn. City dwellers will need to pay extra attention to curb (unnecessary) barking.

EXERCISE

This agile daredevil needs lots of physical exercise to be happy and is therefore not suitable for people who cannot be bothered. In addition to its regular daily strolls you will frequently need to take your dog out with you to give it a chance to romp off-leash. It does not tend to roam.

USES

Pumis are meant for life outdoors. They function best on a farm where they can take on all kinds of jobs as a matter of course. Guarding the yard, keeping (small) livestock together and destroying vermin are jobs you can undoubtedly trust a Pumi to do. There is no reason why you should not keep a Pumi in a built-up area provided you can offer them enough exercise and activity. Agility skills are a sport in which the Pumi can excel and a well-trained Pumi will not let you down at obedience competitions.

Pumi bitch

MUDI

COUNTRY OF ORIGIN	HUNGARY
ORIGINAL FUNCTION	SHEEP HERDERS, HOUND (PARTICULARLY BIG GAME) AND GUARD DOG

APPEARANCE

BODY

The Mudi is a medium-sized dog, with pronounced withers and a straight short back. The groin is moderately wide, slopes slightly and is fairly short. Its ribcage is deep and oval-shaped. The forechest is pronounced. Mudis have straight and well-angulated legs with round and closed feet.

Mudi

HEAD

Long with a slightly rounded skull. Stop and eyebrows are moderate. The nose bridge is straight and the lips are tight and close fitting. The ears are pointed. They are set on high and carried erect. The eyes are oval-shaped and slanting. Mudis have a scissors bite.

SHOULDER HEIGHT

Varies from $13^3/_4$–$18^1/_2$ in (35–47 cm).

COAT

Dense, curly or wavy, with crowns and tufts. Varying in length; its hair is short on the head and at the front of the legs, but longer on the rest of the body.

COLORS

Plain black is most popular among Mudis. Apart from that there are also white, and white and black patchy dogs. The eyes are dark brown and the forenose is always black.

TEMPERAMENT

CHARACTER

Mudis are lively and intelligent dogs, eager to learn. There is no harm in their rather independent nature. They are very observant and watchful, and will defend their owners, families and properties with great conviction and courage. Their great sense of responsibility tends to cause these dogs to bark more than necessary. They have a tendency to attach themselves to one person in the family.

SOCIAL BEHAVIOR

Usually Mudis get on well with other dogs and pets. They are fine with children. Although they instinctively want to guard home and family, they are not over-suspicious towards strangers. Friends of the family are usually greeted warmly.

Mudi

Mudi

Mudi

GENERAL CARE

GROOMING

Its coat does not require a lot of grooming. A regular brush or comb will be quite adequate to keep the coat in good trim. Keep its claws short.

TRAINING

Because these dogs are keen to learn, attached to their owners and highly intelligent, training should not be a problem. Some perseverance might be required, as Mudis can be self-willed. It is best to mix exercises with play, which will keep the dog happy, so it will enjoy its learning, instead of being stubborn. Teaching it not to bark too much is something you need to focus on.

EXERCISE

This dog has ample energy to keep it running and occupied for hours, but it will adjust without a problem if it is given less exercise. Ball games as well as romping off-leash outdoors are favorite pastimes.

USES

The Mudi will turn out to be an excellent watchdog and loyal companion who will not perform badly at all in recreational agility skills.

PULI

COUNTRY OF ORIGIN	HUNGARY
ORIGINAL FUNCTION	SHEEP HERDER

APPEARANCE

BODY

The Puli is a medium-sized dog with an angular built. The transition of the moderately long and muscular neck, into the topline is smooth. The body is of medium-length, the ribs are well arched and the tuck up slopes upward a little. The legs are straight and well angulated. The tail is carried curled over the topline which creates the appearance of the topline sloping upward above the groin.

HEAD

The head is small and fine and appears round when facing it. The muzzle is shorter than the skull and the nose bridge is always straight. The stop is clearly visible. The broad and (rounded) V-shaped ears are set on moderately high. The ears are carried pendulous. Round eyes with an intelligent and lively expression lie below its bushy eyebrows.

SHOULDER HEIGHT

Dogs have an average height of 16–17$\frac{1}{4}$ in (40–44 cm); bitches 14$\frac{1}{2}$–16$\frac{1}{4}$ in (37–41 cm). A deviation of 1$\frac{1}{2}$ in (3 cm) up or down is possible.

WEIGHT

For dogs this will be between 27$\frac{1}{2}$–32 lb (13–15 kg) and for bitches up to 27$\frac{1}{2}$ lb (13 kg).

COAT

The Puli's typical coat is its trademark. A fully-

Black male Puli

to defend their folks and they are very faithful to the family they belong to. Nevertheless they always remain slightly independent by nature. They like to be outside no matter the weather. When they meet strangers they will first tend to keep their distance. They do not take to everybody.

SOCIAL BEHAVIOR

Pulis tend to get on well with other dogs and their association with other pets will rarely cause problems. Pulis and children generally make good combinations. They tend to develop into a one-person-dog in as much

Puli with *maszkos fako* color

grown dog is abundantly covered in long cords of felted hair. The cords on head and legs are approx. $1^1/_4$–$2^1/_2$ in (3–6 cm) long. Elsewhere the length can be $3^1/_4$–7 in (8–18 cm). It may take a number of years before the corded coat has reached full maturity. Apart from this prevalent and desirable fur there are also other types of coats, such as felted plates. Such plates are not always appreciated at shows.

COLORS

Most Pulis are plain black, but we also see white and off-white Pulis, and other colorings. A Puli should not be multicolored or have a chocolate coloring. The maszkos fako, a dog with one coloring and a dark mask, ears and tail, is quite rare. Some white hairs on the toes are allowed in all colors, including a white mark on the chest, which should not exceed 2 in (5 cm). The forenose is black and the skin – also in white dogs – has a very dark pigmentation. The eyes are coffee-colored.

TEMPERAMENT

CHARACTER

Pulis are intelligent, lively dogs full of character. They are excellent watchdogs that do not hesitate

Puli with the rare *maszkos fako* color

that one member of the family in particular can bank on their attention and affection.

GENERAL CARE

GROOMING

Pulis are born with short frizzy hair that begins to felt when they turn one. The soft underlayer will get entangled in the harsher and longer topcoat, which will develop into a corded coat in time. Large pieces of felted hair should be torn into equal strands by hand. The amount of hair lost by a fully-grown Puli is negligible and once the dog

White male Puli

has turned one it need no longer be groomed or combed. This type of coat has a disadvantage because twigs, leaves, sand, etc. will easily become entangled. You should only give this type of dog a wash if it is really necessary and only on a summer's day. It might take a number of days before the thick coat has dried completely. Occasionally it might be necessary to wash the fur round the mouth more frequently, which also applies to the hairs round the groin and under the dog. The corded coat of the Puli will not be fully grown before the age of approx. three, but it may then take another year or so before all the strands have reached equal length. Do check the ear passages and eyes from time to time whenever necessary.

TRAINING

A Puli has enough intelligence to understand your commands quite quickly, but it depends on your approach during the training sessions whether it will actually obey you. If you continue to give your dog the same commands you will meet with its independent and sometimes stubborn nature. It would be better to vary its activities with romping and ball games so that the dog will continue to enjoy its training. Any owner, who responds well to this dog and emphasizes rewarding good behavior, could teach the dog virtually anything in a fairly short period of time. Pulis, particularly dogs, might be rather dominant. Training and the way in which you manage your dog should be very consistent, but above all loving. As they are naturally shy it is advisable to get your puppy acquainted with as many people as possible; to some extent you might be able to prevent their mistrust of strangers becoming extreme.

EXERCISE

Pulis need an average amount of exercise but will adapt to circumstances when their walks are shorter than usual. You will do them an injustice if you condemn them to a boring life. A Puli comes into its own when it can romp and play. Partly because of its typical coat it is a wonderful scene to watch. This breed loves ball games and they usually retrieve.

USES

Together with the right kind of owner a Puli can score highly in types of sports such as agility skills and flyball. These active and varied sports are well suited.

Young male Bergamasco

BERGAMASCO

COUNTRY OF ORIGIN	ITALY
ORIGINAL AND	WORKING DOG WITH
CURRENT JOB	THE HERD (DROVER)

APPEARANCE

BODY

The Bergamasco has a square build, which means that the length of its body is equal to its shoulder height. Its broad chest reaches as far as the elbows. The ribcage is also wide and well arched and the dog has a slightly raised tuck-up. Bergamascos have a straight, wide back and withers protruding above the topline. Its groin slopes slightly and is wide and strong. The tail is set low, broad at the root and tapers towards the end. It reaches down to the hocks. When at rest it will be pendulous, with only the top third bent upward. While moving the tail may be carried gaily.

Bergamasco

The shoulders are strong and solid and the legs are sturdy, straight and parallel. The metatarsals of its forelegs appear to slant forward when observed from the side. The feet are oval (hare feet) with firmly closed and curved toes, with hairs between them. The strong, dry neck is arched at the onset of the neck. The throat and neck, measured from the shoulder to the onset of the neck, ought to be shorter than the length of the head.

HEAD

Fairly long, wide and square. The skull between the ears is arched slightly and the forehead is wide and round. The median groove is well formed, including eyebrows and the occipital peak. Bergamascos have a pronounced stop. Muzzle and skull are equally long and the nose bridge is straight. The muzzle narrows slightly toward the nose, but it is blunt, not sharp. The lips are thin and fit closely. The thin, soft ears are up to $4\frac{1}{4}$–5 in (11–13 cm) long. They are triangular, carried pendulous and set above the line of the skull. The large eyes are oval – almost round – and they are low set in the skull. They should not be too deep or protruding. Bergamascos have a complete and strong scissors bite.

SHOULDER HEIGHT

The dogs are up to $23\frac{1}{2}$ in (60 cm) and bitches $22\frac{1}{2}$ in (56 cm) high. The breed standard permits both sexes to be $\frac{3}{4}$ in (2 cm) shorter.

Bergamasco

WEIGHT

Dogs weigh 70¹/₂–83¹/₂ lb (32–38 kg) and bitches 57–70¹/₂ lb (26–32 kg).

COAT

The Bergamasco has a long and abundant coat. It feels harsh like goat hair on the front part of the body. On the rest of the body and the limbs hair tends to hang in cords (felting). The underlayer is greasy, short and dense. Softer hair on head and shoulders does not felt.

COLORS

Their coloring tends to be plain gray in a number of shades, plain black and speckled gray in shades from very light gray to black, possibly with grayish-yellow or light fawn tints. White markings are acceptable, provided they do not represent more than twenty percent of the area of the coat.

TEMPERAMENT

CHARACTER

Bergamascos are intelligent, balanced, friendly, fairly quiet and self-confident dogs. In spite of the fact that they are rather attached to members of

Young Bergamasco bitch

the family and also very loyal, they do not appear independent or aggressive in their behavior. They are capable of judging situations themselves and acting accordingly. These dogs full of character are very watchful and brave, but they are not great barkers. They are not bothered by adverse weather conditions.

SOCIAL BEHAVIOR

Provided this dog is socialized well at an early age it will not give you any problems mixing with other pets when older. They usually get on well with children. Your dog will however always protect your ("its") children if they are teased by other children, so please bear this in mind. The Bergamasco is an exceptional watchdog, which means burglars will

Bergamasco

certainly have an unpleasant surprise if they visit your house. Bergamascos are a bit shy toward strangers, but when they turn out to be invited guests, they are quite friendly. In general they are tolerant toward other dogs.

GENERAL CARE

GROOMING

A Bergamasco should be combed and groomed until it turns one. The coat will then tend to felt. To avoid larger pieces of felting, broad felt plates should be torn by hand into strands of approximately 1¹/₄ in (3 cm). The hair on the head should be combed regularly. The dog may be washed, but is best to do so in the summer. It may take rather a long time for the coat to dry.

TRAINING

Bergamascos are not difficult to train, provided these dogs do not need to observe commands, which they consider unnecessary. It is best to socialize the puppies well and to remain clear and consistent toward the dog.

EXERCISE

Bergamascos need quite a bit of exercise. Plenty of walks should be adequate and a well-fenced yard will give a Bergamasco opportunity to take care of its own needs. Actually this dog is hardy and with its weather-resistant coat it could be kept outside, provided it gets enough attention from owner and family members. The breed is generally not well suited for life in an apartment or in a busy city.

USES

Today the Bergamasco is still used as a cattle driver. In other countries we rarely see this breed. These dogs are very willing to work which offers good prospects for the owner interested in participating in dog sports.

KOMONDOR

COUNTRY OF ORIGIN	HUNGARY
ORIGINAL FUNCTION	GUARDS HERD AND YARD

APPEARANCE

BODY

The Komondors have a square build, but can be slightly longer than tall. The withers are quite long and clearly visible, the back is short and the loins are of medium length. Its slightly sloping and wide groin is also of medium length. The entire topline is strong and muscular. The tail is set low and carried pendulously, with the end bending upwards. When the dog is walking along or paying attention the tail is carried at the level of the topline. Its barrel chest is moderately deep and

It's unusual "corded" coat protects a Komondor against weather

long and the wide forechest is very muscular. The shoulders are rather steep, but not loose. Its straight legs have solid bones. The thighs are long.

Komondors have big and fairly thickset feet and the back feet are often a bit longer than the forefeet. The dry, moderately long to short neck is often carried in line with the top level when at rest.

HEAD

It is wide but nevertheless in proportion to the body. The arched skull is a bit longer than the muzzle. The stop is moderate. The forehead is arched and the eyebrows are bushy. The nose bridge is straight. Its very wide upper and lower jaws are of medium length and quite muscular. The ears are set at the top of the skull and are carried hanging. The eyes are set straight in the head and the rims fit closely. Komondors have a scissors bite.

SHOULDER HEIGHT

For dogs the minimum standard is $27\frac{1}{2}$ in (70 cm) and for bitches $25\frac{1}{2}$ in (65 cm). It is generally preferable to see heights much taller than this and therefore there is no maximum height.

WEIGHT

Depending on their size, gender and body build Komondors weigh approx. $88–132\frac{1}{2}$ lb (40–60 kg).

COAT

Usually this is the most important distinguishing feature of this breed. Its coat consists of a very long, harsh topcoat and fine woolly hair which tends to felt. The felt-like strands tend to become

Komondor

South Russian Ovtcharka

SOUTH RUSSIAN OVTCHARKA

COUNTRY OF ORIGIN	THE FORMER USSR (UKRAINE)
ORIGINAL AND TODAY'S FUNCTION	LONE SHEEPDOG

APPEARANCE

BODY

The Russian Ovtcharka has a strong build and is a muscular dog with moderately heavy bones. The chest is deep and fairly wide and the belly has a slight tuck-up. Its back is strong and level, with short, broad and rounded loins. The legs are straight and well angulated. The feet are oval shaped. The tail reaches down to the hocks and is carried arched, below the topline. The high-set neck is free from dewlap.

HEAD

This "South-Russian" has an elongated head with a wide forehead and an obvious occiput and cheekbones. The stop is barely visible. The triangular ears are quite small and carried pendent. The eyes are oval shaped and slightly oblique. It has a large nose and a scissors bite.

SHOULDER HEIGHT

The dogs are up to $25^1/_2$ in (65cm) and the bitches are at least 24 in (62cm) high. There is no upper limit.

COAT

The Ovtcharka has a weather-resistant long coat ranging from $4–7^3/_4$ in (10–20cm). It is coarse and tangled, and has a dense undercoat.

COLORS

White or gray/cream in various shades of white with gray plates. The eyes must be dark and the nose should preferably be black.

TEMPERAMENT

CHARACTER

Ovtcharkas are full of character, sober and domineering. They are sensible, tough on themselves, quite watchful and brave. They are also intelligent and independent. They do not need to be told what to do; they assess the situation and do what they think is right. Generally they appear to be calm and self-possessed in line with their character, but they can respond like lightning if they need to. Their temperament is balanced and they do not get agitated. They do not bark much. These dogs like

South Russian Ovtcharka

being outdoors in any kind of weather. They like to stay on their own territory and they are faithful to their handlers. The average "Russian" finds it difficult to get used to a new owner and different surroundings.

SOCIAL BEHAVIOR

South Russian Ovtcharka

This dog naturally gets on well with children. When it grows up among other dogs and pets they will be protected as "part of the family." If an Ovtcharka is well socialized there should not be any problems with cats. They tend to wait and observe when you have visitors and they will certainly not allow unwelcome visitors to step on your premises. Acquaintances, who visit the family regularly, will be accepted as "part of the family."

GENERAL CARE

GROOMING

This breed does not need a lot of grooming. Although sand and dirt tend to stick to their fur, it is easy to brush it out. Thorough grooming once a week will usually take care of the coat. The beard needs brushing regularly and sometimes a wash. Hairs around and between the pads should be checked regularly in case bits get caught in them.

TRAINING

An even tempered and calm owner with natural authority will not find it difficult to train this very unusual and relatively untamed dog. The training should be a matter of mutual respect and the dog needs to be treated fairly. The "Russians" do not like beginners or inconsistent people and you will experience dominant behavior if they are not kept under control. They will never follow commands blindly, but first they appear to "consider" whether it is a sensible command. It is very important to socialize man and dog to avoid the dog becoming shy and suspicious. Do not be afraid that the dog will lose its watchfulness. It is a guard dog by nature.

South Russian Ovtcharka

EXERCISE

Russian Ovtcharkas do not need a great amount of exercise, but they do need space. They will run off their energy provided they have the freedom of a spacious and well-fenced yard. These dogs are not well suited to a busy neighborhood or apartment. They love being outdoors and guarding their terrain.

USES

The Ovtcharka makes an excellent guard and family dog for people who live off the road and who can give the dog sufficient (fenced) space outdoors. It will naturally and almost unnoticeably take over guarding your family, home and property. Its independent nature does not make it a suitable breed for all kinds of dog sports.

South Russian Ovtcharka

KUVASZ

COUNTRY OF ORIGIN	**HUNGARY**
ORIGINAL FUNCTION	**SHEEP GUARDIAN AND SECURITY**

Kuvasz bitch

APPEARANCE

BODY

The Kuvasz is a big, strong, noble dog with a sturdy build but not coarse. The body is slightly longer than tall and the back of medium length, with short sturdy loins and a slightly sloping, broad strong croup. Prolific hair in the croup makes the dog appear over-built. The withers are longer and higher than the back. The tail is set low, reaching down to the hocks. The tail hangs and turns up a little at the end. The chest is deep and the forechest is arched forwards because of the muscles and breastbone. The Kuvasz has a raised tuck-up. The shoulders are long and sloping. The forelegs are straight and the elbows set well, even though not below the body. The hind legs are quite straight. The front metatarsals are straight. The neck is medium length and very muscular without a dewlap.

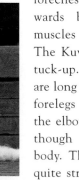

Kuvasz puppy

HEAD

Fairly long but not pointed, with clear but not heavy stop and tight lips. Ears are set high with a blunt V-shape. They hang and are medium length. Almond-shaped eyes with close fitting eyelids are oblique. The Kuvasz has a scissors bite.

SHOULDER HEIGHT

Dogs vary between 28–29½ in (71–75 cm) and bitches between 26–27½ in (66–70 cm.)

WEIGHT

For dogs it ranges from approx. 88–114¾ lb (40–52 kg) and for bitches generally from 66¼–92½ lb (30–42 kg).

COAT

The hair is short on the head, ears, feet and legs – up to ¾ in (2 cm). On the rest of the body it is longer, particularly round the neck, where the fur forms a ruff, and the tail is well-feathered. The outer coat has fairly coarse hairs, harsh and wavy. The undercoat is woolly and much finer.

COLORS

The Kuvasz is only known to have a plain white coat. The skin is slate-colored. The nose, eye rims and lips are black and the eyes are dark brown.

TEMPERAMENT

CHARACTER

This breed is intelligent, honest and equable.

Kuvasz bitch

A Kuvasz is affectionate and loyal and very attached to its owners, but it wants to be seen as independent. A Kuvasz is quite watchful and defends its family, home and contents with lust. They are brave, tough and also domineering. They do not bark often: a good reason to go and inspect if your dog does bark. A Kuvasz can be kept in an outdoor kennel without any problem, provided it has regular contact with its owner and members of the family.

SOCIAL BEHAVIOR

There will not be any problems mixing with cats

Kuvasz

and other pets provided a Kuvasz is well socialized. A high pain threshold and a stable character make them very tolerant to children, but because of their strength, their own initiatives and size,

Male Kuvasz

they should not be cared for by a child. It is important to know that the Kuvasz will protect people and animals belonging to its family; they will therefore protect your children from other children who pester them. A Kuvasz is dominant towards other dogs and once it is challenged it will rise to it.

GENERAL CARE

GROOMING

The Kuvasz has a very dense coat that will protect it from any type of

An older Kuvasz

weather. During shedding periods thorough daily grooming is a definite must. For the rest of the year weekly brushing, preferably with a pin brush, will be adequate. Please keep claws clipped.

TRAINING

The Kuvasz needs balanced, calm, clear and consistent training. It is not the right dog for beginners; the potential owner will need to be strong, both mentally and physically. It does not, however, mean that training should be harsh, on the contrary, your dog will flourish in a harmonious environment and with people that allow it to take its own initiatives.

EXERCISE

These dogs need an average amount of exercise. If you have a large fenced yard the Kuvasz will look after its own need to exercise. This dog tends to inspect the boundaries of its territory several times a day. If this is not possible you will need to take your dog out more often. They need space both physically as well as mentally.

USES

Outside its country of origin the Kuvasz is appreciated as a watchful companion. This breed will not be at its best in a city.

MAREMMA AND ABRUZZESE SHEEPDOG	
COUNTRY OF ORIGIN	ITALY
ORIGINAL FUNCTION	GUARD DOG FOR HERDS

APPEARANCE

BODY

The Maremma and Abruzzese Sheepdog is a big and sturdy dog. Its body is slightly longer than high. The withers are a little above the topline and its wide muscular croup tends to slope. The low set tail is carried down at rest. The belly has a slight tuck-up. The wide chest reaches down to the elbows, which fit closely to the body. The straight legs are heavy boned. These dogs have large cat feet. The hind feet are more oval shaped. The strong neck does not have a dewlap.

HEAD

The head is heavy and long, with the forenose a little shorter than the skull. There is a stop, but it is not obvious. The skull is fairly wide between the ears and shows a smooth transition into the nose. The nose bridge is straight. The small ears are V-shaped and have tips at the ends. When the dog is alert, they are carried semi-erect. The eyes are almond-shaped. Maremmas have a complete scissors bite.

SHOULDER HEIGHT

Dogs are between $25^1/_2$–$28^3/_4$ in (65–73 cm) high and the recommended height for bitches is $23^1/_2$–$26^3/_4$ in (60–68 cm).

WEIGHT

Ranging from $66^1/_4$–$99^1/_4$ lb (30–45 kg).

Maremma and Abruzzese Sheepdog

COAT

Its luxurious coat is long and lies close to the body. The hair feels quite harsh. The dogs have a rich ruff. Hair is short on the face, ears, and on the front of legs.

COLORS

These dogs have a white coat, a black nose and black pigmentation on the rims of lips and eyes. Markings in ivory, pale lemon or orange colorings are acceptable. The eyes are always brown.

TEMPERAMENT

CHARACTER

These dogs are still quite authentic. They are friendly and loyal, sober and tough on themselves, brave, worthy, intelligent and equable. They seldom bark. Maremmas are affectionate, but not dependent or pushy and show considerable maturity in many situations. They make excellent watchdogs and protect their families and homes very convincingly from undesirable characters.

SOCIAL BEHAVIOR

Maremmas tend to get on quite well with other dogs and pets. Generally they are patient and

Male Maremma and Abruzzese Sheepdog

tolerant towards children. With respect to strangers they are reserved. Uninvited guests will not be allowed to set foot on the property.

GENERAL CARE

Maremma and Abruzzese
Sheepdog

GROOMING

This breed needs to be brushed and combed regularly. Especially during the shedding period a daily brush will be necessary to reduce the quantity of dead and loose hairs to a tolerable level.

TRAINING

The Maremma is not a dog to follow your every command slavishly and certainly not when it cannot see the point of it! This does not mean that you cannot teach the dog anything; on the contrary it is intelligent enough to understand what you mean. Its education and training require mutual respect in handling and voice, and above all consistency.

EXERCISE

This breed needs space, mentally as well as physically. Do not condemn this dog to a walk-around three times a day. Ideally the dog should have the freedom of a large fenced yard, where it can indulge itself freely from time to time. This sheepdog will not be bothered by bad weather conditions. It can be kept outside, provided you give it enough attention, but a kennel, whatever the size, is not suitable for this breed. Historically these dogs are used to covering a lot of ground daily and if you give them the chance they will happily disappear for an hour or so.

USES

These dogs are popular as watchful companions. Because they are rather self-willed they will not enjoy dog sports.

Male Maremma and Abruzzese
Sheepdog

Maremma and Abruzzese
Sheepdog bitch

SLOVAK CUVAC

COUNTRY OF ORIGIN	SLOVAKIA
ORIGINAL FUNCTION	GUARD DOG FOR HERDS

APPEARANCE

BODY

It is slightly longer than high. The Cuvac's back is strong and level and slopes gently towards the loins. The croup is strong and square, tilting slightly. Its straight tail is set on low, is carried pendent and reaches down to the hocks. The chest reaches to the elbows and its width is equal to a quarter of its shoulder height. The ribs are well rounded and extend backwards. The stomach and sides are tucked up lightly. The long shoulders slope. The Slovak Cuvac has straight legs, placed directly below the body and they are well angulated. The forefeet are compact, round and close together and the hind feet are slightly longer. The dry neck is as long as the head. The dog will carry its head high when alert.

Slovak Cuvac

HEAD

Its broad and elongated skull is arched to a light degree, but the top of the skull is level. From the side the top of the skull appears to run parallel to its straight nose bridge. The stop is well marked. It has eyebrows and a shallow central furrow. The wide and heavy forenose narrows slightly to the tip of the nose and is a little shorter than the skull. The lips are tight and fit well. The ears are set on high. They have rounded tips and are carried hanging beside the head. The eyes are oval shaped. The Slovak Cuvac has a scissors bite.

SHOULDER HEIGHT

The dogs range between $24^1/_2$–$27^1/_2$ in (62–70 cm) and bitches between 23–$25^1/_2$ in (59–65 cm).

WEIGHT

The dogs weigh between $79^1/_2$–97 lb (36–44 kg).

COAT

Dense and plentiful, the coat should not separate on its back. The outer layer completely covers the short, dense and fine undercoat. The hairs of the outer coat are 2–6 in (5–15 cm) long and wave gently. The dogs have a ruff.

COLORS

The Slovak Cuvac has a plain white coat. A yellow sheen where the ears are set on is permissible, but not desirable. The eyes are brown and nose, rims of lips and eyes are black, as are the pads of their feet.

TEMPERAMENT

CHARACTER

This breed tends to be equable. They are fairly calm and as a rule quite self-assured. Although they can be quite active outdoors, they will be

Maremma and Abruzzese Sheepdog

Young Slovak Cuvac bitch

calm indoors. They certainly mark their territory, they will protect people and property, but also "their" folk, without a doubt. They are very loyal to their owners and families, but also independent. They enjoy company but they are also very happy to amuse themselves for some parts of the day. Their dense coat protects them from any type of weather.

SOCIAL BEHAVIOR

This breed generally likes children and other pets such as cats and (small) livestock should not cause any problems. If they do not know you they will initially be on guard, but they will accept you if their owners say it is fine. The dogs can be a little domineering towards other dogs.

GENERAL CARE

GROOMING

The coat is quite easy to keep tidy. They do tend to shed hair indoors, something the owner will have to put up with, but the coat seldom gets knotted. Give the coat a good brush once a week. In the shedding period this breed will lose a lot of hair in a fairly short period of time, when daily grooming will be essential.

TRAINING

This dog is very adaptable. They can be kept outdoors as a guard dog, but you do need to give them a lot of attention to prevent them from becoming too independent. If you devote enough time and attention to its training, you will have a dog that is happy to listen to you and likes following commands. A Slovak Cuvac needs to make sense of them though. Its training needs to be harmonious and consistent.

EXERCISE

Considering its large size the Slovak Cuvac is quite active. If you have a large well-fenced yard the dog will run off most of its energy of its own accord. If not, you will regularly need to take it for a good walk. If you have a good relationship with your dog and it is well trained, walks off-leash should not be a problem. These dogs do not like ball games, etc.

USES

The breed has different uses in its regions of origin. Elsewhere you will rarely see this type of dog, and if so it will be popular as a watchful companion.

Slovak Cuvac

TATRA MOUNTAIN SHEEPDOG

COUNTRY OF ORIGIN	POLAND
ORIGINAL FUNCTION	WATCHDOG, HERDING DOG

APPEARANCE

BODY

The Tatra is a strong and massive dog, with a straight and broad back, broad and firm loins and a croup that slopes a little. The withers are well defined and broad. The tail reaches down to the hocks and might be slightly curved at the end. The chest is deep and its slanting ribs are a bit flat. The stomach has a slight tuck-up. Its sloping shoulders fit closely. The legs are strong, but not heavy boned. The hindquarters are moderately angulated. The feet are oval and the toes are close to each other. Tatras have a moderately long neck without folds.

HEAD

It will carry its dry head moderately high. The length of its nose is equal to or slightly longer than the skull, interrupted by a clear but not overtly strong stop. The nose bridge is wide and the lips fit closely. The thick, triangular ears are set at the same height as the outer corners of its eyes or a little above and are carried pendent. The eyes of medium size are slightly oblique. A scissors bite is preferable.

SHOULDER HEIGHT

This is $23^{1}/_{2}$–$25^{1}/_{2}$ in (60–65cm) for bitches and $25^{1}/_{2}$–$27^{1}/_{2}$ in (65–70cm) for

Tatra

dogs. Variations up to $^{3}/_{4}$–$1^{1}/_{4}$ in (2–3cm) are acceptable.

COAT

The Tatra has a long, thick outer layer, which feels hard, is either straight or slightly wavy. The undercoat is prolific. The hair on the trousers, ruff and tail is longer while it is short on the head and the front of the legs.

Male Tatra

COLORS

Tatras are always plain white, have a black nose and dark pigmentation of eye rims and lips. The eyes are dark brown.

TEMPERAMENT

CHARACTER

Generally, these dogs are quite calm, sober and equable by nature. They are quite intelligent and even fairly obedient and keen to learn. They are very loyal to their families and protect their members, their home and property from evil-minded people. Most Tatras like to be outdoors and don't feel at ease in an apartment.

SOCIAL BEHAVIOR

Tatras are sociable and most of them get on well with other dogs and pets. The same applies to children, although mind that your dog would no longer support your children if they are rough towards other children. If they do not know folks, they will stand back until their owners say that they are trustworthy. Tatras are not particularly watchful regards strangers, but they will demonstrate that their families come first.

GENERAL CARE

GROOMING

It is best to brush the coat maybe once a week. A daily brush is required during the molt. A coarse comb might be a useful tool, or a brush with metal

Tatra.

pins with ends covered in plastic.

TRAINING

This dog is intelligent and keen to learn. If it is trained in a calm and consistent manner, you will not experience any problems. Harsh training will be counterproductive.

EXERCISE

The Tatra likes being outdoors. Its dense coat protects it from all weather conditions. If you have a spacious, fenced yard, this dog will be able to let off steam. Do take it for longer walks on a regular basis. These dogs generally like swimming.

USES

In its country of origin this breed is used for a variety of tasks. In other countries they are valued as trustworthy family dogs.

Tatra bitch

SARPLANINAC (ILLYRIAN SHEEPDOG)

COUNTRY OF ORIGIN	THE FORMER YUGOSLAVIA
ORIGINAL AND	FLOCK GUARD AND
TODAY'S FUNCTION	WATCHDOG

APPEARANCE

BODY

Sarplaninac

The Sarplaninac is squat and has a very strong build. The body is a bit longer than tall. The chest is deep, medium length and reaches to the elbows. The forechest is wide and muscular. The back is level and slopes down slightly and the loins are broad and muscular. The belly has a tuck-up. The croup flows into the tail almost unnoticeably. The tail should at least reach down to the hocks. It is carried pendulous except when the dog is alert or moving, when the tail may be raised above the topline. The sturdy forelegs have close-fitting elbows and their pasterns slant a little. Their hind feet do not slant as much as their forelegs. The hindquarters are not set as widely apart as their forelegs. Both fore and hind legs are parallel to each other. The feet are strong and oval shaped. The neck is dry and medium length. The set on of the neck is not pronounced.

HEAD

The size of the head balances nicely with the rest of the body and there is a rather rounded, arched skull. The eyebrows are not very pronounced and the stop is faint. The skull is a bit longer than the muzzle. The upper lips hang over slightly, but the corners of the mouth are well closed. The ears are V-shaped. They are carried pendulously. The tips of the ears reach as far as the inner corners of the eye. The almond-shaped eyes should not be too deep-set or be too big. The expression is calm, but not penetrating. Sarplaninacs have a complete scissors bite.

SHOULDER HEIGHT

The dogs are approx. $29^1/_2$ in (75cm) and bitches approx. $25^1/_2$–$27^1/_2$ in (65–70cm). Variations of

Sarplaninac

4 in (10cm) up or downward are acceptable for this specific breed of dog.

WEIGHT

On average the dogs weigh approx. 143$^{1}/_{4}$ lb (65kg) and bitches 99$^{1}/_{4}$ lb (45kg).

COAT

Their double coat has a very dense and prolific under layer and the outer layer is long, coarse and almost flat. The length of the hairs on the withers is 4–4$^{3}/_{4}$ in (10–12cm). The hairs should not be shorter than 2$^{3}/_{4}$ in (7cm), except where it is naturally short: on the head, ears and front of legs.

COLORS

The most common and favorite colors are slate and dark gray. A parti-colored coat or white markings are not permissible, unlike small white markings on chest and toes, although undesirable.

The eyes are dark or light chestnut. Note that skin and mucous membranes have dark pigmentation.

TEMPERAMENT

CHARACTER

This breed is very calm, self-assured, docile and equable. They do not tend to get worked up. The Sarplaninac was introduced to western countries fairly recently, while it is still used for its original task in its region of origin. They are reliable guard dogs that cannot be bribed, without being aggressive or impatient. Guarding and protecting their territory, house and property, including family and pets are a matter of fact. You do not need to train or encourage them to do so.

The dogs do not bark a lot and therefore you should inspect if you hear your dog. They are loyal to their owners and families and demonstrate their affection. They do not need to live indoors, provided they have enough social contact with members of the family.

SOCIAL BEHAVIOR

When the dog has been well socialized with other pets there should not be any problems. The dogs tend to be rather dominant towards other dogs and bitches. People they do not know will either be stopped by means of intimidation, or accepted without any problem, depending on the owner's response. In respect of children a typical Sarplaninac will be friendly regardless whether they are "its" family's children.

GENERAL CARE

GROOMING

A Sarplaninac kept indoors needs quite some grooming. Brush your dog thoroughly at least once a week. During shedding a brush once a day is essential. The coat does not really tangle and resists dirt.

Sarplaninac

TRAINING

Train this dog calmly and harmoniously. If you are honest and consistent, the dog will not disobey your house rules. They are very sensitive to your tone of voice. Quite often you can control them by specific intonation. Do not shout and hit these dogs and as a rule there should be no need to do so. They are not perfectly obedient dogs. They always appear to consider whether the command makes sense. Their self-confidence means that they may decide to take on pack leadership of the family, but they will only do so if they feel that there is little or no leadership, or if their owners are inconsistent and nervous. Calm handlers who know what they are doing and have a natural authority will bring out the best in this dog.

Sarplaninac

EXERCISE

This breed needs a fair amount of exercise. They like to be outdoors, no matter the weather. They are not suited to an apartment or a house with a small yard. They are at their best when they have access to a considerable, fenced yard. You should also take this dog on frequent long walks, when it will generally adapt to your pace and will respond kindly and be interested in anything that comes along.

USES

These dogs are not keen on dog sports. However, they are reliable guard dogs.

Cao da Serra de Aires

CAO DA SERRA DE AIRES (SERRA DE AIRES MOUNTAIN DOG)

COUNTRY OF ORIGIN	**PORTUGAL**
ORIGINAL FUNCTION	**ALL-ROUND HERDING DOG AND GUARD DOG**

APPEARANCE

BODY

The Cao da Serra de Aires has a long back, which might be level or slope down a little. The loins are short and muscular and the croup slopes gently. Its tail is set high and to the hocks. In repose it is carried low and in movement it is raised in a curl. Its deep chest has a normal width. The belly is slightly tucked up. The legs are straight and well angulated. This breed might have single or double dew claws. The feet are round. The neck is devoid of loose dewlap.

HEAD

It is powerful, big and not long. The nose is shorter than the skull. The round skull is longer than wide, with a clearly visible occipital protuberance. The stop is well marked. The strong lips are thin and close well. The ears are set high and hang pendulous. They are triangular. The eyes are round and have an average size. They have a lively, obedient and intelligent expression.
This breed will have a scissors bite.

SHOULDER HEIGHT

Ranging from $16^1/_2$–$20^1/_2$ in (42–52cm) for bitches and $17^1/_2$–$21^1/_2$ in (45–55cm) for dogs.

WEIGHT

Approx. 44–$55^1/_4$ lb (20–25 kg).

59

Cao da Serra de Aires

COAT
It is like goat hair, very long and can be smooth or slightly wavy. There is no under layer. The dog has a beard, mustache and eyebrows, but the eyes remain visible.

COLORS
Permissible colors are fawn, gray, yellow and chestnut. Wolf in different shades is accepted. The most popular color is black with fairly pronounced tan markings (black and tan). A few white hairs or a white patch on the chest are permissible. The eyes should preferably be dark.

TEMPERAMENT

CHARACTER
These sober and tough dogs are rather independent and very persistent. The Cao da Serra de Aires is well known for its liveliness, active nature, intelligence and being a good worker. They are generally well tempered and very loyal to the family they belong to. They will naturally protect their family and defend them from undesirable characters. They like being

Cao da Serra de Aires

outdoors and are resistant to most kinds of weather.

SOCIAL BEHAVIOR
These sheepdogs get on fairly well with other dogs. If they are well socialized they can live with other pets without a problem. They are tolerant towards children. They are suspicious and on their guard with respect to strangers.

GENERAL CARE

GROOMING
A Cao da Serra de Aires coat needs a regular good brush, followed by a comb, especially where it might become tangled. The beard and mustache tend to pick up dirt quickly and need a regular comb through. Clip any excess hair growing between the pads and check ear passages and corners of eyes for debris and dirt.

Cao da Serra de Aires

TRAINING
The Cao da Serra de Aires learns fairly quickly and easily, but consistent training is a prerequisite.

EXERCISE
The Cao da Serra de Aires has extreme stamina and loves being outdoors. Not only does it require exercise but it also needs one or more jobs. Ball games, obedience skills and retrieving will be greeted with enthusiasm.

USES
Good support will help this breed to perform excellently in various types of dog sports, such as flyball and agility skills.

Cao da Serra de Aires

Old English Sheepdog or Bobtail

OLD ENGLISH SHEEPDOG OR BOBTAIL	
COUNTRY OF ORIGIN	ENGLAND
ORIGINAL FUNCTION	SHEEPDOG
	(CATTLE DRIVER)

APPEARANCE

BODY

The Bobtail has a square build and is short and squat. Its over-build is a typical characteristic of this breed, meaning that the loins are higher than the withers. The chest is wide and deep and the ribs are well arched. The loins are very strong, broad and slightly bent. The tail is usually docked in countries where this is permissible. The elbows lie close to the body. The legs are straight, well angulated and they are heavy boned. The round and sturdy feet have arched toes. Any dew claws will be removed. The neck is long and strong with a graceful curve.

HEAD

Bobtails have a fairly square head with a clear stop. Nose and skull are almost equal in length. The small ears are pendulous, carried close to the head. The eyes are wide apart. Bobtails should preferably have a complete and strong scissors bite, but a pincer bite is also accepted.

SHOULDER HEIGHT

Bitches are 22 in (56 cm) and dogs are approx. 24in (61cm). The overall picture is considered more important than the actual size.

COAT

The long, luxuriant coat consists of tough hairs. It must be rough and devoid of curl. The under layer is waterproof. The hindquarters are generally covered more abundantly than the forequarters.

COLORS

Old English Sheepdogs may have any shade of gray, blue or gray, always together with white markings. White marks in colored patches are undesirable and the same applies to brown shades in the coat. This breed may have white socks. The eyes may be either (dark) brown or blue.

TEMPERAMENT

CHARACTER

These dogs are intelligent and honest with an optimistic and uncomplicated outlook on life. They are compliant, obedient and gentle. Their adaptability is considerable. Bobtails may be a little boisterous when they are young, and sometimes also when they are older. They are very affectionate and like the company of their owners and families. A Bobtail would consider a kennel punishment and needs to be among the family. Although most raise their barks when they sense danger, the average Bobtail should not be considered watchful.

SOCIAL BEHAVIOR

Bobtails tend to be sociable and peace-loving. They get on well with other pets, dogs and children. Visitors are welcomed in a friendly manner.

GENERAL CARE

GROOMING

These dogs need considerable grooming. At least once a week the coat needs to be brushed through down to the skin. Do not forget areas where it tends to become tangled, such as trousers and elbows. During the molt the dog will need more care and you might fill half or an entire garbage bag with hair. The required overbuild is emphasized at shows by

Old English Sheepdog or Bobtail

brushing their hair forward from the hindquarters. Dirt and hair need to be removed from the ear passages.

Occasionally you should wash the beard and mustache to prevent discoloring of the hair. The excess of hair between pads needs clipping. The amount of care is so demanding that many Bobtail owners decide to have their dogs' coats trimmed short from time to time. Although it is better than allowing the dog to go through life looking disheveled, you should wonder if it is worth buying a longhaired dog to have its hair clipped.

Young Bobtail bitch

Bobtail

TRAINING

This dog needs gentle and consistent handling during training. It wants to please you and rarely displays dominant behavior, making it suitable for people with little experience of the upbringing of dogs. Because grooming forms so important a part of the general care of this breed, it is important to start brushing it as young as possible. This prevents the grooming ritual degenerating into a wrestling match when the dog is much bigger and stronger.

EXERCISE

A Bobtail needs a considerable amount of exercise, but it will not misbehave if you miss a day due to lack of time. Most of the breed are crazy about playing with a ball and are good at retrieving.

USES

Because of their nimbleness, obedience and intelligence most Bobtails perform excellently in a variety of dog sports, particularly agility. It makes an excellent family dog, but do not underestimate the amount of grooming required.

Bobtail

BEARDED COLLIE

COUNTRY OF ORIGIN	SCOTLAND
ORIGINAL FUNCTION	SHEEPDOG

APPEARANCE

BODY

The Bearded Collie is slim but sturdy. The body is slightly longer than tall (ratio approx.: 5:4). The back is level and the loins are strong. The tail is set low and should reach down to the heel or beyond. The tip of the tail is carried in an upward curve, but not over the back. The chest is deep and the ribs are well arched at the head, but they are not barrel-shaped. The shoulder blades should clearly slope backwards. The forequarters are straight with strong bones, and supple pasterns. The hindquarters are muscular, with bent knee-joints and low heels. The pasterns fall at a right angle to the ground and in a normal stance they are just behind a line vertically below the point of the buttocks. The feet are oval with strong pads and bent toes, lying close to each other. The neck is moderately long and slightly bent.

HEAD

Bearded Collies have a wide, smooth and square skull, which is as broad as it is long. The muzzle has the same length as the skull. The stop is moderately deep. The ears are moderately long and are carried pendulous. When the dog is alert, they are lifted in line with the skull, but never above. The big eyes are set wide apart, and have a lively inquisitive expression. They should not protrude. Bearded Collies have a scissors bite.

Bearded Collie

SHOULDER HEIGHT

The ideal height for dogs is $20^3/_4$–22 in (53–56 cm) and for bitches 20–$20^3/_4$ in (51–53cm). A balanced build is considered more important, however too much deviation in size is not encouraged.

COAT

Bearded Collies have double coats. The upper layer is straight, rough and hard. It should not be woolly or curly, but a slight wave is acceptable. The undercoat is dense, soft and woolly.

COLORS

Slate, reddish-brown, black, blue, sandy-colored brown and any shade of gray with possible white markings.

White markings should however only occur on the muzzle (blaze), tip of tail, chest, neck and legs. White markings on the neck are not permitted

Brown Bearded Collie

Bearded Collie

beyond the shoulder. Nor should white show above the heels on the outside of the legs. Tan markings are permitted, but only on the eyebrows, inside the ears, on the cheeks, below the onset of the tail between the legs. The tan is a kind of barrier between the color of the coat and the white. The color of the nose depends on the color of the coat, but should always be plain like the lips and rims of eyes.

TEMPERAMENT

CHARACTER
This is a cheerful, very lively, high spirited dog, alert and full of self-confidence. It is a very intelligent dog, keen to learn and likes to work with and for its owner. It is affectionate, gentle and sweet. Although a Bearded Collie generally is fairly active and enthusiastic, it is not clumsy. A Bearded Collie belongs with the family and is not a suitable dog to banish to a kennel and a life outdoors.

SOCIAL BEHAVIOR
These dogs can get on very well with anybody by nature. And although any dog will need to be well socialized in order to grow up as a stable and balanced dog, the Bearded Collie is no exception to the rule. They tend to bark when they hear visitors, but that is as far as they go. Visitors will be greeted boisterously.

GENERAL CARE

GROOMING
One of the most important aspects of keeping a Bearded Collie is its grooming. It needs lots of it, more than you would expect. The hair must be brushed and combed several times a week to avoid

tangles. The beard with its longer hairs should be tended to more frequently. Also check the ear passages regularly to remove dirt and an excess of earwax. Clean the ear with a special ear cleaner when necessary. Remove excessive hair between the pads where twigs, thorns and small stones might get caught. At shows longhaired dogs tend to be preferred, and the hair of a Bearded Collie should be parted along the back. It is not easy to keep the coat of a show dog in optimum condition.

TRAINING
The Bearded Collie is an intelligent dog that learns quickly. A soft-handed approach will be better for this sensitive and gentle dog. You will achieve better results by doing so playfully, giving cheerful commands and giving your dog ample praise. Avoid pressurizing it, because it will spoil its receptive and friendly disposition.

Bearded Collie pup

EXERCISE
These dogs are active and lively, always in for any kind of exercise, such as long walks in the woods or along the beach, where the dog is ready to take a plunge into the water. If you are busy building up your own jog-

Bearded Collie

Bearded Collie

ging program, it would be a good way of providing this dog with plenty of exercise running alongside you. This breed has the advantage of having a Shepherd's instinct, which means it will not stray from you when off leash. Because of its great adaptability it will feel at home both in the countryside and in the city and if a walk is inconvenient, it will abide and not misbehave.

USES

Traditionally the Bearded Collie has been a sheepdog, but today the breed is seen at sports such as obedience skills, flyball and agility skills. Bearded Collies can perform extremely well in the latter two sports. This dog is well suited to a sports-loving family that does not mind the considerable amount of grooming.

BRIARD

COUNTRY OF ORIGIN	FRANCE
ORIGINAL FUNCTION	HERDING DOG AND GUARD DOG

APPEARANCE

BODY

Tends to be longer than tall. It has a deep chest with well-arched ribs that continue a long way, a straight topline and a slightly slanting croup. The tail is carried pendulously and the end is hooked. The tail reaches down to its hocks, the muscular legs have strong bones and the elbows fit tightly. The double dew claws on the hind legs are quite obvious. The vertical feet are sturdy and round. The moderately long neck is muscular.

HEAD

Briards have a fairly long head with a clear stop. The muzzle and skull are of equal length. The muzzle should not be narrow or pointed and has a straight nose bridge. The nose is a little square. The eyes are fairly big. Briards have a scissors bite.

Briard

Briard

usually get on reasonably well with children, but only on condition that the children respect the dog and do not tease it. The Briard does not have a sense of humor. In that respect the breed might be more suitable for people with slightly older children.

SHOULDER HEIGHT

For bitches it will range from 22–25$^1/_2$ in (56–64 cm) and for dogs 24$^1/_2$–26$^3/_4$ in (62–68 cm). Dogs failing to reach the minimum height and those more than $^3/_4$ in above the maximum height will be disqualified at shows.

COAT

This will be wavy, long and dry with a light undercoat. The structure of the outer coat will remind you of goat's hair. The eyes are almost completely covered by long hair, and there must be a mustache and a goatee. Dogs with hair shorter than 2$^3/_4$ in (7cm) will be disqualified at shows.

COLOR

Theoretically, all uniform colors are accepted by the standard, with exception of white, two-colored and brown-chestnut. In reality we almost invariably see plain black, mallow-colored and gray tones among the Briards. White markings are undesirable. The eyes are dark and the nose and nails are black.

TEMPERAMENT

CHARACTER

Briards are intelligent, tough and brave dogs that like to work. They guard your family, house and yard with conviction against undesirable characters. They are devoted and loyal to their people and do not accept strangers. Because they like company they are not suited to kennels. These distinctive dogs are very likely to show a dominant streak.

SOCIAL BEHAVIOR

Well-socialized Briards can get on well with cats and other pets. Some can be a little dominant regards other dogs. Unknown visitors are mistrusted; they are not everybody's friend. They

GENERAL CARE

GROOMING

The Briard needs grooming thoroughly once a week to avoid tangles as much as possible. Keep the ear passages clean and pluck excess hairs out of them. Between the pads you might find excessive hair, which you should clip, because it bothers the dog when walking.

TRAINING

The right handler will find the Briard a wonderful, stable and obedient dog that will obey at once. But a thorough training and socialization is essential. A Briard needs to be trained with love, but also firmly. However, do not confuse "firm" with unjust, because such an approach will bring out unexpected traits. It is good for the Briard to live among people and for it to have positive experiences with all kinds of people, children, dogs and a variety of situations during the socializing phase.

Briards

Briards

Briards

EXERCISE

Briards need a fair amount of exercise. They are ready for a long walk through natural surroundings at any time. They do not feel like a walk on their own and walks off-leash will generally be quite relaxed. Running alongside you and swimming are also suitable forms of relaxation. If you need to skip a day, they will generally not mind.

USES

This breed is suitable for all kinds of different dog sports. With the right support they will perform well in sports such as flyball and agility and even advanced obedience skills. Classes for avalanche search or rescue dogs might well be considered.

BEAUCERON (BERGER DE BEAUCE) (BAS ROUGE) (BEAUCE SHEPHERD)	
COUNTRY OF ORIGIN	FRANCE
ORIGINAL FUNCTION	HERDING DOG AND WATCHDOG

APPEARANCE

BODY

The Beauceron is a sturdy and muscular, tough and strongly built dog that should not be coarsely built. Its build is neither exaggerated nor unsophisticated, but average and harmonious in every respect. The back is level and the loins are broad and strong. The croup slopes where the tail sets on. The tail is carried low and reaches down to the hocks or below. It has a light curl in the shape of a "J." The chest is deep and wide with a breastbone set low. The long shoulders slant. The legs are straight, the thighs are vertical and the lower shanks are placed slightly backwards. The hocks, strong and low, are well angulated. The feet are round and powerful. A typical characteristic of this breed is the double dew claws on the inside of the hindquarters, close to the feet.

HEAD

Its long head looks harmonious and chiseled. It has a flat or slightly rounded forehead and a light stop. The straight nose bridge slopes gently down to the nose and from the side it looks in line with the top of the skull. The muzzle is neither pointed nor heavy and has dry, well-pigmented and close-fitting lips. The ears are set high and are carried pendulously, but not too close to the head. They are equal

Male Beauceron

in length to half the size of the head. The round eyes should not be slanting and the shape of the eyelids is slightly almond. The Beaucerons need an open facial expression. They should have a complete scissors bite with strong, white teeth.

SHOULDER HEIGHT

Dogs vary from $25^1/_2$–$27^1/_2$ in (65–70 cm) and bitches from 24–$26^3/_4$ in (61–68 cm). Variations upward of $^3/_4$ in (2 cm) or $1^1/_4$ in (3 cm) are accepted.

WEIGHT

It varies from $66^1/_4$–$110^1/_4$ lb (30–50 kg) according to sex, size and build.

COAT

The coat is solid, close lying, stiff on the body, and short on the head. The trousers of the dog are slightly feathered, like the under part of the body. The undercoat is very short, fine, dense and downy.

COLOR

Beauceron

This breed has two recognized color patterns. The first is black and tan. These dogs are black with squirrel brown markings above the eyes, on the sides of the nose and on the cheeks (but not continuing to the ears), on the chest (preferably two markings), the neck and under the tail. From the toes upward at least one third of the legs is brown. Some white hairs on the chest are accepted, but a marking of $^3/_4$ square inches (5cm^2) or more will lead to disqualification.

The second color pattern is black and tan merle ("harlequin"). The coat consists of equal parts of gray and black: spotted or predominantly black, rather than gray. The tan markings are the same as prescribed for black and tan. The gray markings in this color pattern on puppies and young dogs are brighter than those of adult dogs. The eyes for both color patterns should preferably be dark brown, but in any case not lighter than hazelnut. The mouse gray color of the undercoat should never shine through the outer coat. The claws should be black.

TEMPERAMENT

CHARACTER

The Beauceron is a brave and highly intelligent dog. It will take vigilance of home and family for granted. It is alert and sporty and likes to work for its boss. This breed is extremely loyal and is attached to its owner and family. They are tough, too, sometimes a little independent and dominant, and therefore need good handlers. Their coats

Beaucerons

"Harlequin" Beauceron bitch

pro-
tect them from any kind of weather. They can also be kept in a kennel, provided they have enough attention and exercise.

SOCIAL BEHAVIOR

A Beauceron that has been properly and thoroughly socialized gets along fine with pets, such as cats. It will also be good to children, but very young or busy children will not make ideal company.

A dog might be slightly aggressive towards other members of its sex, but the degree of socializing and upbringing will ultimately decide how well it copes.

A Beauceron will not naturally trust strangers, but if its owner says everything is fine, the dog will accept them.

GENERAL CARE

GROOMING

The coat of a Beauceron does not require a great deal of attention. An occasional grooming with a pin brush, with more attention during the molt, is sufficient. Keep claws short.

TRAINING

A consistent and loving upbringing with plenty of exercise and ample contact with its owner is indispensable for the well-balanced development of a young Beauceron. Without it the dog may become neurotic or aggressive. Allow plenty of time for good socialization. The dog should be able to meet other people, children, dogs, other animals and experience a variety of situations. Good socialization will ensure you have an equable dog that will respond with confidence to all kinds of stimulation, the rest of its life.

Beauceron

EXERCISE

This breed needs more than a round of the block three times a day. Take your dog for regular long walks during which it can run free off-leash and play. Actually nearly all types of physical exercise are suited to the Beauceron. It enjoys retrieving, likes swimming and will happily run alongside you or go on long nature walks.

USES

The breed is trained in its country of origin for hunting, but advanced obedience skills, rescue service, tracking, etc. are also suitable sports and disciplines.

Beauceron

Picardy Shepherd

PICARDY SHEPHERD

COUNTRY OF ORIGIN	FRANCE
ORIGINAL FUNCTION	SHEEPDOG AND WATCHDOG

APPEARANCE

BODY
The build of the Picardy Shepherd is a bit longer than it is tall. The dog looks quaint, elegant and rather sinewy. The topline is level and the belly is tucked up lightly. The deep chest does not stretch beyond the elbows. The tail reaches down to the hocks and is straight with a slight curve at the end. When moving, it is carried a bit higher, but never over the back. The legs are straight and the forequarters have slightly bent wrists. They are well angulated. They are round, short and tight. Dew claws may occur, but are not desirable. The strong and muscular neck carries the head high and proudly.

HEAD
The skull is as long as the muzzle with a very light stop in between. The nose bridge is straight.

The forehead is slightly arched with a slight central furrow. The cheeks are round, but should not be developed too heavily. The ears are medium size (no more than 4–4³/₄ in (10–12cm)). They are straight and have rounded tips. The eyes are medium size.

Properly trained a Picardy Shepherd can perform well in obedience trials.

Picardy Shepherds have a scissors or pincer bite.

SHOULDER HEIGHT
Dogs are between 23¹/₂–25¹/₂ in (60–65 cm) and bitches measure 21³/₄–23¹/₂ in (55–60 cm).

WEIGHT
Dogs range from 66¹/₄–75lb (30–34 kg) and bitches approx. 59¹/₂–68¹/₄ lb (27–31kg).

COAT
Consists of hard, stiff and semi-long hair that should be neither curly nor straight. The average length of hair will be between 2–2¹/₂ in (5–6 cm), with the exception of hairs on the head that are approx. 1¹/₂ in (4cm). The undercoat is fine and dense. Picardy Shepherds have a light goatee and mustache and light eyebrows that should not cover the eyes. The coat is weather-resistant.

COLOR
Gray to dark gray are the most prevailing colors, but gray black, blue or reddish gray shades and light or darker fawn are accepted, too. A small white mark on the chest or white on the toes is not desirable, yet permitted.

The eyes are preferably dark.

TEMPERAMENT

CHARACTER
The Picardy Shepherd is a very energetic and agile dog. It is intelligent and likes to work for its owner. Do not underestimate its cleverness. It is very devoted and loyal, but can be quite stubborn, too. Most Picardy Shepherds develop into a one-person dog; in other words they become very attached to one particular member of the family, usu-

Picardy Shepherds

ally the person who bothers most about the dog. They are not really suited to life in a kennel unless they have enough attention, exercise and activity. They will protect their families with vigor. Otherwise they are sober and tough on themselves. The weather will not bother them.

SOCIAL BEHAVIOR

Picardy Shepherds tend to be distant in respect of strangers. Friends of the family are however greeted kindly. This breed tends to mix well with children and other pets such at cats should not give you any problems if the dog is well socialized. The Picardy Shepherd requires a lot of attention from its owner and should therefore ideally be the only dog in the family.

GENERAL CARE

GROOMING

This breed of dog does not require a lot of groom-

Picardy Shepherd

Picardy Shepherds

ing. It is not advisable to groom the dog too often to avoid damaging the undercoat. Every now and again you could tidy up the coat with a soft brush. Goatee and mustache should however be combed well regularly and in the molt periods you could use a teasel brush to remove loose hairs in the undercoat efficiently. It is best not to spoil the Picardy Shepherd's quaint appearance by over-trimming and grooming. Enthusiasts do not advise washing unless you have no choice.

TRAINING

The Picardy Shepherd might be a little insecure as a puppy and will need some encouragement. It will need to be well socialized with all kinds of different people and animals in order to become an equable dog that responds well to (unknown) stimuli. Picardy Shepherds are intelligent and can learn a lot quite quickly, but they do need handlers who understand them. An approach that is too firm will have a negative effect on their character development and they are susceptible to vibes in the house. Meanwhile you need to remain in control. Give your dog confidence; train it in a calm and harmonious atmosphere and place considerable emphasis on rewarding required behavior. You will have to be quite bold in your approach. Cheerful commands and a lot of variety

Picardy Shepherd

SAARLOOS WOLFHOND (SAARLOOS WOLF DOG)	
COUNTRY OF ORIGIN	THE NETHERLANDS
ORIGINAL FUNCTION	RESCUE DOG, GUIDE FOR THE BLIND, COMPANION

APPEARANCE

BODY

The Saarloos wolfhond is a strong and wolf-like dog with a well-proportioned build. There is a marked difference in appearance between dogs and bitches. The dog is slightly longer than it is tall and has a level, strong topline and muscular loins. The croup slopes normally. The chest is wide and does not stretch below the elbows. The ribs are well arched. The tail is set on low and should not be carried with a curl. The forequarters are well angulated; the hindquarters are normally angulated. Light cow-hockedness is permitted as

will provide the best results. A Picardy Shepherd that is well-brought up and socialized is an equable, and happy dog, willing to work and prepared to do anything for its owner.

EXERCISE

This dog needs a lot of exercise; joining you on a jog, but also swimming, retrieving and walks (off-leash) are excellent ways to channel their enormous amount of energy. They do not tend to stray far from their owners.

USES

If this dog is well supported it can do extremely well in a variety of dog sports, such as agility, obedience and training for hunting.

Group of Saarloos Wolfhounds

Saarloos Wolfhound puppy

Picardy Shepherd

Saarloos Wolfhound

TEMPERAMENT

CHARACTER

Saarloos Wolf Dogs have the blood of wolves and German Shepherds in their veins. The wolves' blood makes them quite unique with a typical personality that resembles that of the wolf. They are intelligent, careful and attentive dogs. They are affectionate and devoted to their handlers and members of the family, but at the same time they are independent and self-willed. They are naturally reserved and cautious towards people, animals, things and situations unknown to them. In addition they have an excellent scent, great stamina and a considerable level of hunting instinct. They do not bark much. On average bitches are on heat only once a year. In threatening circumstances this breed will tend to flee rather than fight. They are not suited as a watchdog or a defense dog.

SOCIAL BEHAVIOR

When a Saarloos wolfhond has been used to children from being a puppy, mixing will not be a problem. They get

Saarloos Wolfhounds

on well with dogs they know or those that are part of the family. It is advisable not to keep a Saarloos wolfhond alone, but to offer it a playful doggy companion, no matter the breed. Cats and other pets are a different story; their hunting instinct requires you to socialize these puppies well with other animals at a very early age. The Saarloos wolfhond will be reserved to strangers and in unknown situations.

GENERAL CARE

GROOMING

This dog is not difficult to groom, but needs some extra attention during the molting season. It is best to remove its shedding undercoat

well as forefeet that turn slightly outward. The feet are a little oval shaped and well closed.

HEAD

It has flat sides and the skull is broad and level, with slight arching between the ears. There is a light stop. The powerful muzzle is about as long as the skull. Its erect ears are set slightly obliquely, and they are medium length and taper a little. The inside of the ears is quite furry. The medium-sized ears are slightly oblique with a reserved and alert expression. The Saarloos wolfhond has a scissors bite.

SHOULDER HEIGHT

For dogs this is between $25\frac{1}{2}$–$29\frac{1}{2}$ in (65–75 cm) and for bitches between 23–$27\frac{1}{2}$ in (60–70 cm).

COAT

It is wiry with a dense and woolly undercoat. Around the neck you will see a clear ruff.

COLOR

Forest-brown and wolf-gray are the most common coat colors. Forest-brown animals have a liver-colored nose and pigmentation and wolf-gray dogs have a black forenose and pigmentation. Light cream to white coats are acknowledged, too. The eyes are preferably yellow.

Saarloos Wolfhound

Saarloos Wolfhounds display many
characteristics of wolves.

the Saarloos wolfhond follow commands that
seem useless from its point of view.

EXERCISE

The Saarloos wolfhond needs an average to
a great deal of daily physical exercise. If you wish
to skip a long walk once in a while, the average
dog of this breed will accommodate, but it is not
the kind of dog that will feel happy leading an
uneventful life. If the Saarloos wolfhond is well
brought-up and thoroughly socialized it can go to
the woods with its owner, off-leash, and safely let
off steam. The Saarloos wolfhond tends to inspect
its surroundings and yard independently; a strong,
high fence is recommended.

USES

One of the original purposes for breeding this type
of dog was to find a dog suited to working as
a guide or rescue dog. However, today Saarloos
wolfdogs tend to be popular as companions. Their
original, natural appearance and typical characteristics will appeal to people who do not like artifi-
ciality. You might consider participating in a training class for agility or obedience skills. The
pleasure it will give to either of you should come
first, not the competitive aspect.

from its coat with a so-called teasel brush to avoid
finding loose hairs all over the house. Keep the
claws clipped.

TRAINING

This breed definitely needs thorough socializing,
preferably starting before its eighth week. Their
natural shyness toward people, animals and things
(including situations) that are new to them, could
lead to undesirable behavior if the dog is not trained in time or adequately. Saarloos wolfhond
handlers need considerable knowledge about dog
behavior and need to put it into practice. They
should also be able to behave like a pack leader to
gain the dog's respect and trust. If these requirements are met, all efforts will lead to a balanced,
socially adjusted dog that can be taken anywhere
and that responds well to all kinds of stimulation.
This breed is intelligent enough to learn commands very quickly, but you should not expect
absolute obedience. It is not a good idea to make

Forest brown male Saarloos Wolfhound

Male Czechoslovakian Wolf Dog

CZECHOSLOVAKIAN WOLFDOG	
COUNTRY OF ORIGIN	THE FORMER CZECHOSLOVAKIA
ORIGINAL FUNCTION	POLICE DOG, ARMY DOG

APPEARANCE

BODY

The Czechoslovakian Wolfdog's body frame is a bit longer than tall (ratio 10:9). The withers are pronounced and muscular and the topline is straight and solid. The muscular loins and croup are short and not wide. The tail is high set and carried pendulously. If the dog is alert the tail becomes saber-shaped and slightly raised. The chest is wide and does not reach down to the tight-fitting and agile elbows. The legs are straight and well angulated and the forequarters are fairly close to each other. The front paws point outward a little and the toes are long and arched. The dry and very muscular neck is long enough for the nose can reach down to

A Saarloos Wolfhound (left) and a Czechoslovakian Wolf Dog

the ground. The neck flows gracefully into the body.

HEAD

From above it has the blunt shape of a dome. The upper skull is arched lightly with a clearly visible occipital protuberance. The stop is moderate. The muzzle is dry, with a straight nose bridge and tight lips. The short V-shaped ears are carried erect. The eyes are small. They are set obliquely and the eyelids fit tightly. Czechoslovakian Wolfhounds have a complete scissors or pincer bite.

SHOULDER HEIGHT

Dogs should not be lower than $25^1/_2$ in (65cm) and for bitches the minimum height is $23^1/_2$ in (60 cm).

WEIGHT

Dogs should weigh at least 57 lb (26 kg) and bitches at least 44 lb (20 kg).

COAT

The wiry hairs make a straight and close lying top layer with a dense, woolly undercoat. There is a marked difference between summer and winter coats.

COLORS

The permitted shades for coats are silver gray to yellow gray, with a typical lighter colored mask. Below the neck and on the chest the color is lighter. A dark gray coat is also acceptable.

TEMPERAMENT

CHARACTER

Czechoslovakian Wolf-dogs have wolves' and German Shepherds' blood running through their veins. Unlike the Saarloos wolfhond this breed is less cautious and reserved in character. They are relatively playful and remain so until a high age. However,

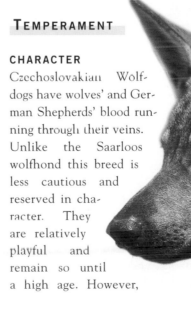

Czechoslovakian Wolf Dog bitch

they still have some wolves' blood in them, which means that they are very authentic animals with typical wolf-like features. They like digging. Czechoslovakian Wolfdogs are very intelligent, attached to their owners and alert to whatever is happening around them. In general they are more obedient and easier to train than the Saarloos wolfhond, but will always retain a degree of independence. Their scent and stamina are excellent and also their hunting instinct is quite obvious. Czechoslovakian Wolfdogs bark very little. Many – but not all – bitches are on heat only once a year.

SOCIAL BEHAVIOR

This breed generally gets on well with other dogs belonging to the same pack and with dogs they know well. It is best to find them a companion. Toward other dogs they do not know, particularly the males, they can be dominant. If a Czechoslovakian Wolfdog has been socialized with children from the start it will be able to live with them in harmony. In practice it will also mix well with other pets in the family – provided they have grown up together from the start – but mixing with other animals might cause some problems when there hunting instinct takes the overhand. They do not like strangers and may be rather reserved toward them.

Male Czechoslovakian Wolf Dog

GENERAL CARE

GROOMING

The coat needs grooming with a coarse brush about once or twice a week. In the molt seasons, which are heavy for this breed, you might need the teasel brush to remove loose hairs from the undercoat. Keep claws short.

TRAINING

Czechoslovakian Wolfdogs can be trained relatively quickly and well, provided the owner has

Czechoslovakian Wolf Dogs like to dig.

a greater knowledge about dog behavior and knows how to apply it. You will achieve the best results by giving the dog a varied training, and providing it with new challenges. A repeat of the same exercises will have a dulling effect. Thorough socialization is a decisive factor in giving your dog a chance to grow up into an equable dog, responding to all kinds of situations in a stable fashion.

EXERCISE

They need a lot of daily exercise. You need to allow 45 minutes a day for long walks, giving the dog – provided it is well trained – an opportunity to stretch its legs. Teach it to jog along with you. Their hunting instinct and excellent scent mean you need to fence your garden well; certainly if you frequently allow your dog in the yard without supervision.

USES

In the country of origin and very occasionally elsewhere, this breed is used for training for hunting and police work. They are not as easy to train as the Mechelen (Belgian) and German Shepherds, but the results are not bad at all. In addition they are extremely well equipped for tracking dog work.

Czechoslovakian
Wolf Dog bitch

SHETLAND SHEEPDOG OR SHELTIE

COUNTRY OF ORIGIN	SCOTLAND (SHETLAND ISLES)
ORIGINAL FUNCTION	SHEEPDOG

Sable Sheltie

APPEARANCE

BODY

The Shetland Sheepdog or Sheltie, for short, looks like a miniature copy of the Scottish Sheepdog. Its body is slightly longer than it is tall. The back is level and the croup slopes gradually. The chest reaches down to the elbows. The ribs are well arched, although they taper a little downward. The tail is set low and reaches at least to the hocks. Usually it is carried slightly upward in a curve, but should not be raised above the topline. The well-angulated legs are straight and have strong bones. The feet are oval shaped and have tightly closed and arched toes. Shelties have well-arched necks, long enough to carry their heads proudly.

HEAD

It is long and wedge-shaped, with a flat skull between the ears and flat cheeks that flow into the round muzzle. Muzzle and skull are equal in length. From the side they appear to run parallel and are separated by a slight stop. The high-set ears are small and triangular and when the dog is alert they are carried erect, with dropping tips. The almond-shaped eyes are set obliquely in the head. Shelties have a complete scissors bite.

Three-color Sheltie

SHOULDER HEIGHT

Dogs are $14\frac{1}{2}$ in (37cm) and bitches $13\frac{3}{4}$ in ($35\frac{1}{2}$ cm). Variations of 1in ($2\frac{1}{2}$ cm) upward or downward are acceptable.

COAT

Shelties have a double coat. The undercoat is soft, dense and short and the upper coat is long, rough and straight. Their hair around the neck, on the chest and shoulders is longer than the rest of their body and the hair on the tail and the back of their hindquarters, down to their hocks, is considerably longer. The front and bottom half of the forequarters and the face is short-haired.

Sable Sheltie.

COLORS

Shelties might be sable (from light gold-colored to mahogany with or without black tips), tricolor (black, with tan markings and white), blue merle (silver blue background with black markings and possibly warm brown markings), black brown and black white. All these colors, with the exception of black brown, should preferably be combined with a white chest, ruff, blaze, legs and tip of tail. White markings on other places are not desirable at shows. The eyes will be dark brown in theory, but blue merles may have one or two, or partially blue-colored eyes. The forenose is black.

TEMPERAMENT

CHARACTER

Shelties are extremely intelligent and smart dogs. If they are trained in the right way they will quickly learn commands and they will be obedient, too, but a little stubbornness is also part of their character. They are cheerful and bright and very active. Shelties will bark noisily when they sense danger. They are very faithful to their owners and members of the family and very devoted, too. This breed tends to stick to their territory, which means that they are not inclined to

Sheltie

leave your property of their own accord. They prefer to be near to their families and therefore they are not suited to life in a kennel.

SOCIAL BEHAVIOR

As a rule mixing with other dogs, (small) livestock, cats and other pets does not cause any problems. They tend to get on well with children, provided they are not too noisy and do not tease the dog. Shelties are suspicious of strangers. They do not get on well with just anybody; it might take a while before they give themselves.

GENERAL CARE

GROOMING

It is not overtly difficult to care for this breed, but weekly brushing is essential. Their hair tends to tangle behind the ears, in the armpits and culottes. These areas need some more attention. During the molt season the Sheltie loses a lot of hair and it will be necessary to brush your dog thoroughly down to the skin once every other day to remove dead and loose hairs.

TRAINING

This dog is quite trainable. A Sheltie likes being taught and enjoys following commands. You need to train this dog gently and consistently. Shelties

A blue merle Sable Sheltie bitch

respond well to the intonation of your voice. Commands given cheerfully and with plenty of variation will achieve the best results. Allow yourself more time for good socialization, so that the dog can mature into a stable representative of its breed.

EXERCISE

A Sheltie will adapt to circumstances, but if it gets nervy, it means that it has not had enough exercise for weeks. Shelties need more than a quick trot round the corner three times a day. Wind or rain does not bother Shelties. They love ball games and retrieving and it is good to allow them to let off steam off-leash. They do not tend to stray from their owners and do not have much hunting instinct. A romp in natural surroundings can therefore be a relaxing time.

USES

Although a Sheltie will suit a sporty family without any problem, you will need to pay attention to its intelligence and desire to work, as they will be wasted if they are not "used." Shelties like to have a job to do and ideally you should decide to take this dog to one of the dog sports. Shelties perform extremely well — they are often at the top. Flyball and agility skills are highly suitable sports as well as advanced obedience. You will not fare badly if you take this dog to competitions.

Sable Sheltie bitch

SCOTTISH COLLIE, LONGHAIRED AND SHORTHAIRED	
COUNTRY OF ORIGIN	NORTH OF ENGLAND AND SCOTLAND
ORIGINAL FUNCTION	SHEPHERD

Sable Rough-haired Scottish Collie

APPEARANCE

BODY

The longhaired Scottish Collies' body frame will be slightly longer than tall. The spine is straight and the loins are arched a little. The chest is deep and wide and the ribs are well arched. The lower phalanx of the tail reaches at least down to the hocks. The tail is carried pendent with the tip curved slightly upward. In

Rough-haired Scottish Collie

movement the tail is carried higher, but never in a curl above the topline. The legs are straight and the elbows fit tightly. Scottish Collies have oval shaped feet with well-closed toes. The strong and muscular neck is moderately long and arches slightly.

Rough-haired Scottish Collie

HEAD

The head is bluntly wedge-shaped with a flat skull. The skull gradually tapers toward the front, without protruding cheekbones. The crown of the skull and the nose bridge run parallel, except for a light stop on a level with the ears. The forenose and skull are equally long. The ears are small. If the dog is alert, they are carried erect, with the tips of the ears hanging

Three-colored Rough-haired Scottish Collie

down ("tipped ears"). In repose the dog will fold its ears backward. The almond-shaped eyes should not be too small. They are set obliquely and have an intelligent and gentle expression. Scottish Collies have a complete scissors bite.

SHOULDER HEIGHT

For dogs it ranges from 22–24 in (56–61cm) and for bitches from 20–22 in (51–56 cm).

WEIGHT

Dogs weigh approx. $46^{1}/_{4}$–$66^{1}/_{4}$ lb ($20^{1}/_{2}$–$29^{1}/_{2}$ kg) and bitches $39^{1}/_{2}$–$55^{1}/_{4}$ lb (18–25 kg).

COAT

This breed has two different types of coat. The best known is a very dense and longhaired coat with a much fuller and longer haired ruff and tail. The upper coat is straight and coarse and lies closely. The undercoat is very dense, soft and woolly. The hair is very short on the face, tips of the ears and the lower part of the legs. The lesser-known short-haired Scottish Collie has a short and close-lying coat. The upper coat typically has a rough structure and the undercoat is very dense.

COLORS

Scottish Collies may be saber-colored with white, tricolor and blue merle. Saber includes every shade from light gold to deep mahogany or red, always with black tipped hairs. Pale straw or creamy colors are undesirable. A tricolor Scottish Collie is predominantly pure black, with tan colored markings on feet and forehead and white markings. Blue merle consists of mainly silver blue, spotted black and marbled. Big black plates and a rusty sheen over the coat are

Rough-haired Scottish Collie

highly undesirable in these color patterns. The tricolor patterns may go together with typical white markings, a fully or partly white ruff, a white front (often part of the chest and stomach), white legs and feet and a white tip of the tail. A blaze is also allowed. The color of the eyes will always be brown for tricolored and saber-colored Scottish Collies. Blue merles may also have (partly) blue eyes.

Male sable Rough-haired Scottish Collie

TEMPERAMENT

CHARACTER

Scottish Collies are cheerful, very intelligent and smart, ready to work and energetic. They are sociably minded and sensitive and devoted. They notice what goes on around them and guard extremely well. They tend to protect the younger members of the family. Scottish Collies are firmly attached to their owners and do not bark a lot.

SOCIAL BEHAVIOR

These dogs are very sociable and get on fine with other pets and dogs. They tend to be nice and tolerant to children and they clearly have a tendency towards protecting them. Welcome guests and acquaintances are greeted in a friendly fashion. The dog will be on guard and on the defense with strangers, particularly if nobody is at home.

GENERAL CARE

GROOMING

The longhaired Scottish Collie is a very hairy dog that needs a thorough comb and brush at least once a week. Particularly dense areas need to be groomed to the skin to avoid tangles. During molting you will need to brush and comb your dog almost daily to avoid a surplus of hair in the house. The short-haired Scottish Collie needs less grooming, but should nevertheless be brushed and combed regularly. A teasel brush would be the most efficient tool. They tend to lose relatively large amounts of hair, even outside the molting

Blue merle Smooth-haired Scottish Collie bitch

season. And of course the advantage of a shorter coat is that it does not usually tangle easily. Poor grooming will leave even short-haired dogs with rather unattractive felted plates. Keep claws clipped.

Blue merle Rough-haired Scottish Collie bitch

Blue merle Smooth-haired Scottish Collie

go off on a walk. They can be trusted not to leave their territory and will generally remain near to their owners on walks off-leash. A walk with a Scottish Collie should therefore be quite relaxing. A Scottish Collie is quite calm in the house.

USES
The Scottish Collie is recommended as a very pleasant dog in families with children looking for a friend and with adults who are happy to romp and do sports. Several types of dog sports are highly suitable for this dog, such as flyball, agility and all kinds of obedience training.

TRAINING
The Scottish Collie likes to learn and does so quickly. It also enjoys doing things for its owner. You will achieve the best results if you play with your tone of voice. Do not forget this Scot is a very sensitive dog and that raising your voice, particularly if you are its handler whom it will adore, will hurt it down to the marrow. Harsh training is absolutely out of the question. It is important to socialize the young puppy well, so that it will grow up into an equable and cheerful dog that responds in a stable manner to all kinds of impressions and stimuli.

EXERCISE
Scottish Collies need a fair amount of physical exercise, but if it does not suit you on the odd occasion, it will not bother them. Do take the dog on longer walks on a regular basis. Ball games, retrieving and romping off-leash are their favorite activities. Once fully grown, you can put higher demands on your dog's exercise. One of the big advantages of this breed is that it does not tend to

Three-color and sable
Smooth-haired Scottish Collies

BORDER COLLIE

BORDER COLLIE	
COUNTRY OF ORIGIN	ENGLAND
ORIGINAL AND	SHEPHERD AND
TODAY'S FUNCTION	CATTLE DRIVER

Border Collie.

APPEARANCE

BODY

The Border Collie has an athletic, light and squarely built body. The chest is wide and strong and the ribs are well arched. The loins are wide, muscular and lightly tucked up and the wide and the muscular croup droops moderately to the base of the tail. The tail reaches at least to the heel, is set low and is carried downward. The tail should never be carried above the back. The shoulders slope well and the elbows fit tightly. The well-angulated legs are strong, but the bones should not be heavy. They are vertical and parallel to each other. The feet are oval shaped and have close-fitting bent toes. The powerful and muscular neck is broader at the shoulders.

HEAD

There is a clear stop in a fairly broad skull without a protruding occipital peak. The moderately short and strong muzzle tapers toward the nose. The skull and muzzle are almost of equal length. The moderately big ears are set far apart. They are usually carried half pricked. The eyes are set wide and are oval shaped. They are moderately big and have a lively and wise expression. Border Collies have a scissors bite.

SHOULDER HEIGHT

Ideally dogs should be $20^3/_4$ in (53 cm) and bitches

are a bit smaller.

COAT

There are two kinds of coats: short-haired and (moderately) longhaired Border Collies. The long-haired variety is in the majority. Both short-haired and longhaired dogs have a dense and moderately thick upper coat with a short, soft, dense and weather-resistant

Three-color Border Collie

undercoat. Longhaired dogs have shorter hair on the nose and the legs (underneath and at the front) and longer round the ruff, the culottes and on the tail.

Border Collie

83

Border Collie

COLORS

All colors are permissible, but white should never be dominant. Black and white are the best knows color combination, but also blue merles and tri-color dogs (black and tan with white markings) are quite popular. Except for blue merles that may have (partly) blue eyes, the color of the eyes is always brown.

TEMPERAMENT

CHARACTER

These dogs are utter working dogs, highly intelligent and smart, lively and agile, alert, watchful, nimble, willing to work and often display a considerable amount of toughness and courage. They tend to hang on to one person in particular. Border Collies are not very susceptible to weather conditions and if they have sufficient exercise and things to do, they can be kept in outdoor kennels without any problem.

SOCIAL BEHAVIOR

Border Collies generally get on well with other dogs. Once they are well socialized, mixing with cats and other pets should not be a problem. On the whole they mix well with children although they are not everybody's friends. Consider that they are real working dogs, who are predominantly used for herding and driving cattle. If there is no work a Border Collie will find itself a job, such as playing with your children or herding dogs in the field.

GENERAL CARE

GROOMING

These dogs do not need a great amount of coat care.

It is sufficient to groom these dogs once a week. Keep the ear canal clean and clip their claws.

TRAINING

Border Collies are a breed known throughout the

Blue merle Border Collie

world for their amazing intelligence, smartness and willingness to work. They like to learn commands and follow them and therefore they are very easy to train. Apart from that it is important for this dog to have one real owner, who is very consistent and knows that this is a real working dog. A lenient or inconsistent owner will have a rough deal with this breed for the dog may one day decide to defy authority.

Border Collies are outstanding in virtually every type of dog sport.

EXERCISE

This breed needs a lot of exercise, but the dogs also want to work and must do so. An idle Border Collie will become extremely badly behaved and even aggressive. You cannot blame the dog, but you should hold the owner responsible for choosing the wrong breed. Plenty of physical exercise will not be enough for this dog. It must be able to work, with body and mind as one, carrying out different tasks. These jobs do not have to be performed in a group or together with sheep; even retrieving balls, looking for hidden objects, obedience skills and "tricks" are acceptable to this dog. A Border Collie that is satisfied, will be a dog that behaves excellently at home of in general.

USES

Most Border Collies have a natural ability for driving sheep and other animals, but it is no coincidence that these dogs always score highly in

Border Collie

all kinds of disciplines among the dog sports. They are at the top when it comes to sports as skill, obedience, advanced obedience and flyball. The Border Collie is a gift from heaven for people who are competitive in dog sports or who need a sheep driver. But also people who really like to do things with their dogs alone, teach them all kinds of things, who are happy to spend lots of time doing so, they will be very happy with this breed. The average Border Collie is not meant to be an average family dog of the kind that only goes to the woods on Sundays.

The most common color for Border Collies is black and white.

German Shepherd bitch

GERMAN SHEPHERD

COUNTRY OF ORIGIN	GERMANY
ORIGINAL AND	UTILITY DOG, SUITABLE FOR
TODAY'S FUNCTION	A NUMBER OF OTHER
	PURPOSES

APPEARANCE

BODY

The German Shepherd has a light square angular body frame. The topline is level and strong. It should not be too long between the long withers, which should be of a good height and the long croup, sloping downward lightly. The heavily feathered tail reaches at least to the hocks and is carried pendulously in a light arch at rest. When moving, the tail is carried high, but should not be raised above the topline. The chest is deep, but not broad. The lower chest is as long as possible and the ribs are long and well shaped; that is neither flat, nor barrel-shaped. The belly is tucked up slightly. The well closed shoulder blades are long and have a definite slant. The legs are vertical and well-angulated. German Shepherds have tight-fitting, rounded, short feet. Dew claws should be removed. The neck is strong and dry with well-developed muscles.

HEAD

Overall it is dry and moderately wide between the ears. The forehead is moderately arched with little or no central furrow. The skull and the wedge-shaped muzzle are of equal length, and the straight nose bridge and upper skull are almost parallel. The stop is not clearly marked. The lips are tight. The moderate ears are set high. They are broad at the base and taper into a point. They are carried erect, with the earflaps turned forward. The medium-sized eyes are almond shaped and set a little obliquely in the head. German Shepherds have a complete scissors bite.

SHOULDER HEIGHT

Ideally this should be $24^3/_4$ in ($62^1/_2$ cm) for dogs and $22^3/_4$ in ($57^1/_2$ cm) for bitches. Variations of 1 in ($2^1/_2$ cm) upward or downward are permitted.

COAT

There are three types of coats for the German Shepherd:
– the wire-haired coat has a dense, straight, harsh and a close-lying outer and undercoat.

German Shepherds are the most used working dogs world wide.

The hair is longer on the ruff, trousers, the rear of the legs and the tail, and short on the face and at the front of the legs.

- long wire-haired dogs can be compared with wire-haired dogs, except that they have longer hairs, which are not as close-lying. The hair is considerably longer, particularly by the ears, the tail and the loins.
- longhaired dogs have fairly long hair, usually with little or no undercoat. This variety is undesirable because the coat is often too soft with no undercoat.

Wolf-gray German Shepherds

COLORS

The German Shepherd is seen in black, steel gray, ash or a plain color, or with regular brown, yellow to off-white markings. A black or dark clouded saddle is quite common. Small white markings on the chest or on the inside of the legs are acceptable, but not desired. The nose is always black and the claws and eyes should be as dark as possible.

Black is a rare color for German Shepherds

TEMPERAMENT

CHARACTER

This breed is very intelligent and the dogs like to work. They notice what goes on around them and naturally guard their family members, home and possessions.

They are extremely loyal and affectionate, friendly and self-confident. Although they tend to be friends to everyone in the family, including the children, most of them tend to attach themselves to one person only. Strangers cannot bribe them. They have an excellent scent. Their coat protects them from all weather conditions which means they can be kept in kennels without any problems. Note that the companionship of other dogs can be no substitute for an owner. These dogs focus on their owners and will strive to please them. This breed is not suitable for people who spend a lot of their time away from home; if this kind of owner-focused dog does not get enough attention, it will feel punished.

SOCIAL BEHAVIOR

A German Shepherd can get on well with children provided they respect the dog. Please take into consideration that many of these

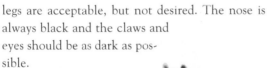

German Shepherd bitch

dogs will defend your children if their games with friends become to rough. They are on their guard toward strangers, but if the owner says everything is fine, they will abide. Friends of the family will be greeted boisterously. If the dog is well socialized, a German Shepherd will not cause any problems with other pets and it will get on well with their other peers.

GENERAL CARE

GROOMING

Head of a German Shepherd

German Shepherds need regular brushing with a teasel brush to remove dead and loose hairs from the dense woolly undercoat. Dogs that live indoors will need more grooming than those kept outdoors; the former tend to molt all year, with an increase in the spring and fall. Keep claws clipped.

TRAINING

German Shepherds are extremely intelligent. They want to learn from their handlers and love following commands. It is not surprising that they are quick to learn. They are sensitive to your tone of voice. If you are clear, honest and consistent, training will not cause you any difficulties. Dogs are bigger and stronger than bitches; therefore it is wise to teach them from an early age not to tug while on leash.

EXERCISE

People who keep German Shepherds as family pets frequently overlook the fact that they need a lot of exercise. The dog will be much happier after long walks, running, retrieving or swimming. Allow yourselves at least one hour a day. German Shepherds will not leave their territory; they know the boundaries of your yard and are not in-clined to explore. If the relationship with the owner is good the dog will not tend to roam independently while off-leash.

USES

This type of dog will not feel happy if it has "nothing" to do; the German Shepherd is the most popular working dog worldwide. It is used by the army and police; it works as a rescue dog, avalanche dog, guide dog, hearing dog or as a tracking and drug sniffer dog. In addition this versatile breed can perform exceptionally well in almost any kind of dog sports, such as training for hunting, agility skills and advanced obedience. The breed is very suitable for sports-loving people who like to try things together with their dog.

German Shepherd bitch

Mechelen Belgian Shepherd

MECHELEN BELGIAN SHEPHERD	
COUNTRY OF ORIGIN	BELGIUM
PREVIOUS FUNCTION	HISTORICALLY A CATTLE DRIVER

APPEARANCE

BODY

The Mechelen Shepherd, called "Mechelaar" by its enthusiasts, displays a combination of strength and elegance. The Mechelen Shepherd dog has a square build, while the bitch's body may be longer than it is tall. They have long, sloping shoulder blades, a deep forechest and clearly defined withers. Back and loins are straight, broad and muscular. The groin is moderately wide and slopes very slightly. The moderate belly continues from the chest in a flowing line. The tail is moderately long and is carried pendent with a light curve at the end. Both front and hind legs are sturdy, parallel and straight, with round forefeet and hind feet. The toes are well arched and close well. The dry neck is a little longer and tapers gradually toward the neck, which is slightly arched.

HEAD

This dog carries its fine and fairly long, dry head with pride. Skull and muzzle are almost the same length, although the muzzle could be a little longer. The muzzle tapers gradually toward the nose. The nose bridge is straight and from the side it appears to run parallel to the top half of the skull. Mechelen Shepherds have a moderate stop. The cheeks are dry and flat, but quite muscular nevertheless. The lips are thin, tightly closed and should have sufficient pigmentation. The high set ears are carried stiff and pricked and are triangular. The eyes are slightly almond shaped and moderately big. They have well-pigmented eye rims and a lively, sensible and questioning expression. These dogs will preferably have a scissors bite, but a pincers bite is accepted, too.

SHOULDER HEIGHT

Dogs are approx. $24\frac{1}{2}$ in (62 cm) and bitches $22\frac{3}{4}$ in (58 cm) high. Variations of $\frac{3}{4}$ in (2 cm) or less or $1\frac{1}{2}$ in (4cm) more are permissible.

COAT

The short-haired coat of the Mechelen Shepherd lies close to the body and has a woolly undercoat. Its hair should not wave. It is very short on the head, the ears and the bottom half of the legs. It is fuller on the tail, trousers and round the neck, where it forms a light ruff.

COLORS

These dogs are only bred in a pale reddish color with black hairtips, and always with a black mask. White markings on the front of the chest and toes are permissible. The eyes should preferably have a dark color.

Mechelen Belgian
Shepherd

TEMPERAMENT

CHARACTER

Dogs of this breed are known for their attentiveness, persistence, courage, toughness, willingness to work, shrewd intelligence and smartness. They are good guardians and very loyal. They will protect their families and their possessions with conviction, when necessary. These high-spirited and agile dogs can be rather domineering. A Mechelen Shepherd can be kept in outdoor kennels without any problems, provided it is not deprived of human contact – they are very attached to their owners.

SOCIAL BEHAVIOR

The Mechelen Shepherd will generally get on well with children. Some of them tend to be a little dominant toward other dogs. The same applies to cats and other pets who need to be with the dogs from the start, so that there will be no problems at a later date. Friends of the family are greeted boisterously, but in other situations they may respond according to circumstances.

GENERAL CARE

GROOMING

The Mechelen Shepherd's coat does not need a lot of care. Only during the molting season you will have to brush the coat with a teasel brush to prevent loose hair in the undercoat from felting. Keep claws short.

Mechelen Belgian Shepherd

TRAINING

The Mechelen Shepherd is a very quick and keen learner. Training will not be a problem, although it requires a calm atmosphere and consistency of the owner. A Mechelen Shepherd that does not sense strong leadership, may one day decide to turn the tables on its owner and family. The owner needs to have

Male Mechelen Belgian Shepherd

a strong personality and should not only train the dog but also regularly do activities together with the dog. A Mechelen Shepherd that is bored, will be unhappy and will display devious behavior. You could spend extra time on thorough socializing, allowing the dog to meet a number of people, animals and all kinds of situations. This will help to build its character.

EXERCISE

These dogs are definite working dogs. These energetic dogs not only need more exercise than the average dog, but they also need to be stimulated mentally. You can do almost anything with this dog, provided you give it a new challenge each day. They can run with you, love ball games, retrieving, swimming and romping off-leash. They are not bothered by adverse weather conditions. It is a great advantage that they do not tend to roam and will stay near to you when off-leash, so that you need not worry on your walks.

USES

Mechelen Shepherds are extremely suited to all kinds of dog sports, such as training for hunting, agility, flyball and advanced obedience. Even in more serious work you will meet Mechelen Shepherds, for instance as tracker dogs, avalanche dogs, rescue dogs and police dogs.

TERVUEREN AND GROENENDAEL BELGIAN SHEPHERDS

COUNTRY OF ORIGIN	BELGIUM
PREVIOUS FUNCTION	HISTORICALLY HERDING DOGS

APPEARANCE

Apart from the coat (see below) these two breeds should look like the Mechelen Shepherd, even their shoulder heights are the similar.

COAT

The Tervueren Shepherd and Groenendaeler have long, close-lying hair over a smooth and a woolly undercoat without waves. Round the ruff, behind the forequarters (upper part), the culottes and the tail the hair is longer and more abundant. It is short on the head, behind the ears and on the lower part of the legs.

COLORS

Tervueren Shepherds might be fawn, gray red, mealy brown gray and every variety of brown to gray, always with a black mask. In the show ring, however, gray blacks are preferred; fallow with black flames. White markings on chest and toes are permissible. Groenendaelers always are deep black, possibly with small white markings on chest and toes.

Male Tervueren Belgian Shepherd

TEMPERAMENT

CHARACTER

Tervueren Shepherds and Groenendaelers are energetic, very lively, sensitive and alert dogs. They are persistent, intelligent and smart, ready to work and very attached to their owners and families. In addition they are very watchful and will guard their folks and belongings with convic-tion if necessary. Most are not suitable for life in a kennel.

SOCIAL BEHAVIOR

If a dog has had good experiences at an early age, it will get on well with other dogs, cats and pets. If the children respect the dog, they will be able to live together harmoniously. They are shy to strangers and on their guard. They do not tend to like everybody, but will greet friends of the family boisterously.

GENERAL CARE

GROOMING

The coats of these dogs do not need a lot of care. It is not generally recommended to comb or brush the dog too frequently because if done too thoroughly it will damage the undercoat. A coarse comb would be most suitable during the molt to remove loose hairs from the undercoat.

Tervueren Belgian Shepherd puppy

TRAINING

The puppies of Tervueren Shepherds and

Groenendael Belgian Shepherd

Groenendael Belgian Shepherd

Male Tervueren Belgian Shepherd

Male Tervueren Belgian Shepherd

Groenendaelers need their self-confidence boosting. Take them to new places and stay with them while you introduce them to all kinds of people, animals and situations. Try to make these encounters positive, noncommittal and cheerful. Thorough socialization will give you an open and happy dog that will continue to respond soundly to all kinds of impressions and events for the rest of its life. These dogs are highly intelligent and learn very quickly. They respond well to the voice of their owners. They tend to have a sensitive nature and harsh words will affect them deeply. Smacking and shouting tends to be counter-productive and should be avoided. A gentle but consistent manner works miracles.

EXERCISE

These high-spirited dogs need more exercise than average. They are always ready for a ball game, swimming, retrieving and romping off-leash. Find ways for the dog to join you when your are involved in running activities, so it can spend its energy. A Tervueren Shepherd or Groenendaeler that has a good rapport with its owner will not leave its owner during a walk off-leash. When both breeds get sufficient outdoor exercise, they will be calm indoors.

USES

Different kinds of dog sports are suitable for both breeds. They go crazy about obedience and flyball competitions in which they excel. They also live up to their reputation when it comes to "serious" disciplines, such as rescue work.

Groenendael Belgian Shepherd
bitch

LAEKEN BELGIAN SHEPHERD

COUNTRY OF ORIGIN	BELGIUM
PREVIOUS FUNCTION	TRADITIONALLY A CATTLE DRIVER

APPEARANCE

Apart from the coat (see below) the Laeken Belgian Shepherd should look like the Mechelen Shepherd, even their shoulder heights are similar.

COAT

The Laeken Shepherd is rough haired. The hair is rough and dry and looks messy. On average the hairs' length right across the body is $2^1/_2$ in (6 cm). The hair around the eyes and below the muzzle should not be too long.

COLORS

The coat will be fallow with dark flamed hairs, particularly on the muzzle and tail.

TEMPERAMENT

CHARACTER

The Laeken Belgian Shepherds are intelligent, alert, lively, hardy, and brave dogs that are keen to work. They have great stamina. They are attached and faithful to their families and will guard and protect their people, home and yard ferociously

Laeken Belgian Shepherd

from undesirable characters. They might be domineering and a bit stubborn. They may well be kept in kennels provided they naturally get enough attention and exercise.

SOCIAL BEHAVIOR

Laeken Belgian Shepherds generally get on well with children. Sometimes they are a little dominant to other dogs. They need to be socialized with cats and other pets from an early age to avoid problems at a later date. Uninvited guests will be stopped and they will initially be a little suspicious of invited guests. These dogs are not everyone's friend.

GENERAL CARE

Laeken Belgian Shepherd

GROOMING

This rough haired dog needs to be plucked twice a year, but a lot depends on the quality of the coat. Dead and superfluous hair needs to be plucked by hand Never be tempted to have a Laeken Belgian Shepherd's coat shorn – it will ruin the coat for many years. Just comb the coat with a coarse comb in between plucking sessions.

TRAINING

It need not be difficult to train a Laeken Belgian Shepherd, provided the dog has a consistent owner who is firm. The dog is intelligent and wants to learn from you. Keep the training varied. The dog will benefit from thorough socialization.

Laeken Belgian Shepherd

Laeken Belgian Shepherd

EXERCISE

These dogs need a fair amount of exercise and they need set tasks. The Laeken Belgian Shepherd does not mind whether you are serious about its training or if you are asking it to retrieve or do exercises for fun, as long as it has something to do. You can take the dog running with you, swimming and for long walks off-leash. Its shepherd's instinct will prevent it from roaming too far from its owner.

USES

Laeken Belgian Shepherds are excellent guard and defense dogs, but they also do well at sports such as agility, flyball and advanced obedience. A variety of jobs such as rescue work and tracking will suit a well-trained Laeken Belgian Shepherd, too.

Laeken Belgian Shepherd

DUTCH SHEPHERD	
COUNTRY OF ORIGIN	THE NETHERLANDS
PREVIOUS FUNCTION	SHEEPDOG

Short-haired Dutch Shepherd

APPEARANCE

BODY

The Dutch Shepherd is a medium-sized dog with a powerful and proportionate build. Its body is slightly longer than tall (ratio 10:9). The back is straight and short and the loins are sturdy. The croup is neither too short, nor does it slope gently. The tail is carried pendulous and may have a slight curve. The deep chest is not too narrow. The shoulders are sloping. The knee joints and hocks of the hindquarters are moderately angulated. The feet are well closed with arched toes. They should not be too long. The neck is dry and not too short.

HEAD

Its size is proportionate to its body. The head has no folds or wrinkles and its shape is elongated rather than heavy. From the side the straight nose bridge and topskull appear to run parallel. Dutch Shepherds do not have a pronounced stop. The lips close tightly. The ears are set high, relatively small and are carried erect, twisted forward. The ears should not be spoon-shaped. The moderately

Short-haired Dutch Shepherd

sized eyes are almond shaped and slightly slanting. Dutch Shepherds have a scissors bite.

SHOULDER HEIGHT
Dogs range from $22^1/_2$–$24^1/_2$ in (57–62 cm) and bitches from $21^3/_4$–$23^1/_2$ in (55–60 cm).

COAT
There are three different kinds of coats:

Shot-haired Dutch Shepherd.

– short hair: these dogs should have harsh hair, which is not too short all over their body, with a woolly undercoat. They have an obvious ruff and trousers, and also the tail has longer hair than the rest of the body

– long hair: longhaired Dutch Shepherds have long, straight, close-lying and coarse hair over the whole body with a woolly undercoat. Head, ears and feet are short-haired. Hair on the hindquarters, from the hocks downward, is short. The hair of the ruff, the back of the front legs and the tail is longer.

– wiry hair: the wire-haired Dutch Shepherds should have a dense, harsh and messy coat with a woolly, dense undercoat. The upper and lower lips are very hairy (mustache and beard) and the eyebrows are rough and stand out. A full pair of trousers is desirable and the tail is well feathered all round.

COLORS
The following colors are acknowledged:
– short and longhaired dogs are accepted with silver and gold brindle coats. Preferably they should have a black mask, but too heavy an outer coat in black is not desirable.
– the wire-haired dog may also be silver and gold brindle, but is also accepted with blue gray and salt and pepper.

TEMPERAMENT

CHARACTER
Dutch Shepherds are highly intelligent, tough, sober and active dogs. They are focused on their owners and families. They are affectionate and obedient and like to work. All three varieties are alert and quite watchful. They bark when they sense danger and if necessary, they will defend their families. Although the three coat varieties are similar, when it comes to character there are a few differences. The short-haired variety appears to be tougher and more aggressive and the wire and longhaired varieties generally appear to be more sensitive and thoughtful.

SOCIAL BEHAVIOR
Dutch Shepherds usually get on well with other dogs. They still have a hunting instinct, but if they have been well socialized and brought up,

Long-haired Dutch Shepherd

95

mixing with cats and other pets will not present any problems. They usually like children, provided the kids show respect and do not tease them. Strangers will be stopped, while friends of the family will be greeted boisterously.

GENERAL CARE

GROOMING
The coats of short and longhaired dogs are fairly easy to keep tidy if they are brushed with a teasel brush or pin brush once a week. During molting a higher frequency of grooming is required. The wire-haired coat should never be brushed, but combed with a coarse comb. It is not recommended to comb the wire-haired too generously. You could have this coat plucked approximately twice a year in a trimming parlor. They will pluck old hair by hand, so that new hair has enough room to come through. The coat will be clipped here and there for the "finishing touch." It is required that you keep the claws trimmed, no matter the variety. You might find too much hair growing in the ear canals of long and wire-haired Dutch Shepherds, which is best removed.

TRAINING
The Dutch Shepherd is intelligent and happy to work and learn from you. They pick up commands very quickly. Long and wire-haired Shepherds are usually not to keen on intensive, repetitive trai-

Long-haired Dutch Shepherd

ning, while the short-haired variety is more willing. Keep the training varied for longhaired and wire-haired Shepherds to keep the dogs interested.

EXERCISE
Your Shepherd will benefit from regular demanding walks or a good run in the woods or across a field. A Dutch Shepherd likes to be active and enjoys working for you. It is suggested that you spend at least half an hour twice a week on obedience skills, retrieving and other activities, because the dog will benefit physically as well as mentally.

Rough-haired Dutch Shepherd

USES
Dutch Shepherds do well when it comes to obedience, skills and flyball. The short-haired Dutch Shepherd is ideally suited to train for hunting.

Rough-haired Dutch Shepherds

SECTION 2   Cattledogs (except Swiss Cattledogs)

AUSTRALIAN CATTLE DOG	
COUNTRY OF ORIGIN	AUSTRALIA
ORIGINAL AND TODAY'S FUNCTION	CATTLE DRIVER

APPEARANCE

BODY

The Australian Cattle Dog is a squat, symmetrical and muscular dog. Its body is slightly longer than its shoulder height (ratio 11:10). The back is straight and strong, the loins are full and powerful. The loins and flanks are wide. Its broad and muscular hindquarters have a long and barely sloping pelvis. The tail is set low, reaches down to the hocks and it will hang with a slight curve, when at rest. In movement the tail should not be above the topline. It has an ample chest, moderately wide. The forechest is well muscled. The ribs are quite arched, but not round. Its strong front legs are sturdy and have round bones. Viewed from the side its pasterns point slightly outward. Note the low-set hocks on its hindquarters. The sturdy feet are short and round, with closed toes and hard, thick pads. Austral-

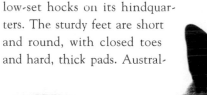

Australian Cattledog

Australian Cattle Dog

ian Cattle Dogs have a moderately long, powerful and muscular neck without any dewlap.

HEAD

It has a broad skull, slightly arched between the ears and flatter towards the front. The stop is light, but well marked. The cheeks need to be muscular, but should not protrude. The muzzle is deep and powerful with close-lying lips. Australian Cattle Dogs carry their medium-sized ears erect. They are a little pointed and set far apart. The medium-sized eyes are oval shaped. Australian Cattle Dogs have a scissors bite.

SHOULDER HEIGHT

For dogs this is 18–20 in (46–51 cm) and for bitches it is 17–19 in (43–48 cm).

COAT

The upper layer is fairly short and weather-resistant, straight and a little coarse. The under layer is short and dense. The hairs on the tail and culottes are longer than on the body. They are shorter on the head, the ears, front legs and lower half of the hindquarters.

COLORS

This breed has coats in different color patterns, ranging from blue to multi-color red. Blue refers to blue or multi-color blue with or without blue or tan-colored markings on the head, legs and body. The black markings of this color pattern are only allowed on the head. Multi-color red means an evenly parti-colored red coat, with dark red markings on the head considered very desirable. Dark red markings are allowed on the body. The nose is always black and the eyes are dark brown.

Australian Cattle Dog

TEMPERAMENT

CHARACTER

These dogs are very intelligent, very loyal to their handlers and show a willingness to work for their owners. Although they are energetic and lively, they strike one as calm and sensible. They are brave, sober and tough on themselves and quite shy, too. Australian Cattle Dogs have a friendly, yet a watchful character and they feel responsible

Australian Cattle Dog

for the well-being of their family members. On the whole they do not bark much.

SOCIAL BEHAVIOR

Australian Cattle Dogs are usually friendly and they make excellent playmates for older children. They usually get on well with peers belonging to the same pack, but when it comes to dogs they do not know, they can be a bit standoffish. They are certainly not the type of dog that play with other dogs in the playing fields. Mixing with pets such as cats does not need to be a problem. They like familiar people but toward strangers a Cattle Dog can be either benign in an off-hand manner, or very much on guard, depending on the circumstances.

GENERAL CARE

GROOMING

The Australian Cattle Dog does not require a lot of brushing. During the molt a teasel brush will come in handy to remove loose hairs from the undercoat. Keep claws short.

TRAINING

The Australian Cattle Dog is a highly intelligent dog that likes you to teach new things and enjoys performing tasks. The training is therefore quite straightforward. To avoid an Australian Cattle Dog from becoming too watchful or far too "controlling", it needs to be monitored during the socializing process.

EXERCISE

This relatively untamed working dog needs a lot of exercise, particularly activities to keep it happy. If it is kept as an average family dog it will get bored. Such a bored dog will make a nuisance of itself and start doing things you might not like. Therefore frequently take the dog on long walks. Retrieving, ball and tracking games, swimming and running are healthy and good ways to exercise and keep this breed occupied. One great advantage is that an Australian Cattle Dog does

Australian Cattle Dog

not tend to roam and is very loyal to its owner. If you have a good rapport with the dog you need not be afraid it will run off when it is off-leash.

USES

You will not be doing the Australian Cattle Dog a favor if you do not provide an outlet. This type of dog is very well suited to sports such as flyball, agility and advanced obedience. Of course you could also consider avalanche and rescue dog training. As long as you give it something to do, it will not let you down.

Australian Cattle Dog

BOUVIER DES FLANDRES (BOUVIER)	
COUNTRY OF ORIGIN	BELGIUM
PREVIOUS FUNCTION	CATTLE DRIVER, WATCH AND DEFENSE DOG

Bouvier

APPEARANCE

BODY

Bouviers have a short and robust body. The front ribs are well arched, the others are bent backward. The back is wide, short and very muscular and needs to be horizontal. The loins are short, wide and muscular. Particularly the dog's flanks are very short. The broad croup is in line with the back and does not slope. In some countries where this is permissible the tail is shortened up to two or three vertebrae. It is set on in line with the back and is carried high. The chest reaches down to the close-fitting elbows. The legs are straight, heavy boned and run parallel. Bouviers have short, round and strong feet, with close-knit toes. The dry neck is strong and the neck is slightly arched. The length of the neck is slightly less than the total length of the head.

HEAD

It looks massive, with a well-developed flat skull that is a little longer than wide. The straight nose bridge and the topskull run parallel to each other. The ratio of skull to muzzle is 3:2 in terms of length. The stop is not well defined, although the hair on the head suggests otherwise. The cheeks are dry and flat. Bouviers have small, triangular

Male Bouvier

Bouviers.

ears set high. They are carried pendulously, close to the head. The eyes are set horizontally, and are elongated and oval. Bouviers have a scissors or pincer bite.

SHOULDER HEIGHT

For dogs this varies between $24^{1}/_{2}$–$26^{3}/_{4}$ in (62–68 cm) and for bitches between 23–$25^{1}/_{2}$ in (59–65 cm). The ideal shoulder height for dogs is $25^{1}/_{2}$ and $254^{1}/_{2}$ in (65 and 62cm).

WEIGHT

Dogs range from $77^{1}/_{4}$–88 lb (35–40 kg) and bitches from $59^{1}/_{2}$–75 lb (27–34 kg).

COAT

Bouviers have a luxuriant, weather-resistant, dry and dull coat, harsh to the touch with a dense undercoat. The hair is approx. $2^{1}/_{2}$ in (6cm) long and slightly tangled without being woolly or curled. The coat does not lie close to the skin. It is very short on the skull, except for the longer hairy beard, mustache and the erect eyebrows. The eyebrows should not cover the eyes.

COLORS

Accepted colors are pale or gray, usually brindle or gray black. Plain black is permissible, but not preferred. Sometimes you will see light-colored, mainly fair coats, but they are undesirable. The nose is always black and the eyes should be dark.

Male Bouvier

Bouvier bitch

TEMPERAMENT

CHARACTER

Bouviers are very loyal dogs, highly devoted to their families. They are extremely watchful and will come to the assistance of their people at any time. You can trust them to guard your property and yard; strangers will not be able to bribe them. Nevertheless they are not busy, shrewd or over-alert. They tend to be quiet and calm and they respond in a stable and kind-hearted manner to any kind of impression. Bouviers are sober and tough dogs. When young they might be a bit restless.

SOCIAL BEHAVIOR

Bouviers are generally quite sociable. If they have been well-socialized there will not be any problems mixing with peers, or cats, or other pets. They make excellent combinations with children, whom they will tolerate and protect very well. Bear in mind that this dog protects "its" children if they are teased by other kids. Strangers are treated with suspicion, but not excessively so if the dog has been well-socialized. If the handler says it is fine, the dog will generally accept them. The Bouvier's priority is its own family.

GENERAL CARE

GROOMING
A Bouvier needs to visit a trimming salon approx. two to three times a year to have its coat clipped and shaped. Loose hairs tend to remain in the coat, which means that a Bouvier loses relatively little hair. It does mean that a weekly, thorough brush is essential to avoid tangles. Too much hair between the pads can bother the dog while walking, and should be cut away. Keep the ear canals clean and the claws short. Do not wash the dog too frequently: it is not good for the outer coat. The grooming of Bouviers for shows will naturally require more attention.

Bouviers

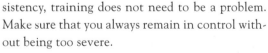

Bouvier

TRAINING
This breed is fairly easy to train, although Bouviers can be a little slow in its understanding than some of the other Shepherd breeds. They do like to please their handlers. If the owner brings up its dog with love and consistency, training does not need to be a problem. Make sure that you always remain in control without being too severe.

EXERCISE
A Bouvier can walk for hours on end if its owner requires it to, but will not become a nuisance if its owner is otherwise inclined. Walks, retrieving, running and swimming are suitable forms of exercise. It is a big advantage that this breed likes to be close to its owner. The breed does not have the tendency to explore beyond the boundaries of its yard and is not likely to run off when off-leash. They are fairly tough and because of their dense coats they can be kept in an outdoor kennel provided the dog is given enough daily exercise and attention. This dog, devoted to its owner will consider too little attention as a form of punishment.

USES
Bouviers can be used for a number of tasks and will perform well in a variety of dog sports, e.g. training for hunting, rescue dog and advanced obedience.

Young Bouvier

Pinscher, Schnauzer, Molossians, Swiss Mountain and Cattledogs

SECTION 1 Pinscher and Schnauzer type

MINIATURE PINSCHER

COUNTRY OF ORIGIN	**GERMANY**
ORIGINAL FUNCTION	**VERMIN DESTROYER**

APPEARANCE

BODY

The same breed standards apply to the Miniature Pinscher as to the German Pinscher, except that this dog has a much smaller and lighter build. It is square and compact and the short topline slopes slightly towards the rear. The croup is lightly rounded up to the base of the high-set tail, which is carried high. In countries where it is permissible, the tail is docked by a maximum of three vertebrae. Its oval and moderately wide chest reaches down to the elbows. The line of the chest is slightly raised towards the back, with a graceful transition into a light tuckup. The shoulder blades are sloping and the elbows are close to the body. The legs are vertical and the feet are catlike. Its noble, arched neck is dry and well fitted into the shoulders.

Miniature Pinschers are alert dogs

HEAD

Robust and long with a slight, but clear stop. The nose bridge is straight and runs parallel to the flat skull. The deep muzzle has a blunt and wedge-shaped nose. The ears are set high and are dropped in a V-shape, although most Miniature Pinschers' ears are initially erect. The dark eyes are oval-shaped and face forwards. The eyelids fit tightly. Miniature Pinschers have a scissors bite.

SHOULDER HEIGHT

This will range from $9^1/_2$–$11^1/_2$ in (25–30 cm).

COAT

It is short and dense, lying closely with glossy hair. It should have no bare spots.

COLORS

Miniature Pinschers are either plain brown (different shades of brown to deer brown red) or two-colored (black and tan). The tan markings should be as dark as possible and clearly defined.

TEMPERAMENT

CHARACTER

These dogs are intelligent, spirited and alert.

Black and tan Miniature Pinscher

Miniature Pinscher puppy

They are good guard dogs and like to bark. They are not squeamish and they are restrained, in other words they are generally content with very little and they are sound and healthy. They adore their masters and families and are loyal and affectionate. Some might be a bit daring.

SOCIAL BEHAVIOR

The Miniature Pinscher gets on well with other pets and children, as long as they do not tease this creature. Strangers are always announced and will initially be regarded with some suspicion. Miniature Pinschers might be a little overbearing towards other dogs in the street, but their behavior depends entirely upon how they were brought up as young pups. Other dogs in the family will generally find they get on well with the Miniature Pinscher.

GENERAL CARE

GROOMING

It is easy to look after the Miniature Pinscher. During the molt you will need a soft rubber brush to remove dead and loose

Male Miniature Pinscher

hair. You can rub the coat with a damp cloth to make it shine. Keep the claws clipped.

TRAINING

A lot of people do not realize that even a little dog like the Miniature Pinscher needs to be kept active, too, which is a shame, because this dog is intelligent enough and keen to learn all kinds of things. On the other hand this dog needs a consistent, decisive training. You will also need to pay considerable attention to house-training. You might not immediately notice the small puddle of a little dog and the Pinscher might be under the impression that you do not mind. If you have a lot of neighbors it may be useful to discourage the dog from barking too much.

EXERCISE

Miniature Pinschers are not meant to spend their lives in a basket or in the arms of their masters or mistresses. They should be given regular opportunities to play and romp off-leash. Most of them like ball games. It is possible for this type of dog to live happily in an apartment and if you have brought up this dog well, you should be able to take it with you anywhere.

USES

These dogs make good companions.

Miniature Pinscher

Affenpinscher

AFFENPINSCHER	
COUNTRY OF ORIGIN	GERMANY
ORIGINAL FUNCTION	VERMIN DESTROYER

APPEARANCE

BODY

The Affenpinscher's body is a little longer than it is high and its back is short and slopes down a little. Its topline and belly line run parallel. The chest reaches deeper than the elbows and the dog is barrel-chested. The bottom ribs and hipbones are not far apart which makes the dog look squat. The tail is set high and carried high. Generally the tail is docked by three vertebrae at the most. The front legs are straight and vertical legs and the hind legs are moderately angulated. The elbows are close. Affenpinschers are cat-footed. The neck is short without any dewlap.

HEAD

It is round and not too heavy, with a clear fore-head, a short muzzle and a straight, flat lower jaw. The ears are V-shaped and set on high. They are carried dropped or erect, depending on their size. The eyes are round, but should not protrude. The facial expression of the Affenpinscher may remind you of a monkey, which explains the name of this breed. Affenpinschers are undershot, with the lower incisors placed in front of the upper jaw.

SHOULDER HEIGHT

This ranges from $9^1/_2-11^1/_2$ in (25–30 cm).

COAT

The Affenpinscher has a full, harsh and rough coat. The harsh and long spiky hair on its head emphasizes the monkey-like expression, which is so typical for this breed: bristly eyebrows, feathered beard, cheeks and crown.

COLORS

These dogs have plain black coats, possibly with brownish or gray tones, which are also accepted. The eyes should be dark.

TEMPERAMENT

CHARACTER

Affenpinschers are lively, friendly and alert. They are affectionate and demonstrate great loyalty to their masters and families. They are quite good watchdogs and like to bark.

SOCIAL BEHAVIOR

Affenpinschers get on well with children, provided they respect the dog and do not tease it, or treat it as a toy. Generally they get on well with other dogs, although Affenpinschers are not keen to share their masters and families with other dogs. You need not expect any difficulties with other pets or cats, provided the dog has had good experiences

Affenpinscher

with cats as a puppy. They are good guard dogs. They are reserved towards strangers.

GENERAL CARE

GROOMING

This rough-haired dog should be plucked at least twice a year depending on the texture of its coat. The old hairs should be plucked by hand which will give new hair a chance to grow. Apart from that this breed does not need a lot of grooming, although you should comb its beard and mustache

Affenpinscher

regularly. Sometimes hairs will grow in the corners of their eyes, which might irritate the eyeballs. It is best to remove the hairs as soon as possible.

TRAINING

Affenpinschers are very intelligent and can learn commands very easily. Be clear and consistent and vary exercises with games, so that the dog continues to enjoy its training.

EXERCISE

These dogs need an average amount of exercise. They will generally adapt to circumstances.

USES

Affenpinschers are generally kept as companion dogs. They are rarely used for their original work of destroying rats and mice, but given the opportunity they will not refuse.

GERMAN PINSCHER	
COUNTRY OF ORIGIN	GERMANY
ORIGINAL FUNCTION	DESTROYING VERMIN AND GUARDING

APPEARANCE

BODY

The German Pinscher is squarely built and compact, with a short back that slopes slightly. The groin is a little rounded to the base of the tail. The high tail is also carried high. In some countries it will be docked by three vertebrae at the most. Its oval and moderately wide chest reaches down to the elbows. The line of the chest is slightly raised towards the back and flows gracefully into the slight tuck-up. The shoulder blades slope and the elbows are well closed. The legs are vertical and the feet are catlike. Its noble and arched neck is dry and well set onto the shoulders.

HEAD

Robust and long with a slight, but clear stop. The nose bridge is straight and runs parallel to the flat skull. The deep muzzle has a blunt and wedge-shaped nose. The ears are set high and are dropped in a V-shape. The dark eyes are oval-shaped and face forwards. The eyelids fit tightly. German Pinschers have a scissors bite.

SHOULDER HEIGHT

This will range from $17^3/_4$–$19^3/_4$ in (45–50 cm).

COAT

It is short and dense, lying closely, with glossy hair. It should have no bare spots.

COLORS

German Pinschers are either plain brown (different shades of brown to deer

German Pinscher bitch

German Pinschers

ly, but if the owner says everything is fine, a well-trained German Pinscher will trust its master. Friends of the family will be greeted boisterously. In general German Pinschers are no trouble to other pets, certainly not if they have been well socialized.

GENERAL CARE

GROOMING

The German Pinscher needs very little grooming. You could brush its coat once a week with a soft

Male German Pinscher

bristle brush and give it a rub with a grooming mitt. During the molt a rubber mitt is useful to remove dead hair. Keep the claws short.

TRAINING

German Pinschers are keen learners. They are good students who like to learn fairly simple new commands and follow them. But the owner should not take training lightly. German Pinschers are quite shrewd and a soft owner will find its dog is always one step ahead. They should be trained with a loving, yet consistent and firm hand.

EXERCISE

This breed needs an average amount of exercise. Take it around the block three times a day and play with it in the yard, and your dog will be happy. If you love sports your dog will adapt and join you on your walks for hours on end without showing fatigue. Most German Pinschers like to leave their baskets for ball games and they enjoy retrieving. In the house this dog will generally be quite calm.

USES

The German Pinscher is a pleasant family dog, but also a high achiever in various dog sports such as flyball, agility and obedience.

brown red) or two-colored (black and tan). The tan markings should be as dark as possible and clearly defined.

TEMPERAMENT

CHARACTER

German Pinschers are very intelligent, smart, energetic, cheerful and alert dogs. They are friendly and playful, but watchful and very protective of their families, homes and possessions. In spite of their watchfulness they are no barkers. They are attached and loyal to their own families. These sober dogs are courageous and not at all squeamish. They have great stamina.

SOCIAL BEHAVIOR

This breed tends to get on well with children. They are very patient. Initially they will warn you if your guests have arrived and approach them suspicious-

German Pinscher bitch

AUSTRIAN PINSCHER

COUNTRY OF ORIGIN	AUSTRIA
ORIGINAL FUNCTION	VERMIN DESTROIER
	AND WATCHDOG

APPEARANCE

BODY

The Austrian Pinscher has a short and muscular back, a wide and deep chest and barrel-shaped ribs. The straight legs are well angulated and the elbows are well closed. Its compact feet are closed and have arched toes. The tail is set on high and is carried in a curl above the topline, if not docked. The neck is powerful and can be either short or medium-length.

HEAD

This dog has a pear-shaped head. The skull is broad, and the stop and cheekbones are clearly defined. Its muzzle is short and powerful, but should not be too wide or simply too pointed. The ears may be folded backwards ("rose ear"), or hang in a V-shape. The eyes are oval-shaped. Austrian

Austrian Pinscher

Pinschers have a scissors bite, but a pincer bite is also acceptable.

SHOULDER HEIGHT

This varies from $13^3/_4$–$19^3/_4$ in (35–50 cm). A shoulder height of around $17^3/_4$ in (45 cm) is the most common.

WEIGHT

Ranging between $26^1/_2$–$39^3/_4$ lb (12–18 kg).

COAT

The short hair feels harsh but is smooth and lies closely, with an undercoat.

Austrian Pinscher

COLORS

These dogs have deer brown, yellow, black and brown coats. These colors may be accompanied by white markings. The eyes are dark.

TEMPERAMENT

CHARACTER

Austrian Pinschers are lively, attentive and energetic dogs. They are sober, very brave and tough on themselves. Most of them like to bark, but some good training will make all the difference. In addition they are intelligent and have an optimistic view of life. These dogs are very affectionate and they are very attached to their families.

SOCIAL BEHAVIOR

The average Austrian Pinscher gets on well with cats and other pets, provided it is well socialized. They are naturally suspicious and on their guard towards strangers. Some dogs can be a little domineering towards other dogs. They are good with kids that belong to the family.

GENERAL CARE

GROOMING

The Austrian Pinscher needs little coat care. Every now and then they need a brush to remove loose hair, which will help to keep the coat in good condition.

TRAINING

This dog should be brought up with a loving and honest heart, but a rather firm hand. They learn fairly quickly.

EXERCISE

Historically the Austrian Pinscher has been a farm dog. Ideally it should be treated as such and be given enough space to let off steam on its own terrain. If you cannot provide the Austrian Pin-

Austrian Pinscher

scher with that amount of freedom you should take it for regular long walks. Austrian Pinschers tend to stay within their perimeters and will not roam.

USES

If it is properly supervised, this dog will do well in various dog sports, agility skills in particular.

Dobermann

DOBERMAN PINSCHER (DOBERMANN)

COUNTRY OF ORIGIN	GERMANY
ORIGINAL FUNCTION	GUARD AND DEFENSE DOG

Dobermans have above average intelligence

APPEARANCE

BODY

The Doberman is a strong, lean and elegant dog. The back is short, stiff and muscular, with clear withers. The croup is not too short and it is slightly rounded. The tail is usually docked by $1^1/_2$–$2^1/_2$ in (4–6 cm) in countries where this is permissible. Its well proportioned chest reaches down to the elbows and the forechest protrudes. The belly is tucked up slightly. The legs are straight and have perfectly round bones. The feet are short, arched and closed.

Male Dobermann.

The dry, muscular neck widens towards the chest.

HEAD

The head is elongated and dry, with a fairly flat top skull and a faint stop. The nose bridge runs parallel to the top skull. The ears are of medium size. They hang tightly against the head. The medium-sized eyes are oval-shaped and have a wise and energetic expression. Dobermans have a scissors bite.

SHOULDER HEIGHT

Ideally this should be $27^1/_2$ in (70 cm) for dogs but certainly not above $28^1/_4$ in (72 cm). A bitch's shoulder height should range from $24^3/_4$–$26^3/_4$ in (63–68 cm).

WEIGHT

Dobermans weigh $70^1/_2$–$92^1/_2$ lb (32–42 kg).

Brown Dobermann bitch

Dobermann

COAT

This breed's hair is short, thick and smooth, and tight to its body.

COLORS

In all countries that are members of FCI these dogs are only bred in black (black and tan) and in brown (brown and tan). The tan markings must be black and dark copper-colored. In other countries you may also see blue with tan and isabella with tan, fainter shades of the previously mentioned colors.

TEMPERAMENT

CHARACTER

Dobermans are very active, alert, intelligent and smart dogs. They are loyal and devoted to their owners and families and will defend and protect their households with vigor. They are quite tenacious in their behavior, courageous and they have a lot of stamina. They can sometimes be noisy. Some Dobermans have a tendency to develop into one-person's dogs.

SOCIAL BEHAVIOR

Provided a Doberman is well brought up and socialized, it will get on with other peers, pets and kids.

Dobermann bitch of almost six months

They will not allow strangers in, but if the owner says it is fine, the dog will abide.

GENERAL CARE

GROOMING

The Doberman's coat does not require much attention. Usually one brush a week with a soft bristle brush and rubbing the coat with a grooming glove will suffice. During the molt use a rubber mitt with a knobbled surface to remove dead and loose hairs. Keep the claws short and from time to time check the teeth for tartar.

TRAINING

This strong, handsome dog requires very careful and consistent training. Strive to ensure everything is harmonious throughout. If you have little experience training dogs, then you are seriously advised not to acquire a dog of this breed. Many Dobermans are neurotic if wrongly brought up (and unfortunately this is all too frequent), making them fearful and/or snappy – whereas their natural character is straightforward and reliable. Always act clearly and fairly with a Doberman; never hit it and make absolutely sure it is not pestered. A calm handler with a natural authority will bring out the best. This

Dobermann bitch

Dobermann

dog learns new commands very quickly and enjoys following them.

EXERCISE

Dobermans are built for speed and have tremendous stamina. A Doberman will not be happy with a daily walk around the neighborhood. It will enjoy any kind of exercise, swimming, running, romping, and ball games and running along with you. Allow yourself approximately one hour a day. This dog will be calm indoors if it gets enough exercise.

USES

This breed is ideal for a variety of dog sport activities. We often see them at training for hunting competitions, in which they excel. Do not start them too early and do not overdo it initially. A Doberman needs to mature before it can start "proper" work. A Doberman will perform well at agility skills, flyball and obedience if well supervised.

STANDARD SCHNAUZER	
COUNTRY OF ORIGIN	GERMANY
ORIGINAL FUNCTION	VERMIN DESTROIER AND WATCHDOG

APPEARANCE

BODY

The Standard Schnauzer is a dog with a square build, looking squat rather than slim. It has a short, slightly arched back that slopes down a little. The tail is set on high and carried erect. In countries where this is permissible, it is generally docked at the fourth vertebra. Schnauzers have oval chests that reach beyond the elbows, and a clear forechest. The belly has a moderate tuck-up. The legs are straight and the elbows fit tightly. Both the forequarters and the hindquarters are well angulated. The feet are short and round with well-closed arched toes. The noble and powerful neck is arched and has no dewlap.

HEAD

The elongated head gradually tapers towards the tip of the nose and displays a clear stop. The nose bridge is straight and viewed from the side, it runs parallel to its flat top skull. The lips fit closely and are always black. The high-set ears are V-shaped and hang pendulous along the head. Schnauzers have oval-shaped eyes, facing forwards, and a complete scissors bite.

SHOULDER HEIGHT

Their size is approx. $17^1/_2$–$19^1/_2$ in (45–50 cm).

COAT

The rugged wire-haired coat should be hard and dense. A Schnauzer typically has a long mustache, beard and eyebrows. The hair on the ears and top skull is shorter than the rest of the body.

COLORS

Standard Schnauzers are solid black and salt and pepper. The latter color pattern might be blended silver gray to steel

Pepper and salt male Standard Schnauzer

gray, preferably with a dark mask. The nose is always black and the eyes are dark.

TEMPERAMENT

CHARACTER

The Standard Schnauzer is a temperamental and intelligent breed with dogs that are eager to learn, sober, reliable, and very dependent on their own families. They have more difficulty adjusting to a new owner than most other dogs. They are not easily led astray with bribes. They are observant and vigilant. Although some dogs are keen barkers, it does not apply to all Standard Schnauzers.

Pepper and salt male Standard Schnauzer

SOCIAL BEHAVIOR

Standard Schnauzers naturally get on well with dogs, other animals, and are extremely tolerant with children, provided they are well socialized. They might approach strangers with suspicion and shyness, but they will greet friends of the family.

GENERAL CARE

GROOMING

Depending on the quality of the coat and whether the dog needs to go to shows, its hair will need to be plucked about twice a year or more often. The old hair will be clipped out by hand or with a blunt clipper to allow new hair to grow. A Schnauzer plucked at the right time generally does not shed a lot of hair in the house and will only need grooming once a week. When necessary, remove any excess hair within the ears – never clip it – and cut away hair between the pads of the feet. Its trimmings, beard, mustache and eyebrows, should be combed regularly to prevent knotting. Keep the claws short.

TRAINING

Schnauzers learn quickly and are eager pupils. It is not difficult to teach them elementary obedience. If the dog trusts its owner it will follow any commands quickly and without difficulty, but it is not keen to repeat the same command. Schnauzers respond best to fair and consistent handling, with the sound of your voice normally being sufficient. It is advisable to socialize these dogs well with people. You need not be afraid that the dog will consequently make friends with everybody and greet any passer-by, because that will not happen, which is a good thing.

EXERCISE

A Standard Schnauzer has an average need for exercise. Despite this, it likes being busy doing things such as swimming, running, playing in the yard, running off-leash in the woods and retrieving. These are all suitable activities for this dog of character. Indoors a Standard Schnauzer will generally be quite calm and it will not get bored if once in a while you do not have enough time for it.

USES

Today we do not see many Standard Schnauzers on breed society and dog school training fields. It does not mean that they lack the capacity, on the contrary, this breed can perform well in sports such as agility, flyball and advanced obedience skills.

Standard Schnauzer

MINIATURE SCHNAUZER	
COUNTRY OF ORIGIN	GERMANY
ORIGINAL FUNCTION	VERMIN DESTROIER
	AND WATCHDOG

APPEARANCE

Theoretically the Miniature Schnauzer should have the same body frame and head as the Standard Schnauzer, except that the dog appears smaller and therefore looks more squat and compact.

SHOULDER HEIGHT

This ranges from 12–13³/₄ in (30–35 cm).

COAT

The coat is identical to that of a Standard Schnauzer.

COLORS

Miniature Schnauzers may have solid black, salt and pepper, black silver and plain white coats. Salt and pepper-colored dogs might be a blended silver gray to steel gray, preferably with a dark mask. The black and silver dogs have black coats with silver markings over the eyes, on their throats and cheeks, the forechest, forequarters and feet, on the inside of the hindquarters and under the tail. White Miniature Schnauzers have been recognized fairly recently and are not yet as common as the other colors. In all color patterns the nose will be black.

Miniature Schnauzer

TEMPERAMENT

CHARACTER

The Miniature Schnauzer's personality compares well with that or its big brother, although there are a few differences. For instance the Miniature Schnauzer can be noisier than the Standard Schnauzer and more active and less cautious in its behavior.

SOCIAL BEHAVIOR

Miniature Schnauzers generally get on well with other pets, and children, if they have been well socialized. Visitors are greeted noisily. This dog is not likely to greet every visitor with a show of affection. Initially they remain on their guard. Do not worry about their behavior towards other dogs, although some may be a little overconfident when they meet other peers.

GENERAL CARE

GROOMING

Please refer to the Standard Schnauzer.

TRAINING

The Miniature Schnauzer needs a confident handler despite its size, and also needs to be handled fairly and with consistency. Schnauzers are quick and bright pupils, although they frequently have their own ideas about your commands. Vary the drills with play and do not repeat them too frequently. Schnauzers tend to bark a lot, it is advisable to discourage barking, particularly if you live in a busy district.

Pepper and salt Miniature Schnauzer bitch

EXERCISE

This dog has enormous amounts of energy. Country walks or a walk downtown will please it, as long

Pair of male Miniature Schnauzers

Giant Schnauzer bitch

Miniature Schnauzer puppy

Male pepper and salt Miniature Schnauzer

GIANT SCHNAUZER (RIESENSCHNAUZER)

COUNTRY OF ORIGIN	GERMANY
ORIGINAL FUNCTION	GUARD AND DEFENSE DOG

APPEARANCE
Theoretically the Giant Schnauzer should have the same build and head as the Standard Schnauzer, except that this dog is bigger and stronger.

SHOULDER HEIGHT
This varies from $23^1/_2$–$27^1/_2$ in (60–70 cm).

COAT
Standard and Giant Schnauzers have the same coats.

COLORS
The Giant Schnauzer's coat is solid black and salt and pepper. Salt and pepper can be blended silver gray down to steel gray, preferably with a dark mask. Both color patterns have a black nose. White markings are not desirable.

TEMPERAMENT

CHARACTER
An alert, good-natured, vigilant, intelligent dog, keen to learn, sober, hardy, and fairly calm. They bond closely with the families they belong to and will do anything to defend them, if necessary. They do not like a change of ownership. They will not be led astray by bribes. They are good guard dogs and you can trust them to defend your family, house, property and yard. They are not outgoing and rash; they tend to be cautious, and determined to achieve their goal. Their stamina is excellent. They do not bark a lot. Unlike their peers they often mature later.

as you take it out of doors as much as possible to play or romp about.

USES
The Miniature Schnauzer used to be popular as a rat and mice catcher, and given the chance, they will show you that they still know how to be one. In spite of its size this dog can cope quite well in dog sports if it is well supervised. Do not hesitate to participate in any sport if that is what you would like to do; there are associations and dog schools with equipment suitable for smaller dogs.

Giant Schnauzer

Giant Schnauzers

SOCIAL BEHAVIOR

The Giant Schnauzer causes few problems with dogs and other pets. The usual caveat applies that the dog must be correctly socialized when young. They are naturally loving and tolerant with children. They are not interested in strangers and tend toward shyness. They will be on their guard and remain vigilant.

GENERAL CARE

GROOMING

Please refer to Standard Schnauzer.

TRAINING

This breed, full of character, requires a sound up-bringing. If the training is consistent, fair and full of variety, your dog will like it. It will not be keen to follow the same command time and time again.

EXERCISE

This is a breed that requires quite a lot of exercise, but will adjust to circumstances. These dogs will be happy to run off-leash, to retrieve, swim and run alongside you. If they can let off steam outdoors they will be quite peaceful indoors.

USES

The Giant Schnauzer is a typical working dog and well suited to all kinds of dog sports such as advanced obedience, agility skills and hunting. They hate boring drills and can be rather obstinate if they find themselves in such a situation.

Giant Schnauzer

DUTCH SMOUSHOND	
COUNTRY OF ORIGIN	THE NETHERLANDS
ORIGINAL FUNCTION	STABLE DOG AND RAT CATCHER

APPEARANCE

BODY

The body of a Dutch Smoushond is powerful and square, but should not be coarse or floppy. It gives the appearance of sturdiness. The topline is level, but arches slightly above the loins. The croup is strong and muscular. The tail is rather short and is usually carried gaily, but not curled above the topline. The shoulder blades slope moderately and the angulations of forequarters and hindquarters are moderate. The legs have strong and oval-shaped bones. The feet are closed, round and small. The neck is short and muscular.

Dutch Smoushonds

HEAD

Viewed from above, the head is wide and short, with a slightly arched skull. The whole muzzle makes up one third of the full length of the skull. The lips are thin, close tightly and the forenose is broad. The thin ears are triangular. They are a bit small and are carried pendulously: they should not stand back or be set below the surface. The eyelashes are well developed. A scissors bite is preferable, but a pincer bite and undershot bite are not considered faults.

SHOULDER HEIGHT

For dogs this will be between $14^{1}/_{2}$–$16^{1}/_{2}$ in

Dutch Smoushond

(37–42 cm) and for bitches 13$^1/_2$–15$^1/_2$ in (35–40 cm).

WEIGHT

A Dutch Smoushond weighs 22 lb (10 kg).

COAT

This dog has a rugged, coarse, harsh, straight and wiry coat with a good undercoat. The length of the hair is approx. 1$^1/_2$–2$^3/_4$ in (4–7 cm). It should not curl, wave or be woolly, nor should it have a tendency to knot. The Dutch Smoushond has a clear mustache, beard and eyebrows. The latter should not obstruct the dog's vision. The hair on the ears is shorter than on the rest of the body.

COLORS

This dog is bred with a plain yellow coat, although there are many different shades of yellow. Straw yellow is preferred. The eyes are dark brown and the forenose, lips and eye rims are black.

TEMPERAMENT

CHARACTER

These friendly, engaging, cunning, energetic and intelligent dogs have considerable adaptability. They are sensitive to the general mood and can be deeply hurt by harsh words. They are playful and dependent, smart and easy to please. A Dutch Smoushond will not bark a lot, although they will make a lot of noise if they sense danger. They have great stamina.

SOCIAL BEHAVIOR

This dog generally likes children. They will accept the family cat and most get on well with their own kind. They will let you know if there is a stranger around, although they

Dutch Smoushond

usually approach people in a friendly and open manner. Their masters always come first.

GENERAL CARE

GROOMING

Depending on the quality of the coat, the Dutch Smoushond generally requires the hairs to be plucked by hand about twice a year, leaving the hair on the head alone as far as possible. Between these grooming sessions, remove any excess hair from inside the ears and brush your dog approximately once a week with a pin brush. They can also be troubled by too much hair between the pads of the feet, so ensure this is trimmed regularly.

TRAINING

The Dutch Smoushond is an intelligent dog, eager to do something for you. Generally the training is quite easy. It is important, though, that you are consistent towards these dogs because some can assert themselves if they get the idea that their handler is rather easy-going. You will see the best

Young Dutch Smoushond

Dutch Smoushond

Molossians (Mastiff type, Mountain type)

ROTTWEILER

COUNTRY OF ORIGIN	GERMANY
ORIGINAL FUNCTION	CATTLE DRIVER, GUARD AND DEFENSE DOG

APPEARANCE

BODY

This dog has a short, squat and powerful body with a level and strong back. The chest is wide, broad and deep. The croup is short and wide. It does not slope and the loins should not be tucked up. The tail is in line with the back and is usually docked down to a stump-like tail in countries where this is permissible. Rottweilers have

results if you vary the training in a playful and cheerful manner.

EXERCISE

This breed is untiring and they enjoy long walks, swimming and retrieving. A good thing about them is that they do not tend to run off. If you have a good rapport with your dog, it will not like to lose sight of you on one of its walks off-leash. Although this doggy likes to romp about in nature, it will also be content with walks on-leash downtown or playing in the backyard. If you occasionally do not have much time, the dog will adjust with no problems.

USES

Today these dogs are basically kept as companions, an important job that should not be underestimated and which this dog does extremely well. Enrolling it in agility skills and flyball would be a rewarding experience for both you and your dog. The Smous is well suited to these activities and enjoys them.

Male Rottweiler

Dutch Smoushonds

straight and strong legs. The feet are round, with closed and well-arched toes. The strong and fairly dry neck is round and broad and the neckline rises from the shoulders in a slight arch.

HEAD

Medium-length with a broad skull and a well-defined stop. The muzzle is as deep as the skull or a little shorter. The skin lies tightly round the head and should only form wrinkles when the dog is attentive. The ears are small and triangular. They are set as far apart as possible, which makes the top skull look broader. The eyes are moderately big with close-fitting eyelids. They have a good-natured and self-assured expression. Rottweilers have a scissors bite.

SHOULDER HEIGHT

Dogs are 24–26³/₄ in (61–68 cm) and bitches 22–24¹/₂ in (56–63 cm) high.

COAT

Rottweilers have a short, coarse and harsh coat with a wire-haired undercoat.

COLORS

The coat is always black with clearly defined mahogany to light brown markings on the muzzle, cheeks, above the eyes, legs and chest. White markings on the chest and toes are undesirable. The eyes are dark brown.

Rottweiler

TEMPERAMENT

CHARACTER

Rottweilers are honest, intelligent, self-confident and equable dogs that are unconditionally loyal to their handlers and families. A Rottweiler will defend its family and property to the end. They cannot be bribed. They do not bark much. They tend to be dominant and brave and they are fearless. Most of them have a tendency to become one person's dogs. They might be a bit posses-sive, particularly if attention has to be shared with other dogs. They are generally calm indoors, but outdoors they are indefatigable workers. They like to work with and for their handlers and have an excellent memory. The average Rottweiler knows its territory and will generally stay within its boundaries; it does not like to explore on its own. It is very attached to its boss so that it is unlikely to run off on off-leash walks.

Working Rottweiler

SOCIAL BEHAVIOR

When a Rottweiler has been consistently brought up and trained, it will be loyal to its family and a good playmate for your children, provided they are fair to the dog. If this dog finds that "its" children are being teased by their friends it will defend them. Cats and other household animals, including livestock, will be accepted unquestioningly if it has had positive experiences with them when young. Rottweilers have hardly any hunting instinct. Particularly dogs can display some dominant traits when they are mature and may be aggressive towards other male dogs. Good socialization and consistent training can make a great difference. Friends and relatives of the family

Rottweiler puppies are irresistible but need strict handling.

Rottweiler

are normally welcomed enthusiastically, whereas strangers are allowed no nearer than the gate or fence of your yard.

GENERAL CARE

GROOMING

The Rottweiler is relatively easy to care for. For the removal of loose and dead hairs during molting it is good to use a rubber glove or brush. Keep the claws short.

TRAINING

Rottweilers need equable, calm handlers who are sure of themselves and who have a natural authority over their dogs. The training needs to be fair and loving, but also consistent and strict. An indulgent or inexperienced owner will otherwise be faced with a dog, particularly a male dog that tends to take over the household. These dogs appear to be strong and tough, which they are to some extent, but they are also sensitive to your tone of voice, so also use it when the dog behaves well. A well-trained Rottweiler can learn many good things and is an absolutely obedient dog. A good socialization among people is important. You should not be afraid of creating a dog that will take to everybody, because that will not happen. There is a big difference in character between dogs and bitches. The latter are gentler and less assertive.

EXERCISE

A Rottweiler has an average need for exercise and

A Rottweiler bitch with two of her fully-grown pups

will adapt to circumstances. Do not forget it is a working dog that likes to be outside and that should not be condemned to simply lazing around. A Rottweiler without enough exercise tends to grow fat. Take the dog on frequent long and varied walks, allow it to swim and run along, and play with it. It adores ball games and retrieving.

Rottweiler

USES

Defense dog sport is suitable for this dog. Most of them have an excellent sense of smell and can learn to track well. Obedience training is not suitable, because it is not challenging enough for this dog.

Rottweiler

HOVAWART

COUNTRY OF ORIGIN	GERMANY
ORIGINAL FUNCTION	FARM GUARD DOG

APPEARANCE

BODY

Hovawarts are medium-sized, strong working dogs with a square build, yet not coarse. There should be a marked difference in the shape of the head between dogs and bitches, but actually this applies to the entire body frame and appearance. The topline is level and strong and the moderately sloping croup should not be too long. The tail is carried low and reaches below the hocks. The chest is wide, powerful and deep in relation to the rest of the body. The legs are straight and strong. The upper arms and shoulder blades are set at right angle. The pasterns should not be too straight. The hindquarters are well angulated and very muscular, with strong hocks. The feet have well-closed toes and hard pads. The neck is dry, strong and moderately long.

HEAD

It is dry and has a broad and arched skull. The nose bridge is straight and is neither too long, nor too wide and short. The muzzle is as long as the skull. The lips are well closed and the nose is well

Hovawart

developed. The triangular ears lie loosely against the head and should not be set on too low. The eyes are almond shaped. Hovawarts are preferred with a complete scissors bite, but a pincer bite is acceptable.

SHOULDER HEIGHT

Dogs vary from $24^1/_2$–$27^1/_2$ in (63–70 cm) and bitches from 23–26 in (58–65 cm).

COAT

The Hovawart has a longhaired, wavy coat which lies flat and there is hardly any underlayer. Any parting of curly hair on the back is considered to be a fault.

Hovawart

COLORS

There are three colors: plain black, blonde and black and tan. Tan may vary from light blonde to gold blonde. A small white marking on the chest and a couple of white hairs on the tip of the tail are permissible.

TEMPERAMENT

CHARACTER

These dogs are good-natured, stable and equable. They are demanding of themselves, tough and remain playful into old age. You will hear their deep bark when there is danger and they will defend their family with vigor, as well as home and yard. Nevertheless they are controlled in their behavior and do not bark much. Although they get on well with all members of the family they tend to become one-person's dogs. They are affectionate dogs, obedient and compliant, but with some degree of independence. They are quite intelligent and have a good scent.

SOCIAL BEHAVIOR

The Hovawart shows good behavior towards other household animals regardless of whether it is a cat or poultry. This is true provided the dog has met these animals when it was young. They are generally very patient with children but sometimes reserved towards strangers. It will protect your property against intruders with great zeal. When its handler indicates that visitors are approved, it will accept them immediately.

GENERAL CARE

GROOMING
The coat does not require a great deal of attention. Occasional grooming with a pin brush will suffice. Keep the claws short.

TRAINING
This dog learns quite quickly what is expected. The best results are required with extremely consistent, loving, and a well-balanced training. These dogs are not suited for long training sessions that do not offer a challenge.

EXERCISE
As a rule, the Hovawart adapts itself to circumstances. Take the dog for regular walks and let it enjoy running and playing off-leash. Most of them like retrieving. Swimming and running are good ways of exercising their bodies. A great advantage of this breed is that it has a highly developed sense of territory and will not readily desert your property. Even on a walk out in the countryside you will find that the dog prefers your company above solitary exploration.

USES
Hovawarts are suited as tracking, avalanche, watch and defense dogs. But they also function well as companions.

Male yellow Boxer

BOXER	
COUNTRY OF ORIGIN	GERMANY
ORIGINAL FUNCTION	ORIGINALLY A FIGHTER DOG, LATER A GUARD AND WORKING DOG

APPEARANCE

BODY
The Boxer has a strong and athletic build. Its dry body, the forequarters as well as the hindquarters, the back as well as the neck are very muscular. The topline is broad, strong and muscular and should be as short and level as possible, with the withers slightly higher. The loins are short, wide and powerful and the broad croup slopes down slightly. The tail is set high and is carried gaily. Usually it is docked by $3^{1}/_{4}$–4 in (8–10 cm) in countries where this is permissible. The deep chest reaches down to the elbows. In depth the chest equals half the dog's shoulder height. The ribs are well arched, but not barrel shaped. They stretch a good way back. The flanks are short and tight and there is a tuck-up. Boxers have long and sloping shoulders that should not be too loaded. Its sturdy and well-angulated legs are straight and parallel. The small feet point forwards and have arched and well-closed toes. Boxers have a fairly long, dry and muscular neck that flows into the topline in a graceful arch. The onset of the neck is clearly visible.

Hovawart

Male brindle Boxer

HEAD

It is as dry as possible and has an arched top skull that should not be flat and round or too wide. The cheek muscles are well developed, but should not bulge. The width of the muzzle should ideally come close to the width of the skull. The central furrow is clearly defined, but not too deep between the eyes. The stop is marked distinctly. The length of the muzzle should be half the length of the skull. The tip of the nose is a bit higher than the base of the nose bridge (slightly turned-up nose). The lower jaw curves upwards and the powerfully developed upper lips lie on the rims of the lower lips. Its small and thin ears are set high and are carried hanging, against the cheeks. The eyes should not show any haw. They have a loyal and serious expression. Boxers have an undershot bite. The teeth should not be visible when the mouth is closed.

SHOULDER HEIGHT

For dogs this is between $22^{1}/_{2}$–$24^{3}/_{4}$ in (57–63 cm). Bitches are between $20^{3}/_{4}$–23 in (53–59 cm) high.

WEIGHT

Dogs weigh approximately $66^{1}/_{4}$–$70^{1}/_{2}$ lb (30–32 kg) and bitches 53–$55^{1}/_{4}$ lb (24–25 kg).

COAT

Boxers have a short smooth-haired coat.

COLORS

They are either yellow or brindle. Yellow may range from light yellow to dark deer red. Brindle dogs have a stripy, black marking over their bright base color. The color brindle can be very light, but also quite heavy, which almost makes the dog look black. Both color patterns may have white markings but the white should not cover more than a third of the dog. A black mask is prescribed for both color patterns. The eyes should be as dark as possible.

TEMPERAMENT

CHARACTER

Boxers are dogs full of character, happy, fair and uncomplicated, with a friendly nature. They are very active and lively, and their spontaneity can make them quite boisterous. They are not suitable for people who treasure objects in their home. They notice what is happening around them, they are watchful, but do not bark a lot. They are stable and self-assured and they are not easily perturbed. They are, however, sensitive to the atmosphere in the home and harsh words will upset them. They bond very closely with their family. You should not underestimate their intelligence.

SOCIAL BEHAVIOR

Boxers and children get on very well, but young kids should be protected from their boisterousness. A well-trained and socialized Boxer is no problem with other dogs and pets, although there are some dogs that will not shun a fight with another male dog. The Boxer naturally guards home and property with conviction, not because it is suspicious. Friends of the family are greeted with great enthusiasm.

GENERAL CARE

GROOMING

A Boxer's coat needs relatively little care. One session a week with a soft brush will suffice. Use a rubber brush or a rubber mitt during molting to remove dead and loose hairs.

TRAINING

This is an intelligent breed and the Boxer will want to please its handler. They learn quickly if the handler approaches the dog in a caring, clear and consistent manner. Harsh words and punishment are seldom needed, but some

Boxer

persistence is required as these dogs are often smarter than their owners imagine. Try to discourage the dog's tendency to jump up against people in its enthusiasm.

EXERCISE

Boxers are energetic dogs and need a lot of physical exercise. As soon as the dog has stopped growing you can let it run. The Boxer loves playing and romping with its kind, but it will not refuse a ball game with its owner or children. They have hardly any hunting instinct and are not likely to roam far from their owners. Walks off-leash will therefore be quite relaxing.

USES

Boxers make excellent companions for sporty families. They are suited to most types of dog sports, from agility skills and flyball to advanced obedience and training for hunting.

ENGLISH BOLLDOG	
COUNTRY OF ORIGIN	ENGLAND
ORIGINAL FUNCTION	ORIGINALLY THIS DOG WAS BRED TO FIGHT BULLS, BUT TODAY IT IS A GOOD-NATURED COMPANION.

Eight-week old English Bulldog puppy

APPEARANCE

BODY

The English Bulldog has a broad, strong and squat build. It is fairly low on its legs. The short and strong topline is broadest over the shoulders and narrows towards the loins. Viewed from the side, the back slopes slightly behind the shoulders, rises up again towards the loins and then down again towards the tail. The highest point of the topline is at the same level as the loins. The chest is roomy, round and very deep, and hangs well between the forequarters. The well-rounded ribs continue far back and there is a tuck-up. The low set tail is thick at the base and tapers into a point. It sticks out sideways and is carried with the tip downwards (screw tail). The tail is naturally short. The straight and sturdy forequarters are far apart and a little shorter than the hindquarters. The hind feet are compact and round and the forefeet, pointing slightly outwards, are nearly always round. The hefty, deep and strong neck tends to be short rather than long.

HEAD

Its massive square skull is very big; its circumference is as long as the height of the shoulders. The cheeks are well rounded and stick out sideways

Brindle Boxer

past the eyes. Viewed from the side the head is very high and short. The forehead is flat, with wrinkles. There is a clear central furrow from the stop to the top of the skull. The very deep and broad muzzle is short and is turned upwards. The nose is almost exactly between the eyes and has wide nostrils. At the sides the broad upper lips drop over the lower jaw, but lie closely against the front of the lower lip so that you cannot see the teeth. The thin and small (rose) ears are set on high and are wide apart. The eyes are set low in the skull, as far as possible form the ears, on a line with the stop. They are round and moderately big.

WEIGHT

The English Bulldog weighs approx. $48\frac{1}{2}$–55 lb (22–25 kg).

COAT

The hair is short, dense, smooth and fine.

COLORS

English Bulldogs may have two color patterns: brindle and red. The red may vary from almost beige to dark deer red and pale brown. They might

Young English Bulldog

have white marking and/or a black mask. In addition there are (almost) white dogs that must have dark pigmentation on the muzzle and eye rims. Black, liver and black and tan are not acceptable colors. The eyes should be as dark as possible.

TEMPERAMENT

CHARACTER

English Bulldogs are good-natured, very equable and gentle dogs. They are cheerful and friendly, spontaneous and enthusiastic in their behavior, but calm indoors. They are sensitive to the mood in the house, but physically demanding of themselves. They are quite intelligent in a thoughtful way and quite obedient. The English Bulldog is very affectionate and prefers to be close to the family. They are not suited as kennel dogs.

English Bulldog bitch

SOCIAL BEHAVIOR

Mixing with other dogs and household pets is usually problem-free partly because they have no hunting instinct. They are extremely tolerant and most of them have a well-developed sense of humor. They are certainly not easily upset. Most of them are friends with everybody, while some are wary and protective.

GENERAL CARE

GROOMING

This dog does not need much coat care. When it molts, it is easy to remove dead and loose hairs with a rubber brush. When necessary, clean the folds in the face – particularly those under the eyes – with a special lotion. The English Bulldog should lie in a draft-free, soft, dry place, and a kennel is definitely unsuitable.

TRAINING

This breed is usually easy to train. They are sensitive to your voice and moods and will often respond to a friendly but determined request. In no circumstances should they be severely treated but do not let them take liberties either. Remain consistent and clear with them at all times. Your dog is keen to please you and if it understands what you want it to do, it will not disappoint you.

EXERCISE

English Bulldogs do not require long walks. This breed will be quite happy with three short outings

Litter of English Bulldog pups at 6 weeks

English Bulldog

a day. For the rest of the time they will be pleased to stay in the house or yard, provided the family is close by. This makes them ideal for less active people. Bulldog puppies have a tendency to keep on running and playing when they are exhausted. Make sure that they get sufficient rest and limit their exercise. They are not able to withstand the heat, so give them somewhere cool to lie on hot days and do not take them out in a car or on a walk.

USES

This dog is popular as a companion in families with or without kids. Although it is an intelligent dog and likes to learn, its build prevents it from participating in a variety of dog sports.

SHAR PEI	
COUNTRY OF ORIGIN	CHINA
ORIGINAL FUNCTION	ITS ORIGINAL TASKS ARE NOT KNOWN, BUT THE SHAR PEI WAS MOST PROBABLY USED AS A HUNTING AND WATCHDOG. SINCE IT HAS BEEN DISCOVERED BY THE WESTERN WORLD IT HAS ONLY BEEN KEPT AS A COMPANION.

APPEARANCE

BODY

The Shar Pei is a compact dog with muscular, sloping shoulders and a broad and deep chest. The length of the body almost equals the shoulder height. The topline is level and strong. This breed has a variety of tails, but mainly screw-tails and tails with a double ring. The legs have strong bones. The hindquarters are moderately angulated with low set hocks. Shar Peis have compact feet with arched toes. The neck is muscular and strong, with loose skin under the neck, but no excessive dewlap.

HEAD

The flat skull is fairly big in relationship to the body. The Shar Pei has clear wrinkles on the forehead, but they should not be in the way of its eyes. The muzzle is almost as long as the skull. It is moderately long, broad

Shar Pei

Shar Pei

too, but it is not highly regarded. The tongue and gums are preferably black blue. Lighter tinted dogs have pink or blotched pigmentation. The eyes are dark.

TEMPERAMENT

CHARACTER

Shar Peis are active, friendly and playful dogs, but they can be a bit self-willed and quite domineering. They are devoted to their owners and families, but they do not follow commands slavishly or show dependency. They are watchful and will defend their folk if necessary, but they are not aggressive or overalert. They tend to make a calm, sober and equable impression. They do not bark a lot.

Two young Shar Peis from the same litter

SOCIAL BEHAVIOR

Shar Peis are generally friendly towards people they do not know, although initially they might be a bit standoffish. They get on well with children, provided they respect the dogs. A well-socialized Shar Pei can live in harmony with cats and other pets. Mixing with other dogs can sometimes present problems. This is because the Shar Pei is a fighter by nature.

on eye level and tapers slightly to the nose. The fairly thick ears are as small as possible. They have a triangular shape and the tips are rounded. The ears are carried close to the skull and the tips point towards the eyes. Erect and semi erect ears are acceptable, but they are not very desirable. The deep-set eyes are moderately big and almond shaped. The eyes should in no way be covered by skin, wrinkles or hair. Shar Peis have a scissors bite. Puppies have wrinkles all over their bodies, but mature dogs should only have them on their foreheads and withers.

SHOULDER HEIGHT

This ranges from $18^1/_2$–$22^1/_2$ in (48–58$^1/_2$ cm).

Shar Pei

WEIGHT

This ranges from $39^1/_2$–$66^1/_4$ lb (18–29$^1/_2$ kg).

COAT

Shar Pei means sand skin. The coat is very short, harsh and bristly without an underlayer. The hairs should not be longer than $1^1/_4$ in (2$^1/_2$ cm).

COLORS

Permissible colors are solid black, blue black, black with a rusty sheen, brown, red and fawn. A cream colored coat may occur,

GENERAL CARE

GROOMING

The Sharp Pei has skin folds over its entire body, especially when young. Check them regularly and clean them if necessary. Some dogs may have tails that lie very close to the body, and these need to be inspected and cleaned to prevent infections. The coat needs

Shar Pei

Shar Pei puppy

to be brushed occasionally with a soft bristly brush. Keep the claws short.

TRAINING

All puppies are endearing, but a Shar Pei puppy with its soft wrinkly skin holds another trump card. It is not easy to train this little, wrinkly body consistently and clearly. It is however essential as the puppy will grow up into a strong dog with a strong self-confident nature.

When a Shar Pei is left without any or with no clear leadership, it might decide to take over the rule of the house. Shar Peis need a calm handler who is consistent, persevering and particularly clear. The right boss will emerge with an obedient dog that knows quite a few commands, following them when asked to. This is not a dog, however that naturally likes to obey its owner. Following commands needs to be beneficial to it. If you reward it for good behavior, possibly by giving it food, a Shar Pei will be a quick learner.

EXERCISE

Shar Peis have a considerable need for exercise. They do not mind if occasionally you do not have time to accompany them on long walks or to throw them a ball. Shar Peis are very adaptable, which means that they feel at ease both in the city and in

the country. They are not suited as kennel dogs. They are fairly peaceful indoors.

USES

Shar Peis are great companions for people who

Shar Pei puppy

like a dog with an unusual appearance. Generally a Shar Pei will not make a good sports dog. They are however quite popular at shows.

Red Shar Pei bitch

PERRO DE PRESA MALLORQUIN (MAJORCAN BULLDOG)	
COUNTRY OF ORIGIN	SPAIN/MAJORCA
ORIGINAL FUNCTION	THIS BREED HAS HAD A NUMBER OF FUNCTIONS, FOR INSTANCE AS A FIGHTING, SHEPHERD AND WATCHDOG.

APPEARANCE

BODY

The Perro de Presa Mallorquin is a powerful, muscular, medium-sized dog with a compact and slightly overbuilt body. The body is fairly short and slightly arched. The croup is wide. The tail is set low and should reach down to the hocks. It is thick at the base and tapers gradually to a point. The tail is not carried above the topline. Its front is wide, with a large, deep chest reaching down to the elbows. The straight and powerful legs are heavy boned. The strong feet have well-closed toes. Its thick and muscular neck displays a slightly loose skin.

Perro de Presa Mallorquin

HEAD

Its almost square skull is very broad and massive with a wide and flat forehead. The stop is clearly marked. The muzzle is broad and strong, just a little shorter than the skull and the nose bridge is straight and slopes upwards slightly. The small ears are set on high and are carried folded over and back (rose ears). The oval eyes are set far apart. They are fairly big and are set in the head with a slight slant. The Perro de Presa Mallorquin has an undershot bite, but the incisors of the lower jaw should not protrude more than half an inch (1 cm) beyond those set in the upper jaw.

SHOULDER HEIGHT

Dogs are $21^3/_4$–$22^3/_4$ in (55–58 cm) and bitches $20^1/_2$–$21^3/_4$ in (52–55 cm).

WEIGHT

Dogs vary between $77^1/_4$–$83^1/_2$ lb (35–38 kg) and bitches between $66^1/_4$–88 lb (30–40 kg).

COAT

The short and coarse hair feels harsh.

COLORS

The Perro de Presa Mallorquin has a brindle, yellow and black coat. White markings are permitted, as long as they do not cover more than 30% of the total surface – a black mask is accepted too. The eyes are dark.

TEMPERAMENT

CHARACTER

This breed is very self-confident and intelligent, watchful and alert. They will naturally guard and protect anything that is precious to them in a very

Perro de Presa Mallorquin

convincing way. They are brave, very tough on themselves and are strongly attached to their owners and their families. They do not generally bark a lot.

SOCIAL BEHAVIOR

This dog will be very friendly and docile towards its own family. They take their task as a guard dog very seriously; they will not allow uninvited guests beyond the front gate. They will however accept newcomers if their bosses tell them it is fine. They tend to be patient with children. These dogs can be quite dominant and ready for a fight with other dogs of their own sex, particularly male dogs. They show little interest in members of the opposite sex. They mix well with one or more cats and other pets, provided the dog has been accustomed to them since puppyhood.

GENERAL CARE

GROOMING

This breed does not require much brushing. A rubber brush will do fine during the molting season. Keep the claws short.

TRAINING

This intelligent dog learns very quickly. They are not suited to long drawn training sessions, but they do like to please their handlers. During their training you need to put considerable emphasis on socialization with people. You need not be afraid that you will create an "all-person's-dog;" the dog will become more stable and easier to manage if it has been well socialized. Its capacities as a guard dog and protector will not be less. A calm and strong master or mistress will bring out the best in this dog.

EXERCISE

The Perro de Presa Mallorquin needs a fair amount of exercise. The dog is happy to accompany you on walks for hours and likes to retrieve sticks and play with balls, etc. If it is not convenient once in a while, the dog will adapt.

USES

These fairly rare dogs are only used as watchful companions.

DETAILS

The Perro de Presa Mallorquin is also officially known as Ca de Bou.

Perro de Presa Canario

PERRO DE PRESA CANARIO	
COUNTRY OF ORIGIN	CANARY ISLANDS
ORIGINAL FUNCTION	THIS BREED HAS HAD DIFFERENT FUNCTIONS: FROM A FIGHTING DOG TO A SHEPHERD AND WATCHDOG.

APPEARANCE

BODY

The Perro de Presa Canario has a square build with a short, level topline. The loin is a little higher than the withers. The high-set tail is thick at the base and tapers to a point. The ribs are well arched and the belly tuck-up is slight. The very broad chest reaches down to the elbows that should be turned neither inward nor outward. The forequarters are set wide. From all sides they look straight and vertical and have heavy bones. The angulations, particularly of the hindquarters are moderate and the hocks are well let down. The feet are round and compact. The hind feet are a little longer than the forefeet. The neck is round, massive and muscular with some loose dewlap.

Perro de Presa Canario

HEAD

The big and massive skull looks square and has a clear, but no abrupt stop. The well-filled muzzle is shorter than the skull. The proportions should ideally be 4:6. The nose bridge is straight. The lips are quite thick and meaty. The upper lips overlap the lower lips slightly. The jaws are well developed. The fairly small to moderately sized ears are set on high and generally they are carried folded backwards. The medium-sized eyes are quite far apart and are oval-shaped. The Perro de Presa Canario has a fitting or slightly undershot bite.

SHOULDER HEIGHT

The dogs are 23–26 in (59–66 cm) and bitches are $21^3/_4$–$24^1/_2$ in (55–62 cm).

WEIGHT

Dogs vary between $99^1/_4$–$125^3/_4$ lb (45–57 kg) and bitches between 88–$110^1/_4$ lb (40–50 kg).

COAT

The harsh short hair lies close to the skin. There is no undercoat.

COLORS

This breed has a brindle coat in a variety of shades, but also in a number of plain sandy colors. A black mask is compulsory. It may stretch over the eyes. Small white markings are accepted. The eyes are brown. The legs and eye rims and the nose should have black pigmentation.

Perro de Presa Canario

TEMPERAMENT

CHARACTER

The Perro de Presa Canario is a fairly calm and equable dog with great self-confidence. These intelligent dogs are very loyal to their own folks and under normal circumstances they are good-natured and friendly. They are territorial and very watchful and protective. Strangers will not be allowed to set foot on your property or in your house. Should any member of the family be threatened, this dog will act immediately. Bitches are generally more manageable than dogs.

SOCIAL BEHAVIOR

This breed mixes well with children provided they are well socialized. They will defend your children if their friends tease them. They get on well with cats and other pets if the dog has been socialized with them from puppyhood. They are quite dominant towards other dogs. They will not shun the opportunity to fight. They are watchful and suspicious regards people they do not know, a characteristic they will demonstrate on their own territory.

GENERAL CARE

GROOMING

This coat needs very little care. The hairs are short and they hardly shed. Brush the dog once a week with a hard bristle brush and keep the claws short. During the molt a rubber mitt is best suited to remove loose hairs from the coat.

TRAINING

This breed is very intelligent and the dogs like to work for their handlers who need to be authoritative and provide good leadership. This type of dog will not suit everyone. The training should not be severe, but consistent, in a harmonious atmosphere. Allow plenty of time for a good socialization process and discourage the dog's tendency to fight its peers.

EXERCISE

These dogs are quite peaceful indoors, but like to be active. Your dog will need taking out frequently. The Perro de Presa Canario likes to be around its own folks, but is quite happy amusing itself in the yard, for instance with a rag or a (safe) ball. Do ensure that the yard is well fenced.

USES

So far this breed has been fairly rare. The dog is mainly used as a watchful companion.

Perro de Presa Canario

CANE CORSO (SICILIAN BRANCHIERO)	
COUNTRY OF ORIGIN	ITALY
ORIGINAL FUNCTION	HUNTING DOG FOR LARGE GAME, HERDING DOG AND FARM DOG

Cane Corso

APPEARANCE

BODY

The Cane Corso is a medium to large sized dog, powerfully built without being squat. Its compact and strong body is approximately 11% longer than its shoulder height. The topline is straight, broad and very muscular. The broad chest is muscular and displays a clear forechest. The tail is set on fairly high. It is usually not docked too short in countries where this is permissible. At rest the tail is carried low. In movement it may be carried in line with the back or slightly above. The legs are straight and well angulated. Cane Corsos have catlike feet that are slightly longer on the hindquarters. The lightly arched neck has hardly any dewlap, it is oval-shaped and very muscular.

HEAD

The skull is wide between the ears and slightly arched. The occiput is not very developed. The Cane Corsos have a clear stop. The broad and deep muzzle is almost as broad as it is long and the nose bridge is straight. The strong lips tend to overlap. Viewed from the front they look like an inverted "U." The eyes are medium sized and they have an alert and intelligent expression. The ears are well in proportion with the head. They are triangular and are carried pendant. Cane Corsos have a slight undershot bite.

SHOULDER HEIGHT

The dogs of this breed have a shoulder height ranging from $25^1/_2$–$26^3/_4$ in (64–68 cm) and the bitches from $23^1/_2$–$25^1/_2$ in (60–64 cm).

WEIGHT

Dogs weigh $99^1/_4$–$110^1/_4$ lb (45–50 kg) and bitches $88^1/_4$–$99^1/_4$ lb (40–45 kg).

COAT

The hair is short, shiny and dense. It should not feel soft.

COLORS

Cane Corsos are recognized in black, various shades of yellow and red and in a number of gray tones and brindle. A black or white mask should not stretch behind the eyes. Small white markings on chest, feet and round the nose are acceptable. The eyes are dark.

TEMPERAMENT

CHARACTER

The Cane Corso is a brave, equable, intelligent, active and also a boisterous dog. It is affectionate and loyal to its family. This breed is not really suited to life in a kennel. Dogs of this breed are very watchful and protective but they make themselves heard when there is real danger.

SOCIAL BEHAVIOR

This dog mixes well with children, but they are suspicious of strangers. It will put up with them if the owners are present. If the dog has been well socialized it will get on well with pets, such as cats. They tend to be ready to fight other dogs.

GENERAL CARE

GROOMING

This breed needs little coat care. Rubber mitts are useful during the molt to remove loose hairs. Keep the claws short.

TRAINING

This breed usually learns quickly and with ease

but it is not suited to beginners. A Cane Corso is an excellent dog for calm people who have a natural authority over the dog. If the puppy is brought up consistently in harmonious surroundings the dog will most certainly grow up into a stable and reliable dog. It will need to meet all kinds of different people, animals and situations as a puppy in order to respond in a stable manner later on. You need

Cane Corso

not be afraid that the dog will become a lesser guard dog or less protective when mature; it is a natural feature of any Cane Corso to be protective and it will act when necessary. You will need to spend extra time socializing this dog with other dogs during puppyhood to prevent the dog going for others of its kind later on when challenged, wanting to prove its strength.

EXERCISE

The Cane Corso is an active and busy dog that will accompany you for hours without any signs of fatigue. Running with you, ball games, retrieving and a number of other forms of physical exercise will appeal to this dog. If you are unable to comply once in a while, your dog will adapt. A Cane Corso that gets enough exercise outdoors will be fairly calm and peaceful indoors.

USES

Cane Corsos have been regarded as good companions up to now, although some people have achieved good results in a number of dog sports with this dog.

Cane Corso

MASTIFF

COUNTRY OF ORIGIN	ENGLAND
ORIGINAL FUNCTION	HUNTING DOG FOR LARGE GAME AND GUARD DOG

APPEARANCE

BODY

The Mastiff, sometimes called Old English Mastiff, has a massive, deep, strongly built body. It must be big and heavy, powerful and in proportion. The back and loins are broad and muscular – flat and very broad for bitches and slightly arched for male dogs. The sides are deep. Mastiffs have a high-set tail that reaches down to the hocks or beyond. The tail is wide at the base and tapers to a point. The tail hangs straight down when at rest, but when the dog is alert it curves. The tail should never be carried over the topline. The broad and deep chest drops down far between the forequarters. The ribs are arched and rounded. The circumference of the chest should be one third more than its shoulder height. The very muscular shoulders are set slanting. The legs are straight and vertical. They are set wide apart, with heavy bones. The feet are large and round, with well-arched feet. The moderately long neck is slightly arched and very muscular. The circumference of the neck is usually 1–2 in (2$^{1}/_{2}$–5 cm) less than the circumference of the skull (measured just in front of the ears).

HEAD

Viewed from all sides its head should make a square and broad impression. The flat forehead only has wrinkles when the dog is alert. The eyebrows protrude slightly and the stop is clearly marked although it is not too abrupt. The short, blunt and square muzzle is wide under the eyes and runs almost parallel to the forenose. The upper lips

Mastiff

hang slightly over the lower lips. The small ears feel thin and are set far apart. They are set on the highest parts of the side of the skull. They are carried pendulously, against the cheeks. The small eyes are set far apart and the eyelids should not flop or be open. Mastiffs have a scissors or light undershot bite, but never so strong that the teeth are visible when the mouth is closed.

Mastiffs

SHOULDER HEIGHT

The mastiff dog should be at least 30 in (76 cm) and bitches at least 27$^{1}/_{2}$ in (70 cm) high.

COAT

Its short hair should be neither thin nor fine on the shoulders, neck and back.

COLORS

The Mastiff might have an apricot, silver, yellow or apricot streaked coat. They always have a black mask and black ears. The black color around the eyes should stretch upwards.

TEMPERAMENT

CHARACTER

The Mastiff is a calm, self-confident, noble dog. It is stable and not impressionable when mature. They are soft-natured and affectionate to their families and do not like to be left alone. They are excellent guard dogs of family, home and property

Mastiff

in a very controlled calm manner. It is not in their nature to jump up and down and bark ferociously behind the fence at passers-by. They bark very little and they know that their appearance is enough to scare wrongdoers. They are definitely intelligent dogs. They are generally obedient and cooperative.

SOCIAL BEHAVIOR

Provided they have been correctly socialized and trained, Mastiffs present no problems mixing with other dogs and household pets, as they hardly have any hunting instinct. Normally its behavior with children is good-tempered and friendly. When strangers visit, it refuses them access unless its handler accepts them. Mastiffs are friendly and will generally accept friends of the family with enthusiasm.

GENERAL CARE

GROOMING

This massive dog does not require much coat care. A good brush once a week with a bristle brush should suffice. During the molting season a rubber mitt or brush may prove useful to remove dead and loose hair. Give a Mastiff a soft place to lie down to avoid ugly pressure marks. Economies must not be made with the young and growing dog's diet. Good nutrition is essential to optimum growth. The dog grows very quickly. It is advisable to ration the dog's amount of exercise to prevent it from overtiring. Like other mastiff types, the Mastiff has a high pain threshold and since it is very demanding of itself, injuries and illnesses can be overlooked until they are truly serious.

Mastiff

TRAINING

Training a Mastiff must be enjoyable, and should be conducted calmly in a harmonious manner. Consistency, lots of love, and plenty of understanding work wonders. Harsh words and punishment are unnecessary and hurtful; these dogs are highly sensitive. You will achieve better results by telling the dog clearly when you are pleased with it and you present its training in a pleasant and cheerful manner. Discourage their pulling on the leash when they are pups, because once they are grown up these dogs will be too strong to be able to change its behavior. Mastiff-pups can be shy and may need encouragement. Give it plenty of time for good socialization and to strengthen its self-confidence.

A fully-grown Mastiff needs an average amount of exercise. It is enough to take the dog round the block at set times and allow it to run and play off-leash several times a week. They are not very keen on ball games or any kind of training. A young Mastiff, a rapidly grow-

Mastiff

ing animal, needs its exercise during puppyhood controlling. If the dog is too strongly pressurized or becomes over-tired, it can have an adverse effect upon the development of bones, joints and muscles.

USES

This dog makes an excellent companion for people with plenty of space in and around the house.

Bull-mastiff bitch

The circumference of the neck is almost equal to the circumference of the skull.

HEAD

Its big and square skull only shows wrinkles when the dog is alert. The circumference of the skull should be equal to the shoulder height of the dog. The wide muzzle is short (no longer than one third of the total length of the head) and looks square. There is a clear stop and a deep furrow between the eyes.

The V-shaped ears are set high and far apart, which accentuates the square appearance of the skull. When the dog is alert the tips of its ears hang in line with the eyes. The eyes are medium-sized. Bull-Mastiffs have a pincer bite, but a light undershot, though not desirable, is permissible.

SHOULDER HEIGHT

Male Bull-mastiff

Male dogs vary between 25–27 in (63$^1/_2$–68$^1/_2$ cm) and bitches between 24–26 in (61–66 cm).

WEIGHT

Dogs range from 110$^1/_4$–139 lb (50–63 kg) and bitches from 88$^1/_4$–110$^1/_4$ lb (40–50 kg).

COAT

Its harsh and short hair lies close to its body.

COLORS

A Bull-Mastiff's coat may be streaked in any color, yellow brown or red, and always with a black muzzle and ears. A bit of white on the chest is acceptable, but not desirable. The eyes are hazel or brown.

TEMPERAMENT

CHARACTER

The Bull-Mastiff is extremely equable, not parti-

BULL-MASTIFF	
COUNTRY OF ORIGIN	ENGLAND
ORIGINAL FUNCTION	THIS DOG WAS BRED SPECIALLY TO PROTECT GAMEKEEPERS FROM POACHERS

APPEARANCE

BODY

Bull-Mastiffs have a compact build with a strong and short topline. The muscular loins are wide and the sides are deep. The high-set tail narrows towards the point. The tail reaches the hocks and is carried straight or curved. The chest is broad and deep, with a roomy forechest. The straight and powerful forequarters are well angulated and the muscular hindquarters have moderately angulated hocks. Bull-Mastiffs have catlike feet. The muscular neck is moderately long and well arched.

Male Bull-mastiff

Bull-mastiff

cularly impressionable, and normally responds in a calm and controlled manner. They are brave and physically tough on themselves. On the other side they are very sensitive to the atmosphere in the home and they are quite soft natured toward members of the family. Although they can be quite energetic outdoors, they are generally calm indoors. They do not bark a lot, but make themselves heard when there is danger. A Bull-Mastiff strongly protects its family, home and property from wrongdoers. They are very affectionate and as a rule quite obedient to members of the household. Their attachment to their handlers means that they will not take to life in a kennel. Keeping them in a kennel tends to have a negative impact on their character. They need to be in a home, among the family.

SOCIAL BEHAVIOR

Bull-Mastiffs are very tolerant towards children but can be rather dominant towards their own kind, both indoors and outdoors. Provided they are properly socialized when young, they can learn to get along with other household pets, such as cats. Friends of the family will be accepted, espe-

cially if the handler signifies approval, but unwanted visitors will be halted in their tracks.

GENERAL CARE

GROOMING

This breed needs fairly little coat care. Occasionally remove dead and loose hairs with a rubber brush or massage mitt. Keep the claws short.

TRAINING

This breed responds best to a fair, stable and consistent approach carried out in a harmonious manner. The Bull-Mastiff is very sensitive to the tone of your voice and is not really difficult to manage, but does require a handler who can assert authority, because of its strength when fully grown and its dominance towards its own kind.

Male Bull-mastiff bitch

EXERCISE

This dog has an average demand for exercise. A couple of outings every day with several opportunities to run and play (on-leash) give it sufficient freedom of movement.

USES

Today the Bull-Mastiff is predominantly used as a watchful family dog. It does however have the physical and mental abilities to do well in various dog sports.

BORDEAUX DOG (DOGUE DE BORDEAUX, FRENCH MASTIFF)

COUNTRY OF ORIGIN	FRANCE
ORIGINAL FUNCTION	GUARD DOG

APPEARANCE

BODY

The Bordeaux Dog looks like a squat athlete. It has a broad chest that reaches below its elbows. The circumference of the body measured behind the elbows, should be $9^1/_2$–$11^1/_2$ in (25–30 cm) more than its shoulder height. Its broad and muscular back is level, with clearly marked withers. The sturdy loins are sufficiently short and the croup slopes down moderately to the base of the tail where it is thick. The tail should not reach beyond the hocks. Bordeaux Dogs have strong and muscular legs, with strong bones and powerful well-closed and fairly short feet. The slightly arched, very muscular neck almost has the same circumference as the skull (measured round the skull, in front of the ears). The dewlaps run from throat to chest.

HEAD

Its very big head is angular, wide and fairly short. For dogs the circumference of the skull is the same as their shoulder height. A bitch's head is not as hefty. The top of the skull is slightly arched. The stop is abrupt and at an angle with the nose bridge. The prominent forehead is much broader than it is high. There are symmetrical deep wrinkles on either sides of the furrow that runs lengthwise. The powerful muzzle is broad and thick, fairly short and the upper profile is slightly concave. The circumference of the muzzle is approximately two thirds of the circumference of the skull. The length of the muzzle varies between one quarter to one third of the total length of the head (measured from the occipital peak to

Bordeaux Dog

the tip of the nose). The broad and strong jaws have a good strong undershot bite. The lower jaw should protrude at least $^1/_4$ in ($^1/_2$ cm) to a maximum of $^3/_4$ in (2 cm). When the dog's mouth is shut, its teeth should not be visible. The fairly small and pendulous ears are set on high, so that the width of the skull is accentuated. The eyes are oval shaped and set well apart. They have an honest and open expression.

SHOULDER HEIGHT

Dogs range from $23^1/_2$–$26^3/_4$ in (60–70 cm) and bitches from $22^1/_2$–26 in (58–66 cm).

WEIGHT

Dogs have a minimum weight of 110 lb (50 kg) and bitches should be at least 99 lb (45 kg).

COAT

Both the undercoat and the top layer have short, fine, soft hair.

COLORS

The coat is either mahogany or fawn, with a read or black

Bordeaux Dog

mask. The latter is rare. The ears are often slightly darker. White markings are only permitted on chest and feet.

TEMPERAMENT

CHARACTER

This dog is a real "rough diamond." It is very brave and physically it is very tough on itself, but it is extremely sensitive to the atmosphere at home. They become very attached to "their" people. They should not be in a kennel. The Bordeaux Dog is a stable, peaceful, compliant and friendly dog. It wants to know what is happening around

Bordeaux Dog

it. The dog is very loyal and affectionate to its owner and family. It does not bark a lot; a good reason why you should check whenever you hear its loud bark. A Bordeaux Dog will protect its family members from wrongdoers and it will naturally guard home and property.

SOCIAL BEHAVIOR

A Bordeaux Dog that has had positive experiences during puppyhood and has consequently established an equable character, will mix well with other pets. They tend to be kind, tolerant and protective to children. They will initially mistrust strangers and approach them warily, but if the boss accepts the people, the dog will immediately accept. Bordeaux Dogs and particularly the males can be very dominant towards other dogs, both in the street and in the house.

Bordeaux Dogs like to cool off in hot weather

GENERAL CARE

GROOMING

Remove dead and loose hairs from the coat with a rubber mitt during the molt season. During the rest of the year a Bordeaux Dog needs relatively little grooming. When necessary you may clean the facial folds and corners of the eyes. Keep the claws clipped.

TRAINING

These dogs learn best when they are trained and educated in a consistent, just and loving manner. They are fairly sensitive to your tone of voice and like your approval for what they are doing. Do reward desirable behavior. They are fairly sensitive; a harsh upbringing is not helpful. Although they are gentle-natured to their owners they are not dogs to suit everyone. Once they are mature they are too big and unmanageable for people without a strong personality. A calm, equable owner with natural authority can bring out the best in a Bordeaux Dog. Although an average Bordeaux Dog would not like to disappoint its owner, it is not a dog that will be pleased with repetitive exercises or being given useless assignments.

EXERCISE

The Bordeaux Dog has a moderate need for exercise. The dog will be happy with several walks a day on-leash and additional running and playing off-leash. Like all big dogs this dog needs a lot of energy to develop a strong body. Good food and the right exercise are recommended during the first eighteen months. This dog will prefer to lie in the shade on hot days and it is advisable not to tire it.

USES

Bordeaux Dogs are excellent watchdogs and companions, but because of their build and mentality they are less suited to various dog sports.

Two young Bordeaux Dogs from the same litter

Young male Bordeaux Dog

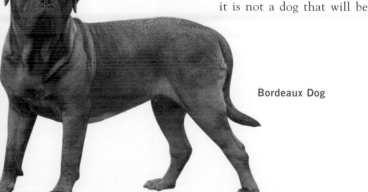

Bordeaux Dog

MASTINO NAPOLETANO (NEAPOLITAN MASTIFF)

COUNTRY OF ORIGIN	ITALY
ORIGINAL FUNCTION	GUARD DOG

Male Neapolitan Mastiff

APPEARANCE

BODY

The Neapolitan Mastiff is a powerful, muscular dog with a rustic and majestic appearance. The skin is loose, particularly on the head. Its body is approximately 10% longer than its shoulder height. Viewed from the side the topline is level and runs in a straight line interrupted only by the withers. From the side the transition between the loins and the back is slightly rounded. The sides are tucked up and the broad and muscular croup slopes a little. The powerful tail is docked down to one third of its length in countries where this is permissible. When in movement the tail is carried horizontally or slightly above the topline. The very muscular chest is wide and reaches down to the elbows or a little below. The long and slanting ribs are well arched and continue quite a way. The muscular shoulders are long and slope a little. The legs have strong bones, are muscular and well angulated and should have no dew claws. The feet are oval, very big, well closed and arched. The hind feet are a little smaller than the forefeet. The neck is short and squat and quite muscular, with a loose dewlap.

HEAD

The massive, short head is slightly wider between the cheekbones than the total length of the head. The stop is pronounced and there is a clear central furrow and occipital peak. From the side the top skull and wide nose bridge appear to run parallel. The length of the optically square muzzle is about one third of the total length of the head. The skin folds that run from the eye corners to the corners of the lips are typical for this breed. Viewed from the side the generous nose should not protrude beyond the lips. The lips are thick, meaty, heavy and droopy. Viewed from the front the corners of the mouth are the lowest point of the lips and you can see slimy skin. The triangular eyes are comparatively small and are carried pendulous, against the cheeks. The eyes are more or less round, but look small and slightly oval due to the floppy skin of the head above them. They are set deep and the eyelids should lie closely against the eyes. Neapolitan Mastiffs have a scissors or pincer bite.

SHOULDER HEIGHT

For dogs this will range from $25^1/_2$–$29^1/_2$ in (65–75 cm) and for bitches from $23^1/_2$–$26^3/_4$ (60–68 cm).

WEIGHT

Dogs weigh between $110^1/_2$–$154^1/_2$ lb (50–70 kg) and bitches between $92^1/_2$–$132^1/_4$ lb (42–60 kg).

COAT

The smooth coat is short (no longer

Neapolitan Mastiff

Male Mastiff

than one in ($1^1/_2$ cm), dense, smooth and fine.

COLORS

The Mastiff's most common coat is blue gray, but coats in gray, black, brown and fox red are also accepted. All colors may be streamed. A little white on the chest or on the tips of the toes is permitted.

Mastino bitch

TEMPERAMENT

CHARACTER

If a Mastiff is well brought up it will be an equable, fairly calm and quiet dog. These dogs are strongly attached to members of the family and their owners, to whom they are faithful, willing and compliant. They are affectionate to their folks and sensitive to the general atmosphere in the house. However, they are not easy dogs; they are brave and tough, fairly dominant and self-assured – and this applies particularly to male dogs. The breed is naturally defensive on its territory and knows if someone has good or bad intentions. They are good watchdogs and protect home and property very well. If the dog senses that its people are threatened or if uninvited guests announce themselves during their absence, it will react. These dogs are not suited to kennels. They need to be in the house amidst people and like to be involved in daily life.

SOCIAL BEHAVIOR

Male dogs might be dominant towards other male dogs in the street and at home; bitches are generally less assertive. These dogs are generally friendly and good-natured to kids, provided the dogs do not tease them. If they have positive experiences with cats and other pets at an early age, there should be no problem. Friends of the family are greeted in a friendly manner, but towards strangers the dog will initially respond defensively. It is not keen on imprudent strangers. It will initially be guarded and only go up to them when it decides to do so.

GENERAL CARE

GROOMING

The Neapolitan Mastiff's coat is quite easy to care for. About once a week you need to brush the coat with a rubber bristle brush. During the molting season it is good to remove dead and loose hair with a rubber brush or massage mitt. These dogs are more likely to slobber because of their

Mastino

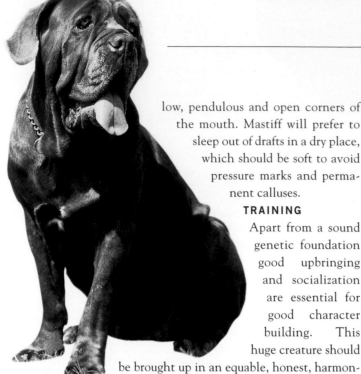

Mastiff
bitch

low, pendulous and open corners of the mouth. Mastiff will prefer to sleep out of drafts in a dry place, which should be soft to avoid pressure marks and permanent calluses.

TRAINING

Apart from a sound genetic foundation good upbringing and socialization are essential for good character building. This huge creature should be brought up in an equable, honest, harmonious and very consistent manner. A calm and consistent boss with natural authority will bring out the best in the Mastiff, but the opposite is also possible – do not tease or excite this dog. Mastiffs are no dogs for beginners and they are not suitable for people who are nervous, busy, soft or changeable. A Mastiff will naturally protect you and your possessions vigorously. It does not need any extra incentives or commands to do so. Take your young dog with you whenever possible and let it have positive experiences with all kinds of people, animals and situations, so that it can grow up into a reliable dog that responds to many impressions in a stable manner. Teach the dog not to pull on its leash from an early age.

EXERCISE

The Mastiff has an average need for exercise. They like to play and romp, but they are no dogs to walk for hours on end. The young Mastiff grows very quickly and you need to ration its exercise. It should not get overtired. Avoid rough games during its growth and take care that it can use all its energy to build up good bone mass and muscles. Indoors the dogs tend to be quite calm to the point of laziness.

USES

This breed is popular as watchful companions.

ARGENTINEAN MASTIFF (DOGO ARGENTINO)

COUNTRY OF ORIGIN	ARGENTINA
ORIGINAL FUNCTION	INDEPENDENT HUNTING DOG FOR LARGE GAME AND DEFENSIBLE GAME, PARTICULARLY PUMAS

APPEARANCE

BODY

The Argentinean Mastiff is quite muscular over all its body, particularly its shoulders and loins. The chest is roomy and the lowest part of the underline is behind the elbows. The strong back slopes down gradually from its withers to the croup. If it is well muscled there is a groove along the backbone, which is clearly visible from above. The tail does not reach beyond the hocks and is carried high, but not in a curl. The legs are straight. The low-set hocks are obvious on the hindquarters. Dew claws are not accepted. The feet have well-closed toes and are shorter on the forequarters than on the hindquarters. The graceful neck is muscular and arched, with a supple dewlap. The arched neck is so muscular that the occipital peak is masked by its muscles.

HEAD

The skull is rounded with the line of the face curving slightly upwards. The muzzle and skull are both equally long. Argentinean Mastiffs have close-lying lips, with slightly overlapping flews. The high-set ears are carried pendulously, alongside the head. The eyes are far apart and they have a lively, but severe expression. This breed has a scissors bite.

SHOULDER HEIGHT

This varies between $24^{1}/_{2}$–$26^{3}/_{4}$ in (62–68 cm) for dogs and between $23^{1}/_{2}$–$25^{1}/_{2}$ in (60–65 cm) for bitches.

WEIGHT

Dogs range from 88–$110^{1}/_{4}$ lb (40–50 kg) and bitches from 88–$99^{1}/_{4}$ lb (40–45 kg). Bitches may be a little bigger and heavier than suggested.

COAT

The Argentinean Mastiff has a short and fairly coarse coat.

Argentinean Dog

COLORS

This breed is always white, with possibly some pigment flecks in the skin. A small black patch between ears and eyes is acceptable, but markings on other places will mean disqualification at shows. The forenose is always black and the lip rims have black pigmentation. The eyelids need not be black, but the eyes are always dark.

Argentinean Dog puppy

TEMPERAMENT

CHARACTER

Argentinean Mastiffs are temperamental, occasionally boisterous, dogs with lots of stamina. They are equable and sober, persistent, brave, tough on themselves and generally quite self-assured, even dominant. They are very loyal to their handlers and families and also show their affection. Most of these dogs are quite watchful and will defend the family when necessary, but they seldom bark. There is some hunting instinct in most dogs. Although the dogs are not very sensitive to weather conditions, they are not suited as a kennel dog. It would numb them.

SOCIAL BEHAVIOR

An Argentinean Mastiff usually gets on well with kids, although their size and boisterousness make them less suited to families with small kids. Visitors are initially eyed with mistrust but friends of the family are greeted happily and boisterously. It is not impossible to expect a good relationship with cats, cattle and other pets. Its hunting instinct might emerge which means the owner needs to spend a lot of time socializing the dog from a very early age. An Argentinean Mastiff rarely behaves sociably towards other dogs. Particularly male dogs may domineer others of its kind, although the ladies might make their presence felt, too. Good socialization and upbringing can make a world of difference.

GENERAL CARE

GROOMING

It is easy to keep an Argentinean Mastiff's coat in good condition. You can remove the loose and dead hairs during molting with a rubber brush. Keep the claws short.

TRAINING

Give the Argentinean Mastiff a consistent training in a fair and calm manner. Severe punishment will have a counter-effect. Considerable time needs to be spent on socializing. Take the dog with you wherever you go and allow it to meet a variety of people, children, dogs and different pets and animals. In general this breed is less suited to inexperienced and insecure people. A calm owner with a natural authority will bring out the best in this dog.

Argentinean Dog

EXERCISE

Argentinean Mastiffs are energetic dogs and they need more than their daily outing. Take the dog on regular longer walks. This dog can let off a fair amount of steam in a large, fenced backyard. It needs to be well under control before you let it run off-leash, considering its hunting instinct and dominant behavior to other dogs.

USES

This breed is still used for its original function in its country of origin, but elsewhere it is predominantly a companion for people who have a lot of space in and around the house.

Argentinean Dog

Fila Brasileiro

FILA BRASILEIRO BRAZILIAN MOLOSSER	
COUNTRY OF ORIGIN	BRAZIL
ORIGINAL FUNCTION	WATCHDOG AND TRACKING DOG, HUNTING DOG FOR BIG CATS AND OTHER ANIMALS

APPEARANCE

BODY

The Fila Brasileiro has a strong, broad and deep body and a square build. One of the typical characteristics for this breed is the loose skin over its entire body, which forms dewlaps in the neck. Another typical trait is that their powerful and long croup lies higher than the chest. The tail reaches down to the hocks, it is broad at the base and tapers to a point. It should not be carried in a curl over the topline. Its broad and deep chest reaches to the elbows. The breastbone protrudes clearly and the ribs are well arched. The chest is moderately tucked up. The legs are straight and have sturdy bones. The knees are moderately angulated. The vertical feet are powerful, with arched toes not too close together. The neck is very muscular

Fila Brasileiro

and appears to be short and the neck is arched slightly at the top.

HEAD

Viewed from above the head has the shape of a trapeze. The muzzle is slightly shorter than the skull. There is a central furrow, which is not too pronounced. The stop is undulating and the eyebrows are well developed. The muzzle is broad, deep and powerful and the nose bridge is straight or slightly arched (muzzle). The thick lips hang over the lower flews. Its large fat ears are V-shaped with rounded tips. They are in line with the eyes, set on fairly far back and are carried pendulously. The eyes are medium to large, almond-shaped, and fairly far apart and set quite deeply. The lower eyelids may droop. Fila Brasileiros have a scissors or pincer bite.

Fila Brasileiro bitch

SHOULDER HEIGHT

Bitches measure $25^1/_2$–$27^1/_2$ in (65–70 cm) and dogs $27^1/_2$–$33^1/_2$ in (70–85 cm) to the withers.

WEIGHT

Bitches weigh at least 88 lb (40 kg) and dogs are at least $110^1/_4$ lb (50 kg).

COAT

The short-haired coat is soft, dense and lies close to the skin.

COLORS

The Fila's coat is known in many different colors of which only white, mouse gray, and spotted or piebald are not accepted. White markings are permissible, but only on the feet, chest and tip of the tail. They should definitely not cover more than 25 % of the total surface. The most usual coat is brindle in a variety of shades.

TEMPERAMENT

CHARACTER

The Fila Brasileiro is a very affectionate, gentle and obedient dog to its family. It always subjects itself to its handler and it has difficulty adjusting to a new owner when it is older. It is a self-assured, brave dog, which is fairly tough on itself. The Fila is very watchful. It is a natural watchdog that needs to defend your property. It will not only defend house and yard, but also all those who are dear to it. It is suspicious of strangers and if it feels its owner is in danger it will act immediately. They tend to be quite peaceful in the house. This dog has an exceptionally well-developed sense of smell and some hunting instinct.

Fila Brasileiro

SOCIAL BEHAVIOR

For the children of its family, the Fila Brasileiro presents no problems but this is not true of their playmates. It will also accept some other household animals, which it has met while young. New pets joining the family are not generally accepted. The Fila Brasileiro is noted for its suspicious nature towards strangers. This can manifest itself as aggression or by being evasive. Obviously this dog should not live in a busy housing area. Regular visitors are generally accepted provided the owner indicates that they are welcome. A Fila can be quite dominant towards other dogs, particularly if they are of the same sex and do not belong to its own pack.

GENERAL CARE

GROOMING

The Fila needs relatively little coat care. You will need to brush the coat once a week with a bristle brush and use a rubber mitt during the molt to remove dead and loose hairs. Filas need somewhere soft to lie to prevent calluses forming on the pressure points. Calluses occur mainly on their elbows.

TRAINING

A Fila Brasileiro is not a suitable dog for people who are indecisive, or for people who are inexperienced with dogs. They have a character that is sometimes difficult to fathom. Future Fila owners need to be sure of themselves, both mentally as well as physically, have a natural authority and plenty of understanding of the character of the dog and dog behavior in general to be able to complete the training successfully. The dog's training should be carried out in a calm and harmonious manner. The future Fila owner needs to know that these dogs can respond like a flash of lightning. Give yourself plenty of time to socialize your dog.

Fila Brasileiro dog and young bitch

EXERCISE

Ideally this dog has the use of a well-fenced yard, where it can determine its own need of exercise. Every now and again you can take the dog out on the leash to explore and experience new terrain.

Fila Brasileiro

TOSA INU (JAPANESE TOSA)

COUNTRY OF ORIGIN	JAPAN
ORIGINAL FUNCTION	FIGHTING DOG AND WATCHDOG

APPEARANCE

Tosa Inu

BODY

The Tosa Inu is a big massive dog and looks impressive. It has a horizontal topline with high withers and the loins are broad and muscular. At the top the croup is rounded. The tail is thick where it is set on and gradually tapers to a point. It is set quite high and reaches down to the hocks. The chest is deep and the ribs are moderately arched. The legs are straight, with moderately angulated hocks and knees. Tosa Inus have compact feet with closed toes and firm pads. The neck is muscular and has a loose dewlap, but not excessively.

HEAD

The skull is broad and the stop is pronounced. The muzzle gives a square impression and is moderately long. The nose bridge is straight. The comparatively small and thin ears are set high. They are carried pendulous, against the skull. The eyes are quite small and have a dignified expression. Tosa Inus have a scissors bite.

SHOULDER HEIGHT

The Tosa Inu dog should be at least 24 in (61 cm) high.

The minimum height for a bitch is 21$^1/_2$ in (55 cm). There is no maximum height, and therefore these measurements are often exceeded considerably.

COAT

Tosa Inus have a short-haired coat that is strong and dense.

Young Tosa Inu

COLORS

The most popular color is solid red brown, but these dogs also have yellow, streaked and black and tan coats. White markings are permissible on the chest, toes, tip of the tail and as a blaze on the forehead. The nose is always black, the eyes are dark brown and dark nails are preferable.

TEMPERAMENT

CHARACTER

Tosa Inus are very self-confident, patient, equable, intelligent and calm dogs. They rarely get upset, except when they feel their families might be threatened or if they are confronted with trespassers during the absence of their folks. They are excellent watchdogs, with a natural instinct to protect their people and territory. They are extremely brave and tough on themselves. They gen-

Tosa Inu

erally do not bark a lot. This dog is affectionate to its people. It does not perform well if it is banned to a kennel. These dogs do not generally slobber.

SOCIAL BEHAVIOR

The Tosa Inu places its family first and foremost. They object to strangers. They are generally shy but they are watchful towards unknown guests, however, if the owner invites them in they will accept. Acquaintances of the family are usually approached in a friendly manner. Generally they are fine with children and very tolerant. Particularly the males can be dominant towards their own sex. Keep your dog away from other dogs, which are raring to fight because an attacker will always come off worse. As a rule you need not worry about cats and other pets, provided the dog is well socialized.

GENERAL CARE

GROOMING

This dog's coat is easy to care for. You may need to brush its coat weekly with a harsh bristle brush and keep the claws short. A rubber brush or rubber mitt will come in handy during the molt to remove dead or loose hairs. The dogs benefit from a soft bed to prevent ugly calluses on pressure points such as the elbows.

TRAINING

This breed requires an equable, loving and consistent approach to its training. They are very sensitive to your voice. If you are clear and in control, you will not need to punish or correct your dog. The dog needs a handler with a mental authority. Discourage pulling on the leash from an early age and spend a lot of time socializing your dog.

Young Tosa Inu

EXERCISE

On a well-fenced and large enough area of land, this dog can happily look after its own exercise demands. Take it with you to the beach, woods or open countryside occasionally for a change of scene. In principle it only requires an average level of exercise. This breed is not keen on ball games. Indoors these dogs are quite peaceful.

USES

This dog is at its best with people who keep it as a companion and who have plenty of space in and around the house.

Black Great Dane

GREAT DANE	
COUNTRY OF ORIGIN	GERMANY
ORIGINAL FUNCTION	PREVIOUSLY A HUNTING DOG FOR LARGE GAME, NOW A WATCHDOG AND FAMILY PET

APPEARANCE

BODY

The Great Dane is a giant dog that combines nobility with robustness and power with elegance. The length of its body is equal to its shoulder height. Bitches may have a slightly longer body. The withers form the highest parts of the strong, short back. The loins are powerful and arch a little, and the full croup slopes down a bit towards the base of the tail. The moderately long tail, set on high, does not extend beyond the hocks. It is thick at the base and tapers to a point. The chest has a good width and reaches down to the elbows. The belly has a good tuck-up towards the back. The shoulder blade is long and set slanting and the elbows fit closely. The legs are long, dry and vertical. The round feet are vertical and have short, strongly arched and well-closed toes. The muscular dry neck is set on high. Its transition is fine with a beautifully arched and well-formed onset of the neck.

HEAD

A Great Dane's head is long, narrow and striking. It should look angular. Great Danes have a marked stop and well-developed eyebrows. The top skull and straight nose bridge run parallel to each other and the skull and muzzle are of equal length. Viewed from the front the head is narrow, with a broad nose bridge and under-

Tosa Inu

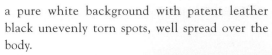

developed muscles of the cheek. The full lips drop down from the nose in a straight line and should show a clear angle. The ears are set on high. They are carried pendant, close to the head. The round eyes are medium size and have close-fitting eyelids. They should have a sensible and lively expression. Great Danes have a scissors bite.

SHOULDER HEIGHT
Minimally this should be $31^1/_2$ in (80 cm) for dogs and $28^1/_2$ in (72 cm) for bitches. There is no maximum height and preferably the minimum measurements should be exceeded.

WEIGHT
A Dane should weigh approx. $121^1/_4$–$187^1/_2$ lb (55–85 kg) or more, depending on size, gender and build.

COAT
All Danes have very short, thick, shiny and close-fitting hair.

COLORS
There are three color patterns:
– Brindles – yellow and streaked yellow:
Yellow dogs have a light golden yellow to dark yellow color with dark eyes, preferably with a black mask. Brindle Danes have the same features, except that they have a strong black stream over a yellow background.
– Black and spotted:
Black dogs are a patent leather black with dark eyes. They may have small white markings. The spotted dogs are known as harlequins. They have a pure white background with patent leather black unevenly torn spots, well spread over the body.
– Some gray or brownish marks are permissible. Harlequin is the only variety permitted to have partially blue eyes and a partially flesh-colored muzzle. Brown eyes are preferable as well as a nose, eye rims and lip rims with black pigmentation.
– Blue:
This color is preferably steel blue, without any yellow or black. Small white markings and light colored eyes are permissible.

Young yellow Great Dane bitch

There are also mantle and blanket Danes that are considered part of the black color pattern. They are not recognized in most of the countries not belonging to the FCI. The black coat of the Mantel Dane covers almost all the dog like a mantel, with white showing on just the chest, neck, blaze, belly, legs and tip of the tail. The other variety has the same markings, but this mantel is broken with white.
The different colors are not interbred.

Blue Great Dane bitch

Blue Great Dane dog

TEMPERAMENT

CHARACTER

These are affectionate dogs that are very loyal to the handler and family. They are sensitive and harsh words will hurt them deeply. They are very

Blue Great Danes

intelligent and curious; they do not miss much. They appear to be sensible and equable. Particularly male dogs are excellent guard dogs; they say that a burglar may enter the house, but will never leave it again if a Great Dane

is on duty. They are not barkers. Great Danes are not very susceptible to pain, like other Mastiff types, and therefore it is possible that an illness or injury may be overlooked for some time. They do not belong in a kennel and are rather fond of comfort and warmth in the house.

TRAINING

The Great Dane grows into a very large dog very quickly. You must therefore teach it as a very young dog that it must not pull on the leash. Train it with understanding in a harmonious manner and with great consistency. They are very sensitive to the intonation of the voice and your friendly request is often sufficient to get them to do what you require. Severe training does not suit this breed. They are not suited to long and monotonous training sessions – they will simply lose interest. You will achieve the best results with variety and positive rewards. Spend enough time on socializing; young Great Danes can be a little shy and need a fair amount of encouragement.

GENERAL CARE

GROOMING

The Great Dane's coat requires very little attention. During molting it is best to remove dead and loose hairs with a rubber mitt. The Great Dane should be given somewhere soft to lie to avoid causing pressure marks. Fast-growing breeds like the Great Dane require care during the growing stage. Good nutrition is a first essential and secondly its exercise should be well balanced and measured. Keep its claws short.

SOCIAL BEHAVIOR

Great Danes are extremely devoted to their families, but they are shy to strangers. Well-socialized dogs will not show excessive behavior in this respect. Friends of the family are greeted with enthusiasm. Generally they get on perfectly well with livestock, other household pets, and children, provided they have been well socialized. Their own kind should be no problem although there are male dogs that like to assert their authority towards others of their sex.

EXERCISE

This strong and elegant dog requires significant levels of exercise. They will enjoy being able to run free and romping, off-leash in open country or woodland. They will seldom wander off and usually remain in the vicinity of their owners. Walks in the rain will generally be short, because most of these dogs dislike rain and cold weather. When a Great Dane gets enough exercise, it is calm indoors. A young Great Dane needs all its strength to develop a strong and healthy body and will need controlled exercise. These dogs are too big for an apartment. In fact climbing stairs is not good for them.

USES

These dogs are now almost only exclusively used as family dogs, but there are Great Danes that are renowned for their achievements in advanced obedience skills. Because of their exceptional sense of smell they are quite good tracking dogs.

Great Danes are very big dogs

Young Caucasian Ovtcharka bitch

CAUCASIAN OVTCHARKA OR CAUCASIAN SHEEPDOG

COUNTRY OF ORIGIN	RUSSIA
ORIGINAL AND TODAY'S FUNCTION	WATCHDOG

APPEARANCE

BODY

The Caucasian Ovtcharka is a big to very big and powerful dog with a coarse body frame. The body is a bit longer than it is tall. The back is straight, broad and muscular and the short and broad loins are slightly arched. The broad croup is long, muscled and flat. The tail is high-set, is carried in a curl and reaches to the hock. The broad, deep chest reaches slightly below the elbows. The belly has a slight tuck-up. The vertical legs are powerful and are parallel to each other. The feet are big, oval shaped and arched. The short and muscular neck is set on moderately high.

Caucasian Ovtcharka

HEAD

The Caucasian Ovtcharka has a massive head with a broad skull, heavy cheekbones and a broad and flat forehead. There is a clear central furrow and a slight stop. The muzzle and skull are of equal length. The lips are thick and close tightly. The ears are set on high and are carried pendulously (in its country of origin they are usually docked short). The small eyes are oval shaped, set deep in the skull. The Caucasian Ovtcharka has a scissors bite.

SHOULDER HEIGHT

This should be at least $25^{1}/_{2}$ in (65 cm) for dogs and $24^{1}/_{2}$ in 62 cm) for bitches. Dogs are preferred to be more than $27^{1}/_{2}$ in (70 cm), bitches more than $26^{3}/_{4}$ in (68 cm).

COAT

The Caucasian Ovtcharka has straight hair with a good undercoat. The hair on the head and the front of the legs is short. This breed has three different kinds of coat: longhaired, short-haired and medium-length hair. Longhaired dogs have collars, well-feathered culottes and a bushy tail (flag). The short-haired dogs have a very dense tail, but without the densely feathered culottes, the collar and bushy tail. The medium kind has medium-length hair, without longer hair on the tail, culottes and collar.

COLORS

These dogs are bred in different shades of wolf-gray with light (whitish) to rust-colored markings, red, wheaten, white, dun, tiger and they can be multi-colored and patterned. A solid black coat is considered a fault, including black spotted and a plain brown coat, which are serious faults.

Male Caucasian Ovtcharka

TEMPERAMENT

CHARACTER

The Caucasian Ovtcharka is an authentic breed that protects cattle herds in its country of origin from two or four-legged wrongdoers. This dog protects its territory, is independent and very brave. The breed is tough, very dominant and has a lot of self-confidence. It is particularly watchful and has a strong urge to defend. Their coats protect them from harsh weather conditions. They can be kept outdoors without any problem.

SOCIAL BEHAVIOR

Everything and everyone who belongs to the

family – and that includes children, cats and chickens or whatever, will be regarded as "its own", and respected and protected. Do not leave the dog alone with your children because if play should become rough when they are together with other children, the Caucasian Ovtcharka will defend your children. The Caucasian Ovtcharka has no time for strangers but will greet family friends warmly. It can be rather dominant towards other dogs.

GENERAL CARE

GROOMING

The longhaired kind requires grooming from time to time with brush and comb, especially where tangles might occur. The coat of the short-haired variety needs less grooming. It is easy to remove loose hairs in the undercoat with a coarse metal comb during the molt.

TRAINING

The potential owner of a Caucasian Ovtcharka needs to be strong in character and physique. This breed is dominant and will not accept a soft owner as its boss. You must never treat a Caucasian Ovtcharka severely or punish it unfairly. The right handler can achieve a Caucasian Ovtcharka, which is obedient and very loyal through mutual respect that will protect the family and home with its life.

EXERCISE

This breed has an average need for exercise. Walks outside its own territory might cause some problems as this dog regards the surroundings as "its" territory. A Caucasian Ovtcharka is not suited to a housing estate. Ideally the dog should have plenty of space surrounding the home or a well-fenced yard where it can attend to its own exercise needs.

USES

This breed is best suited to a family with lots of (fenced) space around the home. You should consider the purchase of such a dog with great care; the dog mistrusts strangers and if you go on holiday or if you need to give the dog a new home, it could create problems because it will not accept leadership or the proximity of a stranger.

SAINT BERNARD	
COUNTRY OF ORIGIN	SWITZERLAND
ORIGINAL FUNCTION	DRAFT AND RESCUE

Long-haired St. Bernard

APPEARANCE

BODY

The St. Bernard has a very broad back, which is completely level up to the loins, where it slopes down slightly towards the croup. The withers are pronounced. Its long and heavy tail is broad and powerful. It is usually carried pendulous, but may curl back a bit at the tip. The well-arched chest reaches down to the elbows. There is a slight tuck-up. The sloping shoulders are powerful and muscular. The forequarters are straight and strong. The hocks are moderately angulated. The feet are broad and almost closed. The neck is powerful and has a pronounced, yet not exaggerated fold. There is a clear furrow where the head sets on.

HEAD

The St. Bernard has a powerful and impressive head, with clear eyebrows and a deep stop. There is moderately developed stop and a fairly developed occipital peak. The central furrow between the eyes is deep, but it becomes shallower towards the occiput. The short and sturdy muzzle is

Long-haired St. Bernard

Long-haired St. Bernard

COLORS

The colors of these dogs can be a variety of red shades to brownish yellow with white or white with red to brownish yellow. White with streaked patches is another type of coat. The St. Bernard must have white markings on the chest, feet, nose-band and blaze. It should have a white tip of the tail and a white neck patch or collar. The dark markings on the head and ears are called its mask.

TEMPERAMENT

CHARACTER

The dogs are good-humored, friendly, and equable, stable and sensitive to harsh words and the atmosphere. They are devoted to the family, show their affection and do not like to be left out. These dogs do not bark much. A St. Bernard will defend you and your possessions if necessary although this is not

Short-haired St. Bernard

its primary role. Most dogs are calm when they mature, but this breed, particularly the short-haired dogs, also has its more active representatives.

SOCIAL BEHAVIOR

St. Bernards get along fine with children and other dogs. Household animals normally present no problems. Peers are accepted but a St. Bernard will not be bullied. Their attitude towards strangers

deeper than it is long. The nose bridge is straight. The powerfully developed lips arch over the lower jaws. The ears are set on fairly high and they are moderately big. They are carried pendulously in such a way that they accentuate the width of the skull. The eyes are medium-sized and set moderately deep. The lower eyelids do not close completely, but eyes that are opened too much are not desirable. St. Bernards have a scissors or pincer bite.

SHOULDER HEIGHT

Dogs are at least $27\frac{1}{2}$ in (70 cm) high and bitches at least $25\frac{1}{2}$ in (65 cm).

WEIGHT

This will depend on the size and build of the dog, but should be at least $132\frac{1}{4}$ lb (60 kg).

COAT

There are both short-haired and longhaired St. Bernards.

Short-haired dogs have a close-lying, harsh but not rough coat. Longhaired dogs have a coat of medium length, which is straight or a bit wavy, but never curled. The tail needs to be very well feathered, but the hairs should not be wavy. The head and ears are shorter

Short-haired St. Bernard

and softer feathered. The forequarters are lightly feathered and the hair on the culottes is longer and denser.

Long-haired
St. Bernard

with pure intentions ranges from indifferent to friendly.

GENERAL CARE

GROOMING

The St. Bernard needs quite a bit of grooming. Its coat should be brushed and combed at least twice a week. During the molt a daily brush, particularly for the longhaired dogs, is quite essential. Keep the ears clean and check drooping eyelids regularly. If necessary you can apply special cleaning drops to their eyes. Keep the claws short.

TRAINING

A St. Bernard is a reasonably obedient dog and can learn commands quite quickly if it is treated in a consistent and clear manner. The dog is fairly sensitive to your tone of voice; a harsh training is inappropriate. They are not suited to lengthy training sessions, so only give commands when necessary. Teach a St. Bernard at an early age that it should not pull on the leash, because you will be unable to change the dog when it is grown up, as it will be too big and too strong. In common with all other mastiffs it also applies to St. Bernard dogs that their training needs considerable understanding. Take care that they are not over extended physically during their growing stage.

EXERCISE

These dogs have an average need for exercise. A walk around the block three times a day with regular long walks when they can run free, off-leash, are all they need.

USES

St. Bernards are nearly always kept as family dogs. You may consider taking these dogs tracking; their smell is excellent and the dogs will really enjoy this activity.

Short-haired St. Bernard

Mastin Español

MASTIN ESPAÑOL (SPANISH MASTIFF)	
COUNTRY OF ORIGIN	SPAIN
ORIGINAL FUNCTION	FLOCK GUARD

APPEARANCE

BODY

The Mastin Español is a big, stocky, muscular dog with a heavy bone structure and a harmonious build. In spite of its heaviness and size the dog clearly has an elegant and light gait. The body is longer than it is tall. The strong and muscular back is level and horizontal. The loins are broad and powerful. The croup slopes a little. The tail is very thick at the base and is carried low at rest, with the tip usually turned up. The belly has a slight tuck-up. The chest is broad and deep, with

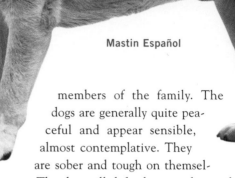

a pronounced sternum. The slanting shoulders are well muscled. The legs have strong bones and are vertical. The hindquarters are reasonably angulated. The Mastin Español has well-closed catlike feet. The neck is broad, powerful and muscular, with a well-developed double dewlap.

HEAD

A Mastin Español has a big and strong head. In length the proportion skull to muzzle is 6:4. The stop is slight. The muzzle tapers a little towards the nose, but should never be pointed. The moderately big, triangular ears are set above the eyes and are carried pendulously. The proportionately small eyes are almond-shaped.

SHOULDER HEIGHT

Male dogs should be at least $30^3/_4$ in (78 cm) high but dogs over $31^1/_2$ in (80 cm) are preferred. Bitches should be at least 30 in (74 cm) high, whereas $29^1/_4$ in (76 cm) is preferred.

Mastin Español

COAT

The Mastin Español has straight hair with a dense underlayer. Its feathering is dense, coarse and smooth over the entire body. The band down its back and tail is a bit longer and coarser.

COLORS

The coats of these dogs may have different colors, although plain colors are preferred. The solid colors might be yellow, red, black, wolf-gray and red-brown. Streaked coats and coats with white patches are accepted, but white should not be too dominant.

Mastin Español

TEMPERAMENT

CHARACTER

The Mastin Español is a very intelligent, fairly independent type of dog with plenty of self-confidence. This breed is gentle and compliant to members of the family. The dogs are generally quite peaceful and appear sensible, almost contemplative. They are sober and tough on themselves. The dog will defend you and your family with all its might against two or four-legged intruders. You will not often hear its heavy bark.

SOCIAL BEHAVIOR

Its own family comes first. The Mastin Español is serious about its job as a watchdog and will not allow any human being or animal to access its domain. This is its natural behavior, you will not need to prompt it or give it commands. It is watchful in a controlled manner and will only apply its strength in a case of emergency. When the boss indicates that guests are welcome the dog will accept. Mixing with other animals does not generally give any problems, certainly not if those animals belong to its own family. The Mastin Español is generally patient and friendly with children. Its behavior towards other dogs, particularly of its own sex, might be less harmonious.

GENERAL CARE

GROOMING

A weekly brush should be adequate for this breed, using a teasel brush. During molting the coat should be brushed thoroughly several times a week. Keep its claws short.

Young Mastin Español bitch

TRAINING

The Mastin Español should be brought up in a balanced, consistent and loving manner. Severe or unfair training will bring out undesirable characteristics. The owner of a Mastin Español should be an even-tempered, calm person with a natural sense of authority. The dog always appears to con-

Young Mastin Español bitch

sider the wisdom of commands, and it is not suited to long training sessions. A good socialization will be beneficial to their character development.

EXERCISE

These dogs can usually satisfy their needs for exercise in a large fenced yard. You do need to take your dog out to the park or woods to widen its experience. They do not tend to roam. The Mastin Español is usually protected from harsh weather conditions by its dense coat and can be kept outside without any problem. The breed is less suited to life in a city.

USES

A Mastin Español is well suited as a reliable guard and family dog for people who have plenty of space both indoors and outdoors.

NEWFOUNDLAND	
COUNTRY OF ORIGIN	CANADA
ORIGINAL FUNCTION	FISHERMAN'S DOG

Black Newfoundland bitch with her brown pup

APPEARANCE

BODY

The Newfoundland is a stately, strong and massive dog with heavy bones. In spite of its size and weight this dog should not appear to be clumsy or slow. Newfoundlands have broad, level backs and well-muscled loins. The chest is broad and deep.

Newfoundlands

Newfoundland bitch

SHOULDER HEIGHT
Male dogs should be approx. 28 in (71 cm) and bitches 26 in (66 cm) high.

WEIGHT
Dogs vary from 142–154^1/$_4$ lb (64–70 kg). Bitches weigh 110^1/$_4$–119^1/$_2$ lb (50–54 kg).

COAT
The Newfoundlands have a water-resistant, double, medium-length, greasy and dense coat. The tail is densely feathered with longer hairs. The feathering at the back of fore and hindquarters is a little longer, too. The hair should not form a frill.

COLORS
Permitted colors of their coats are solid black and solid brown, with some white markings, although this type of coat is rare. In such a case, dogs with beautiful markings, a black saddle and a black head with a white blaze, are preferred. Ticking (small black dots) in the white is undesirable.

TEMPERAMENT

CHARACTER
These dogs are good humored, sociable, gentle-natured, straight forward, tractable and easy to get on with. Generally they are quite peaceful, particularly indoors. They are friendly to people and animals and very affectionate to the family they belong to. Although they are not particularly vigilant, they will protect their families if it should become necessary. The Newfoundland does not bark much, which means you should investigate when it makes a noise. They like to swim, which is typical for this breed, no matter the weather.

The tail reaches a little further than the hocks. It is thick and normally carried pendulous with a faint curve at the tip. When moving, the tail is carried higher, but not above the topline, or as a curl. The elbows fit closely to the body. The legs are straight and heavy-boned, with big, well-formed, forward facing feet. Interestingly, the feet are webbed for better swimming. The strong neck is moderately long.

HEAD
It is heavy and broad. The occipital peak is well developed. The muzzle is short and almost square. Newfoundlands should not have a clear stop. The ears are set on quite far back and they are fairly small. They are carried pendulously, close to the head and the feathering should be short. The small eyes are dark brown and set far apart. The eyelids should close tightly. These dogs should preferably have a scissors bite, but a pincer bite is accepted.

Male Newfoundland

SOCIAL BEHAVIOR

This particular breed produces dogs that make excellent companions. They are not troublemakers, and they will generally greet other dogs in a friendly manner. They are very patient with children, docile and tolerant. They get on reasonably well with pets such as cats, but also with other animals such as (small) livestock. Well-meaning visitors will receive a friendly welcome.

GENERAL CARE

GROOMING

This breed needs quite a bit of grooming. They should be combed and brushed thoroughly. Excessive hair between the pads of their feet and inside their ears should be removed. Although these coats should not be trimmed, unlike those of

Newfoundland bitch

Almost year-old Newfoundland puppy

many terriers, Newfoundlands are quite welcome in a trimming parlor. Generally a Newfoundland will be groomed specially for a show.

TRAINING

This should be conducted in a calm and well-balanced manner. The dogs are very sensitive to your tone of voice. It will not be necessary to punish a Newfoundland if you approach the dog with consistency and make your intentions clear. They will learn new commands fairly quickly, although they do not like training sessions that last too long and speed is not their prime quality. They like to please you, but they are not keen to repeat nonsensical commands.

EXERCISE

This breed has an average need for physical exercise and will adapt well to family circumstances. Avoid all exhausting day-long hikes until the dog is fully-grown. They love to swim and this is an ideal form of exercise for the Newfoundland. Your dog will appreciate a regular chance to swim – definitely on hot days, but even when it is not hot. Their thick coats protect them against cold and wet weather so that they can happily be kept out of doors, provided they are not separated from the family.

USES

This dog is a good family dog, although the owner should never underestimate the amount of groom-

Newfoundland puppy

Black and white Newfoundlands are rare

ing this dog requires. Any water-based activity will appeal to a Newfoundland.

DETAILS

Many of these dogs have a kind of natural "urge to rescue." Many Newfoundlands have attempted to drag their swimming owners from the water. But this does not apply to all dogs of this breed.

Brown Newfoundland

LANDSEER ECT (EUROPEAN CONTINENTAL TYPE)	
COUNTRY OF ORIGIN	CANADA/EUROPE
ORIGINAL FUNCTION	FISHERMAN'S DOG

APPEARANCE

BODY

The Landseer is a big, strong and harmoniously built dog. The back is level and the entire topline is broad and strong from shoulders to croup. The chest is deep and broad. The ribs of the chest are well arched. The belly has a slight tuckup. The flanks clearly show a flat depression between the belly and the muscular loins. The croup is broad and full. The tail reaches no furt-

Landseer ECT

her than just below the hocks. It is carried low at rest, with a very slight arch at the end. The elbows close tightly and the legs are straight, vertical and well muscled. The broad and vertical feet have tight-fitting toes, with strong webs between the toes. The neck is not rounded, but egg-shaped without a pronounced dewlap of the throat or neck.

HEAD

This outstanding and noble head is broad and solid, with a well-developed occipital peak. The stop is clear, but not too pronounced. The length of the muzzle is equal to the depth of the muzzle as far as the stop. The lips are dry – Landseers should not slobber. The medium-sized ears are triangular and slightly rounded underneath. The ears are high, but not set on too far back and they are carried pendulously, close to the head. The almond-shaped eyes are medium-sized and are set quite deeply, with no haw showing. The expression is friendly. Landseers have a scissors bite.

SHOULDER HEIGHT

This ranges from $28^1/_2$–$31^1/_2$ in (72–80 cm) for dogs and from $26^1/_2$ –$28^1/_2$ in (67–72 cm) for bitches.

COAT

Landseers have a straight, dense, long coat that should feel soft to the touch. The underlayer is soft, but not as dense as that of the Newfoundland. The hair on the hips and back may wave a little. The hair on the face is short. The fore and hindquarters are lightly feathered and the tail is very dense and bushy.

COLORS

This breed has a pure white background with clearly separated black patches on the body and the croup. The neck, forechest, belly, legs and tail should always be white. The head is always black with a white, symmetrically marked and not too wide a blaze that runs on. Black dots or ticking are not desirable. The color of the eyes is preferably brown to dark brown, but light brown is acceptable. The nose and lips are always black.

TEMPERAMENT

CHARACTER

The Landseer is an amiable, soft-natured, straightforward, affectionate, docile, self-aware and stable dog. Although these dogs show no signs of aggression they will protect their folk, home and property well if there is an emergency. They are not great barkers. Most of them are keen swimmers.

SOCIAL BEHAVIOR

The Landseer is a fine family dog, which will live in harmony with other dogs and household pets. They will pay kids special attention (in a positive sense). Visitor will be announced, but if they have

The Landseer ECT is mad about water

no evil intentions they will be treated in a friendly manner.

GENERAL CARE

GROOMING

Regular brushing is required, with a pin brush and a coarse comb, paying special attention to areas where tangles are likely to occur. Check the ear passages occasionally to make sure that they are clean, using a special ear cleaner. Trim away any excess of hair between the pads of the feet. In common with all other very big breeds the Landseer grows very quickly. These dogs need special high-quality food while they are growing. You should avoid overtaxing their joints, tendons and muscles. The Landseer can withstand cold and wet weather and should not always lie inside by the warm radiator.

TRAINING

Normally this breed is not difficult to train. Teach the young dog to walk to heel and not to pull on-leash, because when fully grown it is much too strong to control. The Landseer responds very well to the voice and

Landseer ECT's

Landseer ECT puppies

to a calm and balanced upbringing that should be neither severe nor demanding.

EXERCISE

This dog has an average need for exercise, but likes being outdoors and regular long walks off-leash. A well-trained Landseer does not tend to roam, but it is a different matter if there is water nearby. A Landseer loves swimming and it is also its favorite form of physical exercise. Do not take it on exhausting long walks until it is fully grown.

USES

The Landseer is usually kept as a family dog. It will do well at obedience classes and if your dog enjoys it, there is no reason why you should not attend advanced classes.

Landseer ECT

GREAT PYRENEES (PYRENEAN MOUNTAIN DOG)

COUNTRY OF ORIGIN	FRANCE
ORIGINAL FUNCTION	FLOCK GUARD AND LIVESTOCK DOG

APPEARANCE

BODY

Great Pyrenees have a long, broad and strong back with a slightly sloping croup and a fairly long plumed tail. At rest it is carried down in a curve and when the dog is alert it is carried upward in a curl over the back. The withers are broad and muscular. The broad chest is deep, but not too low. The belly has hardly any tuck-up. These dogs have double dew claws on their hind legs. The feet are thickset. Great Pyrenees move elegantly and with ease. They have a strong and fairly short neck showing very little dewlap.

HEAD

This should not be too heavy in relation to the body. The skull is arched and shows a clear occiput. With a gentle curve the skull flows into the broad and long muzzle that tapers towards the end. The lips overhang a little. The fairly small

Pyrenean Mountain Dog

Male Pyrenean Mountain Dog

triangular ears with rounded tips are set on at the same level as the eyes. They are carried pendulously. The eyes are fairly small and are set obliquely in the head. They have a dreamy and intelligent expression. The eyelids fit closely.

SHOULDER HEIGHT
Male dogs reach up to $27^1/_2$–$31^1/_2$ in (70–80 cm) and bitches up to $25^1/_2$–$28^1/_2$ in (65–72).

WEIGHT
Bitches weigh approx. 99 lb (45 kg) and dogs around 132 lb (60 kg).

COAT
The hair is fairly long, close to the body and soft. It is longer around the neck and the tail and may wave slightly. It is very dense on the culottes, woollier and finer.

Pyrenean Mountain Dog

COLORS
Great Pyrenees may have plain white coats or white coats with markings on the head, ears and/or the base of the tail. These markings may be gray (badger-colored), pale yellow, orange or wolf-gray. Gray patches are preferred. One or two markings on the body are acceptable. Their pigmentation is unusual: Great Pyrenees have black noses and black pigmentation of the lips and eye rims, as well as a black palates. The eyes are brown-amber.

TEMPERAMENT

CHARACTER
This breed is intelligent, alert, equable and courageous. They are very watchful and keen to bark. This dog will protect your family, home and property against intruders. They are fairly independent and tough and might be a bit stubborn as well. Generally they are quiet, both outdoors and indoors. They like being outdoors and are not bothered by bad weather. Nevertheless they are not suited to life in a kennel. They do need plenty of contact with members of the family.

SOCIAL BEHAVIOR
In general this breed gets on very well with kids. They are quite tolerant. They will not trust strangers until their owners say everything is fine. Friends of the family will be greeted with enthusiasm. There are no problems with regard to cats and other household animals. Male dogs might be dominant to strong members of their own sex.

GENERAL CARE

GROOMING
Great Pyrenees have abundant coats. To avoid excessive shedding of hair indoors, the dogs should be brushed regularly. Generally a thorough brush once a week should be adequate, but during the molt the dogs will need some more attention.

TRAINING
It is essential to train puppies because when fully grown these dogs are far too strong and too independent. Great Pyrenees need even-tempered owners who are consistent, loving and can respect their dogs' fairly independent nature. These dogs do not tend to be obedient. They will only obey if the command makes sense to them. There is no point in repeating the same command because the dog will only lose interest and disbelieve its owner. Help the dog to overcome its suspicious nature by introducing it to many different people while it is a puppy.

Male Pyrenean Mountain Dog

EXERCISE
This dog is fairly peaceful and has an average need

Young Pyrenean Mountain Dog bitch

for exercise. It regularly needs long walks when it can run and have a good sniff off-leash. This breed is best suited to people who have plenty of space indoors as well as outdoors, but it will also adjust to a smaller home if the owner can provide it with enough exercise. In common with all rapidly growing breeds, they must not be exhausted during the growing stage.

USES

Even today a small number of Great Pyrenees are still used for their original function, the guarding of the flock against two and four-footed predators. Of course it is also a loyal family dog that will naturally take care of home, property and possessions.

ESTRELA MOUNTAIN DOG (CAO DA SERRA DA ESTRELA)	
COUNTRY OF ORIGIN	PORTUGAL
ORIGINAL FUNCTION	FLOCK GUARD AND LIVESTOCK DOG

APPEARANCE

BODY

The Estrela Mountain Dog has a strong body with a level topline, a slightly downward sloping croup and a gradual tuck-up. The tail reaches down to the hocks and has a hook at the end. The hook is a typical trait of this breed and is called a gancho in its country of origin. When the dog is alert, the tail may be carried over the topline, but at rest it hangs down. The legs have round bones, angulated in a normal way. The feet are slightly oval-shaped and have well-closed toes with hair growing in between. Dew claws are acceptable. The strong neck is fairly short and has some dewlap.

HEAD

This bread has a strong, long, big and slightly rounded head with a slight stop. The skull and the muzzle are equal in length and the lips close tightly. Typical for the breed are the thin and fairly small ears, which are carried laid back. This makes the ear canals visible. The oval-shaped eyes are medium size and have an intelligent and peaceful expression.

SHOULDER HEIGHT

Dogs range from $25^1/_2$–$28^1/_2$ in (65–72 cm) and bitches from $24^1/_2$–$26^1/_2$ in (62–68 cm). A variation of $1^1/_2$ in (4 cm) up or down is tolerated.

WEIGHT

They vary between 66–110 lb (30–50 kg).

COAT

There are two types of coat for this breed: longhaired and short-haired. The short-haired variety is almost completely short with a dense undercoat. The longhaired variety has a heavy, thick, but not coarse feathering, a bit like goat's hair. The hair

Cao da Serra da Estrala

may be straight or wavy. Longhaired dogs have a collar with longer hairs around the neck and the feathering of the culottes and tails is longer and more abundant. The undercoat consists of fine and short hair.

COLORS

Yellow is the predominant color, referring to all shades from sandy-colored to deer red, both plain varieties and those with black tips. And of course there are streamed and wolf-colored dogs. A black mask is very desirable. The eyes are amber-colored to dark brown, with black pigmentation of the eyelids preferred.

TEMPERAMENT

CHARACTER

The Estrela Mountain Dog is a sober, intelligent, equable dog that is very devoted to its owner.

Cao da Serra da Estrala

They show their affection to members of the household and they are quite obedient. They find it difficult adjusting to a new owner. On the other hand they can be quite willful and never show dependency. Most of them like to bark, something to be considered if you live in a subdivision. They are very vigilant and will protect their folk and possessions against people with evil intent. The weather will barely bother these dogs.

SOCIAL BEHAVIOR

This dog is suspicious of strangers, but any person or animal belonging to the household, including friends and relatives will be accepted. A good socialization with people will prevent this dog from barking too much and being over-suspicious.

TEMPERAMENT

GROOMING

This breed needs an average amount of grooming. Usually a weekly session will be adequate, but during the molt a daily thorough brush will be necessary. The molt is usually short and severe.

TRAINING

The Estrela Mountain Dog learns quite quickly. Stubbornness and making up their own mind are characteristics of the Estrela but mainly if the dog finds the drills boring or if it feels pressurized. An equable and quiet approach with

Cao da Serra da Estrala

consistency is the key to a successful upbringing of this breed. A good socialization is very important and beneficial to character development. You will not need to increase this dog's vigilance, because it is naturally watchful and protective.

EXERCISE

The Estrelas are happiest when they get enough exercise. Allow yourselves at least an hour and a half per day. The dog can run off its energy in a large, fenced yard, but this will never replace walks – the dog will only get bored. An Estrela that gets enough exercise will be peaceful indoors. In common with all other big breeds these dogs grow fast. Do not overtire the dog and adapt the extent and nature of exercise during the growing stage when it needs all its energy to build healthy bones, muscles and joints.

USES

Outside their country of origin these dogs are only kept as family dogs by people with enough space in and around the house. Estrelas can be very obedient if they are trained well.

Cao da Serra da Estrala puppy

LEONBERGER

COUNTRY OF ORIGIN	GERMANY
ORIGINAL FUNCTION	THIS BREED HAS TRADITIONALLY HAD A VARIETY OF FUNCTIONS, BUT DURING THE PAST ONE HUBDRED YEARS THEY HAVE ALMOST EXCLUSIVELY BEEN KEPT AS A COMPANION

Full-grown Leonberger bitch

APPEARANCE

BODY

The Leonberger is a big, strong, well-muscled and well-proportioned dog. Its body is a bit longer than it is tall and a straight back is desirable. Leonbergers have a semi-pendulous tail, which should never be carried too high or over the back. The chest is deep, but not too barrel-shaped and the loins are strong. The dog should not give an impression of being high on the legs. The forequarters are straight, with close-fitting elbows. The knee joints should be defined sharply and the strong hocks should be well angulated. Dew claws are not permissible. If they occur they are removed at birth. Leonbergers have hare feet. Usually the toes are interconnected by webbing. The dry neck is strong, shows nobility and carries the head with pride.

HEAD

The dry skull is moderately arched and the cheeks are not too heavy. Because the head appears to be flattened sideways, it is deeper than it is broad. The muzzle is moderately deep and should not taper to a point. The lips are tight, do not overhang and the corners of the mouth are closed. Therefore Leonbergers do not slobber. The nose bridge becomes a little rounded and has the same width throughout. The ears are set on high. They are carried pendulously, close to the head. The eyes are medium size and the eye rims close tightly. Leonbergers have a scissors bite.

SHOULDER HEIGHT

The size for dogs is $28^{1}/_{2}$–$31^{1}/_{2}$ in (72–80 cm) and for bitches $25^{1}/_{2}$–$29^{1}/_{2}$ in (65–75 cm). The ideal height is 30 in (76 cm) for dogs and $27^{1}/_{2}$ in (70 cm) for bitches.

Leonberger

COAT

The Leonberger has a soft to firm coat, with quite long, straight hair lying close to the body, with a dense undercoat. The coat should never curl, but is allowed to wave. There should be beautiful manes round the neck.

COLORS

The colors of the Leonberger are yellowish gold to reddish brown with a dark mask and dark to black hair tips. There are also pale yellow dogs with black hair tips. A small white fleck on the chest is permissible, as well as light to white hair on the toes. The nose and pads of the feet, rims of lips and eyes are black. The eyes vary from light to dark brown, although the darkest possible color is preferable.

Leonberger bitch with her pup

TEMPERAMENT

CHARACTER

This breed is peaceful, self-confident and equable. The dogs are straightforward, loyal, intelligent, quick learners and compliant. They are vigilant in a very controlled manner, without being noisy.

SOCIAL BEHAVIOR

Leonbergers are friendly dogs that get on well with other peers, even if they are of the same sex. They are not troublemakers. They like younger as well as older children. They know when a visitor has evil intentions and they will respond in an appropriate manner. They have hardly any hunting instinct and therefore they get on well with cats and other pets.

GENERAL CARE

GROOMING

Brush and comb the coat regularly. Keep the ear passages clean, using an ear cleaner if necessary. The young Leonberger grows so rapidly that you must never economize on a good well-balanced diet, particularly during the growing phase. You need to control its amount of exercise and not allow the young dog to get overtired.

TRAINING

Leonbergers are not usually difficult to train. It is important that you do not force the dog or approach it too severely, because a Leonberger is sensitive and responds well to its owner's voice and likes to please. This dog usually obeys well and quickly, but it is not suited to long training sessions. Do not demand too much. The training needs to be balanced, consistent and harmonious. The dog will understand quickly what is required.

Leonberger

EXERCISE

This dog needs quite a bit of exercise. Take the dog on regular long walks, and allow it to be off-leash provided it is well trained. Leonbergers will rarely stray from their owners.

Leonberger

USES

Although these dogs are almost exclusively kept as companions, it does not exclude the possibility of participating in various types of sports and tasks. If you like doing activities together with your Leonberger, you should consider tracking or a variety of obedience classes.

Young male
Leonberger

Anatolian Shepherd

ANATOLIAN SHEPHERD OR KARABASH DOG	
COUNTRY OF ORIGIN	TURKEY
ORIGINAL FUNCTION	FLOCK GUARD

APPEARANCE

BODY

This strong, powerfully built dog has a fairly short back with a slight upward slope above the loins. The belly has a good tuck-up. The chest reaches down to the elbows. The tail, which is set on fairly high reaches down to the hocks. At repose the tail is carried downward in a curve and when alert or while moving it is carried in a curl over the topline. The muscular and strong neck is slightly arched and has a slight dewlap.

HEAD

The skull is broad and a bit rounded between the ears. The stop is moderately defined. The muzzle is a bit shorter than the skull and has a straight profile. The lips overhang slightly. The eyes are fairly small in proportion to the skull. The ears are triangular and medium-sized. They are carried pendulously. There is a marked difference in appearance between dogs and bitches.

SHOULDER HEIGHT

Dogs have a height ranging from $29^1/_2$–$31^3/_4$ in (74–81 cm) and bitches from 28–$31^1/_4$ in (71–79 cm).

WEIGHT

The Anatolian Shepherd weighs approx. 90–141 lb (41–64 kg).

COAT

It is short and dense with an abundant undercoat. The hair is longer around the collar and the tail.

COLORS

All colors are permitted, but plain creamy to fawn dogs with black masks and black ears are most common. Golden brown is the preferred color of the eyes.

TEMPERAMENT

CHARACTER

This sober, brave, vigilant, dominant and sometimes willful dog is demanding of itself. It can be reasonably independent and reserved toward strangers, but it is devoted to its "own" folk. Anatolian Shepherds are active dogs with an equable character.

SOCIAL BEHAVIOR

This breed generally gets on well with other animals. They are rather unsure of strangers. Kids are not generally a problem. Male dogs tend to be dominant towards other dogs. A lot depends on its socialization. It is advisable to take them

Anatolian Shepherd

with you as puppies so that you give them a chance to meet other dogs, animals and people.

GENERAL CARE

GROOMING

The Anatolian Shepherd does not need a great amount of coat care. During the molt a comb with a double row of metal teeth will be useful to remove dead and loose hairs from the undercoat.

TRAINING

The Anatolian Shepherd is not a dog for beginners. It needs a handler who naturally exudes leadership. A determined, consistent and loving approach will achieve the best results. It is very important to start training quite early because fully-grown dogs are too strong and too big to be corrected. They are intelligent enough to understand commands very quickly and if they have been

Anatolian Shepherd

trained well they will be quite obedient. They do not lend themselves to repeated exercises. Commands need to make sense from their point of view.

EXERCISE

These dogs need a fair amount of exercise. When they can run free in their yard with a surrounding fence, they can decide upon their own exercise needs. This breed is not suited to an apartment.

USES

These are excellent dogs for people with plenty of space in and around the house. They are a little independent which makes them unsuitable for a number of dog sports.

TIBETAN MASTIFF	
COUNTRY OF ORIGIN	TIBET
ORIGINAL FUNCTION	FLOCK GUARD AND FARM DOG

Tibetan Mastiff

APPEARANCE

BODY

The Tibetan Mastiff is an imposing, strong, muscular and solid dog with a body that is slightly longer than tall. The topline is level, strong, well muscled and the chest is broad and deep. It reaches beyond the elbows. The tail is set on in line with the back and when moving it is curled to one side and carried gaily. When carried downward the tail should not reach beyond the hocks. The hindquarters are very muscular and well angulated, with bent knee joints and strong, low heels.

Black and tan male Tibetan Mastiff

Tibetan Mastiffs

Viewed from the back the legs are straight. The tight feet are big and strong, well closed and well feathered between the toes. Dew claws might occur on the hindquarters. The muscular shoulders are well set. The neck is broad and muscular with a slight dewlap.

HEAD

This is fairly wide, heavy and strong. The stop is clearly defined. The solid skull has a very tangible occipital peak. The skull is just as long as the muzzle. The wide foreface looks square from all sides. The nose is broad with good pigmentation and wide nostrils. The lips overhang slightly. The eyes are set obliquely to a slight degree and are very expressive. The medium-sized, triangular ears

Male Tibetan Mastiff

are set on sideways, carried close to the head. When alert they are carried forward. The jaws should preferably have a complete and regular scissors bite, but a pincer bite is acceptable too.

SHOULDER HEIGHT

Dogs have a shoulder height of at least $25^1/_2$ in (65 cm) and bitches are 24 in (61 cm) high.

WEIGHT

A grown dog will weigh between $110^1/_4$–$132^1/_4$ lb (50–60 kg). Bitches are a bit lighter.

COAT

The upper layer is abundant, semi-long, close lying, harsh and stiff with a rather woolly under-coat. The hair makes a well-furnished collar round the shoulders and neck, which runs to the back of the skull. The thighs and bottom half of the tail are heavily feathered with long hair. The face, the ears and legs have short and smooth hair, but they are also well feathered. The back of the forequarters and the heels of the hindquarters have beautiful feathering.

COLORS

Most coats are black or gray with tan markings. Occasionally you will see solid black, gray and gold-colored animals. The tan color may vary considerably, from a very deep to a very light shade. A white patch on the chest is permissible, as well as white markings on the toes, although they should not be too big. Pale beige and cream-colored coats are not accepted.

TEMPERAMENT

CHARACTER

Tibetan Mastiffs are calm, dignified, thoughtful, equable dogs radiating pride. They may be very loyal and devoted to their families and yet they are reserved and independent. They are however sensitive and like to be close to their people. On their own ground they are self-confident. It comes naturally to this Mastiff to guard its family and property and you will not need to encourage this characteristic. They do not bark much, but they will raise their bark if they sense any danger. They tend to be peaceful indoors, but outside they might be quite active from time to time. Tibetan Mastiffs like being outdoors. Their coat protects them from all kinds of weather. In spite of their love for an outdoor life they are not suited to kennels. This dog matures late both physically and mentally.

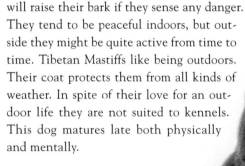

Male Tibetan Mastiff

Male Tibetan Mastiff

SOCIAL BEHAVIOR

These dogs love their families and are extremely loyal. All pets will be marked as "their own" and are treated as such. Provided they are well socialized there are not likely to be any problems with cats, rabbits and (small) livestock. Tibetan Mastiffs are very tolerant, patient and careful toward kids. Strangers will not be allowed in, until the owner indicates that they are to be trusted. This dog will not display territorial behavior outside its domain, but will continue to mistrust strangers. Particularly male dogs can be a bit dominant toward other dogs. They rarely start a fight, but they will not shun a fight either.

GENERAL CARE

GROOMING

In autumn and winter the Tibetan Mastiff has an abundance of hair forming a very thick coat, which needs little care, according to the breed standards. Generally it will be sufficient to comb it once a month or once a fortnight with a very coarse comb. In spring it almost completely sheds its undercoat. During this period daily grooming is essential. Although their size and solidity might make you think otherwise, these dogs are not big eaters.

TRAINING

This dog needs a consistent and fair upbringing, preferably from a calm owner who will not be swayed and has a natural authority. A strict upbringing with too many demands is useless or even counterproductive for this dog. A good approach will help this dog to learn new commands and as a rule it is obedient. They do not like to follow commands that do not seem to make sense.

EXERCISE

The Tibetan Mastiff has an average demand for exercise. They can let off steam if you have a big fenced yard, but will certainly appreciate regular long walks. It will enjoy escorting you to open countryside and in the woods, but it is not the type of dog that enjoys retrieving balls and sticks.

Black and tan Tibetan Mastiff dog

Take care that the bones, muscles and joints of the young dog are not overtaxed during the growing stage.

USES

Tibetan Mastiffs make good family dogs that perform well if they are given plenty of space indoors as well as outdoors. They are natural defenders of your family and possessions. This breed is not particularly suited to dog sports because of its rather thoughtful and independent nature. Nor do they like long obedience training, which will only bring out the dog's stubbornness.

DETAILS

This dog's coat is almost odorless – even on rainy days. Bitches tend to be on heat only once a year.

Male Tibetan Mastiffs

Blue with tan markings Tibetan Mastiff dog

AÏDI OR ATLAS SHEPHERD DOG

COUNTRY OF ORIGIN	MOROCCO
ORIGINAL FUNCTION	GUARD DOG, PARTICULARLY OF FLOCKS

APPEARANCE

BODY

The Aïdi is a powerful, active dog. Its broad back is not very long and should curve slightly. The croup is a little rounded and the hip bones protrude considerably. The chest is big and deep. It stretches down to the elbows or beyond. The ribs are bent slightly and the belly has a bit of a tuck-up. The long tail is set on in line with the croup and stretches down to the hocks or beyond. It is carried down with a slight curve. When the dog is moving or alert, the tail is carried higher, but it should not curl above the topline. The forequarters are well angulated and the angulations of the hindquarters are not too strong. The feet are round and strong. The neck is strong, muscular and dry.

HEAD

In size the dry head matches the body. It is conical with a flat and big skull and a light front furrow. The Aïdi has a slight stop. The muzzle is shorter than the skull. The jaws are strong and the lips are dry and fit tightly. The ears are set on far back and in such a way that they seem to broaden the skull. They fold backward when at rest. The tips of the ears are slightly rounded. The eyes are medium-sized and are set slightly obliquely. The expression is alert and lively.

SHOULDER HEIGHT

The dog's height varies between 20$^{1}/_{2}$–24$^{1}/_{2}$ in (52–62 cm).

COAT

Its semi-long coat is dense and wiry. On the body the hair is about 2$^{1}/_{2}$ in (6 cm), but on the collar and culottes it is decidedly longer. The collar is most noticeable with male dogs. The hair on the face and ears is short.

Aïdi

COLORS

Any color is acceptable. Fawn, white, off-white, red, brindle, black with white and fawn with white, with or without black hair tips are the most common coats.

TEMPERAMENT

CHARACTER

These dogs are equable, sober, active, alert and independent, very vigilant, brave and protective. The Aïdi is devoted to its owner and family, but retains its identity and can be quite self-willed.

SOCIAL BEHAVIOR

This dog naturally gets on well with other pets and children, but the dog needs to be well socialized at an early age. The males tend to be dominant toward other male dogs. They are shy to strangers.

GENERAL CARE

Aïdi

GROOMING

This breed needs average coat care. A good brush once a week is adequate. During the molt daily grooming might be necessary.

TRAINING

The Aïdi was not meant or bred to work together with its owner. In its country of origin it is still used as a farm or flock guard on a daily basis and being able to work independently is one of the necessary prerequisites. This breed will seldom show a "will-to-please." If an Aïdi is socialized and supervised from an early age, it should be possible to teach it some essential basic rules.

EXERCISE

This sober dog needs a considerable amount of exercise. A few short runs a day will not be adequate. Take your dog on frequent hikes. A well-trained Aïdi could run along with you on a bike-walk and a big yard will give it enough space to run off its energy. This is a hardy breed and they are not susceptible to cold weather and harsh weather conditions. The dogs like to be outdoors. Do fence off your yard because an Aïdi tends to roam.

Aïdi

USES

This dog was only recently discovered by dog lovers outside its country of origin, and it is still quite rare outside Morocco. Not much is known about its suitability for various types of dog sports and their suitability as family dogs. But it is probably not well suited, considering its original behavior, independent nature and lack of a "will-to-please." It has a much better record as a guard dog. This dog will only be found in areas remote from our modern society. If you buy a puppy in its country of origin, it might be advisable to choose a very young pup so that you can supervise its socialization as much as possible.

SECTION 3   Swiss cattle drivers

Bernese Mountain Dog

BERNESE MOUNTAIN DOG OR BERNER SENNENHOND, ALSO BERNESE CATTLE DOG

COUNTRY OF ORIGIN	SWITZERLAND
ORIGINAL FUNCTION	THIS BREED HAS NUMEROUS FUNCTION, AS A DRAFT DOG, GUARD DOG AND CATTLE-DROVERS

APPEARANCE

BODY

The trunk of the Bernese Mountain Dog is only a little longer than its shoulder height. The chest is wide and the ribcage has a round and oval-shaped profile. The topline is level and solid, the loins are strong and the croup is slightly rounded. The tail reaches beyond the hocks, but not down to the ground. It is carried saber-fashion. The shoulders are flat and muscular. They are long and set slanting. The straight and sturdy legs are well angulated and they are cat-footed. The neck is medium-length and muscular.

HEAD

The strong head has a flat skull, a clearly defined stop, but the stop is not too prominent and the front furrow is slight. The forenose is powerful but the lips are not well developed. The medium-sized ears are triangular and set on high. They are carried pendulously, close to the head. The almond-shaped eyes should have close-fitting eyelids. Bernese Mountain Dogs have a complete scissors bite.

SHOULDER HEIGHT

Male dogs vary from $25^1/_2$–$27^1/_2$ in (64–74 cm), but ideally this should be 26–$26^3/_4$ in (66–68 cm). Bitches measure $22^1/_2$–26 in (58–66 cm), but ideally they should be $23^1/_2$–$24^3/_4$ in (60–63 cm).

COAT

The hair is semi-long and varies from straight to slightly wavy.

COLORS

Bernese Mountain Dogs have a very deep black ground color with tan-colored and white markings. Tan colored markings should only occur above the eyes, on the cheeks, the legs and the chest. The white markings take the shape of a symmetrical blaze on the head, which should not be too broad or too narrow, and a white cross on the chest. White feet and a white tip of the tail are preferred, although not required. The white feet should not reach beyond the metatarsals. A small white patch on the front or back of the neck is not desirable, but accepted nevertheless. The eyes of these dogs should be dark brown.

TEMPERAMENT

CHARACTER

This is a calm, very stable, happy and friendly dog. Although they are definitely vigilant and will protect their owners and possession from all wrong-doers, they are fairly peaceful. You will only hear their deep bark when there is something seriously wrong. They are alert to what is happening

Bernese Mountain Dogs

Bernese Mountain Dogs

around them and their intelligence is above average. They are loyal to their owners and members of the family, compliant and generally quite obedient.

SOCIAL BEHAVIOR

Bernese Mountain Dogs are normally wonderful with children and will also protect them. They will behave well with cats and other pets, as they have hardly any hunting instinct. In an emergency the Bernese Mountain Dog will be at your side. It is friendly and docile to friends of the family and acquaintances. Some of this breed can be a little domineering toward other dogs, but most of them get on well with their own kind.

GENERAL CARE

GROOMING

The Bernese Mountain Dog needs an average amount of coat care. A weekly comb and brushing session, particularly where the hair readily tangles, will be sufficient. During the molt a brush every other day will be necessary. If there is excessive hair between the toes that will trap blades of grass, small stones, etc. it would be best to trim protruding hair. Keep the claws short.

TRAINING

This dog is a fairly quick learner. It is intelligent enough to understand what you want it to do and it is generally compliant and obedient. They are sensitive to your tone of voice. This breed will respond best if they are treated in a calm, loving and consistent manner.

EXERCISE

This is an active dog. You will have to take it out regularly and allow it to run and play off-leash. Do not forget that a young dog of this breed still needs a lot of rest. Strenuous walks and rough

Bernese Mountain Dog puppies

games will not be beneficial to the development of its bones. The Bernese Mountain Dog has strong territorial instincts and does not tend to explore independently. It is not likely to stray while accompanying you in the woods. These dogs tend to be peaceful indoors.

Bernese Mountain Dog

USES

Bernese Mountain Dogs are usually kept as companions and highly respected as such. You might wish to participate in dog sports with this dog. It will perform very well in advanced obedience skills, especially if it is well supervised.

APPENZELL MOUNTAIN DOG OR APPENZELLER SENNENHOND	
COUNTRY OF ORIGIN	SWITZERLAND
ORIGINAL FUNCTION	THE APPENZELL MOUNTAIN DOG WAS GIVEN A NUMBER OF FUNCTIONS, SUCH AS CATTLE-PROTECTOR AND DRIVER, DRAFT AND GUARD DOG.

APPEARANCE

BODY

The Appenzell Mountain Dog's build is slightly longer than it is tall (a ratio of 10:9). The topline is solid and level. The tail is set on high and is carried sideways and curled above the croup. The chest is deep and broad with a clear forechest. The legs are straight and well angulated with strong cat's feet. The powerful neck is moderately long. The dog has a fairly flat top skull, which is broad between the ears and tapers to the front. The Appenzell Mountain Dog has a slight front furrow and a gradually disappearing stop. The strong foreface tapers a bit toward the nose. It is slightly shorter than the skull. The triangular ears are set on fairly high and are carried pendulously. When the dog is alert, the head and ears together give a triangular impression. The almond-shaped eyes are fairly small and are set obliquely. The Appenzell Mountain Dog has a scissors bite but a pincer bite is acceptable.

SHOULDER HEIGHT

Ideally this should be between $20^1/_2$–22 in (52–56 cm) for dogs and between $19^1/_2$–$21^1/_2$ in (50–54 cm) for bitches.

Appenzeller Sennenhonds

Appenzeller Sennenhond dog

COAT

The Appenzell Mountain Dog has a wiry coat. The dense, shiny upper coat is close lying and covers the woolly undercoat.

COLORS

The most popular color for this breed is the tricolor black with tan and white. But dogs with chocolate brown as their main color are also recognized, although they are rare. The white should have the shape of a blaze on the face, running from the forehead, across the muzzle, continuing without any interruption to the neck and chest. The feet and tip of the tail should be white too. A white neck patch and half a white collar are acceptable. The tan color appears under the tail, on the legs, either side of the muzzle and cheeks, above the eyes, on the belly and on either side of the chest.

TEMPERAMENT

CHARACTER

This is a tough and sober working dog. It is lively and active and has a cheerful and lively expression. They have a boisterous, but equable character and they are very intelligent. The Appenzell Mountain Dog likes to bark, is quite vigilant and brave with a natural keenness. They focus on their owners and families. They will not be bribed by strangers.

SOCIAL BEHAVIOR

The Appenzell Mountain Dog generally gets along with other dogs, although male dogs can be domineering toward other males. If they have been well socialized since puppyhood they will mix with other pets. They are shy and vigilant toward strangers although they will greet friends of the family boisterously. A well-trained Appenzell Mountain Dog gets on well with children. Do keep an eye on it when little friends come to play because your dog may protect "its" children if the game gets too rough. This dog is a family dog and yet it tends to attach itself to one person in particular.

GENERAL CARE

GROOMING

The Appenzell Mountain Dog needs little coat care. A teasel brush will help to remove dead and loose hair. Keep the claws short.

TRAINING

This breed responds best to an equable manner of training that is consistent in its approach. Try to ensure that it meets with all kinds of situations, people and other animals as positively as possible. Poor socialization often produces a dog that cannot stop barking and is over-vigilant. The Appenzell Mountain Dog is very intelligent and likes to be active. This dog learns quite quickly.

EXERCISE

An Appenzell Mountain Dog likes being outside and adverse weather conditions will not bother it. Not only do they need quite a bit of exercise but plenty of activity as well. If they are kept on a farm they will keep themselves occupied by rounding up small livestock, guarding the yard and destroying vermin in the stables. If you live in a sub-division you will have to think of ways to entertain your dog in a sporty way. Ball

Appenzeller Sennenhond

Appenzeller Sennenhond

games, retrieving, bike-walks, obedience skills, etc. are all suitable activities for this breed. Fortunately these dogs do not tend to roam. Off-leash they will seldom stray from their owners. Although an Appenzell Mountain Dog likes to be outdoors this does not mean it will enjoy life in a kennel, because it does not like being left alone.

USES

This breed performs well in dog sports such as agility skills and fly-ball.

The Appenzeller Sennenhond has a penetrating gaze

ENTELBUCH MOUNTAIN DOG OR ENTELBUCHER SENNENHOND	
COUNTRY OF ORIGIN	SWITZERLAND
ORIGINAL FUNCTION	CATTLE-DRIVERS AND FARM DOG

APPEARANCE

BODY

The Entelbuch Mountain Dog has a fairly elongated trunk. The body is a little longer than it is tall; the ratio shoulder height to trunk is 8:10. The chest is deep and wide and the topline is level and strong. The tail is naturally short on some dogs, but will be docked in other cases in countries where this is permissible. The long shoulders are set slanting and the legs are strong and straight. The hocks are well angulated. The feet are fairly round and closed. The Entelbuch Mountain Dog has a short and thickset neck.

HEAD

The skull is flat with a light stop and a strong muzzle. There is a clear transition from the skull and cheeks to the muzzle. The lips are not well developed. The high-set ears with rounded tips are triangular, not too big and they are carried pendulously against the head. The eyes are fairly small and have a lively expression. These dogs should preferably have a scissors bite, but a pincer bite is tolerated.

Entlebucher Sennenhond

SHOULDER HEIGHT

Dogs vary from $17^1/_2$–$19^3/_4$ in (44–50 cm) high and bitches from $16^1/_2$–$18^3/_4$ in (42–48 cm). Variations up to $^3/_4$ in (2 cm) upward are acceptable.

COAT

The hair is short, hard and shiny and is close lying.

COLORS

These dogs are only bred in a black ground color with tan-colored and symmetrical white markings. There should be white on the face (blaze and white muzzle) the neck, chest and legs (feet). The tan, which may vary from yellow to rusty brown, is found on the legs, either side of the muzzle and cheeks, over the eyes, on the belly, under the tail and on either side of the chest. The tan color on the chest and legs always lies between the white and the black. The nose is black.

TEMPERAMENT

CHARACTER

The Entelbuch Mountain Dog is a lively and high-spirited dog with keen intelligence and a happy nature. These dogs are very devoted to their owners and families and they make good watchdogs. They are equable and stable, brave and sober, and cannot be bribed by strangers. Although they are generally obedient, they do show some initiative and they are certainly not slavish. This breed should not be kept in kennels, they like being outdoors, but with their owners.

SOCIAL BEHAVIOR

Traditionally this breed has lived on farms and it still shows in their approach to poultry and cats. They get on perfectly well with them. Of course good socialization is necessary. Their contact with peers is quite good too and the same applies to children. The Entelbuch Mountain Dog might be a little aloof or vigilant towards strangers. Nobody will be allowed to enter the yard or house while you are away. The dog will also defend you if a disaster befalls you.

GENERAL CARE

GROOMING

This breed needs little coat care. Outside the molting season you only need to brush the coat with

Entlebucher Sennenhond

Entlebucher Sennenhond

Entlebucher Sennenhonds

and they often enjoy learning new commands. However, they object to monotonous drills. Variety and change keep them alert and motivated. The Entelbuch Mountain Dog responds best to an equable, caring handler who is always consistent. Use the socialization period well to give the dog plenty of positive experiences with other animals, people and situations.

EXERCISE

This dog is an unspoiled working dog that needs plenty of activity and exercise. It becomes moody and insecure if its life is boring. The Entelbuch Mountain Dog is quite territorial which means it is not likely to run off. When it is off-leash in the countryside it will not stray from its owner.

USES

This rare breed is predominantly kept as companion dogs. If they have the right owners they will perform well in dog sports such as flyball and agility skills. Tracking suits them too.

a hard bristle brush once a week. If the dog molts you can remove the loose hairs from the undercoat with a teasel brush. Keep the claws short.

TRAINING

Entelbuch Mountain Dogs will learn new commands quite quickly

Entlebucher Sennenhond

Greater Swiss Mountain Dog

GREATER SWISS MOUNTAIN DOG

COUNTRY OF ORIGIN	SWITZERLAND
ORIGINAL FUNCTION	DRAFT DOG AND GUARDIAN

APPEARANCE

BODY

The Greater Swiss Mountain Dog has a trunk that is a little longer than it is tall (10:9). The topline is moderately long, strong and level and the withers are high and long. The long and broad groin slopes down in a slight curve. The fairly bushy tail is carried down in repose and reaches down to the hocks. When moving the tail lifts, but should not curl or be carried above the topline. The belly is tucked up slightly and is not too rounded. The chest is deep, broad and beautifully arched toward the front. The flat-lying, well-muscled shoulders are long and set obliquely. They are at an obtuse angle with the upper arm. The strong legs are well angulated. The strong feet point straight forward and the toes are close fitting. Dew claws should be removed. The strong and muscular neck is moderately long and should not have any loose dewlap.

HEAD

This dog has a strong head, but it is not heavy. The skull is flat and broad with a slight furrow. The muzzle and skull are almost equal in length, interrupted by a slight stop. The nose bridge is straight and broad. Just before the nose the nose bridge displays a slight arch. The medium-sized eyes are triangular and set on high. They are carried pendulously, close against the head. The moderately big eyes should not be prominent or deep set and the eyelids close tightly. Greater Swiss Mountain Dogs have a scissors bite.

SHOULDER HEIGHT

Dogs range from $25^1/_2$–$28^1/_4$ in (65–72 cm) and bitches from $23^1/_2$–27 in (60–68 cm).

COAT

The Greater Swiss Mountain Dogs have a wiry-haired coat. Hairs of the outer layer are moderately long.

COLORS

These dogs have coats that are always black with rusty brown and symmetrical white markings. The white is limited to the head (blaze and white muzzle), the feet, chest and tip of the tail. The tan should always be a buffer between the black and white, with the exception of the tan-colored flecks above the eyes, which should be surrounded by black. A white patch in the neck and a white collar are acceptable. The nose and lips should be black and the color of the eyes should be hazel to chestnut brown.

Greater Swiss Mountain Dog

TEMPERAMENT

CHARACTER

These intelligent dogs are calm and equable. They are friendly and good-natured, but they are excellent watchdogs and will jump to your rescue when needed. It is a natural feature and it does not need to be learnt. They are devoted to their people and will not be bribed. They like to work and they are generally quite obedient. They are boisterous while they are young for quite a time. The average Greater Swiss Mountain Dog only barks when necessary, but there are exceptions. They should not be banished to kennels.

SOCIAL BEHAVIOR

These dogs generally mix well with cats and other pets, although they need to be well socialized. They get along with other dogs, although male dogs will make their presence felt. This Swiss dog will defend your kids if they are teased. Invited guests will be met in a friendly manner, although the dog will retain its distance. The house will be guarded while you are away, but this dog will not approach strangers in a threatening manner or bark loudly.

GENERAL CARE

GROOMING

These dogs do not need a great deal of coat care. A weekly brush will suffice. During the molting season you can remove dead and loose hairs with a coarse rubber brush. Keep the claws short. Like all big dogs the Greater Swiss Mountain Dogs will benefit from controlled exercise until they have stopped growing. Do not allow this dog to tire itself, try to avoid stairs and keep rough games to a minimum. Give this dog high-quality food so that its joints will grow and develop well.

TRAINING

This dog will not suit everybody even though it will be very devoted to you and your family. The Greater Swiss has a strong personality and needs a handler who is equally strong. The

Greater Swiss
Mountain Dog

Greater Swiss Mountain Dog

Greater Swiss Mountain Dog

dog needs to be given a chance to grow up equably. It needs to know where it stands and to be given time to bond with the family. Always be fair to this dog and certainly consistent. A harsh approach will ruin its character.

EXERCISE

The Greater Swiss Mountain Dog likes to be busy. Take this dog on regular long walks off-leash. Most of them like to retrieve. This breed does not tend to roam and will respect the boundaries of your yard. You might be too busy one week to pay full attention and the dog will adapt without behaving badly. This dog needs a lot of space. An apartment or small house without a yard is not a suitable environment for this breed.

Its intelligence and love to work will make this dog a versatile and faithful working dog provided it finds the right handler. It can do well at obedience training and other kinds of dog sports. Its size and weight do not make it suitable for sports such as training for hunting and agility skills.

Terriers

7

SECTION 1 Long-legged terriers

Wire Fox Terriers are crazy
about balls

FOX TERRIER

COUNTRY OF ORIGIN	ENGLAND
ORIGINAL FUNCTION	TRADITIONALLY A VERMIN DESTROYER AND HUNTER USED FOR FOXES AND BADGERS

APPEARANCE

BODY

Fox Terriers have a short, level back, with pronounced withers and powerful, very slightly arched loins. The hindquarters are solid. The tail is set high and is carried gaily, but not over the

Smooth Fox Terrier

back or curled. In countries where this is permitted, the tail is customarily docked to a minimum of four inches (10 cm) in adult dogs. The chest is deep but not broad. The front ribs are moderately sprung, while the back ribs are deep and carried well back. The shoulders are sloping and the elbows are perpendicular to the body. The legs are perfectly straight. The knee joints are moderately angulated and the hocks are well let down. Fox Terriers have round, close-knit feet, with moderately arched toes and strong pads. The feet are pointing forwards. The fairly long neck is muscular and dry, and gradually widens to the shoulders.

HEAD

The head has a flat and fairly narrow skull that gradually tapers to the eyes. The cheeks must not be too full. The small ears are V-shaped and should drop forward close to the cheeks. The eyes are small, as round as possible and rather deeply set. Fox Terriers have a scissors bite.

SHOULDER HEIGHT

Ranges from $13^3/_4$–$15^1/_2$ in (35–$39^1/_2$ cm). Bitches may be a little smaller and dogs a little bigger, provided overall balance is retained.

WEIGHT

Fox Terriers are about 15 1/2–18 lb (7–8 kg).

COAT

There are two coat varieties in this breed:

– the Smooth Fox Terrier has a short, dense, straight, hard, smooth coat, that should not be bare anywhere, including the belly or the groin.

– the Wire Fox Terrier has a dense, wiry coat with a woolly undercoat. The hair may have a slight wave, but must not be curly, woolly or soft. The longer hair on the foreface is a characteristic feature of the Wire Fox Terrier.

COLORS

A predominantly white color with tan or black markings is desirable for both coat varieties. The nose should be solid black and the eyes dark.

TEMPERAMENT

CHARACTER

Fox Terriers are high-spirited, perky, extrovert, cheerful and alert with an uncomplicated and honest disposition. They are hardy, courageous, self-assured and certainly no cowards. They are single-minded: when they want something, they will not be swayed. Fox Terriers are intelligent and also pretty smart. Although they like to be near their masters, they are quite capable of entertaining themselves for an hour or even longer, playing and romping around with

Fox Terriers are extremely intelligent and can learn much.

a ball or a rag. Digging is one of their favorite pastimes.

SOCIAL BEHAVIOR

This breed generally gets on well with children and makes good playmates for them. They are sturdy with a high tolerance threshold. Males can be aggressive towards their own sex. Introduce your Fox Terrier to cats and other pets when young, so that it will not chase them later on. Fox Terriers are vigilant and will bark when something is wrong, but they are not unfriendly to people. Friends of the family are greeted warmly.

Wire Fox Terrier dog

GENERAL CARE

GROOMING

The coat of the Smooth Fox Terrier needs little attention. Brushing the coat with a firm bristle brush once a week is sufficient. During the molt you can remove loose hairs efficiently using a rubber mitt. If the hair on the back of the tail grows too long you can trim it shorter. The coats of Wires need more attention, especially if you value a well-groomed appearance. This coat is usually trimmed a few times a year. Old and very long hairs are hand-plucked and then the dog is clipped so that its coat looks neat and tidy. In addition to these trims, you will need to brush the coat several times a week, ideally with a small slicker brush. Show-dogs require rather more grooming. This is a highly skilled task, which is best left to professional groomers.

Smooth Fox Terrier

TRAINING

Fox Terriers are highly intelligent and with the right approach they can learn a lot relatively quickly. However, the handler needs to be self-assured, maintain iron discipline and always be one step ahead of the dog. Fox Terriers are pretty shrewd and know how to fool their masters. Do not give in, but be clear and above all consistent at all times. This breed is not suitable for indulgent people, as they would end up with a dog that does as it pleases and takes no notice of anyone or anything.

EXERCISE

Fox Terriers like to be busy and are full of energy. Ball games are particular favorites; nothing is too rough for them and they can never get enough. Give your dog regular opportunities to release its energy off-leash, but only in places where this is safe or where you can be sure that you can recall the dog. Although these dogs enjoy long walks through the woods and retrieving sticks for their owners, they have just as much fun playing in the yard.

USES

With the right owner these nimble, energetic dogs can do pretty well in sports such as flyball and agility. They will also do well as companions, provided they get enough exercise.

Wire Fox Terrier bitch

WELSH TERRIER

COUNTRY OF ORIGIN	WALES
ORIGINAL FUNCTION	HUNTING DOG USED FOR PESTS, SUCH AS BADGERS AND FOXES

APPEARANCE

BODY

The Welsh Terrier is a compact dog of medium size with a short, straight back and a deep, moderately broad chest. The tail is customarily docked in countries where this is permitted. The legs are straight and well angulated, with round, tight cat's feet. The neck is moderately long and thick, and slightly arched.

HEAD

The head is flat with an indistinct stop. The ears are small, set on fairly high and carried folded forward. The small eyes must not be round. They have a high-spirited expression. Welsh Terriers have a complete and powerful scissors bite.

SHOULDER HEIGHT

The maximum size of a Welsh Terrier is 15¹/₂ in (39 cm).

WEIGHT

These dogs weigh approx. 20 lb (9 kg) or slightly more.

COAT

The coat of the Welsh Terrier is wiry and hard, and should be dense and abundant, with an undercoat.

Welsh Terrier

COLORS

The most common and popular color is reddish brown with black, or reddish brown with black and gray. Welsh Terriers should have no black on the toes and black markings or black hairs below the hocks are highly undesirable. The eyes are dark.

TEMPERAMENT

CHARACTER

The Welsh Terrier is a watchful, vigilant, courageous, cheerful and active dog. It has an uncomplicated, equable disposition and is generally self-assured. As a rule, these intelligent dogs are affectionate and fairly obedient for a terrier. They are strongly attached to their masters and their families. Most enjoy digging. If you have a well-kept yard, then you should bear this in mind.

SOCIAL BEHAVIOR

Welsh Terriers are generally patient and tolerant towards children. They are fairly tough. Their terrier-like qualities will emerge if they are not socialized with cats and other pets; these will then be

Welsh Terrier bitch

viewed as prey. However, well-socialized Welsh Terriers can get on okay with other animals, although outdoors you need to be prepared in case they notice any strange cats. This terrier can be aloof towards strangers. Some males are dominant towards other dogs, although bitches tend to be a little milder in this respect.

GENERAL CARE

GROOMING

The amount of coat care depends on the quality of the coat and on the dog's "purpose." A dog that is not shown and that has a good coat will need to be plucked no more than twice a year. Outside these trims a Welsh Terrier that is kept as a pet needs to be thoroughly brushed and combed at least once a week and its beard and mustache need to be cleaned and combed as required. A slicker brush is an ideal tool for this. Show-dogs need

Welsh Terrier dog

Welsh Terrier dog

(considerably) more plucking and trimming sessions to stay ahead of the competition in the show-ring. This normally involves clipping the neck and the topline, the sides, the tail and the head, leaving the hair a little longer on the legs, on the lower abdomen and the facial features (beard, mustache and short eyebrows.)

TRAINING

The Welsh Terrier is smart enough to quickly grasp what you are trying to say, but can also use its cleverness to take advantage of you. Dogs of this breed benefit from a varied, cheerful training and consistent leadership. Too much pressure brings out its stubborn traits in this breed.

EXERCISE

These dogs are full of energy and are tireless outdoors. They are always ready for a ball game, a tug of war or a good romp around off-leash. If you need to skip a day, then this terrier will usually adapt.

USES

With the right owner, this nimble, intelligent dog can achieve great results in sports such as agility and flyball.

Welsh Terriers

AIREDALE TERRIER

COUNTRY OF ORIGIN	ENGLAND
ORIGINAL FUNCTION	INDEPENDENT HUNTER USED FOR OTTERS

APPEARANCE

BODY

The Airedale Terrier is also known as "The King of Terriers" because of its large size. It is a muscular dog with a fairly compact build and a short, level back. The ribs are well developed and the loins are short and muscular. The chest reaches to the elbows, but should not be too broad. The tail is set high and is carried erect. In countries where this is permitted it is customarily docked to such a length that the tail tip is in line with the top of the skull. Airedale Terriers have long, sloping shoulders. The legs are straight with small, compact round feet. The neck is dry and muscular.

HEAD

The head has a long, flat skull that is not too broad. The powerful muzzle and the skull are equal in length, separated by an almost imperceptible stop. The jaws must not be too well developed. The lips are tight. The ears are small and V-shaped. They are carried folded to the side and forwards, with the fold slightly higher than the top of the skull. The small eyes have a lively and intelligent expression. They should not be round. A scissors bite is preferred, but a pincer bite is also allowed.

SHOULDER HEIGHT

In dogs $22^3/_4$–24 in (58–61 cm) and in bitches approx. 22–$22^3/_4$ in (56–58 cm).

COAT

The upper coat is hard, stiff and wiry. It should not be too long.

Airedale Terrier

Airedale Terrier dog

The undercoat is shorter and softer. The hairs may be curly or slightly wavy, but a curly coat is highly undesirable.

COLORS

Airedale Terriers are tan-colored with a black or gray saddle, which extends to the ribs, the loins and the croup. The top of the tail is black or gray. Around the neck and along the sides of the skull black or gray markings can also occur. Some white hairs on the chest are permitted. The eyes are dark in color.

TEMPERAMENT

CHARACTER

Airedale Terriers are playful, equable, active, intelligent, persistent and attentive dogs. They are vigilant, courageous and tough on themselves. Although very fond of their own people, they can be willful at times. Airedales tend to bark little. In spite of their liveliness they are generally calmer than other terriers.

SOCIAL BEHAVIOR

In general, Airedale Terriers are patient with children. They can be dominant towards other dogs, but this depends upon their training and the temperament of the individual dog. Visitors are

Airedale Terrier bitch

its daily short walks, then your dog will be perfectly happy. If you enjoy long walks through the countryside, then this terrier will love to keep you company and will show no signs of tiring. Airedale Terriers love to play ball games, retrieve objects and swim. Once it is fully grown, an Airedale Terrier will also enjoy running alongside you on your regular jogging sessions.

USES
Airedale Terriers are kept mainly as companion dogs, usually to everyone's satisfaction. With the right handler and supervision these dogs will do well in various types of dog sports and in training for hunting.

announced. In non-threatening situations an Airedale will be open and friendly towards strangers, but in an emergency it will always jump to the defense of its owner and the family members. They have an above-average hunting instinct. If you keep animals such as chickens and rabbits, you will have to teach the dog from an early age that these animals are part of the family.

GENERAL CARE

GROOMING
The coat of these dogs is plucked about twice a year. This involves plucking the old hairs from the coat by hand to allow the new hairs to come through. Apart from this, little grooming is required. Brushing the coat through once a week with a slicker brush is sufficient. Trim any excess hair between the pads when necessary. Show-dogs require more coat care.

TRAINING
The Airedale Terrier is an intelligent dog that can learn new commands fairly quickly. However, in true terrier style, this dog will not be happy to follow the same command repeatedly. If you demand too much of the dog then you will get to know its willful and occasionally stubborn nature. Try to vary the training and emphasize rewarding good behavior. This will ensure that the dog will continue to enjoy the training and that you bring out the best in your Airedale.

EXERCISE
The Airedale Terrier has average exercise needs. If you let it frolic off-leash regularly, in addition to

Airedale Terrier

Border Terrier

BORDER TERRIER

BORDER TERRIER	
COUNTRY OF ORIGIN	NORTH OF ENGLAND
ORIGINAL FUNCTION	HUNTING DOG USED FOR FOXES AND OTHER GAME

APPEARANCE

BODY

Border Terriers have a deep, narrow and fairly long body. The ribs are carried well back, but are not oversprung. The tail is moderately short, thick at the base and tapers to a point. It is set high and carried gaily, but not erect or in a curl over the back. The legs are straight and not too heavily boned. The feet are small (cat's feet).

HEAD

The Border Terrier's head looks like that of an otter. It is moderately broad in the skull, with a short, powerful muzzle. The small V-shaped ears drop forward, hanging close to the cheeks. The

Young Border Terrier

eyes have a keen expression. A scissors bite is preferred, although a pincer bite is also allowed.

SHOULDER HEIGHT

The breed standard makes no mention of the shoulder height.

WEIGHT

In dogs this may range from 13–15$^{1}/_{2}$ lb (6–7 kg) and in bitches from 11$^{1}/_{2}$–14 lb (5–6$^{1}/_{2}$ kg).

COAT

Border Terriers have a hard, dense coat, with a close undercoat.

COLORS

This breed comes in red, wheaten, gray with brown and blue with brown. A black nose and dark eyes are preferred.

TEMPERAMENT

Border Terrier

CHARACTER

This breed is highly intelligent and fairly cunning. They are playful, perky and active with a cheerful outlook on life. In line with their original function these sober dogs are not easily intimidated, show great persistence and can take a blow. They are also affectionate and love the company of people. The average Border Terrier is totally unsuited to kennel life.

SOCIAL BEHAVIOR

Most Border Terriers get on very well with children and will often seek out their company. Contact with their own kind is generally okay, although this breed will always behave like a true terrier. It will accept a household cat without any problems provided the dog has grown up with it, but when it encounters a cat outdoors its hunting instinct will often emerge. Border Terriers are real people lovers. Although not all specimens are vigilant, they will usually announce the arrival of visitors, but will certainly leave it at that. Any visitors, both welcome and unwelcome, can expect a very friendly reception.

GENERAL CARE

GROOMING

Border Terriers need relatively little coat care.

Seven-month old Border Terrier

Depending upon the quality of the coat it needs to be plucked once to three times a year. This involves hand-plucking the dead hairs from the coat, so that the new coat can come through. Apart from this, it is sufficient to groom the dog thoroughly once a week. Keep the claws short.

TRAINING

These dogs are highly intelligent and they like to be active. In line with their lively, sporty character they love variety and challenges. Do not bore

Little escapes the attention of a Border Terrier

this dog with long, repetitive training sessions. A very consistent, loving training and varied exercises will bring out the best in this breed. Teach the dog at a young age to return to you when called.

EXERCISE

Border Terriers are real working dogs that love being outdoors. They will happily accompany you on your walks for many hours and will be delighted to leave their baskets for a couple of ball games in the yard. Because a Border Terrier does possess a certain amount of hunting instinct, it should only be allowed off the leash in areas where there is no traffic and where you can be sure the dog will return to you promptly when called. Make sure your yard is well fenced to prevent this adventurer from going off on its own. A Border Terrier that is restricted to a quiet life indoors will find itself something to do, which will lead to activities that its owners might not appreciate.

USES

This breed is particularly suited to active, varied sports that are challenging, such as flyball and agility skills. A Border Terrier will also do well in a sports-minded family with plenty of time to spend with the dog.

Border Terrier

IRISH TERRIER

COUNTRY OF ORIGIN	IRELAND
ORIGINAL FUNCTION	THIS BREED HAS HAD VARIOUS FUNCTIONS, FROM INDEPENDENT HUNTER USED FOR SMALL GAME, TO GUARD DOG AND VERMIN DESTROYER ON FARMS

Young Irish Terrier

APPEARANCE

BODY

Irish Terriers are dogs with a powerful build that are never cobby, but show a "racy" outline. The body is moderately long. The straight, strong back should not display any slackness behind the shoulders. The slightly arched loins are broad and powerful. The tail is set quite high and is carried gaily, but not over the back or curled. It is customarily docked in countries where this is permitted. The chest is deep, but not wide and must not protrude. The ribs are nicely sprung and deep rather than rounded. The ribcage is well developed. The shoulders are sloping, dry and long. The straight legs are moderately long. The elbows should be free from the body. The stifles are moderately angulated and the hocks are well let down. Irish Terriers have fairly round, strong and moderately small feet. The neck is dry, fairly long, and is carried well.

HEAD

The narrow head is long and dry with a flat skull. The lips are close fitting and not pendulous. The ears are small and V-shaped. They are dropping forward, close to the cheeks. The small eyes should not be prominent and they have a lively, fiery expression.

SHOULDER HEIGHT

Approx. $18–19^1/_2$ in (46–50 cm).

WEIGHT

The ideal weight for dogs is $26^1/_2$ lb (12 kg) and for bitches $24^1/_2$ lb (11 kg).

COAT

The upper coat is very harsh ("as hard as wire") while the undercoat is softer and finer in texture. The coat should not be so long as to hide the outline of the body and should certainly not curl or grow in tufts. The hair on the head, legs and ears is shorter than on the rest of the body. A slight beard that must not be too long is a characteristic feature of the breed.

COLORS

The coat is solid yellow red, wheaten or pale red. Small white markings on the chest are acceptable, but white markings on the feet are undesirable. Black nails are highly desirable. The eyes are dark hazel.

TEMPERAMENT

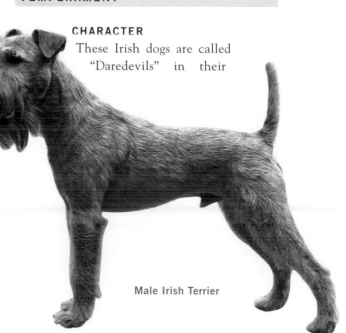

CHARACTER

These Irish dogs are called "Daredevils" in their

Male Irish Terrier

country of origin. Smart, high-spirited and very courageous, these dogs are not afraid of anything and have a vigilant and protective disposition. This means that the dog does not merely bark when it senses danger, but also that it does not shrink from intervening when it feels action is required. Irish Terriers are not friends to everyone. They form a very close bond with their own people and are extremely affectionate and even gentle towards them. They regard it as punishment if they are left on their own for any length of time. They are playful, untiring when playing or working and are pretty intelligent. As a rule, the females of this breed are calmer and more compliant.

SOCIAL BEHAVIOR

This distinctive breed tends to be aggressive towards other dogs, particularly the males. Such behavior can be controlled to some extent with good training and proper socialization, but can never be completely stopped. Teach the young puppy that you disapprove when it chases cats and other animals. A puppy that has been introduced

Irish Terriers are real working dogs

to a calm household cat will be able to live in harmony with it. These dogs are friendly and often very good-natured and tolerant towards children. They will protect and defend their property and their people against intruders, but are not suspicious towards strangers.

GENERAL CARE

GROOMING

An Irish Terrier that is kept as a pet should be taken to a trimming parlor about twice a year. The old hair should then be hand-plucked from the coat, to allow the new hair to grow through. Apart from that, the dog should be groomed once or twice a week with a soft slicker brush. The coat care of show-dogs will be more time-consuming. Because these dogs should always look their best, their coats are plucked and neatly trimmed more frequently. Also make sure you clip any excess hair growing between the pads and obviously keep the claws short.

TRAINING

This high-spirited breed needs a handler that exudes authority. An Irish Terrier should be trained very consistently and firmly, but also sensitively and lovingly. When this dog is in a good mood it

Male Irish Terrier

can learn anything, and it enjoys working for its master. Keep the training varied so that the dog's attention will not waver.

EXERCISE

The Irish Terrier has traditionally been a tireless working dog and modern specimens also need a fair amount of exercise. Take your dog out regularly. If you have a good relationship with your pet, then it will not wander very far. However, in view of its hunting instinct it is a good idea to teach the dog to return promptly when called. Every Irish Terrier loves a ball game in the yard or likes to frolic in the countryside. A dog that is well exercised will be calm in the house.

USES

This breed is kept predominantly as a companion dog by people who like its high-spirited character and natural appearance. Irish Terriers are used in

Irish Soft-coated Wheaten Terriers

SOFT-COATED WHEATEN TERRIER	
COUNTRY OF ORIGIN	IRELAND
ORIGINAL FUNCTION	HUNTING DOG
	AND GUARD DOG

APPEARANCE

BODY

The Soft-coated Wheaten Terrier has a short, deep body with powerful, short loins. The chest is deep and the ribs are well arched. The tail is set on high and is carried gaily. In countries where this is permitted it is customarily docked to one third of its length. The sloping shoulders are fine, muscular and well laid back. The legs are straight and muscular. The hocks are well let down. Soft-coated Wheaten Terriers have small, tight feet. The strong neck is dry and moderately long.

Pair of Irish Terrier bitches

various types of dog sports on a small scale and can do quite well but only with a handler who knows a lot about dog training and behavior.

Young Irish Soft-coated Wheaten Terrier

Irish Soft-coated Wheaten Terriers

HEAD

The head is long and powerful, with a flat skull and a pronounced stop. The muzzle must not be longer than the skull. The ears are small to medium in size. They are carried folded forwards and at the level of the skull. The eyes should not be too large. Soft-coated Wheaten Terriers have a pincer or a scissors bite.

SHOULDER HEIGHT

This is approx. 18–18³/₄ in (46–47¹/₂ cm) for dogs.

WEIGHT

Approx. 33 lb (15 kg). Bitches are a little smaller and lighter.

COAT

The coat is soft and silky, slightly wavy to curly. A wiry coat is highly undesirable. Puppies and young dogs do not have this coat texture. It can take 18–30 months for the ultimate coat to grow.

COLORS

These dogs come in every shade from light wheaten to a reddish golden shading. Puppies are always born with a dark color. It can take a year

or longer for the final coat color to appear. The preferred eye color for Soft-coated Wheaten Terriers is hazel.

TEMPERAMENT

CHARACTER

Soft-coated Wheaten Terriers are cheerful, extrovert, active and playful. They are fairly intelligent, eager to learn with an even-tempered, reasonably calm disposition. They form a very close bond with their families and make excellent guards. They are affectionate without being subservient. Although this breed is self-confident, a well-trained Wheaten is usually obedient and loyal to its master.

SOCIAL BEHAVIOR

A well-trained Soft-coated Wheaten Terrier generally gets along fine with children. Contact with cats and other pets should not be a problem, provided the dog has been introduced to these animals as a puppy. Wheatens get on reasonably well with their own kind, although they will always be true terriers. Because of this it is not advisable to keep two male dogs. Soft-coated Wheaten Terriers will bark to announce the arrival of visitors. If the master indicates that it is okay then the visitors will be greeted boisterously. These dogs are vigilant, but also tend to be friendly to both familiar faces and strangers.

GENERAL CARE

GROOMING

The adult coat does not shed in the spring or fall and any loose hairs will

Irish Soft-coated Wheaten Terrier dog

Irish Soft-coated Wheaten Terrier bitch with two pups

a challenge; when it finds the drills too tame it will lose its enthusiasm. Plenty of variety and action will keep this dog motivated.

EXERCISE

Wheatens are active dogs. When they can release their energy outdoors, they tend to be quiet in the house. You can take this dog for long walks, but it will also appreciate the chance to frolic and play ball games in the yard. Although they do possess some hunting instinct, they can be recalled fairly easily once they are properly trained and you need not worry that your dog will run away.

USES

Dogs of this breed are eminently suited for various types of dog sports, particularly agility and flyball. They can also do well in advanced obedience, if it is presented in a fun way. The most important thing is that the dog continues to enjoy it, otherwise it will quickly lose interest.

largely stay behind in the coat. These should be combed out once a week so the coat will not tangle. A well-groomed Soft-coated Wheaten Terrier sheds very little in the house. There are quite a few international differences in coat texture and consequently in presentation. The heavier coats of American Wheatens often require considerably more grooming and are elaborately clipped for the show-ring. The softer coats of English Wheatens, however, allow for a much more natural presentation and the coat of these dogs is therefore less labor-intensive. The coat is always trimmed in such a way that the facial features (mustache, beard and eyebrows) and the hair on the legs, at the bottom of the neck, on the chest and the belly are kept slightly longer. Wheatens are not plucked.

TRAINING

In common with other dogs, this breed needs to be taught the difference between what is and what is not allowed. Because they are intelligent, they will quickly grasp what is expected of them. This dog needs to regard its training as

Irish Soft-coated Wheaten Terrier

Irish Soft-coated Wheaten Terrier pups look quite different to full-grown dogs

LAKELAND TERRIER

COUNTRY OF ORIGIN	ENGLAND
ORIGINAL FUNCTION	INPENDENT WORKING HUNTER, USED MAINLY FOR FOXES

APPEARANCE

BODY

The Lakeland Terrier is a compact dog with a moderately short, strong back and well-muscled hindquarters. The chest is fairly flat. The tail is well set on and is carried gaily, but not over the back or curled. In countries where this is permitted the tail is usually docked. The shoulders are well laid back. The forelegs are straight and the well-bent stifles and low, straight hocks are a striking feature of the hind legs. The feet are small, compact and round. The reachy and slightly arched neck is free from throatiness.

HEAD

The skull is flat, with powerful jaws and a muzzle that is neither too broad nor too narrow. The distance from the nose to the stop should not exceed that from the stop to the occiput. The moderately small ears are V-shaped, set neither too high nor too low and are carried alertly. The almond-shaped eyes should be set slightly obliquely. Lakeland Terriers have a scissors bite.

Irish Soft-coated
Wheaten Terriers

SHOULDER HEIGHT

This should be no higher than 14¹/₂ in (37 cm).

Male Lakeland Terrier

WEIGHT

Dogs weigh on average 16 lb (7¹/₂ kg) and bitches are approx. 15¹/₂ lb (7 kg).

COAT

Lakeland Terriers have a dense, hard and water-resistant outer coat with a good undercoat.

COLORS

This breed comes in black and tan, blue and tan, red gray, red, wheaten, liver-colored, blue or black. Small white markings on the chest and feet do occur, but are not desirable. Mahogany or dark tan-colored dogs are also not desirable. The eye color is dark or hazel.

TEMPERAMENT

CHARACTER

Lakeland Terriers are sporty, self-confident, friendly and even-tempered with a cheerful, honest disposition. These intelligent dogs are full of character, although they are generally a bit

Lakeland Terrier

more tractable than many other terriers. Affectionate and loyal, they are excellent guards, but they do not bark excessively.

SOCIAL BEHAVIOR

Lakelands generally get on extremely well with children. Contact with other dogs is no problem either, something which is not common among terriers. This breed can be reserved towards strangers, but normally not excessively so. As Lakeland Terriers do possess some hunting instinct, it is advisable to socialize them well with cats and other pets. Once they have been introduced to cats there will be no problems.

GENERAL CARE

GROOMING

The Lakeland Terrier needs to be plucked about twice to three times a year. This means that the old hairs are plucked from the coat by hand so the new hair can grow. Outside these plucking sessions you should brush the coat with a slicker brush about once a week. Trim any excess hairs from the ear passages and between the pads. Keep the claws

Lakeland Terrier bitch

short. The coats of show-dogs need more attention.

TRAINING

This sporty, intelligent dog is a quick learner. Be consistent, clear and fair, and make sure the exercises are varied and challenging. Good socialization will pay off.

Lakeland Terrier bitch

EXERCISE

Lakeland Terriers like to be active and a quiet existence in front of the fireplace is not for them. You can take your dog for long walks, provided it is well trained, although this breed also loves ball games in the yard. Most specimens like digging and you should bear this in mind if you value your yard. A Lakeland Terrier can be kept in an apartment. If it gets plenty of exercise outdoors then it will usually be quiet indoors.

Lakeland Terrier

USES

Lakelands are certainly suitable for various types of dog sports, but particularly for flyball and agility. They also make excellent companion dogs.

PARSON JACK RUSSELL TERRIER	
COUNTRY OF ORIGIN	ENGLAND
ORIGINAL AND TODAY'S FUNCTION	BARKING AT FOXES AND BADGERS BELOW GROUND, SO THEY WILL LEAVE THEIR DEN AND CAN BE HUNTED

APPEARANCE

BODY

The Parson Jack Russell Terrier is a dry and muscular dog. The distance from the top of the shoulder to the tail-set is the same as that from the top of the shoulder to the ground. To enable this breed to go to ground after its prey it should be possible to span its chest with two hands.

The level, strong back is slightly arched at the loins. The straight tail is set high. In countries where this is permitted it is customarily docked to such a length that the tip is level with the ear set when the dog walks. The hindquarters are strong and well angulated. The forelegs are straight with compact feet. The neck is strong and muscular.

HEAD

The head has a flat, moderately broad skull. The muzzle is strong with powerful jaws. The small ears are hanging on the side of the head. The eyes are almond-shaped with an intelligent expression. Parson Jack Russells have a scissors bite.

SHOULDER HEIGHT

The ideal size for dogs is $13^3/_4$ in (35 cm) and for bitches 13 in (33 cm). The provisional minimum size for both dogs and bitches is

Smooth-hair Parson Jack Russell Terrier

$10^1/_4$ in (26 cm). No maximum size is given, although the dog's size is limited by the rule that it must be possible to span the chest with two hands.

COAT

Parson Jack Russell Terriers have a double coat, which means that they have an outer coat and an undercoat. They come in both smooth and rough coats. Both types are stiff, close and dense. Rough-haired Jack Russell Terriers should not be woolly or curly.

COLORS

White dogs and dogs with markings on the head and the tail-set are preferred. These markings may be black, brown, lemon or black and brown (black and tan). Brindle markings are undesirable.

TEMPERAMENT

CHARACTER

These dogs are active, agile and enterprising. They are intelligent and full of tricks. Alert to what goes on around them, they make excellent guards. They have always had to work fairly independently. Because of this they are still independent and often cheeky dogs with a ten-

Rough-haired Parson Jack Russell Terrier

dency to recklessness. They exude self-confidence and can be dominant. As a rule, these are sober dogs that are happy with very little.

SOCIAL BEHAVIOR

Parson Jack Russell Terriers are generally uncomplicated and honest. They love playing with kids and can take a blow. They usually leave the family cat alone, but as true hunting dogs they are always tempted to chase after a fleeing cat outdoors. Very dominant dogs can be a little dominant towards their own sex. Visitors will be announced, but a well-trained Jack Russell Terrier will then usually react friendly.

GENERAL CARE

GROOMING

The coat of the Smooth Parson Jack Russell Terrier is easy to care for. During the molt loose hairs should be removed daily with a rubber brush. Outside the molt weekly brushing is sufficient. The rough-haired Jack needs to be plucked three to four times a year, which involves removing the dead hairs from the coat by hand.

TRAINING

Parson Jack Russell Terriers are generally easy to train. They are highly intelligent and can learn new commands very quickly. However, do remember that they were traditionally bred to chase bad-

Smooth-haired Parson Jack Russell Terrier

gers and foxes from their dens independently. Such a dog needs plenty of courage and stamina, and must be able to act swiftly and on its own initiative. You should always allow for these charac-

ter traits. Do not give in to their mischievous attitude; they know perfectly well that this may fool you. It is very important that this dog is treated consistently and is well socialized from a very young age.

Parson Jack Russell Terriers have boundless energy

EXERCISE

Parson Jack Russells are active dogs with a lot of energy which they need to release on a daily basis. They like to play and romp around. Digging holes in the yard is another favorite pastime – something you should bear in mind if you are a keen gardener. Ball games are also popular with this breed. A Parson Jack Russell Terrier will not usually let you know when it is tired, even though it certainly needs its sleep, especially during its growth. You should therefore only take this dog on long walks from the age of one. By that stage it can also be trained to join you on your daily runs, provided you build things up slowly. Because its hunting instinct will regularly emerge during off-leash walks, your dog needs to be taught as a puppy to return to you immediately when called.

USES

This nimble, strong and active breed is eminently suited for sports such as agility and flyball. The variety and challenges of such sports will certainly appeal to them. They can make themselves

Parson Jack Russell Terriers need lots
of varied activity

extremely useful on farms as destroyers of mice
and rats, but they will also do well as a companion
dog in a sports-minded family.

DETAILS

Apart from the Parson Jack Russell Terrier there is
also a short-legged Jack Russell Terrier. The Jack
Russell Terrier is reasonably popular but has not
yet been officially recognized by the FCI. The
Jack Russell Terrier belongs to breed group 11.

KERRY BLUE TERRIER

COUNTRY OF ORIGIN	IRELAND
ORIGINAL FUNCTION	HUNTING DOG, VERMIN DESTROYER AND GUARD DOG

APPEARANCE

BODY
The Kerry Blue Terrier is a sturdy, well-knit, well-
proportioned and muscular dog. The back is
moderately long and straight. The loins are not
long. The tail is customarily docked in countries
where this is permitted. It is thin and is carried
gaily. The deep chest is of moderate width and the
ribs are well sprung. The shoulders are dry. The
legs are well boned and straight when viewed from
the front. The thighs are muscular and well developed. Kerry Blue Terriers have strong hocks and
the hind legs are well positioned under the body.
Dew claws and evidence of their removal are
highly undesirable. The feet have strong, round
pads and the toes are close-knit. The neck is well
proportioned and moderately long.

HEAD
The strong head has a slight stop and the muzzle is
moderately long. The jaws are strong and muscular. The thin ears are medium size. They are carried forward or to the sides of the head. The well-
positioned eyes are medium size. Kerry Blue
Terriers have a heavy, regular white set of teeth.

SHOULDER HEIGHT
Approx. $17^1/_2$–$18^1/_2$ in (45–48 cm).

WEIGHT
Dogs are approx.
33–$39^1/_2$ lb (15–18 kg)
and bitches slightly
less.

COAT
The Kerry Blue Terrier
has a soft, abundant
wavy coat, with no
undercoat. The coat
must not be harsh,
wiry or bristly.

COLORS
The coat color is light
to dark blue, but blue
and brown (blue with

Pair of Kerry Blue bitches

tan-colored markings on the legs and the head) is also permitted. The latter is very rare. A very

Kerry Blue Terrier

small amount of white on the chest is allowed but not desirable. The eyes should be dark or dark hazel. The claws, gums and palate are black. Kerry Blue Terriers are always black at birth and it may take up to eighteen months for the ultimate blue color to develop.

TEMPERAMENT

CHARACTER
The Kerry Blue Terrier is full of character, perky and lively. It is self-confident, hardy and courageous, fairly vigilant and sometimes noisy. These Kerry Blues are fairly intelligent with an excellent memory but also with a mind of their own. They can be fairly stubborn and willful. They form a close bond with their masters and families, and have an honest, predictable character.

Kerry Blue Terrier dog

SOCIAL BEHAVIOR
They are friendly and docile towards children. Socialization with cats and other pets should take place early under close supervision. If this has taken place then the dog will usually live in harmony with other household pets. But vigilance is always required outdoors when the dog might see a cat running off in the street or game fleeing in the woods; in such cases the dog's hunting instinct will prevail. Some enjoy doggy companions, whereas other specimens prefer not to share their masters. As a rule, these dogs – particularly the males – are dominant and aggressive towards other dogs, especially if these do not belong to their own pack. They may initially be reserved and vigilant towards people they do not know, but that is usually all.

GENERAL CARE

GROOMING
The coat of the Kerry Blue Terrier is a striking feature. The beauty of this dog is shown to its best advantage when the coat is groomed, clipped and styled to perfection. A Kerry Blue Terrier that is kept as a family dog will need to visit the trimming parlor about every two months, but the coat of a show-dog obviously requires considerably more attention. Apart from these trimming sessions you need to brush the coat, particularly on the head and the legs, with a slicker brush from time to time. This coat has the

benefit that it does not shed and is not prone to tangling.

TRAINING

The Kerry Blue is not a dog for beginners. It is active, self-confident and stubborn, a combination that demands a resolute handler who is able to exert authority. Vary the training sessions and make sure they are sufficiently challenging. If the drills and exercises are too monotonous to the dog's liking then its stubborn streak will show. Outdoors this breed may be tempted to attack other dogs, which is something that you should never tolerate.

EXERCISE

This sporty dog likes to accompany its master on long walks, either on the leash through the city or off-leash through the countryside. Nearly all Kerry Blue Terriers are fond of ball games. If occasionally you cannot spend a lot of time with the dog, it will usually adapt.

USES

The Kerry Blue Terrier has a certain flair for sports such as flyball and agility. If you want your dog to take part in a dog sport, make sure that the dog continues to enjoy it and it will not disappoint you.

The color of this Kerry Blue Terrier is not to the breed standard

BEDLINGTON TERRIER	
COUNTRY OF ORIGIN	**ENGLAND**
ORIGINAL FUNCTION	**VERMIN DESTROYER AND HUNTER USED FOR HARE, BADGER AND FOX**

Liver Bedlington Terrier

APPEARANCE

BODY

The Bedlington Terrier is a graceful, lithe and muscular dog. Its chest is broad and deep and the flat ribs are carried well back. This breed is also characterized by flat, sloping shoulders, a roach back with well-arched loins and muscular hindquarters. The moderately long tail is set low and tapers to a point. It is carried in a graceful curve, but never above the topline. The forelegs are straight and when seen from the front the distance between the forefeet is shorter than that between the elbows. The hind legs give the impression of being longer.

Bedlington Terriers have long hare feet with thick, tight pads. The long, tapering neck is free from throatiness and set on in such a way that the head can be carried fairly high.

HEAD

The head is pear-shaped with no stop. The jaws taper to the front and the lips are close fitting. The moderately large ears are set on low and are carried hanging, close to the cheeks. The deep-set eyes are triangular, with a gentle expression at rest. Both pincer and scissors bites are permissible.

SHOULDER HEIGHT

The size is approx. 16$\frac{1}{2}$ in (40$\frac{1}{2}$ cm). Bitches may be one inch (2$\frac{1}{2}$ cm) smaller and dogs one inch (2$\frac{1}{2}$ cm) bigger.

Bedlington Terrier

COAT
This "wolf in sheep's clothing" has a thick, frizzy coat that stands out from the skin and must not be wiry. The hair should have a tendency to curl. The ears are short and covered with fine hair with a fringe of longer hair at the tip.

COLORS
Bedlingtons come in solid blue, blue and brown and solid liver-colored, but solid blue is most common. Liver color is slightly less common and blue and brown dogs are fairly rare. Puppies are born with a black, black and brown or

brown coat. The coat becomes considerably lighter over time, so much so that the coat looks virtually white. Blue and blue and brown dogs have a black nose and liver-colored dogs have a brown nose. The eyelids of blue and browns and browns are lighter than those of the blues.

Bedlington Terrier

TEMPERAMENT

CHARACTER
Bedlington Terriers are courageous, tenacious, cheerful, intelligent and equable dogs that are normally peaceful, compliant, affectionate and good-natured indoors. Outdoors they are lively and active, playful and tireless. Although loyal to their owners, Bedlingtons tend to bond closely with one person in particular. As a rule they are obedient, though not subservient, and always retain a certain degree of dignity. They do not bark much, but will become vocal when something is wrong.

Bedlington Terrier

Black Russian Terrier

COAT

The rough, full coat is coarse in texture and lies flat against the skin. Black Russian Terriers have a dense undercoat. The guard hairs are approx. two inches (5 cm) long. The hair above the eyes and on the muzzle is longer and softer, forming the characteristic facial features of this breed.

COLORS

The color is solid black or black with a few gray hairs in the coat. The eyes are always dark.

TEMPERAMENT

CHARACTER

This intelligent and generally obedient breed is extremely loyal to its own people and has an uncomplicated, sober and self-confident disposition. Black Russian Terriers make excellent guards that protect

Black Russian Terrier

and defend their people, home and property convincingly. They tend to bark little and are fairly quiet in the house. Although compliant towards their owners and families, they also show some initiative. Imports from the country of origin and neighboring countries may be a little sharper and tougher in character than specimens bred in Western Europe.

SOCIAL BEHAVIOR

Black Russian Terriers get along well with children and have a high tolerance threshold when it comes to kids. If properly socialized with cats and other pets, then contact with these animals will be no problem. Friends of the family are greeted warmly, but strangers will not stand a chance of entering your property or your house. This breed is reserved towards strangers but when the master says it is okay then the dog will accept them. Males can be a little dominant towards other dogs.

GENERAL CARE

GROOMING

The Russian Terrier's coat is hand-plucked about three to four times a year. This is necessary to maintain the coat's hardness and to give the new hair the chance to come through. Between trims you can clip the long hair that grows between the pads and keep the ears free from excess hair. The beard and mustache need to be combed regularly to avoid tangles. A Black Russian Terrier that is plucked regularly will shed little in the house.

Black Russian Terrier

TRAINING

These dogs are eager to learn and love to work for their handlers, but can also be a little dominant. This makes them less suitable for people with little or no experience of training these dogs. Russian Terriers will do best with a handler who is consistent and clear in his training. They respond well to the voice; punishments will rarely be necessary with an owner who exerts authority.

EXERCISE

Black Russian Terriers like to be active and can walk or run for hours without tiring. Off-leash walks in the countryside and swimming are suitable forms of exercise for them. If you need to skip a day, then they will usually adapt without becoming a nuisance.

USES

In Russia this dog is specifically bred for police work, so it is hardly surprising that these dogs excel in training for hunting. There are not many dog sports and disciplines for which this breed is unsuitable. A Black Russian can be trained to do rescue work and tracking, but it can also excel in advanced obedience.

GLEN OF IMAAL TERRIER	
COUNTRY OF ORIGIN	IRELAND
ORIGINAL FUNCTION	THE GLEN OF IMAAL TERRIER WAS USED FOR VARIOUS PURPOSSES: AS A HUNTER USED TO HUNT BADGERS AND AS A GUARD DOG AND VERMIN DESTROYER ON FARMS

APPEARANCE

BODY

The Glen of Imaal Terrier is a low-legged, muscular dog of very powerful build showing maximum substance for its size. The body is longer than tall and the topline rises slightly. The chest is wide and strong. The tail is wide at the root and is carried gaily. In countries where this is permitted it is customarily docked, although this is optional. The forelegs are a little bowed with sturdy, close-knit feet that turn outward slightly. The hind feet are also close-knit, but point straight ahead.

Glen of Imaal Terrier

HEAD

The head is of good width and length. The skull tapers to the nose. The muzzle is powerful and the stop is pronounced. The ears are small and carried folded backwards (rose ear). The round eyes are medium size and set well apart. Glen of Imaal Terriers have a complete, strong scissors bite.

SHOULDER HEIGHT

Must not exceed 14 in (35$^1/_2$ cm).

WEIGHT

In spite of its small size this is a sturdy dog. Glen of Imaal Terriers weigh around 33–35¼ lb (15–16 kg).

COAT

The Glen of Imaal Terrier has a harsh outer coat of medium length with a soft, dense undercoat.

COLORS

The coat may be any shade of blue, brindle and wheaten. The eyes are brown.

Glen of Imaal Terrier

TEMPERAMENT

CHARACTER

Dogs of this breed have a lot of self-confidence and are equable, courageous, fairly tough on themselves and intelligent. Although loyal and affectionate towards their own people, they can also be willful. When young, but often even when they are older, these dogs are playful, perky and boisterous. Glen of Imaal Terriers are usually calm in the house and do not bark much. They will bark when they sense there is something wrong and will not hesitate when their people are threatened. A Glen of Imaal Terrier usually matures late.

SOCIAL BEHAVIOR

Glen of Imaal Terriers are generally okay with children. If they have had positive experiences of cats and other pets when young, they will get along fine with them. Males can be dominant towards other dogs. Welcome visitors are greeted, but unwelcome visitors will get a less friendly reception. They are certainly not everybody's friend.

Glen of Imaal Terriers

GENERAL CARE

GROOMING

If your Glen of Imaal Terrier is kept as a pet then its coat needs to be hand-plucked about twice a year. Coats of show-dogs need more attention. Clip the long hair that grows between the pads and remove any excess hair from the ear passages.

TRAINING

It should not be difficult to train this breed. They are intelligent and eager to learn, although they can also be dominant and obstinate. Be consistent at all times and regularly vary exercises with play.

Glen of Imaal Terrier

Emphasize the dog's socialization with people and animals.

EXERCISE

Glen of Imaal Terriers are tireless in the field, can walk or play for many hours and are always ready for a ball game. In spite of this, it is not strictly necessary to exercise these dogs a lot. If you need to skip a day then they will adapt.

USES

This still comparatively rare dog is now mostly kept as a companion dog. With the right handler and supervision this breed can take part in dog sports such as agility and flyball, although it will not excel.

Glen of Imaal Terrier

Glen of Imaal Terrier

GERMAN HUNT TERRIER	
COUNTRY OF ORIGIN	GERMANY
ORIGINAL AND TODAY'S FUNCTION	THIS BREED IS USED MAINLY TO HUNT FOXES, BUT ALSO FOR SCENTING, AS A HARRIER AND (WATER) RETRIEVER

German Hunt Terrier

APPEARANCE

BODY

The back is strong, level and not particularly short. The loins and the croup are well muscled. The tail is carried level rather than erect. The chest is well sprung and the strong shoulders are set obliquely. The muscular legs are straight, with bones that are coarse rather than fine. The feet are tight. The forefeet are often wider than the hind feet. The powerful neck is not too long and is carried slightly raised.

HEAD

The head is flat with a slight stop. The muzzle is shorter than the skull. The V-shaped ears are set high and are carried pendulously, more or less against the skull. The eyes are small and deeply set, with close-fitting eyelids. German Hunt Terriers have a complete and powerful scissors bite.

SHOULDER HEIGHT

Ranges from 13–15³/₄ in (33–40 cm).

WEIGHT

Dogs are 20–22 lb (9–10 kg) and bitches are 16–18³/₄ lb (7¹/₂–8¹/₂ kg).

COAT

There are two coat varieties: short and rough. The rough-haired coat is close and dense, while the short-haired coat is strong, hard and not too short.

COLORS

The most common color is black and tan, but brown and black and gray dogs with tan markings also occur. Some white on the chest and/or the toes is permitted. The eyes should be dark.

TEMPERAMENT

CHARACTER

Dogs of this breed are energetic, high-spirited and active with considerable stamina and a strong hunting instinct. They are very courageous, sober

German Hunt Terrier

and hardy, love to use their voices, but do not bark excessively. Self-confident, often dominant and not easily intimidated, German Hunt Terriers are alert to what goes on around them and are excellent guards. Although devoted to their masters and families, this breed is not usually considered suitable to be an "average" companion dog because of its high-spirited nature.

SOCIAL BEHAVIOR

German Hunt Terriers tend to do well with children, provided they do not pester the dog. Because of their sharpness and their hunting instinct it is unlikely that they will live in harmony with cats and other pets, although thorough socialization may help. A German Hunt Terrier can be snappy towards other dogs, particular those of its own sex. When visitors arrive then this dog will be vigilant at first, but will soon thaw; it is not aggressive towards people.

GENERAL CARE

GROOMING

Both coat varieties need comparatively little attention. The texture of rough-haired coats is such that plucking will not be necessary or only rarely. Keep the claws short.

TRAINING

These dogs should be trained consistently and with a firm hand. In that case this breed will be fairly obedient. However, its hunting instinct will always remain its weakness: the dog may play deaf when it is in pursuit of any real or imaginary prey.

The German Hunt Terrier has fearsome jaws

EXERCISE

German Hunt Terriers need a great deal of exercise and activity. They are ready for anything, from ball games to retrieving and from swimming to frolicking. In spite of their small size these dogs can be trained to join you on your daily runs, provided you build things up slowly. If you let the dog walk off the leash then there is always the risk that it will go off hunting on its own. So make sure your yard is well fenced. A German Hunt Terrier is usually fairly agile and affectionate both outdoors and in the house.

USES

This breed is used exclusively as a hunter both in its country of origin and elsewhere. While many terriers have lost some of their keen hunting instinct over decades, this breed still possesses all the original characteristics and the mentality that a working terrier needs for its job. This explains why this breed is predominantly owned by hunters, who have adopted a stringent placement policy. For non-hunters it is quite difficult to acquire a puppy of this breed.

German Hunt Terrier

MANCHESTER TERRIER	
COUNTRY OF ORIGIN	ENGLAND
ORIGINAL FUNCTION	RATTER

Manchester Terrier

APPEARANCE

BODY

The Manchester Terrier is an elegant dog with a compact build and a narrow, deep front. The body is short with well-arched ribs. The hindquarters are strong and muscular. The tail is thick at the base and tapers to a point. It is rather short and is not carried above the topline. The legs are perfectly straight and well bent at the stifles. The feet are small and strong, with well-arched toes. They are somewhere between cat and hare feet in shape. The clean shoulders are sloping. The dry neck is fairly long and tapers from the shoulders to the head.

HEAD

The long, narrow, wedge-shaped head is flat in the skull. The cheek muscles are not visible and the lips are tight. The small, V-shaped ears are carried above the topline of the skull and are hanging close

to the head, above the eyes. The small eyes are almond-shaped and should not be prominent. Manchester Terriers have a regular scissors bite.

Manchester Terrier

SHOULDER HEIGHT

The ideal size for dogs is $15^3/_4$–$16^1/_4$ in (40–41 cm) and for bitches 15 in (38 cm).

COAT

The coat is dense, smooth, short and glossy with a firm texture.

COLORS

Manchester Terriers are bred exclusively in black

Manchester Terrier

and tan. Brown on the backs of the hind legs is undesirable and the black should not run into the brown or vice versa anywhere on the body. The markings should be clearly divided. The nose is always black and the eyes are dark.

TEMPERAMENT

CHARACTER

Dogs of this breed are high-spirited, intelligent, eager to learn, fairly active, sporty and agile. They are lively and courageous, but rarely nervous or aggressive. They make excellent guards but only bark when necessary. They bond closely with their people.

SOCIAL BEHAVIOR

This nimble breed generally gets along fine with kids, although some specimens can be dominant towards their own kind. They are excellent rat and mole catchers and in view of their keen hunting instinct, early and thorough socialization with cats and other pets is very important, so that they can happily live under the same roof. Manchester Terriers are not particularly large dogs, but if they feel that their master or a member of their family is in trouble they will not hesitate to act. In normal circumstances they are friendly to both familiar faces and strangers.

GENERAL CARE

GROOMING

The coat of the Manchester Terrier does not need

Manchester Terrier

a lot of grooming. It is very short and sheds little. During the molt a rubber brush can be used to remove dead and loose hairs from the coat. Afterwards a damp hound glove can be used to make the coat shine. Keep the ears clean and the claws short.

TRAINING

The Manchester Terrier is intelligent, loves to please its master and is a relatively quick learner. They respond well to the tone of your voice.

Manchester Terrier

EXERCISE

Dogs of this breed are fairly active and need a considerable amount of exercise. In addition to their normal daily walks, let them run and play off-leash regularly. Manchesters can run extremely fast and can keep up their speed for a long time.

USES

Traditionally, there has never been a better ratter than the Manchester Terrier. In the old days this dog was specifically bred to kill as many rats as quickly as possible for a bet. Whenever they get the chance they will prove that they have not forgotten this skill. A Manchester Terrier can provide a very useful service on a farm or at the stable. This breed is rare and is kept primarily as a companion dog. However, it can also excel in sports such as agility and flyball and do pretty well in obedience trials.

Manchester Terriers

SCOTTISH TERRIER

COUNTRY OF ORIGIN	**SCOTLAND**
ORIGINAL FUNCTION	**HUNTING OF FOXES, RABBITS**
	AND OTHER SMALL PREY

Scottish Terrier

APPEARANCE

BODY

The Scottish Terrier is a squat, short-legged dog with a muscular, but proportionately short back. It has remarkably strong hindquarters with big, broad buttocks. The tail is carried straight up or slightly curved and is moderately long. The tail is broad at the base and gradually tapers to a point. The chest is broad and has a clear forechest. The well-arched ribs are well laid back. Scottish Terriers have vertical legs with close-fitting elbows. The front feet are a bit bigger than the hind feet. The well-muscled neck is moderately long.

HEAD

It looks rather big and long in proportion to the body. It has an almost flat skull and a powerful deep foreface of equal length. The jaws do not protrude. A slight but distinct stop is clearly visible just in front of the eye. Viewed from the side the line from the nose to the chin appears to slope down backward. The ears are thin, sharp and pointed. They are carried erect. The almond-shaped eyes are set far apart. Scottish Terriers have a scissors bite.

SHOULDER HEIGHT

They are about $9^1/_2$ in ($25^1/_2$ cm) high.

WEIGHT

Scottish Terriers weigh approx. $18^1/_2$–23 lb ($8^1/_2$–$10^1/_2$ kg).

COAT

Their double coats lie close to the skin. The upper coat is wiry, hard and dense while the undercoat is dense, short and soft. Scottish Terriers have a distinct beard and eyebrows. They are plucked in such a way that their hair on the flanks, lower chest, belly and legs appears to be considerably longer than the rest of the body.

COLORS

The coat of the Scottish Terrier can be solid black, have various brindle shades and possibly wheaten.

TEMPERAMENT

CHARACTER

This Scottie is calm, cautious, straightforward and sober and devoted to "its" people, but at the same time it remains independent and proud. Scotties appear to be reserved, but in fact they are very loyal to the family. They are watchful, brave, self-assured, intelligent and even sporty little dogs. They like digging. They do not bark a lot.

Scottish Terrier dog

A rare wheaten Scottish Terrier

be combed thoroughly once every other day and the same applies to the longer hair underneath the body. Keep the claws short and occasionally check the eye corners for dirt. Scottish Terriers have a tendency to become obese, so please ensure that their intake of calories matches their activities.

TRAINING

For the right handler this aristocrat of a dog is easy to train. Remember though that for all its loyalty to you, this is an independent dog. It is not in its nature to do the same things over and over again. Simply asking is not enough. If this type of dog is trained in a strict manner it may become quite obstinate. The training needs to be founded on mutual respect, but should also be consistent and clear. Scottish Terriers need to be well socialized, as it will benefit their character development.

EXERCISE

The Scottish Terrier will adapt its exercise demands to the circumstances. It is usually peaceful in the house.

USES

Scotties have taken on their role as companions with character and excellence.

SOCIAL BEHAVIOR

The natural inclination of a Scottie is to get on well with other household animals and its own kind. Provided kids respect this dog, they will get along well together. Much depends upon their social training as a puppy. They are reserved towards strangers, will bark if they sense danger, but that is all.

GENERAL CARE

GROOMING

The amount of coat care depends on whether you need to take your dog to shows. A Scottish Terrier kept as a family dog, needs to be hand-plucked about twice a year by an expert, although the exact frequency depends on the quality of the coat. Between the plucking sessions the hair should be brushed or combed regularly. The facial hair features (its longer tufts of hair) should

Scottish Terrier bitch

WEST HIGHLAND WHITE TERRIER	
COUNTRY OF ORIGIN	SCOTLAND
ORIGINAL FUNCTION	FOX, BADGER AND VERMIN HUNTER

West Highland White Terrier

APPEARANCE

BODY

The West Highland White Terrier has a compact and strong body frame with a deep chest, a level topline and short loins. The ribs are well sprung. Westies should naturally have a short tail (approx. $4^3/_4$–6 in ($12^1/_2$–15 cm) long. It is carried gaily. The shoulders of these dogs are well laid back. The upper arms are quite straight. The thighs are well muscled, as well as the broad hindquarters, with good angulation of the knees and the hocks. The strong, short legs are straight and vertical and well placed under the body. The feet are round. The front feet are bigger than the hind feet. The neck is long and muscular. It is broad at the base and tapers towards the head.

HEAD

The head is set straight or at a slight angle on its muscular neck. The skull is arched a little. There is a clear stop with a slight median furrow and eyebrows. The muzzle is full, particularly below the eyes and overall it is a bit shorter than the skull. The small ears are strong and are carried erect. They end in a point. The medium-size eyes are set a little deeper in the head and have a penetrating expression. The nose is relatively big. Dogs of this breed have a strong and big scissors bite.

West Highland White Terrier

SHOULDER HEIGHT

The West Highland White Terrier is approx. 11 in (28 cm) high.

WEIGHT

This is around $16^1/_2$ lb ($7^1/_2$ kg).

COAT

The topcoat is rough and hard, approximately 2 in (5 cm) long and should not be curly. The ears should be naturally short and smooth haired.

COLORS

This breed will only have a white coat. The color of the eyes should be as dark as possible and the nose is always black. The nails and pads of the feet are preferably black.

West Highland White Terriers

TEMPERAMENT

CHARACTER

These lively and extrovert dogs bristle with self-confidence. They are not easily impressed. They rely on their abilities, they are brave, fearless and persistent. Westies are aware of everything happening around them and they make themselves heard if they sense danger. They are loyal to their owners and families, definitely affectionate, but they can also display a fair amount of stubbornness and independence. Bad-tempered Westies are a rarity; they are generally playful and cheerful dogs and you should not underestimate their cunning and ingenuity. Their presence adds spice to life.

SOCIAL BEHAVIOR

Westies can usually get on well with kids that are old enough to play and romp about with their dogs. They can withstand rough play. Westies generally get on well with their own kind although a Westie cannot resist challenging members of its own sex in the street. Good training and socialization can curb this characteristic. This breed needs to be taught at an early age that it should not chase cats and other animals. Once again good socializing and training will work wonders. Although they are vigilant and alert Westies are not at all shy.

GENERAL CARE

GROOMING

A West Highland Terrier, kept as a family dog, will need to have its coat trimmed once every three months. The hair on the back, neck and sides in particular, needs plucking short by hand. In between the trimming sessions the coat will need a good brush once or twice a week. It is best to use a slicker brush. If necessary you should clip excess hair between the pads of the feet and comb the beard and mustache daily. The West Highland Terrier should have a hard coat and therefore it

West Highland White Terriers

should not be washed too frequently. Washing makes the hair go lank, although there are special shampoos without this side effect. The structure of the hair allows you to brush away dirt and mud quite easily once it is dry. The coats of show-dogs will require more grooming. It needs the expertise of someone who is accustomed to taking dogs to shows.

West Highland White Terriers

TRAINING

The straightforward and cheerful character of this dog should not tempt you to let it get away with whatever it likes. Westies can persist in bad habits and they can bark more than necessary. This dog needs a firm handler who will train it consistently and will not be fooled. With some good supervision a Westie can learn a lot of commands in a short period of time. If there is no clear guidance the dog will find its own pastime, one which will generally not be appreciated by its owner.

EXERCISE

This dog deserves more than a few obligatory runs round the block each day. Westies are active dogs that love ball games, rope pulling, romping and playing. They like to be outdoors and are not bothered by the weather. They enjoy digging, so be warned if you take pride in your well-furnished yard.

USES

Westies are not used for their original hunting jobs, although they are still considered to be the best vermin destroyers. They are intelligent and agile enough for sports such as flyball and agility skills, but they do need good training and supervision. These are excellent family dogs provided the family is sports minded.

Cairn Terrier

CAIRN TERRIER

COUNTRY OF ORIGIN	SCOTLAND
ORIGINAL FUNCTION	VERMIN DESTROYER, HUNTER, TERRIER TRIALS

APPEARANCE

BODY

Cairn Terriers have a level topline of medium length. The hindquarters are strong and muscular and the loins are strong and flexible. The ribs are well arched and deep. The shoulders are set obliquely. Cairn Terriers have a short tail carried gaily, but not curled over the back. The legs are moderately long, strong, well angulated and have close-fitting elbows. The front feet are a little bigger than the hind feet and may point slightly outward.

HEAD

The small head is in proportion to the body. The skull is broad and there is a clear dip between the eyes. The stop is pronounced. The muzzle is strong, as are the jaws, but it is neither too long, not too heavy. The small ears are not too close together. They are pointed and are carried erect. The eyes are set far apart. They are deep set and moderately big. Cairn Terriers have a complete and strong scissors bite.

SHOULDER HEIGHT

Cairn Terriers are approximately $11-12\frac{1}{2}$ in (28–31 cm) high, but their height should be in proportion to their weight.

West Highland White Terrier

WEIGHT

A Cairn Terrier weighs approximately 16 lb (7 kg).

COAT

The Cairn Terrier has a double-layered coat of which the topcoat is hard and abundant, and the undercoat is soft and short. The hair may not curl or part. The eyes and the tail should not be feathered too heavily.

COLORS

Permitted colors are wheaten, cream (blonde), gray to almost black (but not solid black) or red. Streamed is permissible in all colors. Dark markings on the ears and muzzle are highly regarded. The eyes are hazel.

TEMPERAMENT

CHARACTER

Cairn Terrier

Cairn Terrier

This dog is intelligent, cheerful, uncomplicated, equable and extrovert. It is very lively and playful, indefatigable at play and hunting, very brave and not squeamish. Cairn Terriers are alert to what is happening in their surroundings and most of them are quite watchful. They are devoted to their owners and like to be involved in the family's activities. However they will always be a bit stubborn and independent.

SOCIAL BEHAVIOR

The Cairn Terrier makes a first-class friend for kids; it can tolerate rough play and has a well-developed sense of humor. They can also get on reasonably well with other dogs, although some dogs of this breed will stand their ground. They are not unfriendly towards strangers, but they are alert if they sense something is wrong. They will mix well with cats and other pets provided the dog has been socialized with these pets from an early age.

GENERAL CARE

GROOMING

Cairn Terriers have plucking coats, which means that about twice a year the dead hairs need to be plucked out by hand. A trimming parlor can do

Cairn Terrier

this, but it is good to learn how to do it yourself. In between sessions the coat will need to be combed and brushed regularly. From time to time remove excess hair form the ear passages. Excessive hair growing from the feet between the pads should be clipped and the claws should be kept short. Originally a Cairn Terrier must have had a rough and rustic appearance. The breed experts typify its appearance as that of a broom. It will not be groomed excessively for a show, but any excess hair on the legs, ears and tail will be removed before a show.

Cairn Terrier

TRAINING

A Cairn Terrier needs a loving but definitely a strict and consistent training. This vagabond will take privileges, no matter whether the owner approves. The antics of the puppy are often the cause of laughter but do not forget that the tricks of the puppy become less amusing when the dog has grown up. Teach this dog early to get on with cats and other household pets, so that it will not chase them when older. Cairn Terriers need an owner who can set limits, in which case the dog will obey the rules and become a cheerful – though sometimes mischievous – and fairly obedient dog.

Cairn Terrier puppy

EXERCISE

The Cairn Terrier is bursting with energy and needs to be able to play and run. It is an ideal dog for a sportive family. It likes to be taken for a walk in the woods or in open countryside or on the beach where it can run free, but make sure before you do so that the dog will return to you when you call it – their hunting instinct is so strong that they can take off. They make good playmates for older kids who like to play ball games and can romp around with them in the yard for hours on end. The average Cairn Terrier likes to dig. Something you need to take into consideration if you value your well-furnished yard.

USES

This dog is well suited as a family dog in a sporty family. They can perform quite well in dog sports such as agility skills and flyball.

Cairn Terriers

CESKY TERRIER OR BOHEMIAN TERRIER	
COUNTRY OF ORIGIN	CZECH REPUBLIC OR SLOVAKIA
ORIGINAL AND TODAY'S FUNCTION	HUNTER OF FOXES AND OTHER PESTS, TERRIER TRIALS

APPEARANCE

BODY

The Cesky Terrier has a moderately long body. The topline arches slightly over the well-muscled loins. The muscular croup is well developed, moderately full and arched. The tail is approximately 7–7³/₄ in (18–20 cm) long and is not set too high. In repose the tail is carried down or in a sickle curve. The ribs are well sprung and the belly has a slight tuck-up. Cesky Terriers have well-muscled shoulders. The elbows are not turned inward or outward. The circumference of the trunk, measured just behind the elbows, should

Cesky Terriers

ideally be 17¹/₂–17³/₄ in (44–45 cm). The legs are vertical. They are parallel to each other and are well angulated. The feet are fairly big and the toes are arched. The hind feet are smaller than the front feet. The strong neck is moderately long and slopes upward from the shoulders. The dog is quite throaty but has no dewlap.

HEAD

The head is fairly long, yet in proportion to the rest of the body. There is a visible, but not a pronounced stop. The nose bridge is straight. The occipital peak and central furrow are barely marked. The high-set and medium-sized ears have a triangular shape. They are carried pendulously and cover the opening of the ear. The eyes are moderately big, are set fairly deep and are almost completely hidden under the eyebrows. Cesky Terriers have a scissors or pincer bite.

SHOULDER HEIGHT

Varies from 10–12¹/₂ in (25–32 cm). The ideal height for dogs is 11¹/₂ in (29 cm) and for bitches 10¹/₂ in (27 cm).

WEIGHT

Cesky Terriers should be no lighter than 13¹/₂ lb (6 kg) and no heavier than 22¹/₂ lb (10 kg).

COAT

Its thick, long hair shines like silk and waves slightly. The long hair on the head forms a beard and eyebrows. The Cesky Terrier is trimmed

Cesky Terrier

according to a particular style for this breed (see Grooming).

COLORS

The most usual color is blue-gray in different shadings. Light brown is rarer, though recognized. Both colors are permitted, with and without white, yellow or grayish markings on the head, neck, chest, belly, lower part of the legs and under the tail. A white collar and tail tip are accepted too. Blue-gray Cesky Terriers are always black at birth and the light coffee colored variety will have a chocolate brown color at birth. The coat changes to a lighter color in due course. Some dogs may not have their definite color until they are two.

TEMPERAMENT

CHARACTER

Cesky Terriers are intelligent, good-humored, stable, affectionate and sociable dogs. They are very adaptable and therefore they will feel at ease both in an apartment as well as in the countryside. They are quite peaceful indoors, but outdoors in the open they will show the sporty, brave and per-

Cesky Terrier

Cesky Terriers

severing side of their character. Contrary to most terriers that are used in semi-terrier trials, the Cesky Terrier is quite obedient, gentle and compliant. It has an excellent scent.

SOCIAL BEHAVIOR

This sociable dog gets on well with its own kind and with other household animals. In addition, it is always loving to children. They can be somewhat cautious of strangers, but not extremely so, if they have been well socialized.

GENERAL CARE

GROOMING

The great advantage of this type of coat is that the Cesky does not molt. Its hair does however grow, and therefore it needs to be trimmed regularly, whereas the hair on the belly and legs is left long, as well as hair on the muzzle and eyebrows. Pets are usually trimmed four times a year in this style. Depending on the quality of the coat, longer hair needs to be brushed thoroughly twice or more often per week and combed afterwards to prevent tangles. Clip the excess hair between the pads of the feet and remove loose hairs in the ear canals. Show dogs need more grooming.

TRAINING

The training of this breed is not very demanding. The dogs are intelligent and prepared to please their owners. It is important to let the puppy meet with various people and different animals and to experience a variety of situations to enable it to grow up to be an equable adult.

EXERCISE

The Cesky Terrier has an average demand for exercise. This dog likes to frolic and play but it also enjoys walks through a wood or across open countryside. It will not bother the dog if you have to miss a day. You need to watch your dog because it is happy to wander off, although a well-trained Cesky Terrier will come back quickly if its owner calls it.

USES

In its country of origin this breed is still used for its original function but otherwise it is predominantly loved for its companionship.

Cesky Terrier

SKYE TERRIER	
COUNTRY OF ORIGIN	SCOTLAND
ORIGINAL FUNCTION	HUNTER OF FOX, BADGER AND OTTER

APPEARANCE

BODY

Skye Terriers have a long body with a long and level topline. The loins are short and the hindquarters are strong, full and well developed. The upper half of the tail hangs down and the lower half curves forward. The tail should be carried no higher than the backline. The chest is deep and the ribs are oval. Skye Terriers have short, muscular and well-angulated legs. The front feet are generally bigger than the hind feet and they point straightforward. The neck is long and slightly arched.

HEAD

The head is long, strong, moderately wide and tapers gradually to the foreface. The stop is moderate. The majority of Skye Terriers have erect ears, but some have pendulous ears. The medium-sized, expressive eyes are set close together. Skye Terriers have a scissors bite.

SHOULDER HEIGHT

These dogs are only $9^1/_2$–$10^1/_2$ in (25–26 cm) high, but the length of the body, measured from nose to tail tip might be over $39^1/_2$ in (100 cm). Bitches can be a little shorter.

WEIGHT

These dogs weigh $22^1/_2$–$26^1/_2$ lb (10–12 kg).

COAT

The Skye Terrier has a double-layered coat. The topcoat is long, hard and straight, without curls, and the undercoat is short, soft and woolly.

COLORS

The coats can be black, various shades of gray and roe-deer brown. Another usual color is

Skye Terrier

Skye Terrier puppy

blonde with dark markings on the ears, nose and tail. A white patch on the chest is permitted. The eyes should preferably be dark brown.

TEMPERAMENT

CHARACTER

These equable, dignified dogs are full of character. They are highly adaptable, and will feel entirely at ease in a busy city as well as on a farm. They display plenty of courage and they are quite watchful without being barkers. On average they are compliant. They are loyal and affectionate

Skye Terriers hail from the Scottish island of Skye

towards the family and they tend to become one-person-dogs.

SOCIAL BEHAVIOR

This breed is well known for being reserved with strangers. They do not generally like everybody. A well-socialized Skye Terrier will not be un-friendly to your guests but it does not like to be treated with too much enthusiasm. It generally mixes well with dogs, although some dogs can be a little domineering to members of their own sex. When the dog is well socialized it will not be a problem to other pets, such as cats. They can get on well with kids, but they do not understand or appreciate teasing.

Skye Terriers

GENERAL CARE

GROOMING

The Skye Terrier re-quires little grooming, even though the coat would appear to sug-gest otherwise. A good brushing once or twice a week is sufficient to keep it in good condi-tion. The hair should fall into a parting from the center of the back. The hair round the muzzle will have to be brushed and combed more frequently. Re-move loose hairs and dirt from the ear canals and it is also advisable to trim excess hair between the pads of the feet.

Skye Terrier

TRAINING

Dogs of this breed need to be trained with mutual respect, by an owner who is fair and consistent, and gives the dog freedom to develop its own ini-tiative. If you pay considerable attention to its socialization, it will benefit its character.

Skye Terriers

EXERCISE

The Skye Terrier has a moderate need for exercise. It loves to accompany you in woodland or open countryside, but a walk downtown will make it happy too. If you do not feel like a walk one day, the Skye Terrier will adapt to the situation and not misbehave. Indoors the dog is quite peaceful. Traditionally the Skye Terrier was a hunting dog. Its hunting instincts are still noticeable, though in a weakened form. Bare this in mind when you allow your dog off-leash in an area with plenty of game and ensure that your dog returns to you when you call it.

USES

This dog is hardly used for its original function. Today it has exclusively become a companion.

Skye Terrier

AUSTRALIAN TERRIER	
COUNTRY OF ORIGIN	AUSTRALIA
ORIGINAL FUNCTION	VERMIN DESTROYER

APPEARANCE

BODY
The Australian Terrier's body is fairly squat and it is low on its legs. The trunk is long in comparison with its height. The topline is level and the ribs are well sprung. The tail is usually docked in countries where this is permitted. The legs are straight and have small, well-closed feet.

HEAD
The long head has a flat skull and a long and strong jaw. The ears are small, they are carried erect and they must be set on high. The small eyes have a penetrating expression. Australian Terriers have a scissors bite.

SHOULDER HEIGHT
Approx. $9^1/_2$ in (25 cm).

WEIGHT
On average these dogs weigh $12-14^1/_2$ lb (5–6 kg).

COAT
The hair is straight with an extremely harsh structure. It should not be wavy or woolly. Its length is about 2 in (5 cm), except for the short hair on the ears and feet.

COLORS
The Australian Terrier has a blue trunk and a deep tan color on its legs and face. The cowlick could be blue, silver, or even pure sandy colored or red. The eyes are dark.

TEMPERAMENT

CHARACTER
These dogs are well known for their vigilance, watchfulness and cou-

Australian Terrier

rage. They are very lively and self-confident, a little self-willed and independent. Their intelligence is above average and they are quite playful and cheerful. They are good guard dogs and keen to bark.

SOCIAL BEHAVIOR

Australian Terriers get on quite well with children provided they are not teased. Unknown visitors will not be accepted immediately, but it is not right to say that the Australian Terrier is suspicious by nature. If the dog is socialized with cats at an early age, there will be no problems later on. It is typical for a terrier to be domineering towards its peers.

Australian Terrier

GENERAL CARE

GROOMING

Australian Terriers with the right harsh coat texture do not need a lot of grooming. The coat will need a good brush and comb about once a week, and plucking from time to time. The old hair needs to be plucked by hand to allow new hair to grow. Ensure that no hair is growing in the ear canals and pluck excess hair by hand. An Australian Terrier that is well cared for will shed little hair indoors.

Australian Terrier

TRAINING

The Australian Terrier needs strict training because this self-confident freebooter will sometimes only follow its own ideas. A lenient handler will end up with an impossible dog that will not listen to any instructions and will go its one way. If these dogs are trained well and the rules are clear, they can learn new commands very easily. Make sure that you control their barking habits during their upbringing. The command to come to heel should be taught at a very early age.

EXERCISE

The adaptability of the Australian Terrier is phenomenal, and they will be quite happy living in an apartment. However, they are active working dogs that love to romp outdoors. Ball games are their favorites.

USES

A well-trained Australian Terrier can be registered for flyball and agility classes. Do not expect any laurels because these dogs do not perform well consistently. They need to enjoy what they are told to do and can be quite stubborn once they lose interest.

Australian Terrier

NORFOLK AND NORWICH TERRIERS	
COUNTRY OF ORIGIN	ENGLAND
ORIGINAL FUNCTION	MUCH USED AS A TRUE TERRIER (A DOG WHICH HUNTS ANIMALS SUCH AS BADGERS AND FOXES UNDERGROUND) AND AS A VERMIN DESTROYER

APPEARANCE

BODY

Norwich and Norfolk Terriers are two separate breeds, but this split did not come about until 1964. Until that time these two breeds were known as the Norwich Terrier, split into one variety with erect ears and one with folded ears. Now there are two separate breed standards, which have a lot in common (understandably), but obviously they differ according to the position of their ears. The Norwich has medium-sized erect ears with pointed tips and the Norfolk has V-shaped folded ears dropped forward close to the cheeks. Both breeds typically have a small and compact body build. They are low down on the legs and have a short, level topline. The tail is set in line with the back and is carried erect, but not too gaily. In countries where this is permitted the tail is usually medium docked. The legs are short, strong and straight. The feet are round and have thick pads.

Norfolk Terrier

HEAD

This terrier has a broad skull that is slightly rounded. The length of the wedge-shaped and powerful muzzle is shorter than the length of the skull. The stop is clearly marked. The eyes are oval shaped and very expressive. Norwich and Norfolk Terriers have a big and strong scissors bite.

SHOULDER HEIGHT

Their size is around 9¹/₂–10 in (25–26 cm).

Norfolk Terrier

Norfolk Terrier

WEIGHT

Both breeds weigh between 11¹/₄–15¹/₂ lb (5–7 kg).

COAT

These dogs have hard, close-lying wire-coats. The

Norfolk Terrier

hair on the neck and shoulders is longer, and shorter on the head and the ears, with exception of the (light) mustache, beard and eyebrows.

COLORS

The Norfolk and Norwich Terrier come in a variety of red shades, straw-yellow or wheaten, black with rusty-brown or gray-colored. A small amount of white is permissible although not preferred. The eyes are dark.

TEMPERAMENT

CHARACTER

These breeds are renown for their foolhardy and courageous character. They are cheerful, friendly, uncomplicated and lively, as well as playful and enterprising, impudent and cunning, full of initiative and sometimes a little stubborn.

SOCIAL BEHAVIOR

These dogs get on fairly well with other dogs. There are seldom problems with children; on the contrary they make excellent playmates. Visitors are greeted noisily, but they soon stop and make friends. If the dog is well socialized there will be no problems with cats or other pets.

Norfolk Terrier

GENERAL CARE

GROOMING

These breeds need a brush and a comb about once a week. The beard and mustache might need more frequent care because they get dirty more quickly. Plucking excess and old hair is usually done by hand about twice a year. This is a job you can do yourself or leave to a professional dog trimming parlor. Excess hair between the pads of the feet must also be trimmed.

TRAINING

Both Norwich and Norfolk Terriers are intelligent dogs and learn quite quickly. They are and will

Norwich Terriers

always be real terriers and quite self-willed. Make sure you are consistent and vary their drills to have the best results. Do not forget to reward them by giving them food or playing with them and they will respond quickly.

EXERCISE

Although both breeds are very energetic and they will accompany you on long walks for hours on end, they usually adjust to different circumstances. The weather conditions have little effect on these breeds. They are always ready for a walk or a ball game. Their true nature will force them to grab any opportunity to dig in your yard. If you are attached to your well-furnished yard you need to bare this in mind.

USES

These dogs make excellent family dogs. You might wish to try agility skills with these dogs, but do not expect consistent results; the pleasure it gives you and your dog should be most important.

Norwich Terrier

Dandie Dinmont Terrier

DANDIE DINMONT TERRIER	
COUNTRY OF ORIGIN	ENGLAND
ORIGINAL FUNCTION	INDEPENDENT HUNTER, PARTICULARLY OF RABBITS

APPEARANCE

BODY

According to the breed standards the Dandie Dinmont Terrier's body compares with that of a weasel. It owes this description to the typical topline: the back is quite low at shoulder level and rises again over the loins to drop again at the base of the tail. The tail is about $7^3/_4$–10 in (20–25 cm) long. It is thick at the base, broadens in the middle and ends in a point. It is carried slightly over the topline, in saber-fashion. The well-developed chest hangs low between the forequarters and the ribs are rounded. The shoulders are well laid back, but should not be too heavy. The muscular legs are short and straight, with well developed bones and they are set quite far apart. The hindquarters are a bit longer than the forequarters, with well-angulated knee joints and low hocks. The feet are round, with well developed feet pads. The front feet are bigger than the hind feet. They are vertical or turned slightly outward. The neck is well muscled and strong.

HEAD

The sturdy and big head is in proportion with the rest of the body. Its skull is wide between the eyes and tapers towards the eyes. The forehead is arched. The deep, strong muzzle is shorter than the skull (3:5) and tapers a little towards the tip of the nose. The thin pendant ears are set far back and fairly low. They are about $2^3/_4$–4 in ($7^1/_2$–10 cm) long and have tassels that are typical for the breed. The eyes are set low and far apart.

Dandie Dinmont Terrier

They are big, full and round, but should not bulge. Dandie Dinmont Terriers have a scissors bite.

SHOULDER HEIGHT

The breed standards do not stipulate any guidelines regards shoulder height. These dogs tend to be about 9 in (23 cm) high.

WEIGHT

They vary from $17^1/_4$–24 lb (8–11 kg) with lighter dogs preferred at shows.

COAT

A Dandie Dinmont Terrier has a unique coat, with a soft underlayer and a harder outer coat. It should be crisp to the touch and there should be no parting on the back. The hair on the head and the face, ear tips and underneath the dog is soft-textured.

Dandie Dinmont Terrier

Dandie Dinmont Terrier

COLORS

The Dandie Dinmont coat comes in two color patterns:
- pepper runs from dark-blue to silver-gray. A middle shade is preferable and the topknot is always creamy white.
- mustard varies from reddish brown to beige.

Both color patterns are accepted with some white hair on the chest, as well as white claws. The eyes are always deep hazel.

TEMPERAMENT

CHARACTER

These are cheerful, equable, fairly calm, intelligent dogs. They behave in a dignified cautious manner. They sense the atmosphere in the home and in those respects they differ from most terriers. What they share is their watchfulness and perseverance. A Dandie Dinmont is devoted to its handler and family.

SOCIAL BEHAVIOR

Dandie Dinmonts are quite sociable. They can usually get on quite well with other dogs, both indoors and outdoors.

Dandie Dinmont Terrier

They will not easily be tempted to play, they prefer to do their own thing. If the young puppy has been well socialized with cats and other pets there should be no problems. The Dandie Dinmont is usually quite friendly and gentle to kids. They will bark if they hear visitors, but that is all. They are friendly dogs.

GENERAL CARE

GROOMING

The Dandie Dinmont needs to be taken to a trimming parlor about twice a year to have the dead hair plucked out by hand and the coat needs to be

Dandie Dinmont Terriers

re-styled. Of course the dog should be combed and brushed regularly, preferably with a small slicker brush. You yourself can clip excess hair from between the pads of the feet. Dogs that are to be shown will require additional grooming.

TRAINING

Fortunately this dog is not difficult to train. You will see the best results if you reward the dog when it behaves as required and if you provided plenty of variety during the training sessions. A Dandie Dinmont Terrier is intelligent and will know what you require of it, but it will not show much enthusiasm for lengthy drills that do not seem to make sense. In such a case the dog can be stubborn and very contrary in its behavior.

EXERCISE

If you are an avid walker, this dog will be happy to accompany you. If you are less sporty the dog will not mind: even if you do not have enough time once in a while the dog will adapt. A well-trained Dandie Dinmont is a dog you can take

Sealyham Terrier

Dandie Dinmont Terrier

SEALYHAM TERRIER	
COUNTRY OF ORIGIN	WALES
ORIGINAL FUNCTION	INDEPENDENT HUNTING DOG OF FOXES, BADGERS, OTTERS AND OTHER GAME

with you wherever you go. They are peaceful indoors.

USES

These dogs make good companions.

APPEARANCE

BODY

The Sealyham Terrier is a long-legged strong dog with a long body. Its medium-sized trunk has well sprung ribs and strikingly powerful hindquarters. In countries where this is permitted the tail is usually docked. It is set on in line with the back and is carried erect. Viewed from the side the buttocks stretch beyond the onset of the tail. The chest is broad as well as deep and is set low between the front legs. Viewed from the side the highest point of the shoulder should be in line with the hindquarters of the close-fitting elbow. The legs are short and straight, with round and vertical feet. The fairly long neck is powerful and muscular.

HEAD

The skull is wide between the ears and slightly arched without overhanging jaws. The jaw is square and long. The medium-sized ears are carried pendant along the cheeks and have rounded tips. The eyes are moderately big and round. Sealyham Terriers have a powerful and relatively big scissors bite.

SHOULDER HEIGHT

Sealyham Terriers should not be any higher than $12^{1}/_{2}$ in (31 cm).

Dandie Dinmont Terrier

Sealyham Terrier

WEIGHT

Dogs are approx. 22¹/₂ lb (10 kg) and bitches weigh a little less.

COAT

The long, hard, wire-haired outer layer of the coat covers a weather-resistant underlayer.

COLORS

The coats of Sealyham Terriers come in solid white or white with lemon-yellow, brown, blue, or badger-colored markings on the head and/or ears. The eye rims are preferred with black pigmentation, but it is not compulsory. The nose should be black.

TEMPERAMENT

CHARACTER

Sealyham Terriers are equable, friendly, brave and tough dogs. They are active outdoors, but indoors they are very quiet. You will only hear their deep bark if there is danger. Although they are very devoted to their handlers and families they are fairly self-willed. They remain playful to a good old age and most of them love digging.

SOCIAL BEHAVIOR

The Sealyham gets on reasonably well with other dogs, but it needs to have socialized with cats and other pets from a very early age. Provided this dog has had positive experiences with kids since it was a puppy, it will be able to mix well with children when it is grown up. The way in which the dog responds to familiar and unfamiliar visitors depends on its socialization, but a well-trained Sealyham usually behaves perfectly.

GENERAL CARE

GROOMING

These breeds need to be taken to a trimming parlor about twice a year to have the dead hair plucked out by hand and the coat needs to be re-styled according to the current fashion. Usually the hair on the head (except for the furnishings), the ears, neck, back and tail are trimmed, while the hair on the legs, the lower part of the forechest, the belly and the thighs are left long. The coat will need a good regular brushing and combing, particularly the furnishings (mustache, beard and eyebrows) need extra attention. You will not need to worry about tangles because the texture of the coat is not prone to tangling. It is easy to brush dirt and mud from the coat once it has dried.

TRAINING

In general the Sealyham Terrier is an intelligent dog that is keen to learn but it may occasionally try to evade you if it is up to mischief. A consistent and direct approach is essential to achieve a successful training. Good socialization with all kinds of people and animals is important for their character development.

Sealyham Terrier

EXERCISE

The Sealyham Terrier has an average need for exercise and generally adjusts to circumstances. They will be quite happy in an apartment. Nevertheless the Sealyham likes to leave its bed for a walk off-leash in the woods or the park, and ball games will meet with its approval, too. Sealyhams like to dig up the soil, something the avid gardener should not forget.

USES

This fairly uncommon dog is a popular companion. Given the chance this dog will keep your yard, farm and stables free of vermin.

Sealyham Terriers

Bull Terrier

BULL TERRIER	
COUNTRY OF ORIGIN	ENGLAND
ORIGINAL FUNCTION	THIS DOG WAS BRED TO BE A FIGHTING DOG AROUND THE MIDDLE OF THE NINETEENTH CENTURY, BUT TODAY IT IS KNOWN AS A FRIENDLY COMPANION

APPEARANCE

BODY

Bull Terriers have short, strong backs and broad, well-muscled loins. The short tail is low-set and it is carried horizontally. The tail is thick at the base and ends in a point. Viewed from the front the chest and ribs are deep and well arched. The shoulders slope. The well-angulated legs are set parallel and have strong, round bones. Bull Terriers have round, sturdy feet with well arched toes. The dry neck is muscular, long and arched.

HEAD

The long head is strong and deep to the end of the muzzle, but it is not coarse. Viewed from the front it is egg-shaped and has no hollows or dints. The skull between the ears is almost flat. The ears are small and thin, They are set close together and are carried totally erect. The small eyes are triangular and are set obliquely. Bull Terriers have a scissors bite.

SHOULDER HEIGHT

The breed standards have set no guidelines concerning size and weight. However, it is essential for the build to create an impression of a substantial dog.

COAT

The shiny coat is short, feels hard and lies close to the body.

COLORS

Bull Terriers may be plain white, white with markings on the head and brindle. There are also red, black brindle, fawn colored (roe-deer) and tricolor dogs. With non-white animals, one color must predominate. The eyes should be as dark as possible.

TEMPERAMENT

CHARACTER

This is a friendly, spontaneous and cheerful dog. When they are young their boisterousness and enthusiasm can cause them to break a thing or two. They are brave and physically very tough on themselves, almost without any sensitivity to

The striking profile of a Bull Terrier

pain, and consequently you might not notice an ailment until it is almost too late. Generally they are healthy dogs. They are very devoted to the family but they can be quite self-willed, even stubborn.

SOCIAL BEHAVIOR

Bull Terriers usually get on excellently with children. They are quite tolerant and can stand a fair amount of rough and tumble. They might be a little too boisterous for very small kids. Cats and other pets should give no problems either once the dog is well socialized. Some Bull Terriers are rather keen to fight other dogs, depending on their nature and the way in which they were socialized and brought up. It is not advisable to introduce a male dog if you already have a male dog in the house, no matter the breed. There is bound to be a confrontation, even though it

Bull Terrier

might take years. A Bull Terrier will bark at visitors, but that is as far as it will go. It is naturally friendly to grown-ups and kids. In a critical situation this dog will not desert you.

GENERAL CARE

GROOMING

A Bull Terrier requires very little coat care. It is sufficient to groom the dog once a week with a soft bristle brush. During the molt a rubber massage mitt or a rubber brush is the best way to remove dead hairs from the coat. Keep the claws short. The ear canal needs to be cleaned occasionally with a special ear cleaner.

Bull Terrier

White dogs may need to be washed, but try to limit this to a minimum. Give this dog a soft bed, because otherwise it might develop calluses on pressure points.

Bull Terrier

TRAINING

These dog needs to be trained from a very young age. Once they are mature they are too strong and uncontrollable for you to change them. Particularly pulling on the leash could be a problem. The Bull Terrier is intelligent and can learn quite quickly, but it is also stubborn. The trainer needs a lot of patience, and must be consistent, while showing understanding and care. If its training is varied the dog will not lose interest, nor give up. Take your puppy to a good obedience training course.

EXERCISE

Bull Terriers need quite a bit of exercise. Whether you take your dog on long walks downtown or in the woods, play ball games in the yard, take it swimming or on bike-walks, they all make suitable exercise for

Bull Terrier

USES

This breed is almost entirely kept as a much-appreciated family dog. The average Bull Terrier does not like dog sports, most certainly not if they are competitive, but it will not mind if it the sport is meant for fun.

Bull Terriers

this breed. Do not take this dog on a bike-walk before it is fully-grown and never for too long.

Bull Terriers

Miniature Bull Terrier

Miniature Bull Terrier

choose the Miniature Bull Terrier. It is a pity that this attractive breed has been overshadowed by its big brother for many years, because it deserves more notice. In most countries there will be one or more breeders or fans that wish to perpetuate and promote this breed.

MINIATURE BULL TERRIER
COUNTRY OF ORIGIN	ENGLAND

APPEARANCE

The breed standard of the Miniature Bull Terrier is no different to that of the Bull Terrier, the only difference being size: the shoulder height of a Miniature specimens will not reach beyond $13^3/_4$ in (35 cm). This dog needs to have a maximum substance in accordance with its size.

DETAILS

Miniature Bull Terrier

The characteristics of the Miniature Bull Terrier and Bull Terrier are potentially the same. The Miniature Bull Terriers however, has a smaller stature and although they are noticeably strong considering their shoulder height, the Miniatures are much more manageable. People who like Bull Terriers, but who would prefer a smaller dog, will naturally

Miniature Bull Terrier

Staffordshire Bull Terrier

STAFFORDSHIRE BULL TERRIER

COUNTRY OF ORIGIN	ENGLAND
ORIGINAL FUNCTION	A FIGHTING DOG, NOW
	A RELIABLE FAMILY DOG

APPEARANCE

BODY

Staffordshire Bull Terriers have a compact and muscular body, with a level topline and short loins. The tail is moderately long, set on low and is carried down. The forequarters are wide with a deep forechest and well-arched ribs. The elbows should not be loose. The straight legs have strong bones. They are set quite far apart. The strong and

Staffordshire Bull Terrier

moderately big feet point outward slightly. The muscular neck is short and dry.

HEAD

The short and deep head, with a broad skull has a clear stop and visibly strong-developed jaw muscles. The lips fit tightly. Their ears are either rose or half prick, but neither should be too long or too heavy. The eyes are round and moderately big. Staffordshire Bull Terriers have a solid and complete scissors bite.

SHOULDER HEIGHT

Their size varies from $13^1/_2$–$16^1/_2$ in ($35^1/_2$–$40^1/_2$ cm).

WEIGHT

Dogs range between $27^1/_2$–$37^1/_2$ lb (13–$17^1/_2$ kg) and bitches between 24–32 lb (11–15 kg).

COAT

The short, smooth and close coat lies close to the skin.

COLORS

Staffordshires have black, red, roe-deer, blue and many kinds of brindle coats, with or without white. Any amount of white is permitted, whether it is a small patch on the chest or an almost completely white dog. Plain white dogs are possible too. Black and tan and liver colored coats are undesirable colors.

TEMPERAMENT

CHARACTER

The Staffordshire Bull Terrier, sometimes called an English Staff, is a stable, intelligent, affectionate and fairly obedient dog. It has a cheerful and positive outlook

Staffordshire Bull Terrier

235

on life and possesses a fair amount of self-confidence. It tends to be very brave and tough on itself. In general these are active and playful dogs, that can be rather boisterous in their enthusiasm. They notice what is happening around them and they will certainly bark if they suspect danger. They are very adaptable and can live happily on a farm as well as in an apartment in the city.

SOCIAL BEHAVIOR

These dogs generally get on quite well with kids. They do not mind a rough game and they seldom feel snubbed. Provided a Staffordshire Bull Terrier is well socialized, cats and other pets will give no problems. Puppies mix well with their peers, but once they are mature the Staffs prefer to be lord and master. Particularly male dogs will be ready to fight other males. These dogs will bark if they sense something wrong, but generally they are friendly to anybody.

Staffordshire Bull Terrier

GENERAL CARE

GROOMING

The Staffordshire Bull Terrier needs very little coat care. It is sufficient to brush it once a week with a soft bristle brush. During the molt you can easily remove dead hairs with a rubber massage mitt. Keep the claws short.

Staffordshire Bull Terriers are big dogs in a compact form

TRAINING

The Staffordshire Bull Terrier is very intelligent and learns quite quickly. A consistent and loving upbringing with plenty of variety and action is what it needs. Pay a lot of attention to its socialization, as this is beneficial to its character development.

EXERCISE

These dogs are very energetic and love games; the rougher, the better. Particularly rope tugging is a favorite activity, but do teach the dog to let go when enough is enough. They can jump very high, and love playing with balls and retrieving. They will be happy to accompany their owners on long walks and it does not matter if they are taken downtown or into the countryside. If a Staff has enough exercise it will be peaceful indoors.

USES

This breed rarely participates in dog sports, but that does not mean the dogs do not have the ability. Considering their energy, agility and intelligence they should do quite well in agility skills and flyball. The Staffordshire Bull Terrier is a suitable family dog for people without sufficient space to keep a big dog, but who would very much like to have a "big" dog.

Staffordshire Bull Terrier

AMERICAN STAFFORDSHIRE TERRIER	
COUNTRY OF ORIGIN	USA
ORIGINAL FUNCTION	IN THE NINETEENTH CENTURY THEY WERE BRED AS FIGHTING DOGS, BUT TODAY THEY ARE RELIABLE COMPANIONS

APPEARANCE

BODY

American Staffordshire Terriers are very muscular dogs with a squat body frame. Their powerful impression should be in accordance with their size. The topline is short and strong and the ribs are well arched. The tail is short considering the size of the dog. It is set on low and tapers to a point. The tail should not curl or be carried over the back. The chest is broad and deep. Its width causes the forequarters to be set wide apart. They are vertical on the compact feet and they have round bones. The medium-sized neck is heavy, without any dewlap and arches slightly.

HEAD

This dog has a medium-sized skull and pronounced muscles of the cheek. The stop is clear and the jaws are distinct. The medium-sized muzzle has well-closed lips. The ears are set on high and are carried erect (prick ear) or partly laid back (rose ear). The round eyes are set low and wide apart. American Bull Terriers have a scissors bite.

SHOULDER HEIGHT

Dogs should preferably be 18–19 in (45^1/$_2$–48 cm). For bitches this can be 17–18 in (43–46 cm). However, a good height and weight ratio is more important.

COAT

The short hair feels stiff. It lies close to the skin and should be shiny.

American Staffordshire Terrier bitch

American Staffordshire Terrier

COLORS

Any color is permitted. However, plain white, more than 80 % white, black and tan and liver are not preferred at shows. The most common colors are different shades of brindle, red and beige, possibly with white markings and a black mask.

TEMPERAMENT

CHARACTER

American Staffordshire Terriers, sometimes called

American Staffordshire Terrier dog

Am Staffs by dog lovers, are honest, extrovert, uncomplicated, affectionate, active and boisterous dogs. They are watchful, very courageous and persistent, and quite tough on themselves. They are very loyal to their families and generally quite obedient too. Male dogs can be a little domineering.

SOCIAL BEHAVIOR

Am Staffs generally get on well with children and are quite tolerant, but because of their boisterous nature they make better playmates for bigger kids. Mixing with peers can be problematic. Particularly male dogs may make their presence felt, although a lot depends on the socialization and upbringing of the dog. A well-trained Am Staff will guard home and property, but will not be unfriendly towards strangers. It will however demonstrate its worth if its family is in danger. Once it has been well socialized with cats and other pets there should be no problems.

GENERAL CARE

GROOMING

Their coats need minimal care. From time to time you will need to remove the dead and loose hairs with a rubber massage mitt or brush.

TRAINING

These dogs are intelligent and keen to learn new things. They pick up many things in a short time and as a rule they enjoy their tasks. An Am Staff is not suitable for indulgent, inconsistent folk with little experience of dogs.

This breed's strength is awesome and if the handler is not in control it will not be a pleasure

American Staffordshire Terrier

taking the dog out for a walk. The handler needs to be consistent and start the training at an early age. Teach the dog not to tug at its leash and if necessary you should discourage its tendency to attack other dogs.

EXERCISE

Am Staffs are active dogs and can run and play for hours on end. They need quite a lot of exercise although they will not mind if you cannot manage every day. In a large yard where the dog can play with a ball, it can take care of its own need for exercise. Ball games are favorites, and bike-walks or swimming are all suitable activities for this dog.

USES

The right owner can supervise this dog in numerous dog sports where it will perform well. There are plenty of examples of Am Staffs that have won obedience certificates. Some of these dogs, though not many, have been used successfully for serious working tasks, such as avalanche and guide dogs.

American Staffordshire Terrier

SECTION 4   Toy terriers

YORKSHIRE TERRIER

COUNTRY OF ORIGIN	**ENGLAND**
ORIGINAL FUNCTION	**VERMIN DESTROYER AND COMPANION**

APPEARANCE

BODY

The body of the Yorkshire Terrier is strongly built and well in proportion with a compact trunk and a flat topline. The legs are straight and the round feet have black claws. The tail is carried a little above the topline. It is usually docked to a medium length in countries where this is permissible.

HEAD

The fairly small head has a flat skull with a muzzle that is not overtly long and is carried proudly. The eyes are moderately big, with an intelligent expression and the eyelids have a dark pigmentation. They are set forwards facing. The ears are small and V-shaped. They are carried erect or semi-erect and are covered with short hair.

WEIGHT

Yorkshire Terriers are small dogs and on average they weigh $6^1/_2$ lb (3 kg).

COAT

This breed has a very long, silky coat with a straight parting down the back to the tail. The shiny coat is straight and should not wave.

Yorkshire Terrier

COLORS

Yorkshire Terriers are steel-gray with a rust-brown tan and golden-brown hair on the head. The brown color on the head should not stretch down over the neck. There should be no other colors among the tan or the blue. The eyes are dark. Puppies are black and tan when they are born. Their coats become a lighter color after a while.

TEMPERAMENT

CHARACTER

These dogs are lively and active, courageous (sometimes overconfident) and intelligent. They are attached to their families and affectionate, but also quite stubborn. Yorkshire Terriers are noisy, alert and very vigilant.

SOCIAL BEHAVIOR

Provided kids do not treat them as a toy and do not invade their territory, these dogs will not cause any problems. Yorkshire Terriers can be rather foolhardy in their courage towards other dogs, but they get along fine with cats if they have been together since they were young. There could be problems with other pets such as rodents, as they

Yorkshire Terriers need a lot of grooming

Yorkshire Terrier

TRAINING

The Yorkshire Terrier learns quite quickly, but it can also display some obstinacy. If you are consistent and teach the dog positively, with fun and variety, this dog will generally learn to listen quickly. Unfortunately the Yorkshire Terrier is a little over-alert and can bark incessantly and unnecessarily. Never encourage vigilance because it will only exacerbate the situation, but rather teach the dog that a few barks will do.

EXERCISE

The Yorkshire Terrier adapts to the family in its need for exercise. They are active indoors as well as outdoors. Digging and romping is something they love doing. Their size makes them easy to keep in an apartment.

USES

Although this dog is intelligent and agile,

Yorkshire Terrier

you will seldom meet it at agility classes. It is very suited as a small family dog – preferably not with very young kids – and it is a respected and popular show dog.

are a natural prey to this little terrier. Good socialization with all pets in the household could prevent such difficulties. Strangers will be announced noisily and it might take a while before the Yorkshire Terrier accepts them.

GENERAL CARE

GROOMING

The Yorkshire Terrier requires intensive daily grooming, which is why these dogs often have short trimmed coats, particularly if they are pets. Like this it is much easier to keep the coat in good condition, and a regular comb or brush will be adequate. The grooming of show dogs needs far more expertise and time on behalf of the owner. The coat of show dogs is usually protected to keep its condition by rolling it up with curling papers and washing it with special products to keep its resilience and shine. The hairs are usually tied back from the eyes with a rubber band or ribbon.

Yorkshire Terrier

Silky Terrier

SILKY TERRIER

COUNTRY OF ORIGIN	AUSTRALIA
ORIGINAL FUNCTION	RATTER

APPEARANCE

BODY

The Silky Terrier has a low body approximately one fifth longer than its shoulder height. The topline is level with a light arch towards the croup. The tail is usually docked in countries where this is permissible. It is set on high and is carried straight and gaily. The chest is moderately wide and reaches beyond the elbows. The well-angulated legs have light bones without heavy muscles. The long neck is slightly arched at the top.

HEAD

The Silky Terrier has a wedge-shaped head with a skull that is slightly longer than the muzzle. The skull is flat and should not be too long between the ears. The stop is not too deep. The small ears have a V-shape. They are high set on the head and are carried erect. The eyes are small and full of expression. Silky Terriers have a scissors bite.

Silky Terrier

SHOULDER HEIGHT

This varies from 9–9³/₄ in (22¹/₂–25 cm).

WEIGHT

Silky Terriers range between (3¹/₂–4¹/₂ kg).

COAT

Their hair is smooth, shiny and silky. They do not have an undercoat. The hair on the body of adult dogs should be 4³/₄–6 in (12–15 cm) long. On the head the hair forms a long cowlick, but the hair on the muzzle and cheeks should not be too long. There is a clear parting on the back from the neck to the base of the tail.

COLORS

Silky Terriers are exclusively bred in blue with tan. The blue coat may be silver-blue, dove-blue or slate-blue and the tan should be a strong blue. Silky Terriers are born as black and tans. The blue color develops later. The claws are dark, and so are the eyes.

TEMPERAMENT

CHARACTER

These dogs have lots of character, they are cheerful, full of energy, agile and intelligent. They are loyal and devoted towards their owners and in general they are quite submissive and obedient. They are small, yet very vigilant and do not hesitate to act if they feel their family is being threatened. They like being near to their owners and do not like being left alone. This is not necessary because you can take a well-trained Silky Terrier with you wherever you go and it will not embarrass you.

SOCIAL BEHAVIOR

Silky Terriers generally mix well with children. They need to be well socialized with other pets otherwise they are

Silky Terriers

Silky Terrier

likely to chase them. Initially they tend to be vigilant with people they do not know, but only mildly. They get on well with other dogs, but once challenged they will stand their ground.

GENERAL CARE

GROOMING

This breed does not need as much care as you might think. Fifteen minutes of grooming on a daily basis is quite adequate. The dog might need to be washed occasionally with a special dog shampoo. Check the teeth from time to time to see that there is no tartar and keep the claws short. A Silky Terrier hardly sheds any hair.

TRAINING

Silky Terriers are very easy to train. They are quite intelligent and keen to learn. Devote plenty of time to their socialization, as this is beneficial to their character development.

EXERCISE

The Silky Terrier will fit in with its family as far as exercise is concerned. It makes this breed suitable for sporty people as well as those who are less sports-minded. It will be happy in a house with a yard, as well as in an apartment. Ball games are their favorites.

USES

These dogs are popular as companions. They are rarely seen at dog sport competitions, but that does not refer to their unsuitability. If they are well supervised they will do well at agility skills. Of course the track will need to be adapted to their size.

Dachshunds

8

Rare on two counts: smooth-haired *Kaninchen* Dachshund with a tiger-like dappled color

DACHSHUND	
COUNTRY OF ORIGIN	GERMANY
ORIGINAL FUNCTION	HUNTING DOG USED FOR GAME ABOVE AND BELOW GROUND, SUCH AS BADGERS, RABBITS, WILD BOAR, ROE DEER AND FOXES

APPEARANCE

BODY

The Dachshund has long, high withers, a level back, slightly arched loins and a long, broad and muscled croup. The tail forms a continuation of the topline and must not be too curved. The belly is moderately tucked up. The forequarters are muscular, low and broad, and the thorax is oval when viewed from the front. The deepest point of the well-developed chest is exactly behind the forelegs. The breastbone is heavy and so prominent that a depression appears on either side. The shoulders are long and well laid back. The straight legs are well angulated and parallel. The feet are close, with arched toes. The dry, muscular neck is carried high and has a slight arch.

HEAD

The long head gradually tapers uniformly towards the tip of the nose, but is not pointed. The stop is not prominent – the less prominent, the better – and the nose bridge is slightly arched. The lips are narrow and fit tightly. The high-set ears are nicely rounded; they should not be pointed or folded. The front edge of the ears lies close to the cheeks. The eyes are oval and of medium size. They must

Long-haired black and tan Dachshund

not have a piercing expression. Dachshunds may have a scissors or a pincer bite.

CHEST SIZE AND WEIGHT

Dachshunds are divided into three sizes, which are not crossed:

- the Standard Dachshund has a chest size of $13^1/_2$ in (35 cm). It should weigh no more than 20 lb (9kg);
- the Miniature Dachshund has a chest size of $11^1/_2$–$13^1/_2$ in (30–35 cm) and weighs from 11–15 lb (5–7kg);
- the Kaninchen or little rabbit has a chest size less than $11^1/_2$ in (30 cm) and weighs approx. $8^3/_4$ lb (4kg).

COAT

This breed comes in three coat varieties: smooth, wire-haired and longhaired, which are not crossed. The Smooth Dachshund has short, dense, sleek hair that lies flat on the body. The whole body of the Wire-haired Dachshund is covered with a close, dense, wiry coat and a dense undercoat. The muzzle is furnished with a beard and a mustache, and the eyebrows are bushy. The hair on the ears should be very short in the wire-haired variety. Long-haired Dachshunds have a long, glossy, smooth and silky coat. The feathering is longer on the lower part of the body, the trousers, the tail and the ears.

COLORS

Dachshunds are bred in many different colors:

- solid red. This color varies from yellowish red to dark red, with or without any interspersed black hairs in the coat. White markings are undesirable. Animals with a pure red coat are preferred in this color pattern;
- bicolor dogs. These have black or brown as

Dachshunds loved to dig, including this wire-haired Miniature

Rode kortharige Teckel

a ground color, with rusty or yellow tan markings above the eyes, on either side of the mouth, on the lower lip, inside the ears, on the legs, on the underside of the tail and around the anus. White or extensive tan markings are undesirable;

- dappled (tiger-like or brindle) dogs have a black, red or gray ground color evenly marked with light-colored patches. None of the colors should dominate. Blue eyes, also known as wall eyes, do occur in Dachshunds with tiger-like markings, but are not desirable. Brindle animals are red or yellow with darker stripes. These are uncommon.

In addition to these three color patterns, other colors are also permitted, including "wild boar" which is so popular in the wire-haired. Although many different coat colors are permissible for all varieties of coat, Smooth and Long-haired Dachshunds are mainly bred in solid bright red and in black and tan – occasionally also in brown and tan and rarely in brindle. The wire-haired variety comes almost exclusively in wild boar and less often in black and tan.

TEMPERAMENT

CHARACTER

Dachshunds are lively and known for their intelligence, resourcefulness and cleverness. They are not the most obedient of dogs and can be willful in an almost comical fashion. These dogs are full of contrasts. They display great courage, toughness and tenacity in the field, but in a family set-

Red short-haired Dachshund

ting they like their home comforts, crave attention and are visibly deeply upset by harsh words. They are devoted to their owners and do not like being left alone, although they do have a tendency to take off on their own if they are gripped by their hunting instinct. Most Dachshunds are fairly energetic and active, but not boisterous. A Dachshund will bark when it hears unfamiliar noises and the bravest specimens will not shrink from stopping intruders in their tracks. These dogs have an excellent nose. They are determined in

their behavior and once they have set their minds on something, they are very skillful at manipulating their owners.

SOCIAL BEHAVIOR

Its own people come first and the Dachshund has little time for strangers. This is shown by a rather reserved manner towards people the dog does not know. When socialized with children it tends to get on well with them, but it will not tolerate being used as a plaything. Since we cannot expect too much from very young children in this respect, a Dachshund is generally better suited to a family with older kids. Dachshunds usually get on well with other dogs but will put up a fight if challenged. Because of its strong hunting instinct, this breed is not suitable as a pet with small pets such as rabbits. However, a Dachshund can live in harmony with cats provided the dog has been properly socialized with them from an early age.

GENERAL CARE

GROOMING

The coat of the Smooth Dachshund needs little attention. Brushing it with a soft rubber brush or mitt from time to time is sufficient to remove dead and loose hairs. The Wire-haired Dachshund needs to have its coat plucked about twice a year, depending on the condition of the coat. The hair on the head should be kept very short and close. In addition to regular plucking, you could occasionally brush the coat with a firm bristle brush. The Long-haired Dachshund is happy with occasional grooming, especially in areas that are prone to tangling. In the Long-haired and the Wire-haired varieties you

Long-haired Dachshund pup

Smooth-haired black and tan Dachshund

advisable to take your Dachshund to a good puppy training course and possibly to a follow-up course as well. It will help build its character if a Dachshund is introduced to all kinds of people, animals and situations.

EXERCISE

Although Dachshunds are quite able and happy to accompany their owners on long walks, they will usually adapt to circumstances. Nevertheless, it is a good idea to give this dog plenty of exercise, so that it stays in good condition. If you let your Dachshund run off-leash there is a great risk that its hunting instinct will emerge and the dog will suddenly run off. For the same reason these dogs will not always respect the boundaries of your yard either, and a solid fence around your property is therefore recommended. Dachshunds are generally strong and healthy and can live for a long time, but in view of their long backs, climbing stairs and overfeeding should be avoided.

USES

In many countries Dachshunds are still used for hunting. They can also be trained for various hunting trials. However, they are mainly kept as companion

need to clip excess hair growing between the pads because thorns, little stones and the like can get stuck in it. In all three varieties you will need to check the ears for dirt regularly and clean them with a suitable lotion, if necessary. Keep the claws short. Most Dachshunds like their food and often manage to get more than is healthy for them because of the imploring look in their eyes. Do not give in because a fat Dachshund is an unhealthy one. Excess weight puts (too much) strain on its long back and causes many other problems.

TRAINING

The Dachshund has a mind of its own and is strong-willed, a temperament that calls for a consistent training. With plenty of patience and understanding, it is possible to teach a Dachshund a great deal, although it will never slavishly follow your commands. Dachshunds can be very upset and may sulk if they feel they have been punished unfairly. It is

Long-haired black and tan Dachshund

dogs. They are not suitable for dog sports such as flyball and agility because of their long backs, while their willfulness makes these remarkable dogs less enthusiastic about advanced agility training.

DETAILS

The Smooth Dachshund is the original strain of this family of dogs. The Wire-haired and Long-haired varieties were attained by crossing the Smooth Dachshund with other breeds. Occasionally, a litter is born in which one or more puppies turn out to be a different variety to that of their parents. If there is any doubt about the correct size of the adult dog, then the body size is measured just behind the elbows and if necessary, the pedigree is adjusted accordingly.

Wire-haired Dachshund

The most common color for wire-haired Dachshunds is this "wild boar" coat

9 Spitz and other primitive breeds

Siberian Husky

SIBERIAN HUSKY

COUNTRY OF ORIGIN	ALASKA
ORIGINAL AND TODAY'S FUNCTION	SLED DOG, BRED FOR SPEED

APPEARANCE

BODY

The moderately solid body should not be too short or too cobby. The strong, level back is moderate in length and the taut loins are slightly arched. When the dog is at attention, the tail is carried over the back in a sickle curve. It trails down in repose. The chest is strong and deep, but not too broad and the ribs are well sprung. The shoulders are powerful and well laid back. The legs are straight and muscular, not too heavily boned. The stifles are well bent. The feet are oval-shaped, medium size and solid. The neck is of medium length, strong and arched.

HEAD

The head is medium size and slightly rounded on top. The muzzle and skull are roughly the same length. The ears are set on high and relatively close together. They are medium size, carried erect and well furred inside. The eyes are set slightly obliquely, with a friendly, interested expression. Siberian Huskies have a scissors bite.

SHOULDER HEIGHT

Dogs range from $20^1/_2$–$23^1/_2$ in (53–60 cm) and bitches stand 20–22 in (51–56 cm) tall.

WEIGHT

Dogs weigh approx. 44–60 lb (20–27 kg) and their female counterparts weigh $35^1/_4$–$35^1/_4$ lb (16–$22^1/_2$ kg).

Siberian Husky

Siberian Husky

COAT
Siberian Huskies have a double coat. The undercoat is dense, soft, fluffy and of sufficient length to support the outer coat. The very dense outer coat is smooth and soft.

COLORS
All colors and markings are permitted. The eyes may be brown or blue. There are also Huskies with one blue and one brown eye, as well as Huskies with different colors in a single eye.

TEMPERAMENT

CHARACTER
The Siberian Husky is a friendly, good-natured and gentle dog with lots of energy, initiative and a considerable hunting instinct. It is fond of its owners and its family – and displays its affections – but in spite of this will always be independent and slightly willful in temperament. A Husky is usually not vigilant.

SOCIAL BEHAVIOR
Siberian Huskies tend to get on fine with their own kind, but they will not be bullied. Their contact with other pets should be carefully supervised. Animals such as cats, rabbits and chickens are not ideal pets for a Siberian Husky because of its hunting instinct. Most Huskies get along very well with children and are quite tolerant. Huskies, more so than many other dogs, are pack-oriented and as they usually find it hard to be left on their own it is advisable to keep more than one Husky. Although indifferent towards strangers, they will never be aggressive to people.

GENERAL CARE

GROOMING
The degree of care required with this breed is strongly linked to the way the dog is kept and to the time of year. Dogs that are kept outdoors often have a nicer coat and shed less than their colleagues who are kept as pets. A teasel brush is an efficient tool for removing loose hair from the coat during the molt.

TRAINING
An aspiring Husky owner should realize that this dog is an out and out sled dog. This breed was never meant to bond closely with a handler or to be a perfectly obedient pet for its owner. You will

Siberian Huskies must not work during hot weather

need a bold and consistent approach to teach your Siberian Husky anything. This also requires considerable patience and an understanding of the archetypal character of Arctic dogs. Although a great deal can be achieved with the right approach you will never be able to turn a Husky into a perfectly obedient dog. A Husky will only obey a command if it sees the point of it and will not let itself be bribed with kind words or tidbits.

EXERCISE

The Siberian Husky needs a tremendous amount of exercise and this is an absolute must. Allow at least an hour and a half each day to go running with the dog or to take it for a long walk. Lonely Huskies that are locked up with too little exercise and few activities will howl and become destructive. This is not the fault of the dog but entirely that of the owner who has chosen the wrong dog or assumed that the dog would be easy to train.

Siberian Husky

The Siberian Husky is in its element in snow

Always take a Husky out on a leash and make sure your yard is well fenced, otherwise it is likely to run off. Siberian Huskies will usually be happy to share an outdoor kennel with one or more other dogs. Their dense coat protects them bril-

liantly from the cold. However, these dogs should not be worked in the summer, as their constitution is not able to cope with exertion on hot days.

USES

If you would like to learn more about sled dog sports and become actively involved then you have chosen the right breed. This dog is renowned for its speed worldwide. Nearly all sled dog races with pure-bred dogs are won by a team of Siberian Huskies. This dog will also do well in a very active family but is not suitable as an "average" companion dog.

Siberian Husky

ALASKAN MALAMUTE

COUNTRY OF ORIGIN	ALASKA
ORIGINAL AND TODAY'S FUNCTION	SLED DOG, SPECIFICALLY FOR PULLING HEAVY LOADS

APPEARANCE

BODY

The Alaskan Malamute has a powerful, compact body, with heavy bones and strong muscles. The level back slopes gently down from shoulder to hip, and the loins are muscular. The tail is set level with the topline and is carried above the back like a waving plume, not in a stiff curl or hanging down. The chest is deep. The legs are straight and muscular, heavy in bone, with large, compact feet. The strong neck is moderately arched.

HEAD

The head is broad and powerful. The skull is broad between the ears and gradually narrows to the eyes. The large muzzle narrows slightly towards the forenose and is neither too snipey nor too full. The wedge-shaped ears are comparatively small. They are carried erect and forward when the dog is at attention, and are set at the side of the head. The eyes are almond-shaped. They are moderately large and set obliquely. Alaskan Malamutes have a scissors bite.

SHOULDER HEIGHT

For dogs the ideal size is approx. $25^{1}/_{2}$ in (64 cm) and for bitches approx. $22^{1}/_{2}$ in (58 cm).

WEIGHT

Dogs are approx. $83^{1}/_{2}$ lb (38 kg) and bitches approx. $68^{1}/_{4}$ lb (31 kg).

Alaskan Malamute

An Alaskan Malamute needs a real boss

COAT

The Alaskan Malamute has a double wiry coat; the outer coat is thick and coarse and the undercoat is dense, oily and woolly. In the summer months the coat is obviously shorter and less dense.

COLORS

Permitted colors are light gray to black, always with white on the belly and the legs. A cap-like or mask-like marking on the face is required and a white spot on the neck or a white collar is permissible. A solid white coat color is also allowed, but is rare. There are also specimens with a brownish coat. This color is not accepted worldwide. The eyes are always brown.

TEMPERAMENT

CHARACTER

This intelligent breed is fairly independent, friendly and loyal, but also dignified, with a mind of its own and can be dominant. Subservience is foreign to its nature. The average representative of the breed has plenty of self-confidence and an

Alaskan Malamute

equable disposition. It is sober and hardy with a coat that provides excellent protection against adverse weather conditions. It can be kept in an outdoor kennel, provided it has (close) contact with its handler or another dog. Alaskan Malamutes do not like to be alone.

SOCIAL BEHAVIOR

Alaskan Malamutes generally get on well with children, and they are friendly with everyone. This makes them totally unsuitable as watchdogs. They can display dominant behavior towards other dogs of the same sex, but this is the exception rather than the rule. The owner should be aware of this and strongly discourage his dog from

Alaskan Malamute

an early age from displaying dominant behavior towards other dogs in the street. Cats are not really suitable as companions in the same house, unless the dog has grown up with the cats since puppyhood. In this case there should be no problem. Because these dogs have a keen hunting instinct it is advisable to socialize them with all kinds of other animals – including cattle.

GENERAL CARE

GROOMING

The weather-resistant coat of the Alaskan Malamute does not need a lot of grooming. Dirt and mud can be simply brushed off when dry. An Alaskan Malamute is a heavy shedder, particularly during the spring and the fall. During the molt it is best to use a coarse comb with a double row of metal teeth to remove loose hairs from the undercoat.

TRAINING

Despite its friendly nature, this dog needs a firm hand in its training, as the average Malamute needs consistent supervision. A calm, equable handler who is physically strong and exudes a natural authority will get the best out of this breed. If these requirements are met, then Malamutes are fairly obedient and capable of learning relatively many commands quickly. Do bear in mind, though, that the exercises should be fun for the dog. Monotonous drills will inevitably lead to protests and the dog will simply refuse to do them. During the training particular attention should be paid to the "Come here" command. Alaskan Malamutes are good eaters, and using food as a reward will help you achieve great results. Good socialization, which should ideally begin with the breeder, has

Alaskan Malamute

Alaskan Malamute

GREENLAND DOG

COUNTRY OF ORIGIN	**SCANDINAVIA**
ORIGINAL AND **TODAY'S FUNCTION**	**SLED DOG AND HUNTING DOG**

a very positive influence on character building, but the opposite is also true.

EXERCISE

Perhaps the most important aspect of keeping an Alaskan Malamute, apart from attention and company, is its huge exercise needs. If you do not fancy taking the dog out for a run or a brisk walk for an hour each day then you should look for a different breed. When taking your Alaskan Malamute for off-leash walks, you should make sure that it is well-trained and can be recalled promptly.

USES

In many countries there are organizations that arrange sled dog trials or trials with wheeled carts when there is no snow. Under the supervision of an experienced trainer with an understanding of the dog's character the Malamute can even take part in other sports such as agility. There have also been a few Malamutes that performed well as avalanche search dogs and in obedience trials. These sports should be done purely for fun, because this breed is usually outperformed by one of the sheepdog breeds.

APPEARANCE

BODY

The Greenland Dog is a strong dog built for stamina. The trunk is slightly longer than the shoulder height. The body is strong and muscular, with a broad chest, a level back and straight, wide loins. The croup slopes slightly. The rather thick tail is set high and is carried curled over the back. The legs are straight, with heavy bones and strong muscles. The elbows are held close to the body, but can move freely. The hind legs have slight angulation. The feet are round, fairly thick and powerful. The neck is strong and fairly short.

HEAD

Greenland Dogs have a broad, slightly domed skull and a pronounced – but not exaggerated – stop. The broad nose bridge is perfectly straight. The wedge-shaped muzzle tapers to the tip of the nose, but should not be snipey. The lips are thin. The triangular, erect ears are fairly small with rounded tips. The eyes are set slightly obliquely in the skull and should neither protrude nor be set too deeply. Greenland Dogs have a strong scissors bite.

SHOULDER HEIGHT

The dogs of this breed should have a minimum size of 23¹/₂ in (60 cm). The minimum size for bitches is 21³/₄ in (55 cm). There is no maximum size.

COAT

The Greenland Dog has a double coat. Its undercoat is soft and dense, and the outer coat is dense, straight and harsh. The coat is free from curl or wave. The hair is thick and longer on the underside of the tail.

COLORS

All coat colors and color combinations are allowed in this breed, except albino. The nose is black, but may be flesh-colored in winter. Dark eyes are preferred, although lighter shades occur in dogs with a light colored coat.

TEMPERAMENT

CHARACTER

Greenland Dogs are archetypal Arctic dogs with a temperament to match. This breed is not terribly suitable as a companion dog, as it lacks the right disposition. They are confident and calm, equable, independent and headstrong, as well as sober and undemanding, fairly tough on themselves and dominant. The Greenland Dog is a sociable animal that finds it difficult to be alone. It rarely barks, but howls

quite a lot. This breed has an amazing amount of energy and tremendous stamina.

SOCIAL BEHAVIOR

Greenland Dogs cannot stand being left on their own. If you are considering buying such a dog then you should get at least two but ideally several specimens. They are perfectly happy together in an outdoor kennel. They can display dominant behavior towards dogs from outside their pack. Because of their keen hunting instinct, they do not usually get on well with cats and other pets. Friends and strangers alike are usually greeted boisterously, often with excited howling. Although their size and appearance may scare off intruders, these dogs are not suitable as guard dogs.

Greenland Dog

GENERAL CARE

GROOMING

The care required depends on the climate where the dog lives and on how it is kept. Dogs kept outside in colder areas need very little grooming, but the coats of dogs living in warmer climes and/or of specimens that frequently come indoors should be combed and brushed regularly. A comb with a double row of metal teeth is the most efficient tool during the molt when the dead undercoat is shed.

TRAINING

The Greenland Dog is difficult to obedience train, as it is rather headstrong, dominant and

Greenland Dog

independent. Although fond of its handler, it generally prefers to follow its own instincts. A lot of patience and understanding is needed to teach it the basics, but its owner should not expect too much. The Greenland Dog is primarily a sled dog, that is used to and bred for working in a harsh climate. This is not a companion dog.

EXERCISE

It should be obvious that the Greenland Dog needs a great deal of exercise. The best form of exercise you can offer this breed is by letting it pull a sled or a wheeled cart. If this is not an option for you then you are better off looking for a different breed. Greenland Dogs are generally too strong to accompany you when you go bike-walking as they can easily pull you over. The urge to walk for many hours is deeply rooted in them and they are capable of covering huge distances. If they are given the chance – for instance, because of a faulty fence around a yard – they love to take to their heels and may stay away for days. For the same reason it is not recommended to let them walk off-leash.

USES

This breed is eminently suited in front of a sled and people who want to use this dog for this purpose make an excellent choice. This dog should not be worked when it is hot, which means temperatures above 59 °F (15 °C.)

Samoyed

SAMOYED	
COUNTRY OF ORIGIN	NORTH WESTERN SIBERIA
ORIGINAL FUNCTION	SHEEPDOG, HUNTING DOG AND SLED DOG

APPEARANCE

BODY

The Samoyed is slightly longer than tall, with a medium-length, muscular and level back. The abdomen is moderately tucked up. The ribs are well sprung and the chest reaches nearly to the elbows. The legs are muscular with strong bones. They are well angulated with strong, supple

Greenland Dog

Samoyed

wrists. The supple feet are oval and the slightly arched toes are not too tightly closed. The tail is set high and reaches to the hocks. It is carried over the back or to the side when the dog is alert or in movement. The moderately long neck is strong and carries the head proudly.

HEAD

Samoyeds have a powerful, wedge-shaped head with a pronounced but not too prominent stop. The powerful muzzle is roughly the same length as the skull and tapers to the well-developed nose. The nose bridge is straight. The corners of the mouth are turned up slightly, which in combination with the slanting eyes creates the impression that the dog is always smiling. The mobile, comparatively small ears are set high and are triangular in shape. The deep-set eyes are almond-shaped and set slightly obliquely, with an intelligent and vigilant expression. Another important feature is the gait, which should be

effortless, light, full of drive and powerful. Samoyeds have a scissors bite.

SHOULDER HEIGHT

Dogs are $22^1/_2$ in (57 cm) at the shoulder and bitches stand $20^3/_4$ in (53 cm) tall. Deviations of $1^1/_2$ in (3 cm) up or down are permitted.

COAT

The outer coat is hard, harsh and stands away from the body, while the undercoat is short, soft and dense. Samoyeds have a collar around the neck and shoulders and the tail is also profusely coated.

COLORS

The coat color is white, cream or white with biscuit markings. Samoyeds have black pigment. The nose may pale slightly during the winter months. The eyes are dark brown.

TEMPERAMENT

CHARACTER

The Samoyed is a dog of contradictions: it is friendly and cheerful, highly intelligent and intuitive, reasonably obedient, though never subservient and occasionally even downright stubborn. It is sensitive, gentle-natured and affectionate, but not obtrusively so. The Samoyed loves to roam, has tremendous stamina and remains playful into old age. Samoyeds are rather vocal and can be reasonably vigilant, although this is not true of all specimens.

Samoyed

SOCIAL BEHAVIOR

Samoyeds are gentle-natured and patient with children, but they tend to ignore strangers. As a rule, they get on fairly well with other dogs, although this breed does have its more dominant specimens. Socialization with cats and other pets is very important. Remember that the Samoyed has traditionally been used as a hunting dog and it will not stick to simply chasing after other animals.

Samoyed

Keep the claws short.

TRAINING

This breed should be obedience trained very early and the training should be based primarily on consistency. Make sure there is plenty of variety in the drills. A monotonous training will have an adverse effect on the Samoyed and its stubbornness will take over. Teach the dog from a very young age to come to you when called and let it experience as many positive encounters with cats and other pets as possible. Show your authority but always with a friendly yet firm touch. You will not win the respect of this breed by using harsh words and physical punishments.

GENERAL CARE

GROOMING

Do not brush the coat of a Samoyed excessively, because this could damage the undercoat. During the molt a coarse comb with a double row of metal teeth is an ideal tool for removing loose hairs from the undercoat.

Male Samoyed

EXERCISE

The Samoyed is built to walk and run for long distances. It needs plenty of exercise and is impervious to the weather. Once the dog is fully grown, take it for long daily walks to keep it in good shape. If the dog gets enough exercise then it tends to be calm in the house. Samoyeds can have a tendency to roam, so a well-fenced yard is essential.

USES

The Samoyed belongs to a select group of officially recognized sled dogs breeds. You could consider taking up sled racing with your dog, but bear in mind that this will demand a lot of time and effort and is more a way of life than a hobby. This dog will also do well as a companion dog in an athletic family.

Samoyed bitch

Scandinavian hunting dogs

WEST SIBERIAN LAIKA

COUNTRY OF ORIGIN	WESTERN SIBERIA AND NORTHERN URALS
ORIGINAL AND TODAY'S FUNCTION	IN ITS REGION OF ORIGIN THE WEST SIBERIAN LAIKA IS USED FOR VARIOUS HUNTING DUTIES FROM TRACKING TO RETRIEVING AND POINTING BIG AND SMALL GAME, BOTH INDIVIDUALLY AND IN SMALL GROUPS. IN ADDITION, THESE DOGS ARE USED AS SLED DOGS AND AS WATCHDOGS.

APPEARANCE

BODY

The West Siberian Laika has a slightly rectangular build. The back is level and strong with pronounced withers. The loins are short and the croup slopes gently. The abdomen is tucked up. The high-set tail is carried in a stiff curl over the back or loin. The legs are well angulated. The oval-shaped feet have close-knit toes. The muscular neck is devoid of dewlap.

HEAD

The dry head has the shape of an isosceles triangle. The stop is not pronounced. The muzzle is long and the lips are dry. The erect ears are triangular in shape. The oval eyes are set obliquely. West Siberian Laikas have a scissors bite.

SHOULDER HEIGHT

Dogs stand 22–23$^1/_2$ in (56–60 cm) tall and bit-

West Siberian Laika

ches are 20$^1/_2$–22$^1/_2$ in (52–58 cm).

COAT

The coat is double and consists of a straight, rough outer coat with a dense undercoat.

COLORS

West Siberian Laikas are permitted in nearly all colors, including white, pepper and salt, any shade of red and gray, black and parti-colored. Black and white spotted dogs are permitted, but not desirable. The eyes are brown.

West Siberian Laika dog

TEMPERAMENT

CHARACTER

Dogs of this breed are even-tempered, honest, sober and uncomplicated animals. They have an open, friendly disposition and are blessed with a fair amount of intelligence. They are also eager to learn. West Siberian Laikas have an iron constitution and are impervious to the weather.

SOCIAL BEHAVIOR

This pure breed gets on well with its own kind and is usually gentle and friendly with children. Your visitors will be announced but then greeted warmly. However, in a real emergency they will be reliable guards and defenders.

West Siberian Laika

GENERAL CARE

GROOMING

The West Siberian Laika needs relatively little grooming. During the molt, which is usually brief but heavy, you can easily remove loose hairs from the coat using a metal comb with a double row of teeth.

TRAINING

West Siberian Laikas are not difficult to train. They learn commands quickly and love to work. Like any other breed, this dog also needs a consistent approach to its training but a firm hand is not recommended.

EXERCISE

These dogs can walk for many hours at a time. In addition to the regular daily walks, you should allow at least one hour every day to let the dog burn off its energy by running or playing off-leash.

USES

In its country of origin this breed is still in demand as a versatile hunting dog, but also as a sled dog and a watchdog. A well-trained West Siberian Laika can do well in nearly all areas of dog sports, such as obedience and agility. It can

West Siberian Laika

also be used as a working dog, for instance as a tracker or avalanche rescue dog.

West Siberian Laika bitch

KARELIAN BEAR DOG

COUNTRY OF ORIGIN	FINLAND
ORIGINAL AND TODAY'S FUNCTION	HUNTING DOG USED FOR LARGE GAME

APPEARANCE

BODY

The Karelian Bear Dog is a medium-sized dog of sturdy build. The body is slightly longer than tall. The back is level and muscular with a broad, strong and slightly sloping croup. The tail is set on high, of moderate length and is carried in a curve over the back with the tip touching the body on either side or on the back. A natural bobtail is acceptable. The ample chest is moderately wide and reaches roughly to the elbows. The brisket is clearly visible, but not very wide. The ribs are moderately sprung and the belly is slightly tucked up. The shoulders are sloping and, particularly in dogs, well developed. The elbows are pointing backwards and are set perpendicular to the shoulders. The hindquarters are strong and muscular, straight and parallel, with wide, long, muscular thighs. The moderately bent stifles are pointing forwards. The powerful forelegs are straight and parallel. The closed forefeet are well arched, round and pointing forwards, while the hind feet are slightly longer and less arched. The gracefully arched neck is muscular and of medium length. Karelians have no dewlap.

HEAD

The head is wedge-shaped. The broad skull is slightly round when viewed from the front and the side. The stop is weak, fairly long and gradually tapers to the skull. The brow ridges are slightly developed. The deep muzzle gradually tapers to the nose

Karelian Bear Dog

and the nose bridge is straight. The forenose is large. The lips are thin and tight and the jaws are very strong. The eyes are relatively small and oval in shape with an alert and fiery expression. The erect ears are set fairly high and are medium size with rounded tips. Karelian Bear Dogs have a scissors bite.

SHOULDER HEIGHT

The ideal size is $22\frac{1}{2}$ in (57 cm) for dogs and $20\frac{1}{2}$ in (52 cm) for bitches, with a deviation of approx. $1\frac{1}{2}$ in (3 cm) permitted.

WEIGHT

Dogs weigh $55\frac{1}{4}$–$61\frac{3}{4}$ lb (25–28 kg) and bitches $37\frac{1}{2}$–44 lb (17–20 kg).

COAT

The outer coat is coarse and straight. The hair on the neck, the back and the backs of the upper legs is longer than on the rest of the body. The undercoat is soft and very dense.

Karelian Bear Dog

COLORS

The coat color is black, often mat with a bear-brown glow and usually with sharply-defined white patches on the head (blaze), neck, chest, belly and legs and also on the tip of the tail. The forenose is black. The eyes are various shades of brown, but never yellow.

TEMPERAMENT

CHARACTER

The Karelian Bear Dog is vigilant, clever, aggressive, quick, independent and extremely headstrong, but also sensitive at the same time. Its aggressiveness means that it will not budge if provoked by another dog. Its speed, strength and ability to calculate its chances will usually help it emerge from a fight unscathed. Tough on itself and able to cope with all weathers, it can be kept in an outdoor kennel, provided it is not denied close contact with its family.

SOCIAL BEHAVIOR

In spite of its rather antisocial tendencies towards its own kind, the Karelian Bear Dog is free from any aggressiveness towards people. They are very loyal to their own people and will accept friends of the family without any problem. They are aloof towards strangers and any attempts at getting acquainted should come from the dog itself. Potential owners are strongly advised not to keep several males, while females could also create problems amongst themselves. A dog and a bitch will often live together in harmony. Contact with other pets should be properly supervised. The Karelian Bear Dog is certainly not an average companion dog.

GENERAL CARE

GROOMING

The coat of this dog requires relatively little attention. During the molt it is sufficient to remove loose hairs with a teasel brush. Do not use a metal comb or a slicker brush, because these will damage the hair. In common with most Scandinavian dogs, Karelian Bear Dogs do not have a typical "doggy odor."

TRAINING

The Karelian Bear Dog needs a handler who exudes a natural authority and who can appreciate its headstrong temperament. Slavish obedience is out of the question. The relationship with a Karelian should be based on mutual respect. Because of its sensitive nature it finds it hard to cope with any unfairness or punishments

Karelian Bear Dog

Karelian Bear Dog

and it can take days until it is prepared to forget any affront.

EXERCISE

Karelian Bear Dogs have above-average exercise needs. They should be able to stretch their legs for at least an hour each day. Taking it out for a run or a bike-walk would be an option, provided the owner has the dog under control. Off-leash walks are only really feasible if the dog is very well trained. Free runs around the house are only possible if the yard or area is properly fenced. They have a strong urge to escape and can disappear for hours or even days.

USES

In its country of origin the Karelian is used almost exclusively to hunt for big game. Its exceptional nose makes it eminently suitable for scenting. Active sports such as agility might be possible for the Karelian, except that the presence of other dogs could cause problems. This is not a dog for team sports. There are quite a few potential devotees who are wondering if this breed is suitable for freighting. Because of its independent disposition and its lack of aggressiveness towards people this is not advisable. If the dog is forced to freight, then this could lead to uncontrollable, dangerous situations.

Lundehund

LUNDEHUND

COUNTRY OF ORIGIN	**NORWAY**
ORIGINAL FUNCTION	**THE LUNDEHUND (LUNDEFUGL IS NORWEGIAN FOR PUFFIN) SPECIALIZES IN ROBBING PUFFIN NESTS OF YOUNG BIRDS TO TAKE THEM TO ITS HANDLER. PUFFIN NESTS ARE OFTEN FOUND ALONG THE COAST, HIGH UP ON THE CLIFFS AND IN ROCKY CREVICES. THIS TYPE OF HUNTING HAS NOW BEEN BANNED IN THE COUNTRY OF ORIGIN.**

APPEARANCE

BODY

The Lundehund has a relatively long body with a strong, level back and a short, long croup. The short tail is set high and is carried curled over the back. The chest is long and spacious and the belly is not tucked up. The legs are straight and strong. The hind legs are well angulated. The feet have at least five well-arched toes. The medium-length neck is dry and strong. The head is carried fairly low.

HEAD

The head is wedge-shaped, with a moderately broad, not particularly domed skull and striking supraorbital ridges. The stop is sharply defined and the nose bridge is somewhat concave. The ears are broad at the base and are carried erect. The dog is able to fold its ears backwards in such a way that the ear opening is closed off. The eyes should not protrude. Lundehunds have a scissors bite.

SHOULDER HEIGHT

Dogs stand $13^{3}/_{4}$–15 in (35–38 cm) tall and bitches are $12^{1}/_{2}$–$13^{3}/_{4}$ in (32–35 cm).

WEIGHT

Dogs weigh approx. $15^{1}/_{2}$ lb (7 kg) and bitches are generally a little lighter.

COAT

The close-lying, double coat is dense and feels fairly rough. The hair on the head and on the front of the legs is shorter than on the rest of the body. It is longer on the tail, the backs of the legs, the front of the neck and the underside of the chest.

COLORS

The most common color is reddish brown to fallow with more or less black hair tips, combined with white markings. Gray and black specimens are also allowed but (extremely) rare. The nose is black and the eyes are brown.

The Lundehund is the only breed that can bend its front legs laterally

TEMPERAMENT

CHARACTER

Dogs of this breed are cheerful, mischievous, very agile and spirited. They are self-willed, but not obstinate. Lunde-

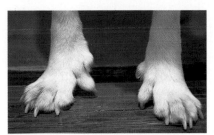

The additional toes of a Lundehund

hunds are intelligent and cunning. Although affectionate, they can also entertain themselves quite well. A Lundehund rarely barks, but will certainly use its voice if there is something wrong.

SOCIAL BEHAVIOR

This dog generally gets on well with its own kind and with children. Contact with other pets should be no problem either. Towards strangers it usually adopts an indifferent attitude and tends to remain cautious.

GENERAL CARE

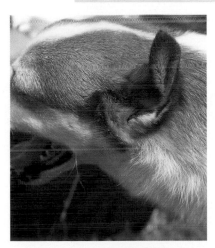

The Lundehund can fold its ears closed

GROOMING

The coat of the Lundehund needs an average amount of care. During the molt a good comb, such as a teasel brush, can be used to remove loose hairs. Keep the claws short.

TRAINING

The training should be as varied as possible. If this dog has to repeat the same exercises over and over again it will certainly rebel. If the exercises are presented to the dog in a fun way then a Lundehund can learn commands very well and fairly quickly and will usually be obedient. Make sure that you are consistent and clear at all times.

EXERCISE

This breed has average exercise needs, but does like to be kept busy. The normal daily walks, supp-

lemented with playing in the yard, provide sufficient exercise for the Lundehund. It is remarkable that this dog can entertain itself reasonably well with ball games and the like. If you love going for long walks, then your Lundehund will have no problems with that; it can walk for many hours without tiring.

USES

This rare breed is no longer allowed to perform its original function and is nowadays mainly kept as a companion dog. In view of its speed and nimbleness a sport such as agility could be worth considering.

DETAILS

Experts cannot agree whether this exceptionally rare breed is indeed a member of the Canis familiares (domesticated dog). It is possible that the breed is part of the Canis ferus (primitive wild dog) because it possesses a number of features that are unknown in any other breed of dog. To protect its very sensitive ears from dirt and dust when creeping through rocky crevices the dog can quite literally close its ears. This ability is sometimes also used when the owner issues a command the dog does not like. In addition, this breed has six toes and eight pads on each foot compared with five toes and six pads in other dogs. Lundehunds are also the only dogs that can spread their front legs out to the side. Another characteristic unknown in any other dog breed is its ability to bend its head completely backwards over the back, which is useful for crawling through narrow rock crevices.

Lundehund puppy

Norbottenspets

legs are well angulated with small, compact and supple feet. Dew claws are permitted but not desirable in this breed. The dry, muscular neck is fairly long and is carried high.

HEAD
The head is wedge-shaped. The skull may be either straight or slightly domed. The muzzle is dry, with thin, tightly closed lips. The stop is well pronounced. The medium-sized ears are carried erect and pointing forwards. The dark eyes are moderately large, with a vigilant expression. The Norbottenspets has a scissors bite.

SHOULDER HEIGHT
Dogs stand approx. $17^3/_4$ in (45 cm) tall and bitches are a little smaller: approx. $16^1/_2$ in (42 cm).

COAT
The coat is double, consisting of a rough, hard outer coat and a soft undercoat.

COLORS
All coat colors are permitted in this breed, although white animals with sharply defined yellow or reddish brown markings are preferred. The nose is black.

TEMPERAMENT

CHARACTER
The Norbottenspets is a vigilant, fairly independent dog with a friendly,

NORBOTTENSPETS (POHJANPYSTYKORVA)	
COUNTRY OF ORIGIN	SWEDEN
ORIGINAL AND TODAY'S FUNCTION	HUNTING DOG USED FOR FEATHER. THIS DOG TREES FEATHER GAME, STAYS ON THE SPOT AND BARKS UNTIL THE HUNTER ARRIVES. THIS BREED HAS ALSO BEEN USED AS WATCHDOGS.

APPEARANCE

BODY
The Norbottenspets is a small dog with a square body outline and a cobby yet light build. The back is level and powerful and the well-developed croup slopes slightly. The tail is set high and is carried to the side. The abdomen is slightly tucked up. The straight

Norbottenspets

though somewhat headstrong temperament. It is extremely active, very vocal, intelligent and smart. Dogs of this breed have tremendous stamina. They are energetic and love to roam. As a rule, these are strong, healthy dogs.

SOCIAL BEHAVIOR

This dog tends to get on well with other dogs.

Norbottenspets

Visits from strangers will be announced, but that is usually all. They are friendly with everyone. Animals that are part of their own family will be accepted without any problems, provided they have been used to them from puppyhood. Contact with children will rarely be a problem, although these dogs will not meekly accept everything from them.

Norbottenspets

GENERAL CARE

GROOMING

This dog needs relatively little grooming. Occasional brushing, particularly during the molt, is sufficient to keep the coat in good condition. Keep the claws short.

TRAINING

The Norbottenspets is self-willed, which means that its owner needs plenty of patience, persuasiveness and insight into the dog's character to be able to teach the dog the basics. Once it is taken off the leash the average Norbottenspets turns a deaf ear to its handler's calls. The dog's hunting instinct is often stronger than the bond with its owner. Make sure you emphasize the "Come Here" command during obedience training. In common with many breeds, these dogs like their food. This can be useful as a tool to speed up the training exercises and to keep the dog motivated.

EXERCISE

The Norbottenspets is very energetic and needs plenty of exercise. In spite of its small size it can happily join you on your daily runs, provided you build things up slowly. Make sure your yard is well fenced to prevent the dog from stretching its legs when it feels like it.

USES

This breed is still extremely rare outside its country of origin and is rarely kept as a companion dog.

Typical stance of a Norbottenspets

NORWEGIAN ELKHOUND

COUNTRY OF ORIGIN	NORWAY
ORIGINAL FUNCTION	HUNTING DOG USED FOR LARGE GAME

Norwegian Elkhound bitch

APPEARANCE

BODY

The Norwegian Elkhound has a square, compact and short build, yet should look athletic without any hint of coarseness. The back is level. The tail is set high and is carried tightly curled over the back. The muscular loin is only slightly tucked up. The chest is well developed, with well-curved ribs. The elbows are held close to the body. The legs are firm, with plenty of bone. The feet are oval, tightly closed and straight. The neck should be of a reasonable length in proportion to the length of the back.

HEAD

The head is wedge-shaped with the forehead and back of the head slightly arched and a visible but not too pronounced stop. The wide muzzle is rather long and gradually tapers to the tip of the nose. The muzzle is slightly longer than the skull.

The nose bridge is straight and the lips are tightly closed. Elkhounds have high-set, firm and comparatively small, erect ears that taper to a point. The eyes should not protrude. Norwegian Elkhounds have a scissors bite.

SHOULDER HEIGHT

The ideal size for bitches is $19^{1}/_{2}$ in (49 cm) and for dogs $20^{1}/_{2}$ in (52 cm).

WEIGHT

Depending upon the sex and build an Elkhound weighs $41^{3}/_{4}$–$50^{1}/_{2}$ lb (19–23 kg).

COAT

The coat consists of a soft, woolly undercoat and a longer, coarse outer coat. The thick coat is profuse and should be hard and weather-resistant. The hair is longer around the collar, on the breeches and the underside of the tail, but short on the head and the front of the legs and the feet.

COLORS

In common with most Northern breeds, the undercoat of this dog is very light in color, bordering on white. The color of the outer coat consists of shades of gray with black hair tips. The belly, the legs, the underside of the tail and the chest are lighter in color. The eyes are dark brown.

TEMPERAMENT

CHARACTER

The Norwegian Elkhound is an active, uncomplicated and self-confident dog with a friendly, even-tempered disposition. It is sober and fairly hardy, with an excellent sense of smell. Norwegian Elkhounds will bark if they sense anything wrong and in an emergency they will defend their family. In spite of this, they are not guard dogs. They are pretty intelligent and although they love to be close to their family they are undeniably independent with a mind of their own.

Elkhound

Elkhound dog

SOCIAL BEHAVIOR

The Norwegian Elkhound is somewhat reserved, though not unfriendly, towards strangers but friends of the family are usually greeted boisterously. They get along very well with children, but will not be pestered. Their behavior towards other dogs is generally no problem, but this breed does have its more dominant specimens. If the dog is not used to cats and other pets then mixing may be a problem, but once they are well socialized they generally get on fine.

Elkhound

GENERAL CARE

GROOMING

The Elkhound needs relatively little grooming. A wooden comb with a double row of metal teeth can be used to remove loose hairs during the molt. In common with most other Arctic dogs, the Elkhound has no doggy odor. Its coat is both water and dirt-repellent, which means that the coat dries quickly after a shower or a swim and any dirt can be easily brushed off.

TRAINING

Although Norwegian Elkhounds are somewhat headstrong and will certainly not lie down submissively at the feet of their owners, they are less independent in character than various other dogs of this type. It is important to be firm yet very loving and above all fair with this dog during its training. Harsh punishments and a demanding training regime are disastrous for its character building. If an Elkhound feels it is punished unfairly, it can be deeply offended and will show this by ignoring the person who has committed this offense for a long time. During the training a lot of attention should be paid to the "Come Here" command.

EXERCISE

Although many dogs of this breed have been kept as a companion dog for decades, the Norwegian Elkhound is still close to nature. This is an aut-

Elkhound puppy

Elkhound

hentic working dog that should be allowed to let off steam for at least one hour each day. You could take the dog bike-walking or for long hikes. Running free through the woods is something that every dog loves, including a Norwegian Elkhound, but if it catches wind of game then its hunting instincts will take over. An Elkhound that gets plenty of exercise will be calm indoors.

USES

In its country of origin this breed is used for hunting elks in particular, but elsewhere it is kept mainly as a companion dog. You could consider taking part in a sport such as agility trials with this dog, but only if having fun is your first priority.

DETAILS

There are also solid black Elkhounds, which may have a few white markings. These dogs are classed as a separate breed (Black Norwegian Elkhound) and are relatively uncommon.

FINNISH SPITZ	
COUNTRY OF ORIGIN	FINLAND
ORIGINAL AND TODAY'S FUNCTION	HUNTING DOG USED FOR BIRDS, PARTICULARLY BLACK GROUSE AND CAPERCAILLIE

APPEARANCE

BODY

The Finnish Spitz is a dog with an almost square outline. The back is level and strong, the chest is deep and the belly is slightly tucked up. The tail should reach to the hocks. It curves forward and tightly down from the root with the tip extending to middle of the thigh. The shoulders are comparatively well laid back and the elbows are strong and straight. They should be neither too loose nor too tight. The legs are strong. Slightly round feet are preferred. The neck may appear short in males because of the heavier ruff than in the females with medium-length hair.

HEAD

The dry head is medium-sized and must not be coarse. The forehead is slightly arched and the stop is pronounced. The narrow, dry muzzle is wedge-shaped when seen from above and from the sides. The lips are thin and tightly closed. The

Finnish Spitz

Finnish Spitz puppy

pointed ears are erect and very mobile. The medium-sized eyes have a lively expression.

SHOULDER HEIGHT

Dogs stand $17^1/_4$–$19^1/_2$ in (44–50 cm) tall and bitches are $15^1/_2$–$17^3/_4$ in (39–45 cm). The ideal height for dogs is $18^1/_2$ in (47 cm) and for bitches 17 in (43 cm).

WEIGHT

Finnish Spitzes weigh $28^1/_2$–$37^1/_2$ lb (13–17 kg).

COAT

The Finnish Spitz has a double coat. The hair on the body is fairly long and semi-erect. The hair on the back of the neck and on the back is stiffer. The coat is longer on the breeches, the tail and around the neck, where it forms a noticeable ruff particularly in males. The coat is short and close-lying on the head and the legs (except on the back) and the ears are covered in fine hair. The undercoat is short, soft and dense.

COLORS

The color of the outer coat is reddish-brown or red gold. The undercoat is always lighter in color. Small white markings on the chest and feet are permitted, as are black hairs on the lips and sparse black pointed hairs on the back and tail. The

forenose should always be pitch black and the eyes should preferably be dark. Puppies are usually born very dark but the black hairs in their coats will gradually fade.

TEMPERAMENT

CHARACTER

Dogs of this breed are very lively, alert, intelligent and inquisitive. They are homely, cheerful, with a stable, confident disposition, and are fairly independent, enterprising and anything but domineering. They can keep themselves amused for hours playing with a ball or a piece of cloth. In spite of this, they also enjoy the company of their family. Finnish Spitzes are fairly vigilant and will certainly let you know if anything is amiss, but sometimes they will also bark for no (apparent) reason. Though loyal to their own people, they will never adopt a subservient attitude towards them. They are very sensitive to the atmosphere in the house and will respond to it. Their sense of smell is excellent, as is their hunting instinct. These dogs have tremendous stamina and are courageous, sober and hardy. Because of their toughness any illness or injuries may sometimes only be discovered in an advanced stage. Finnish Spitzes love digging, something to bear in mind if you value your immaculate yard.

A typical Finnish Spitz dog with his thick neck

Finnish Spitz

SOCIAL BEHAVIOR

Finnish Spitzes generally are no problem when mixing with other dogs, even if these are the same sex. Most get along fine with children. Whenever any strangers arrive they will be announced, but that tends to be all; they do not behave as defenders of the house. Their hunting instinct is generally well developed, which makes it essential to teach them to get along with other animals such as rabbits and cats from an early age. Though aloof towards people they do not know, they are not unfriendly and aggressiveness is completely foreign to them.

GENERAL CARE

GROOMING

In common with many other dogs of this type, the Finnish Spitz has a "self-cleaning coat" that dries quickly after a shower or a swim. Dirt and dried mud will rarely stick to the coat and the dog usually gets rid of any residual dirt itself; Finnish Spitzes keep themselves naturally very clean. This coat has the additional benefit that it does not carry any doggy odors. Washing a Finnish Spitz will therefore not usually be necessary. Regular brushing and combing is required, but excessive grooming will damage the undercoat. During the molt, which is fairly severe in this breed, you can easily comb loose hairs with a teasel brush or a comb with a double row of metal teeth.

TRAINING

People who are looking for a dog that is perfectly obedient will be better off without a Finnish Spitz. These dogs are devoted to their owners and very fond of them, but they are also loyal to themselves and fiercely independent. With patience and understanding, consistency and clarity it is possible to teach the dog the basics of obedience training. Make sure that the exercises are presented in a fun way, so that the dog will be happy to please you.

EXERCISE

Finnish Spitzes need a fair amount of exercise. They love being outdoors and are virtually impervious to the weather. This does not mean, however, that they cannot thrive in an urban environment. Usually they will do very well in the city, provided the owner takes the dog out for very frequent walks. Off-leash walks in the country are

Finnish Spitz

something which any Finnish Spitz loves, but they may leave their handler behind a little further than might be desirable. Make sure that you bond well with your dog, so that it will return to you when called and do not let it walk off-leash in areas where this might be risky. Their adventurous spirit and their hunting instinct may take them beyond your fence. If you regularly let the dog play in your yard unsupervised then a solid fence would be a wise investment.

USES

This breed is still popular as a hunting dog in its country of origin and in Sweden, but elsewhere it is mainly kept as a companion dog. The average Finnish Spitz is too independent to warm to sports such as obedience trials, but you could consider agility at a recreational level.

SECTION 3 Scandinavian guard and herding dogs

SUOMENLAPINKOIRA (FINNISH LAPPHUND)

COUNTRY OF ORIGIN	FINLAND
ORIGINAL FUNCTION	SHEEPDOG AND REINDEER HERDER, FARM ESTATE DOG AND WATCHDOG

APPEARANCE

BODY

The powerful body of the Finnish Lapphund is slightly longer than tall. The back is level and solid and the croup is slightly sloping. The tail is set high, is not too long, and is carried curled over the back when the dog is alert. The chest is deep and the abdomen is slightly tucked up. The legs are straight, moderately angulated and well boned. Finnish Lapphunds have oval feet with tightly closed toes. Dew claws are undesirable. The neck is of medium length and muscular.

HEAD

The head is fairly broad, with a well-developed muzzle that should not be snipey. There is a pronounced stop. The lips are tight fitting and the nose bridge is straight. The ears are triangular in shape and are set well apart. They are carried erect, but semi-erect ears are also permitted. The eyes are oval-shaped. Finnish Lapphunds have a scissors bite.

SHOULDER HEIGHT

Dogs stand 18–20$\frac{1}{2}$ in (46–52 cm) tall and bitches are 16–18$\frac{1}{2}$ in (41–47 cm).

COAT

The Finnish Lapphund has a profuse

Finnish Lapphund

coat. The outer coat is long, coarse and straight and the undercoat is soft, thick and dense. Hair on the front and sides of the legs and on the face is shorter, and longer on the tail, the breeches and around the neck. Males, in particular, have a substantial ruff.

COLORS

All colors are allowed, in the sense that the main color should predominate. The most common color is black with tan or silvery white markings.

Finnish Lapphund

Finnish Lapphund

TEMPERAMENT

CHARACTER

The Finnish Lapphund is even-tempered, friendly, cheerful and sociable. These dogs are pretty intelligent, eager to learn and love working for their handlers. They are active and energetic but not boisterous, fairly tough and brave, and generally undemanding. Dogs of this breed are dedicated, affectionate and gentle-natured pets.

SOCIAL BEHAVIOR

These dogs are naturally very sociable They generally get on extremely well with children and can usually take a great deal from them. Contact with household pets, such as cats and livestock, is rarely a problem. This dog is vigilant in the sense that it will bark when visitors arrive, but it is too gentle-natured to defend your property.

The Finnish Lapphund is gaining popularity because of its fine character

GENERAL CARE

GROOMING

The coat of this breed requires little attention, as its texture is such that it rarely tangles. It also dries fairly quickly after a shower or a swim. During the molt a large part of the undercoat will shed and this does require nearly daily combing. Using a coarse metal comb you can easily remove the loose hairs from the coat. Keep the claws short.

Finnish Lapphund

TRAINING

Finnish Lapphunds are fairly easy to train. This dog is highly intelligent, eager to learn and usually enjoys following commands. This breed can be trained with a gentle hand, but this should not be confused with an inconsistent approach. Punishments are usually not necessary. Cheerful commands and plenty of praise produce the best results.

EXERCISE

This dog needs a fair amount of exercise and will not be happy lounging in front of the fire all day. Its coat provides excellent protection from the weather. Regularly take the dog out on long hikes and give

it the chance to release its energy off-leash. If you have a good relationship with your dog then you need not worry that it will wander off; it is not in its nature to take off on its own.

USES

In their country of origin Finnish Lapphunds are still frequently used for various duties and for

Finnish Lapphund

sheepdog trials. In other countries they are not very common. In view of the increasing number of imports in recent years and the enthusiasm of owners this is probably only a matter of time. Although they certainly make a great companion dog, it is advisable to undertake some kind of activity with the dog. This breed can excel in sports such as flyball and agility.

Finnish Herder

LAPINPOROKOIRA **(FINNISH OR LAPPONIAN HERDER)**	
COUNTRY OF ORIGIN	FINLAND (LAPLAND)
ORIGINAL FUNCTION	REINDEER HERDER

APPEARANCE

BODY

The Finnish Herder has a rectangular build. The back is strong. The low-set tail of moderate length is carried hanging down. The tail is raised saber-fashion when the dog is in action, but should not be carried above the topline. The chest is deep and spacious. The abdomen is slightly tucked up. Both the front and the hind legs are well angulated, straight and well-boned. The neck is not too long and should be free from throatiness.

HEAD

The Finnish Herder has an elongated head with a slightly domed skull. It has a slight stop, a distinct central furrow and obvious brow ridges. The muzzle narrows slightly towards the forenose. The nose bridge is straight and the lips are tight. The ears are medium size, triangular in shape and carried erect. They are fairly wide apart. The eyes are oval in shape. Finnish Herders have a scissors bite.

SHOULDER HEIGHT

The ideal size for dogs is 20 in (51 cm) and for bitches 18 in (46 cm). Deviations of 1$\frac{1}{2}$ in (3 cm) up or down are permitted.

COAT

The coat consists of an outer coat and an undercoat. The outer coat is moderately long, coarse and straight, while the undercoat is soft and dense. The feet and ears should be well furnished with hair.

COLORS

The most familiar color in this breed is black, but there are also gray and reddish brown specimens. These animals usually sport silvery white or tan markings above the eyes, on the inside of the ears, on the throat and muzzle, the cheeks, on the chest, the legs and on the underside of the tail. White markings on the neck, chest and feet are acceptable. The preferred eye color is dark, but the eyes may be lighter in light-colored dogs.

TEMPERAMENT

CHARACTER

The Finnish Herder is a friendly, open and even-tempered dog that forms a close bond with its handler but will always retain its own identity. These dogs are fairly independent and intelligent. They are excellent guards of their owner's house and property, but will only bite in an emergency.

SOCIAL BEHAVIOR

This breed gets along well with its own kind, although males especially can be a little dominant. Provided the opponent does not challenge the dog, this will rarely lead to a fight. Their association with pets such as cats and small livestock

Finnish Herder puppy

Finnish Herder

is generally excellent and these Finnish dogs also get along well with children. A Finnish Herder shows little interest in strangers but is not unfriendly towards them. It will bark when visitors arrive but leaves it at that.

GENERAL CARE

GROOMING

The coat of these dogs requires little attention. Regular brushing with a teasel brush, particularly during the molt, is usually sufficient. Keep the claws short.

TRAINING

This breed is fairly easy to train, provided the owner bears in mind that this dog dislikes monotonous drills. A varied training, with emphasis on rewarding desirable behavior and not too much pressure on the dog, will achieve the best results. These dogs have an outstanding memory.

EXERCISE

The Finish Herder has above-average exercise needs. It loves going on long hikes, enjoys ball games and will happily join you on your daily jogging run. If this breed gets plenty of exercise, then it will be calm in the house. These dogs are able to withstand all weathers and can be kept in an outdoor kennel, provided they also get plenty of attention and activity.

USES

In their country of origin these dogs are used as sheepdogs, watchdogs and guide dogs. Elsewhere this breed is rare and mainly used as a companion dog. The action and variety offered by a sport such as agility will certainly appeal to this breed.

ICELANDIC DOG

COUNTRY OF ORIGIN	ICELAND
ORIGINAL FUNCTION	SHEEPDOG

Icelandic Dog

APPEARANCE

BODY

This medium-sized, lightly built, Spitz-type dog has a strong, fairly short body that is not too heavy. The tail is of medium length and is carried curled over the back. The chest is broad and deep. The belly is well tucked up and the shoulders are straight. The legs are muscular and straight, and the hocks should not be too bent. The feet are oval in shape. The short, strong and slightly arched neck carries the head high.

HEAD

The light head is broad between the ears. The muzzle is short rather than long and the pronounced stop is not very deep. The lips are short and tight.

SHOULDER HEIGHT

Dogs stand $16^1/_2$–19 in (42–48 cm) tall and bitches are 15–$17^1/_4$ in (38–44 cm).

WEIGHT

Icelandic Dogs weigh approx. $30^3/_4$ lb (14 kg).

COAT

The Icelandic Dog has a double, close-lying coat. The outer coat is of moderate length and fairly harsh. The hair is longer around the neck, on the tail and the culottes, and shorter on the legs and the head.

Finnish Herder

COLORS

The most common color is light fawn with black hair tips. White with pink markings and occasionally black, sometimes with white markings, also occur.

Icelandic Dog with her pups

TEMPERAMENT

CHARACTER

The Icelandic Dog is cheerful, friendly, sociable, highly intelligent and eager to learn. Even-tempered and stable in character, this breed is not easily ruffled. They are alert to what goes on around them and also fairly vigilant. At work they are hardy, brave and tireless. They are very affectionate towards their handler. The Icelandic Dog loves to bark. Dogs of this breed want to be part of the family; if they are put in a kennel or have to spend large parts of the day on their own then they will regard this as severe punishment.

SOCIAL BEHAVIOR

The Icelandic Dog is generally very patient and good-natured with children. If socialized with cats and other pets from an early age, contact with these animals will be no pro-

Icelandic Dog

blem either. Icelandic Dogs normally get on extremely well with their own kind. They are friendly towards familiar and unfamiliar visitors, but they will always announce the arrival of strangers.

GENERAL CARE

GROOMING

The Icelandic Dog needs relatively little grooming. During the molt you can comb the coat twice a week with a teasel brush or a coarse comb to remove the loose undercoat. In addition to this combing, weekly brushing is sufficient. Keep the claws short.

Male Icelandic Dog

TRAINING

This breed is generally quite easy to obedience train. These dogs are intelligent enough to grasp what is expected of them. They flourish with a cheerful, friendly, consistent and clear approach to the training. They learn faster if the exercises are varied and sufficiently challenging. Monotonous drills are not for them.

EXERCISE

This pleasant companion dog needs a fair amount of exercise and activity to feel happy. Take it for long hikes regularly and also let it run and play off-leash now and then. Icelandic Dogs do not tend to wander off on their own; they prefer to

Icelandic Dog

stay close to their master. They are always in for ball games.

USES

Icelandic Dogs are very suitable as companion dogs and also do well in agility and flyball trials.

Young Icelandic Dog bitch

NORWEGIAN BUHUND	
COUNTRY OF ORIGIN	NORWAY
ORIGINAL FUNCTION	SHEEP HERDER AND FARM ESTATE DOG

APPEARANCE

BODY

The Norwegian Buhund is a medium, well-balanced Spitz with light, square build and open temperament. Difference between male and female should be clear. The back and loins are short and level. The croup slopes slightly. The high-set tail is short, thick, and tightly curled over the middle of the back. When straightened, it reaches the hock joint. The deep chest reaches to the elbows. The shoulders are held close to the body. The forelegs are straight. The strong, muscular hindquarters are moderately angulated. The weight of bone should be proportional. Dew claws are undesirable. Feet are rounded, with closed toes. The neck is carried well and fairly short.

Norwegian Buhund dog

HEAD

The wedge-shaped head is not too heavy and almost flat. The stop is slight. The relatively short muzzle gradually narrows towards the nose. The nose bridge is straight. The lips are smooth and tightly closed. The erect ears are pointed and suit the head in terms of shape and size. Norwegian Buhunds have a scissors bite.

SHOULDER HEIGHT

Dogs are 17–18$^{1}/_{2}$ in (43–47 cm) and bitches 16–17$^{3}/_{4}$ in (41–45 cm).

Norwegian Buhund

WEIGHT

Dogs weigh 33–41³/₄ lb (15–19 kg) and bitches weigh approx. 28¹/₂–37¹/₂ lb (13–17 kg).

COAT

The Buhund has a dense, full and harsh but smooth coat. The undercoat is soft, dense and woolly. On the head and the front of the legs the coat is short and longer on the neck, shoulders and chest.

COLORS

The most common color in this breed is wheaten, similar to the Norwegian Fjord horse. The color may vary from very pale to reddish yellow. Black hair tips and a dark mask are permitted, but a solid color is preferred. Black also occurs and these specimens should ideally be completely black, although a white blaze and some white on the neck and the feet is allowed. The black should have no brown glow. The eyes should be as dark as possible in both color patterns and the nose should be black.

TEMPERAMENT

CHARACTER

These dogs are intelligent, strong, energetic and tireless outdoors but normally calm in the house.

They are affectionate, devoted to their owners and their families, alert and vigilant. Most specimens love to bark. They are brave, confident and very adaptable. Norwegian Buhunds are uncomplicated creatures that go through life with a cheerful disposition.

SOCIAL BEHAVIOR

Norwegian Buhunds generally get on very well with children and also with dogs and other pets. They give a penetrating warning when visitors arrive but that is all; they are no defenders.

GENERAL CARE

Norwegian Buhund

GROOMING

The coat is fairly easy to care for. During the molt you can simply remove any loose hairs from the undercoat and the outer coat using a "teasel brush." Keep the claws short. A Buhund in good condition produces no "doggy odors."

TRAINING

The Norwegian Buhund is eager to learn and intelligent, but also rather sensitive. Firm training is therefore not recommended with this breed. Consistency and variety is called for in the training, as dull, repetitive exercises do not suit a Buhund.

Norwegian Buhunds

Norwegian Buhund puppies

Norwegian Buhund

EXERCISE

The Buhund is an energetic dog of tremendous stamina that likes to be active. Let it run free off the leash regularly without any fears that it might take off. Its shepherding instincts will make the dog want to stay close to you. If you need to skip some of its activities for one day, then this dog will adapt.

USES

Its lively and intelligent nature makes the Norwegian Buhund very suitable for active sports such as agility and flyball. However, repetitive obedience drills are not ideal for this dog.

VÄSTGÖTASPETS (SWEDISH VALLHUND)	
COUNTRY OF ORIGIN	SWEDEN
ORIGINAL FUNCTION	THIS BREED WAS USED FOR CATTLE DRIVING ("HEELER")

APPEARANCE

BODY

The Västgötaspets is a short-legged dog with a body that is considerably longer than it is tall. The ideal ratio is 3:2. The back is level. The broad croup is short and slightly sloping. The chest is long, well sprung and deep. The lowest point of the chest lies close behind the back of the foreleg. The sternum is clearly visible, but should not be too pronounced. The abdomen has a slight tuck-up. The sturdy legs are well angulated both at the front and the back. The forelegs are straight when viewed from the side, but slightly bent when viewed from the front. The feet are pointing straight ahead. They are oval in shape and should be solid, short and close-knit. A litter can comprise both puppies with and without tails. A long tail is normally carried over the back in a loose curl. The neck is long and muscular.

HEAD

The head is dry and long, with a pronounced, but flat stop. Viewed from above, the head tapers toward the nose, but the muzzle and nose should not be pointed. The muzzle is shorter than the skull. The medium-sized ears are pricked and pointed. The almond-shaped eyes are also medium size.

SHOULDER HEIGHT

The ideal size for dogs is 13 in (33 cm) and for bitches 12 in (31 cm).

COAT

Västgötaspetses are wire-coated. The outer coat is hard and dense, with a very dense and soft undercoat.

COLORS

The most common and most popular color is wolf, which is steel gray with dark guard hairs and lighter markings on

Västgötaspets

Västgötaspets.

the chest, legs, muzzle and throat. A reddish yellow with lighter patches in these areas is highly desirable as well. Gray brown or brown yellow coats are less desirable, though still permissible. Small white markings are acceptable, provided they do not cover more than one third of the dog's coat. White toes and chest patches are very common in this breed. The eyes are dark brown in color and the nose is black.

Västgötaspets like to be active

TEMPERAMENT

CHARACTER

The Västgötaspets is alert, active, eager to work and keen to learn. Self-confident and intelligent, it is loyal and devoted to its owner and the family. When required, this dog emerges as a good, reliable guard and a courageous defender. It is tireless when at work.

SOCIAL BEHAVIOR

This dog is very sociable by nature. Contact with other pets and small livestock should not present any problems, although the degree of socialization obviously also has something to do with this. They usually get along fine with other dogs and are known for their gentleness and patience towards children. Anybody that they do not know, particularly when the master is away, will

be stopped courageously and convincingly. They will initially be somewhat reserved towards invited guests. The master and family members will always come first with this dog.

GENERAL CARE

GROOMING

These distinctive dogs need little care. Weekly brushing and combing is sufficient. During the molt they shed part of their undercoat and a daily combing is necessary. Loose hairs can be removed with a "teasel brush". Keep the claws short.

Västgötaspets

TRAINING

These dogs are fairly easy to obedience train. They are intelligent and love to please their owners: an ideal combination.

EXERCISE

The Västgötaspets is primarily a working dog, so needs plenty of activity. Its small size, the Västgötaspets is suited to an apartment, but only if it gets to run and play every day. This dog adores ball games and retrieving. A Västgötaspets will happily join you on long hikes, on or off the leash.

USES

This dog is an excellent house dog, but likes to keep busy. You will do it no greater pleasure than by taking it to an agility class or similar activity. This breed will also do well in trials.

Västgötaspets

SECTION 4   European Keeshonds

DWARF KEESHOND (POMERANIAN), SMALL KEESHOND (SMALL GERMAN SPITZ) AND MEDIUM KEESHOND (STANDARD GERMAN SPITZ)

COUNTRY OF ORIGIN	GERMANY
ORIGINAL FUNCTION	THE MEDIUM KEESHOND WAS ORIGINALLY A VERMIN DESTROYER, YARD DOG AND COMPANION DOG, THE SMALL AND DWARF KEESHONDS WERE ORIGINALLY COMPANION DOGS

APPEARANCE

BODY

Keeshonds have a short, level back, a deep chest and a slightly tucked-up belly. The moderately long tail is set high and is curled over the back and to one of the sides, in a ring. The moderately long legs are solid and straight, with small, round cat's feet.

HEAD

The head is medium size, narrowing evenly toward the tip of the nose when seen from above. The nose bridge should ideally be slightly arched

Medium Keeshond

Dwarf Keeshond

(ram's nose) and the stop is moderate. The lips are tight fitting. The small, triangular ears are set high and closely together. They are carried erect. The medium-sized eyes are oval in shape and set somewhat obliquely in the head. Keeshonds have a scissors bite.

SHOULDER HEIGHT

Dwarf Keeshonds are a maximum size of $8^1/_2$ in (22 cm), Small Keeshonds are 9–11 in (23–28 cm) at the withers and Medium Keeshonds may be $11^1/_2$–$14^1/_4$ in (29–36 cm) tall. The ideal shoulder height of Medium Keeshonds is $12^1/_2$ in (32 cm).

COAT

Consists of long, erect hairs with a dense undercoat. The hair around the collar and shoulders stands out straight from the body and is also longer. The trousers and the tail are well feathered.

The face, the ears, the front and lower part of the back of the legs are covered in short hair. The hair should not be wavy.

COLORS

The following colors are permitted:
- Dwarf Keeshond: Solid white, brown, black, blue, orange, wolf and cream.
- Small Keeshond: Solid white, brown, black, orange and wolf.
- Medium Keeshond: Solid white, brown, black, orange and wolf.

The eyes should be dark in all varieties and color patterns.

Medium Keeshond

TEMPERAMENT

CHARACTER

Keeshonds are lively and cheerful, active and energetic, with a fair amount of intelligence and extremely eager to learn, loyal to their handlers without being forceful, vigilant and they love to bark. The smallest variety, the Dwarf Keeshond, may be tiny in stature but certainly does not give that impression and can be a little overconfident. All Keeshonds know the extent of your property and are fairly yard-bound.

Dwarf Keeshond

SOCIAL BEHAVIOR

These dogs generally get on fine with their peers, but if attacked or bullied by a (much) larger dog some tend to forget all about their own modest size. Make sure you protect such specimens from themselves. A Dwarf or Small Keeshond is a less appropriate choice with boisterous children, because too much commotion and noise can make them nervous. Mixing with pets such as cats is usually no problem. These dogs are vigilant towards strangers and the family always comes first.

GENERAL CARE

GROOMING

Although abundantly furnished with hair, these dogs generally need very little grooming. The texture of their coats is such that it does not tend to tangle. Every two weeks you should thoroughly brush the coat with a very coarse comb and then lightly comb it through. Frequent or very thorough grooming is not recommended, as this could damage the undercoat. However, daily combing is useful to keep your house free from dog hairs during the molt when the undercoat will shed substantially. Keep the claws short and regularly check the teeth – particularly the back molars – for tartar.

TRAINING

As a rule, Keeshonds are fairly easy to train. They are intelligent and can quickly learn new commands. One sore point in this breed is its readiness to yelp. Make sure you teach the dog early on that it should only bark a few times when something is going on (doorbell, visitors) and then be quiet. With a consistent and clear approach such undesirable barking can be overcome. Use the socialization period well. Take the young puppy with you as much as possible and let it get used to all kinds of different animals, people and children in a relaxed and informal way. This will allow the puppy to grow up into a stable dog that is able to respond confidently to various impressions.

Small Keeshond

EXERCISE

These dogs are happy with a few short walks each day if they can also regularly play and frolic in the yard. If longer walks are more your style, then these dogs will be delighted to keep you company. They are not bothered where you take them, either through a busy city or out in the countryside. They are very adaptable and will also do well in an apartment. One major advantage of these dogs is that they will seldom take off on their own. Roaming is not in their nature and during off-leash walks they prefer to stay close to their owners.

USES

These breeds are almost exclusively kept as companion dogs, but their nimbleness and intelligence in combination with the right supervision can lead to unexpected training results.

LARGE KEESHOND AND WOLFSKEESHOND (WOLFSPITZ)	
COUNTRY OF ORIGIN	GERMANY
ORIGINAL FUNCTION	VERMIN DESTROYER, YARD DOG

APPEARANCE

BODY

Keeshonds have a very short, level back that slopes backwards slightly. The high-set tail is moderately long and is curled over the back. The chest is deep and the ribs are arched. The belly is slightly tucked up. The solid, straight legs are of medium length. The hind legs are slightly angulated in the hocks. The feet are round and should be as small as possible, with arched toes. The neck is moderately long.

HEAD

The medium-sized head narrows into a wedge

Wolfskeeshond

shape toward the tip of the nose when viewed from above. The stop is moderate. The muzzle should not be too long and a slight ram's nose is desirable. The lips should fit tightly and there should be no fold in the corners of the mouth. Keeshonds have small, erect, triangular and high-set ears that should be as close together as possible. The eyes are medium size and oval in shape. They are set slightly obliquely in the head. Large Keeshonds and Wolfskeeshonds have a scissors bite.

SHOULDER HEIGHT

The ideal size for a Large Keeshond is 18 in (46 cm). Deviations of $1^1/_2$ in (4 cm) up or down are allowed. The Wolfskeeshond has an ideal shoulder height of $19^1/_2$ in (50 cm). Deviations of two inches (5 cm) up or down are allowed.

COAT

The profuse, long, stand-off coat is characteristic of these Keeshonds. The hair is loose and stands off from the body, particularly around the neck and shoulders. It should not form a parting on the back. The hair is longest on the tail and under the neck, but short on the face, the ears and on the front and sides of the legs.

COLORS

The Wolfskeeshond has a wolf color, which is a silvery gray coat with black hair tips. The Large Keeshond comes in solid black, brown or white. The eyes should be dark in all color patterns.

TEMPERAMENT

CHARACTER

These dogs are cheerful, even-tempered, intelligent and eager to learn. Very loyal to their owners and the family, they are vigilant and alert and will not be bribed by strangers. They have a moderate temperament and tend to bark very little. Their coats provide excellent protection from the elements. Although these dogs love the outdoors, they would regard a kennel existence as a punishment. They want to be near their families and do not like being excluded.

SOCIAL BEHAVIOR

Large Keeshonds and Wolfskeeshonds generally get along extremely well with their own kind. Their contact with children is usually fine, especially with any children from their own families.

Wolfskeeshond

Although Keeshonds have very little hunting instinct, it is still a good idea to let the dogs get used to cats and other pets when young. Once properly socialized they can live with them in harmony. Keeshonds are always a little vigilant towards strangers, but rarely to a serious extent.

GENERAL CARE

GROOMING

The coat of these Keeshonds is easy to care for, since the hair stands off from the body and will not easily tangle. However, during the molt when a large part of the undercoat is shed the dog needs to be combed very regularly and thoroughly with a coarse comb. Frequent combing or brushing outside these periods is not recommended, as that could damage the undercoat. Keep the claws short.

TRAINING

The Large Keeshond and Wolfskeeshond are intelligent dogs that are eager to learn and enjoy obeying commands. Training these dogs should therefore present no problems.

EXERCISE

These dogs will adapt their exercise needs to their family. Ball games and long hikes are always popular with them.

USES

These breeds are very suitable as companion dogs. They will adapt either to city life or to a farm existence. Keeshonds can do well in various types of dog sports, including agility.

SECTION 5 Asian Keeshonds and related breeds

JAPANESE SPITZ

COUNTRY OF ORIGIN	**JAPAN**
ORIGINAL FUNCTION	**COMPANION DOG**

APPEARANCE

BODY

The body of the Japanese Spitz is slightly longer than tall with a short, level back. The chest is deep and broad, and the abdomen is well tucked up. The moderately long tail is set high and is carried over the back. The feet are round, with close-knit toes (cat's feet) and thick pads. The forelegs are straight and the elbows are held close.

HEAD

The head has a pointed muzzle and a pronounced stop. The skull is rounded. The small, triangular ears are set high and facing forward. The almond-shaped eyes are set slightly obliquely. Japanese Spitzes have a strong scissors bite.

SHOULDER HEIGHT

Dogs stand 12–15 in (30–38 cm) tall. Bitches are a little smaller.

COAT

The double coat consists of a long, straight and stand-off outer coat and a dense, soft and short undercoat. The hair is more abundant around the neck, withers and brisket, where it forms a dense ruff, as well as on the tail. The hair is significantly shorter on the face, the ears and on the front of the legs.

Japanese Spitz

COLORS

Japanese Spitzes are always pure white in color, with dark (black) pigmentation on the lips, nose, eye rims, nails and pads. The eyes are dark.

TEMPERAMENT

CHARACTER

Dogs of this breed are high-spirited, playful and intelligent, with a moderate temperament. They are generally fairly obedient and vigilant. They love to bark.

SOCIAL BEHAVIOR

This dog generally gets along fine with children. They tend to be a little wary of strangers, but friends of the family are greeted loudly. Mixing with their own kind and other pets does not usually lead to any problems.

Japanese Spitz

Japanese Spitz

GENERAL CARE

GROOMING

The Japanese Spitz needs an average amount of coat care. Although this breed has fairly long hair, its texture is such that it hardly tangles. During the molt a coarse comb with a double row of metal teeth can be used to remove loose hairs from the undercoat. Do not comb and brush the Japanese Spitz too often; there is a risk that this will damage the undercoat.

TRAINING

The Japanese Spitz is reasonably obedient and intelligent, qualities that make for a fairly quick learner. Of course this dog, like any other, should be trained consistently. If you live in a busy city street then you need to keep its tendency to bark under control.

EXERCISE

Japanese Spitzes have average exercise needs and will easily adapt to circumstances. Three walks a day and regular opportunities to run and to play off-leash are sufficient to keep the dog mentally and physically in good condition. These dogs generally love ball games and retrieving.

USES

With the right supervision, dogs of this breed can perform very well in sports such as agility and flyball.

AKITA INU	
COUNTRY OF ORIGIN	JAPAN
ORIGINAL FUNCTION	THE AKITA INU HAS BEEN USED FOR VARIOUS TASKS OVER THE YEARS, RANGING FROM HUNTING AND GUARD DOG TO COMPANION DOG OF NOBLEMEN

APPEARANCE

BODY

The Akita Inu is slightly longer than high. The level, short back has high withers and the loins are wide. Akitas have a deep, well-developed chest. The ribs are moderately arched. The abdomen is well tucked up. The tail is set on high and is carried over the back in a single curl which should reach almost to the hocks. The legs are straight and solid and the elbows are held close. The pasterns are slightly inclined. The feet are round, with close-knit toes. The neck is thick and muscular.

HEAD

The skull is flat, broad at the front, with a pronounced stop and a furrow across the forehead. The cheeks are well developed and the powerful muzzle is moderately long. The small, thick and triangular ears, which are erect and pointing slightly forwards, are characteristic of the breed. The eyes are fairly small and almost triangular in shape. They are set well apart and slanting. Akita Inus have a strong scissors bite.

Akita Inu bitch

Young brindle Akita Inu dog

SHOULDER HEIGHT

Dogs stand 26¹/₂ in (67 cm) tall and bitches are 24 in (61 cm). Deviations of 1¹/₂ in (3 cm) up or down are permitted.

COAT

The undercoat is dense and soft, whereas the outer coat is coarse and straight. The hair is a little longer on the tail. Longhaired dogs will be disqualified from the show ring.

COLORS

Permitted coat colors are red, white, brindle and sesame. All colors, except white dogs, should possess "urajiro." This is a whitish color on the side of the muzzle and cheeks, underneath the mouth, on the neck, the chest and the belly, the bottom of the tail and on the inside of the legs. This urajiro is highly characteristic of the Akita Inu. A black mask is not permitted. The eyes should be dark brown or even darker.

TEMPERAMENT

CHARACTER

Akita Inus are even-tempered, sensible and thoughtful, intelligent and friendly, but also a little independent and at times domineering. They are excellent guard dogs that will convincingly come to their people's rescue. It is not in their nature to be yappy, overly alert and excited; an Akita always gives an impression of being calm and unruffled. They are devoted to their owners and the family and reasonably obedient, but their attitude is friendly rather than subservient. Like the Japanese themselves, this breed has a certain dignity and restraint which could be described as inscrutable.

SOCIAL BEHAVIOR

Most Akita Inus have no time for people they do not know and tend to be a little reserved or vigilant towards them. They are not particularly amiable with other dogs and can be dominant towards those of their own sex. Because of their hunting instinct they need to become acquainted with cats and other pets but then will get on reasonably well with these animals. They are usually fine with children and are very protective of them, although they could never be considered a playmate.

GENERAL CARE

GROOMING

Dogs of this breed molt heavily twice a year when a teasel brush should be used to remove loose hair from the coat. Outside the molt weekly brushing is sufficient.

Akita Inu dog

TRAINING

With a handler who is confident and consistent in his approach, the Akita Inu can learn a great deal. This is not the type of dog that can be compelled to show respect through hitting, shouting and force. These dogs do best if the drills remain challenging and are not constantly repeated. Akita Inus are reasonably obedient, but will always have a mind of their own.

EXERCISE

The Akita Inu has tremendous stamina and above-average exercise needs. Three short walks around the block each day are not enough to keep

Akita Inu

USES

Although Akita Inus are a common sight on the trial field in different countries where they are used in various disciplines, there is no particular dog sport that is ideal for this breed or in which it excels. You could consider entering your dog in an agility class, where fun rather than performance comes first.

DETAILS

In addition to the Japanese type Akita Inu described above, which is the only one recognized by the FCI and Japan, there is also another type or rather another breed. This "American type" Akita Inu is very common in countries like Great Britain and the USA, but also on the European Continent. This breed developed when Akita Inus were crossed with mastiffs and sheepdogs and is characterized by a heavier and coarser build with heavier bones. There are also differences in character. These dogs can be distinguished by a wider range of colors, such as black masks which are permitted. Since January 1, 2000 this type of Akita Inu no longer belongs to this breed category but to FCI Group 2, with the breed name Great Japanese Dog.

Akita Inu

this dog in good condition. The Akita needs regular runs out but is not keen on ball games or retrieving. This breed is usually quiet indoors.

Pair of young Akita Inus

Shiba Inu

SHIBA INU	
COUNTRY OF ORIGIN	JAPAN
ORIGINAL FUNCTION	HUNTING DOG USED FOR BOTH FEATHER AND FUR AND BIG GAME

APPEARANCE

BODY

The Shiba Inu is a compact dog with a body that is slightly longer than tall (ratio 11:10). The shoulders are well developed and moderately sloping and the back is short and level. The tail is set on high, reaches to the hocks, and is carried curled or curved as a sickle. The abdomen is slightly tucked up. The chest is deep, with well-sprung ribs. The legs are straight and the pasterns are slightly sprung. The elbows are set close to the body. The thighs are long. Shiba Inus have round feet with well-knuckled toes. The neck is heavy and solid.

HEAD

The head is broad, with well-developed cheeks. There is a marked stop and a slight central furrow. The muzzle is pointed and of good depth, with a straight nose bridge and tight lips. The ears are small and triangular. They are carried pricked and tilted slightly forward. The comparatively small eyes are triangular and set well apart. The outer eyelids are slanting slightly upwards. Shiba Inus have a scissors bite.

SHOULDER HEIGHT

Dogs stand $15^{1}/_{2}$ in (40 cm) tall and bitches are $14^{1}/_{2}$ in (37 cm). Deviations of $^{3}/_{4}$ in ($1^{1}/_{2}$ cm) up or down are permitted.

COAT

The Shiba Inu has a hard, straight outer coat with a soft, dense undercoat.

COLORS

Permitted colors are red, sesame, red sesame, black sesame and black and tan. In practice Shiba Inus with a red coat or sometimes sesame and black and tan are the most common. The eyes are dark brown.

TEMPERAMENT

CHARACTER

This breed is even-tempered, alert, inquisitive and cheerful. They rarely bark, but can be vigilant. Shiba Inus bond closely with their owners, but remain independent. Usually fairly obedient, they are also adaptable and generally calm, quiet and circumspect.

SOCIAL BEHAVIOR

The Shiba Inu generally gets on well with dogs of the opposite sex, although

Shiba Inus

Shiba Inu

shed and regular thorough brushing is required in these periods. Keep the claws short.

TRAINING

The Shiba Inu is generally easy to train, provided the owner is aware that this dog may display a few independent traits. Vary the exercises with play to make sure the dog keeps enjoying them and emphasize desirable behavior. These dogs can be motivated with tasty treats. A Shiba Inu will usually adapt to your circumstances and behave exemplary if you take it somewhere, but it will not lend itself to circus tricks and endless and monotonous training sessions. This breed has traditionally been used as a hunting dog and in some specimens their hunting instincts will emerge during off-leash walks. Make sure you pay particular attention to the "Come here" command.

EXERCISE

The Shiba Inu will adapt to your circumstances. It can be perfectly happy with three short walks a day supplemented with regular opportunities to play in the yard or a weekly romp in the park. However, if you enjoy daily ramblings through the woods then this dog will be delighted to accompany you. The Shiba Inu does not mind whether it walks in a city or out in the countryside; it feels at home wherever it goes. This type of dog is therefore also suitable for a busy city district or an apartment.

USES

Because of their adaptability this breed will feel at home in different surroundings and is a suitable companion dog for people of all ages.

specimens belonging to the same sex will be challenged if they live under one roof. If you want to keep two dogs of this breed, then it is better to opt for one male and one female. Mixing with household pets such as cats is usually no problem and any visitors are also greeted warmly. Shiba Inus tend to be good with children, provided they do not use the dogs as playthings.

GENERAL CARE

GROOMING

The coat of the Shiba Inu needs relatively little attention. This dog keeps itself very clean and the texture of the coat is such that it does not soil quickly. The coat is also virtually odorless. However, during the molt large amounts of hair are

Shiba Inu

Chow Chow

CHOW CHOW

COUNTRY OF ORIGIN	CHINA
ORIGINAL FUNCTION	THE CHOW CHOW HAS HAD VARIOUS FUNCTIONS IN THE PAST, INCLUDING AS HUNTING DOG. THIS BREED HAS LONG FEATURED ON CHINESE MENUS.

APPEARANCE

BODY

The Chow Chow is a compact, short-coupled and proportionally built, leonine dog. The level back is short and strong and the loins are powerful. The tail is set on high and carried well over the back. The chest is broad and deep, with well-sprung

Chow Chow bitch

ribs. The forelegs are straight. They are of moderate length, with good bone. The minimal angulation of the hocks produces the breed's characteristic stilted gait. The hocks should not flex forward. The feet of the Chow Chow are small, close-knit and round (cat's feet). The strong, full neck must not be short, is set obliquely in the shoulders and is slightly arched.

HEAD

The skull is flat and broad. The broad muzzle is of moderate length and does not taper to a point.

The comparatively small eyes are almond-shaped and free from entropion (eyelids turned inwards). The small, thick ears are slightly rounded at the tips. They are set well apart and are carried erect and tilting slightly forward. They should tilt slightly towards each other, giving the dog its characteristic "scowl" (frowning expression). Chows have a complete scissors bite.

SHOULDER HEIGHT

Dogs stand 19–22 in (48–56 cm) tall and the size for bitches is 18–20 in (46–51 cm).

COAT

There are two types of coat. The longhaired is the best known and the most common variety. Longhaired Chows have profuse, dense, straight and stand-off hair. The outer coat is rather coarse in texture, while the undercoat is soft and woolly. The

Chow Chow puppy

coat is longer around the neck, where it forms a ruff, and on the culottes. The short-haired Chow has short, straight, abundant, dense and

Smooth-hair red Chow Chow bitch

them and guard and protect their people and the family home convincingly against intruders. They are not friends to everyone. They are not at all squeamish and display great courage whenever it is called for. These dogs are full of character.

SOCIAL BEHAVIOR

Most Chow Chows are slightly dominant towards other dogs. However, they generally get on well with children, provided they do not pester the dog. There should be no problems with cats and other pets once they are well socialized with them. Chows are reserved and vigilant towards strangers.

GENERAL CARE

GROOMING

The longhaired Chow Chow needs regular thorough brushing, particularly in areas that are prone to tangling. Get the young dog used to this ritual, so that grooming does not become a battle of wills when it is fully grown and stronger. Looking after the short-haired Chow's coat is significantly less demanding, although it should still be brushed thoroughly, especially during the molt. Keep the claws short.

TRAINING

Chow Chow puppy

The Chow needs an owner who is calm and even-tempered and who exudes a natural authority. With such a handler the Chow will be able to develop well. Do not expect any miracles from a Chow in terms of obedience; it is born stubborn and with a mind of its own. Of course, this breed can certainly learn quite a few things, but it is not suited to prolonged exercise drills. Be consistent at all times.

EXERCISE

The Chow Chow is a very quiet dog that needs relatively little exercise. It does like to be outside

upstanding hair. The hair should give a velvety impression and should not lie flat.

COLORS

Chows come in solid black, red, blue and cream. The most common colors are red (fawn) and black. The tongue is always bluish black, as is the palate. The gums are preferably black and the eyes are always dark.

TEMPERAMENT

CHARACTER

Chows are calm, dignified and proud. Although very loyal to their owners and the family, they will always remain a little self-willed and independent. They are assertive with plenty of self-confidence. They are alert to what goes on around

in the yard where it will find itself a peaceful spot from where it will warn you if anything is wrong. This is not the type of dog that will pace up and down restlessly. You can take this dog out for long walks, but make sure it does not exert itself on hot

Cream-colored Chow Chow dog

days. This dog prefers to withdraw to a shady spot in the summer.

USES

This breed does not have the right temperament to be a sporting dog. However, it is eminently suitable as a spirited companion dog for people who also like a bit of peace and quiet.

EURASIAN

COUNTRY OF ORIGIN	GERMANY
ORIGINAL FUNCTION	COMPANION DOG

APPEARANCE

BODY

The Eurasian has a powerful body, which is slightly longer than tall. The withers are pronounced, the muscular back is level and solid, and the croup is straight, broad, long and muscular. Eurasians have a round tail of moderate thickness, carried forwards or to the side over the back in a curl. The chest reaches to the elbows and the ribs are moderately arched. The brisket is well developed but not too pronounced. The belly and flanks are tucked up. The shoulders are moderately long and well laid back. The legs are moderately long, with solid bone. The forelegs are straight and the angulation of the shoulders is moderate. The stifle and hock joints of the hind legs are slightly angulated when viewed from the side. The feet are round and tight, with well-arched toes. The muscular, deep, broad neck is moderately long and is carried outstretched.

HEAD

The head is wedge-shaped when viewed from above. The skull and muzzle are nearly equal in length. The skull has a flat crown with a distinct central furrow and a well-defined occipital peak. The stop is slight. The nose bridge is straight and the muzzle narrows gradually towards the forenose. The corners of the mouth are closed because of the tight lips. The ears are triangular and medium size. They are carried erect, with the opening pointing forward. The medium-sized eyes are almond-

Eurasian

Eurasian

short on the head, the front and sides and the lower part of the legs, but longer on the tail, the back of the forelegs and the culottes. The neck is covered in slightly longer hair than the body. A mane is undesirable.

COLORS

All colors are permitted, except white, white patches or liver. Eurasians mainly come in red to blonde, wolf, black and black with markings in other colors (similar to black and tan, where the tan may also be white or silver, for example). The forenose and the rims of the lips and eyes should always be black.

TEMPERAMENT

Eurasian

CHARACTER

Eurasians are calm, even-tempered and friendly, intelligent and reasonably obedient, but they do have a mind of their own. They are vigilant and will certainly bark when something is wrong. However, normally these dogs do not bark much. They are loyal to their own people and like to be part of the family. They are not suited to kennel life.

SOCIAL BEHAVIOR

Dogs of this breed get on well with their own kind and with children. They are reserved though not unfriendly towards strangers. Good socialization with pets such as cats is essential and will ensure that there are no problems in this respect.

GENERAL CARE

GROOMING

In spite of its dense coat this breed needs very little grooming. The texture of the coat is such that it rarely tangles, except during the molt when the undercoat sheds. A teasel brush or a comb with a double row of metal teeth will then be useful to remove the shed undercoat efficiently. Frequent

shaped and set slightly obliquely. They should not be too deep. Eurasians may have either a scissors or a pincer bite.

SHOULDER HEIGHT

Dogs stand $20^1/_2$–$23^1/_2$ in (52–60 cm) tall and bitches are 19–22 in (48–56 cm).

WEIGHT

Dogs are approx. $48^1/_2$–$66^1/_4$ lb (22–30 kg) and bitches $39^1/_2$–57 lb (18–26 kg).

COAT

Eurasians have a dense undercoat and a medium-length, loose lying, thick outer coat. The hair is

Eurasian pup

brushing or combing outside the molt is not recommended, because this would remove too much of the undercoat and would also encourage continuous shedding with this type of coat. The coat is virtually self-cleaning, so that it dries quickly and any mud or dirt will not stick to it. Keep the claws short.

TRAINING

The Eurasian is generally not difficult to train, although the owner should be consistent and clear towards the dog. This breed responds well to a varied training regime which emphasizes desirable behavior. Training a Eurasian in a friendly manner, with plenty of understanding and patience and a loving approach will bring out the best in this breed.

Eurasian puppy

Eurasian

EXERCISE

A Eurasian needs a fair amount of exercise. In addition to regular daily walks it is advisable to let the dog burn off its energy for about an hour each day. They love playing and romping around off-leash and are also fond of retrieving. They are not prone to wandering off very far from their owner.

USES

With the right supervision this dog can do very well in sports such as agility and obedience. Having fun should be the main priority for both you and your dog. This is not the type of dog that will get very far in dog trials.

Primitive breeds

Basenjis

BASENJI	
COUNTRY OF ORIGIN	AFRICA
ORIGINAL AND	ORIGINALLY AN INDEPENDENT
TODAY'S FUNCTION	HUNTER OF SMALL GAME

APPEARANCE

BODY

The Basenji is a lightly built, finely boned, aristocratic-looking dog that moves gracefully. This dog stands comparatively tall. The horizontal back is short and level. The tail is set high and is carried in a tight single or double curl

Basenji

over the back and close to one thigh. The deep chest gradually flows into a well tucked-up belly. The ribs are deep and oval. The shoulders are muscular, well laid back but not loaded. The elbows are held close. The legs are straight with small, narrow and compact feet and well arched toes. The strong neck is arched gracefully, with a high and proud carriage of the head.

HEAD

Basenjis have a moderately broad skull with a slight stop. The length of the skull is slightly greater than that of the muzzle. The skull tapers slightly towards the nose. The small, pointed ears are carried erect and slightly forward. When the dog is alert, the breed's characteristic fine wrinkles appear on the forehead. The almond-shaped eyes are set obliquely. They should be inscrutable in expression and present an impression that the dog is always looking into the distance. Basenjis have a scissors bite.

SHOULDER HEIGHT

The ideal size for dogs is 17 in (43 cm) and for bitches $15^1/_2$ in (40 cm).

WEIGHT

Dogs weigh approx. $24^1/_4$ lb (11 kg) and bitches 21 lb ($9^1/_2$ kg).

COAT

The short, smooth coat is fine in texture and lies very close to the skin. Basenjis have no undercoat.

COLORS

Basenjis come in red and white, black and white and tricolor (black and tan with white markings). White markings are required on the feet, the chest and the tail tip. White legs, a white collar and a blaze are optional. Brindle coats do occur, but are not (yet) recognized by the FCI. A black nose is preferred, but a pale pink nose is not considered a fault in outstanding specimens. The eyes are dark.

Basenji

Basenjis

Basenji

TEMPERAMENT

CHARACTER

Basenjis are independent and self-willed, but also devoted to the family and appreciate their company. Intelligent, clever and inquisitive, they are alert to what goes on around them. They are vigilant and will let you know if anything is amiss. This breed has a number of remarkable characteristics. Basenjis do not bark but produce a kind of yodeling sound. They are cat-like in the way they lick their coats clean. Another distinct feature is that females of this breed usually come into heat only once a year.

SOCIAL BEHAVIOR

These dogs get on well with children, provided they do not pester the animals. Basenjis can never be considered real playmates, though. This breed is reserved towards strangers and dislikes people who are overly familiar towards them. Contact with other dogs is generally no problem, although some specimens can be a little headstrong. This breed has a fairly strong hunting instinct, which necessitates good supervision during the period of socialization with cats and other pets.

GENERAL CARE

GROOMING

Basenjis are very clean animals. They shed little and therefore do not need much grooming. During the molt, you can use a soft rubber brush and a grooming glove to remove the few dead hairs from the coat. Outside these periods you should groom the coat once a week using a soft grooming brush. Keep the claws short. Most Basenjis cope well with the heat, but detest rain and cannot stand cold or drafts. This makes them unsuitable for kennel life.

Basenjis

TRAINING

If you want to own a perfectly obedient companion dog, then you should really look for a different breed. Basenjis are too independent to take pleasure in obeying all kinds of commands. In spite of this, you certainly can teach these dogs any number of commands, although this requires a great deal of cunning from the trainer. Allow plenty of time and attention to their socialization with other animals and to the "Come Here" command.

EXERCISE

A Basenji is a fairly calm and placid dog that usually adapts to your circumstances and is quiet in the house. Nevertheless, this dog deserves more than just a few short walks each day. This breed is well suited to apartment life. If you enjoy long hikes then a Basenji will happily accompany you without tiring. Bear in mind that this breed has a tendency to take off on its own; make sure your yard is well fenced and only let the dog run free where this is safe.

USES

This breed is mainly popular as a companion dog. In view of its independent streak it is not suited for the various types of dog sports.

PHARAOH HOUND	
COUNTRY OF ORIGIN	MALTA
ORIGINAL FUNCTION	INDEPENDENT HUNTER THAT WORKS BY SIGHT, SOUND AND SCENT, PARTICULARLY SMALL GAME SUCH AS RABBITS

APPEARANCE

BODY

The Pharaoh Hound is an elegant dog of powerful build. The topline is almost level with the croup sloping down slightly. The chest reaches to the elbows and the ribs are well sprung. The abdomen is slightly tucked up. The medium-set tail is wide at the root and tapers to a point. It reaches to the hocks and is held downwards at rest – but never between the hind legs. The tail is raised in a curve when the dog is in action. The legs are straight, with strong feet. The long, slightly arched neck is muscular and dry.

Pharaoh Hound

HEAD
The head is wedge-shaped and has a long, dry skull. The muzzle is usually slightly longer than the skull. In profile, the top of the skull runs parallel to the nose bridge, divided by a slight stop. The moderately high-set ears are fairly large and carried erect. The eyes are oval in shape, with an intelligent expression. Pharaoh Hounds have a strong scissors bite.

SHOULDER HEIGHT
The ideal size for dogs is approx. 22 in (56 cm) and for bitches $20^{1}/_{2}$ in (53 cm).

COAT
Pharaoh Hounds have a short, glossy coat.

COLORS
The coat color is light to dark reddish brown. A white tail tip is highly desirable. Some white on the chest and toes and a narrow white blaze are permissible.

TEMPERAMENT

CHARACTER
Pharaoh Hounds are playful, intelligent, friendly and reasonably obedient and affectionate. They form a close bond with their owners and the family without becoming clingy and they tend to be very quiet in the house. They are equable and good-natured, as well as fairly vigilant and brave. The Pharaoh Hound has a lot of stamina and a highly developed hunting instinct.

SOCIAL BEHAVIOR
Dogs of this breed can be dominant towards their own kind at times. While Pharaoh Hounds generally get along fine with children, they are somewhat reserved towards strangers but certainly not aggressive or shy. Cats and other small household animals are not the most ideal of pets for a Pharaoh Hound, as the dog regards them as prey. With the right approach and very early training this dog can be taught to live together with a quiet household cat.

GENERAL CARE

GROOMING
The Pharaoh Hound needs very little coat care. During the molt you can easily remove dead and loose hair from the coat with a rubber brush. For the finishing touches you can also use a soft cloth and some grooming lotion to polish the coat. Keep the claws short.

Pharaoh Hound

TRAINING
The Pharaoh Hound is generally not difficult to train. It is reasonably pliable by nature and rarely shows any signs of rebellion. The "Come Here" command requires particular attention during the training. This is because its hunting instinct can get the better of the dog once it is off-leash, which could cause problems in a well-populated area or in places with busy roads. Snacks and friendly words can sometimes work wonders here.

EXERCISE
The Pharaoh Hound needs plenty of exercise. Allow at least one hour each day to go running with this dog or to take it on a long walk. Pharaoh Hounds do have a tendency to take off when they catch wind or sight of any game. Make sure your yard is surrounded by a sturdy and high fence. These dogs can jump very high.

USES
Rabbit hunting, for which this breed was originally bred, is illegal in most countries. However, coursing is an excellent alternative for unemployed Pharaoh Hounds.

Pharaoh Hound

DETAILS

The Pharaoh Hound is sometimes considered "half Greyhound," because it hunts not just by sight but also by scent and sound.

MEXICAN HAIRLESS DOG OR XOLOITZCUINTLE	
COUNTRY OF ORIGIN	MEXICO
ORIGINAL FUNCTION	THIS ANCIENT AZTEC BREED WAS USED AS A WATCHDOG, BUT ALSO AS A SACRIFICIAL ANIMAL AND FOR CONSUMPTION

APPEARANCE

BODY
The Xolo should look similar to a large Manchester Terrier, being elegantly built with sturdy yet slender legs. It has a fairly long body with a level back, a rounded croup and a muscular, tucked-up belly. The chest reaches to the elbows and is narrow. The legs are straight, with tight elbows and strong thighs. Xolos have hare feet. The low-set tail tapers to a point and should reach at least to the hocks. The long, slightly arched neck is set high and is free from wrinkle or dewlap.

HEAD
The long, pointed muzzle is longer than the comparatively large skull. There is a slight stop. The ears are large, thin and delicate. They are carried erect when the dog is alert. The eyes are medium size and slightly almond-shaped. Xolos have a scissors bite, which does not need to be complete.

SHOULDER HEIGHT
Xolos come in two sizes: the miniature Xolo has a shoulder height ranging from $9^1/_2$–13 in (25–33 cm) and the standard and most common variety has a shoulder height of at least 13–22 in (33–56 cm).

COAT
Xolos have no coat but are nude, often with the exception of a stiff short-haired wisp on the forehead and some longer hairs on the tail tip. The skin feels smooth and warm.

COLORS
They come in various colors including black, elephant gray, dark bronze or gray black. Lighter patches are permitted, provided they are not too

Mexican Hairless Dog

prominent. Dark eyes are preferred, but light eyes also occur.

TEMPERAMENT

Mexican Hairless Dog

CHARACTER

The Xolo is affectionate towards its own people, including the children, and is calm, even-tempered and dignified in character. These intelligent and obedient dogs are very adaptable. The larger specimens in particular make excellent guards. They do not bark, but produce a kind of howling sound. Indoors they tend to be quiet.

SOCIAL BEHAVIOR

These striking, rare dogs generally get on well with their own kind and once properly socialized they are also fine with other pets. They tend to be patient with children and somewhat aloof towards strangers. They are not friends to all-comers, but if the master says it's okay then strangers will be accepted.

GENERAL CARE

GROOMING

Although the Mexican Hairless Dog requires no grooming, the skin does need to be treated regularly. Handlers regularly scrub the skin (using a scrub cream intended for humans) to remove

Mexican Hairless Dog

Mexican Hairless Dogs

dead skin cells and to keep the skin soft. The main point is that the skin remains supple and even and is protected from drying out. A good lotion or cream is excellent for this purpose, but sometimes it is necessary to rub the skin with oil. Because it burns easily, the skin must be protected from the sun using a good quality oil or cream in the summer. One advantage of this breed is that it is not a very attractive habitat for fleas, and you will obviously not find any hairs on your clothes and carpets.

TRAINING

The Mexican Hairless Dog is not difficult to train. These dogs are intelligent and fairly quick learners. They do retain their dignity at all times and do not relish having to follow the same command repeatedly. A consistent training based on mutual respect will bring out the best in this breed.

EXERCISE

This dog needs very little exercise. It is perfectly happy if it can frolic and play regularly, or even if it can come along with its owner on a leash. Nearly all Xolos are usually quiet in the house.

USES

This breed makes an excellent companion dog for families with or without children who would love to own an unusual dog. This breed is under-represented in the various branches of dog sports.

SECTION 7   Primitive hounds

PODENCO IBICENCO (IBIZAN HOUND)

COUNTRY OF ORIGIN	THE BALEARIC ISLANDS
ORIGINAL FUNCTION	INDEPENDENT HUNTING DOG WORKING BY SIGHT, SOUND AND SMELL AND SPECIALIZING IN SMALL GAME SUCH AS RABBITS

APPEARANCE

BODY

Ibizan Hounds have a level back with high withers, arched loins and a sloping croup. The chest is deep and narrow, with a prominent breastbone. The ribs are slightly arched. The tail is set fairly low and reaches at least to the hocks. It is carried low between the legs and slightly higher when the dog is in action. There is no preference for curled or raised tails. The legs are very long and straight, with sturdy, straight hare feet. The long, dry neck is slightly arched.

HEAD

The long, narrow head is wedge-shaped with a narrow forehead and an indistinct stop. There is a prominent occipital peak. The skull and muzzle are equal in length. The nose bridge is slightly arched and the lips are tight. In profile the nose reaches beyond the lower jaw. The medium-sized, long, diamond-shaped ears are set on at eye level and carried erect when the dog is alert. The small eyes are set obliquely in the skull and

have an intelligent expression. Podenco Ibicencos have a pincer bite.

SHOULDER HEIGHT

Dogs are from 26–28$\frac{1}{4}$ in (66–72 cm). Bitches stand 23$\frac{1}{2}$–26$\frac{1}{2}$ in (60–67 cm) tall.

COAT

The Podenco Ibicenco comes in short, long and rough coats. The short-haired is the most common and the longhaired fairly rare. The long-haired has slightly longer rough hair, which is fairly soft in texture.

COLORS

Red and white dogs are preferred, but solid white or red dogs are also acceptable. The standard also permits a fawn coat, provided the dog is exceptional in all other areas. The eyes are light amber.

Smooth-hair Podenco Ibicenco

TEMPERAMENT

CHARACTER

These even-tempered, intelligent dogs are very loyal to their own people, reasonably eager to learn and obedient. They are affectionate, but at the same time reasonably independent as well. They are alert to what goes on around them and will certainly bark if they sense there is something amiss. Podenco Ibicencos are calm and affectionate in the house. Outdoors they are energetic, playful and active, and inexhaustible when playing or hunting. They are fairly tough on themselves and have a well-developed hunting instinct. This dog is not suited to kennel life.

SOCIAL BEHAVIOR

Ibizan Hounds generally get along well with children but tend to be a little reserved towards

Rough-hair Podenco Ibicenco

strangers. But once they realize the strangers mean no harm they thaw very quickly. Podenco dogs can be dominant towards other dogs at times. There will be no problems with any cats, provided the dogs have been introduced to them when young. Cats outside will often be chased, though.

GENERAL CARE

GROOMING

Dogs of this breed, irrespective of their type of coat, need very little grooming. The short-haired Podenco can be brushed with a soft rubber brush now and then during the molt. The coat can then be polished with a soft cloth and some grooming lotion. The rough and longhaired varieties should be brushed about once a week or slightly less frequently. Plucking or clipping is not necessary.

TRAINING

This breed is not difficult to train. The Podenco Ibicenco is a dog that is eager to learn and intelligent enough to quickly grasp what is expected. It responds well to its owner's voice and punishments will rarely be necessary. A friendly request achieves more than a grouchy command. The "Come here" command requires special attention.

Once the dog has caught sight of a rabbit or a different prey then it is difficult to recall.

EXERCISE

Dogs of this breed are very adaptable and provided they get plenty of exercise they are also suitable for apartment-life. You could consider letting the dog run alongside you when you go bike-walking, but only once the dog is fully grown. Podencos can sometimes follow their noses or their eyes when they discover something interesting, so make sure that your yard is well fenced; this breed can jump

Podenco Ibicenco

6½ feet (2 meters) high from stance and can allegedly also climb fences. Most Podencos love retrieving.

Podenco Ibicenco

USES

Coursing is a very appropriate sport for this breed. With the right supervision and, above all, the right attitude from their handlers, this breed can also take part in other types of dog sports, such as agility and obedience. However, this should be taken in perspective. Do not expect a top performance from a dog that has basically been bred for hunting game on its own.

DETAILS

The Podenco Ibicenco is sometimes considered half Greyhound, because it does not just hunt by sight but also by scent and sound.

Cirneco dell'Etna

CIRNECO DELL'ETNA (SICILIAN GREYHOUND)

COUNTRY OF ORIGIN	SICILY
ORIGINAL FUNCTION	HUNTING DOG. IT HUNTS PREY, MAINLY RABBITS, INDEPENDENTLY USING ITS SCENT, SOUND AND SIGHT.

APPEARANCE

BODY

Dogs of this breed have a square build, which means that the length of the trunk is equal to the shoulder height. The back is long and level. The fairly long tail is set low and is carried saber-fashion at rest. When the dog is in action the tail is curved over the croup. The chest is narrow and the chest muscles are poorly developed. The abdomen is tucked up. The shoulders are long and powerful. The legs are long, straight, lightly boned and dry. The hocks are well let down. The feet are oval in shape with well arched, closed toes. The muscular, dry throat is well arched at the top, with the neck sharply defined.

HEAD

The skull is narrow and long and the muzzle is slightly shorter than the skull or equal in length. The nose bridge is straight and the cheeks are flat. In profile, the large nose extends beyond the poorly developed receding chin and lower jaw.

The lips are delicate, tight and close fitting. The triangular ears are large and carried erect. The ears should never be longer than half the total length of the head. They are set high and fairly close together. The slanting eyes are normal size, but because they are deep set they seem a little small. They are oval in shape. Cirneco dell'Etnas have a scissors bite.

SHOULDER HEIGHT

Dogs are 18–19$\frac{1}{2}$ in (46–50 cm) and bitches 16$\frac{1}{2}$–18 in (42–46 cm).

WEIGHT

Dogs weigh 22–26$\frac{1}{2}$ lb (10–12 kg) and bitches approx. 17$\frac{1}{2}$–22 lb (8–10 kg).

COAT

Cirneco dell'Etnas have a smooth, close-lying coat, which is approx. 1$\frac{1}{2}$ in (3 cm) in length on the body and tail. The hair is shorter on the head, the ears and the legs.

COLORS

Nearly all solid shades of red are permitted, including diluted shades such as isabella and sandy. A white blaze, patch on the chest, feet, belly and tail tip are permitted. A white neck ring is less desirable. Solid white coats, white with orange blankets and all shades of red, mingled with lighter and darker hairs are uncommon but acceptable.

TEMPERAMENT

CHARACTER

Cirneco dell'Etnas are friendly, intelligent, com-

Cirneco dell'Etna

pliant and good-natured. Outdoors they are agile and energetic, but in the house they tend to be quiet. This dog will certainly warn you if anything is wrong, but unfortunately it may also bark without any particular reason. This breed is known for its loyalty and affection. In return these dogs do demand plenty of attention. They are devoted to their owners and do not usually cope very well when they are left on their own. They are not suited to kennel life.

other animals that they would normally hunt is not recommended. This breed is patient with children and reasonably tolerant. The arrival of strangers is marked, but that is usually all. These dogs are not natural defenders of the home.

GENERAL CARE

GROOMING
This breed requires little grooming. Brush the coat with a soft grooming brush now and then and polish it with a grooming glove or a hound glove. Check the ears for debris occasionally and keep the claws short.

TRAINING
The Cirneco dell'Etna is devoted to its owner and intelligent enough to grasp what is expected. It is generally reasonably obedient, although not suited to prolonged exercise drills. Optimum obedience should not be expected from this dog. A consistent and loving training is essential.

Cirneco dell'Etna

An older Cirneco dell'Etna

EXERCISE
The Cirneco needs plenty of exercise and you should allow at least an hour each day. Running off its energy is a good form of exercise for this breed. However, only let a Cirneco dell'Etna run off-leash when you can be sure there is no game nearby otherwise it may be tempted to go hunting on its own initiative. Cirnecos can jump very high, which is a good reason to enclose your yard with a solid, high fence.

USES
Coursing is a highly appropriate sport for this breed.

SOCIAL BEHAVIOR
This breed can be somewhat reserved with other dogs and they like to keep their owners to themselves. However, they generally do get along reasonably well with other specimens from their own breed and similar dog breeds. Contact with the family cat is no problem, provided they have been socialized with cats from a young age, but strange cats outdoors are usually chased. Because of their strong hunting instinct mixing with rabbits and

SECTION 8   Primitive hounds with a dorsal ridge

THAI RIDGEBACK DOG

COUNTRY OF ORIGIN	THAILAND
ORIGINAL FUNCTION	HUNTING AND GUARD DOG

APPEARANCE

BODY

The Thai Ridgeback Dog is medium-sized with a rectangular build and well-developed muscles. The back and loins are strong and the croup is slightly arched. The tail is thick at the root and tapers to a point, reaching to the hocks and carried raised.

The chest is deep and spacious and the ribcage is moderately arched. The abdomen is tucked up. The legs are straight and parallel to each other. The feet have close-knit toes. The neck is of medium length and muscular. The head is carried proudly.

HEAD

The head has a flat skull, a moderate stop and a long muzzle. A striking feature are the fine wrinkles on the forehead that appear when the dog is alert. The nose bridge is straight. The lips are dry and tight fitting. The large ears are triangular in shape. They are fairly wide apart and are always carried pricked, pointing slightly forwards. The medium-sized eyes are oval in shape. Thai Ridgeback Dogs have a scissors bite.

SHOULDER HEIGHT

The size for dogs: 21–23$^1/_2$ in (52$^1/_2$–60 cm), for bitches 18$^3/_4$–21$^3/_4$ in (47$^1/_2$–55 cm).

Thai Ridgeback Dog

Thai Ridgeback Dog

COAT

The coat is very short and feels velvety. The "ridge" on the back is characteristic of the breed. This is a line of hair growing in the opposite direction from the rest of the coat. The ridge should be straight, not too wide and should ideally run from the shoulders to the croup.

COLORS

Thai Ridgeback Dogs come in various shades of solid blue, very pale brown and black. The most common color is blue. The eye color depends on the coat color.

Thai Ridgeback Dog

TEMPERAMENT

CHARACTER

These fairly authentic and striking dogs are intelligent, active and nimble. They are alert to what goes on around them and fairly vigilant. Their stamina is tremendous. Although loyal to their owners, they will never be subservient. Thai Ridgebacks can be fairly self-willed at times. They display a lot of initiative and are also reasonably independent. Most bitches come into season only once a year.

SOCIAL BEHAVIOR

There are a number of individual differences in terms of social behavior within this breed that may be due to their early youth. Thai Ridgeback Dogs growing up in the Western world that are well socialized usually get on reasonably well with household pets such as cats. Their reaction to strangers is well-balanced, although invariably somewhat reserved and vigilant. They dislike strangers that behave too freely towards them but most specimens get along well with children, provided they do not pester the dog. However, dogs from the country of origin often have problems of adjustment. This is why it is better to buy a puppy from a breeder in your own country.

GENERAL CARE

GROOMING

This breed has minimum care requirements. The coat is very short and sheds little. Brush the coat with a soft grooming brush now and then and keep the claws short.

TRAINING

The Thai Ridgeback Dog is highly intelligent and

Thai Ridgeback Dog

is able to learn quite a bit, but also has a mind of its own and may not always do as it is told. The owner should therefore be cunning and very patient. Always be consistent and unambiguous towards the dog and try to make the training exercises as varied and fun as possible. This will keep the Thai motivated, so it will be more inclined to follow your commands. Do not make the mistake of treating this breed harshly; you would merely lose the dog's respect and it would act accordingly.

EXERCISE

The Thai Ridgeback Dog needs a fair amount of exercise. Regular runs or long hikes are a must to keep the dog mentally and physically in good condition. Most Thai Ridgebacks are not keen on ball games and similar activities, and they are not accomplished swimmers either. However, Thai Ridgeback Dogs do possess a certain amount of hunting instinct. If you take the dog out off-leash, make sure you let it run free in places where this is safe.

USES

Outside its country of origin this still relatively rare dog is used mainly as a companion dog. There are examples of specimens that have successfully completed various classes, but in general these dogs are not suitable for the various dog sports.

Thai Ridgeback Dog

Thai Ridgeback Dog

Hounds and related breeds

BLOODHOUND OR ST. HUBERT HOUND

COUNTRY OF ORIGIN	BELGIUM
ORIGINAL FUNCTION	TRACKING AND SCENT DOG

APPEARANCE

BODY

The Bloodhound has a strong back and powerful, deep and slightly arched loins. The shoulders are muscular, the chest is well let down between the forelegs, while the ribs are well sprung. The long tail tapers to a point and is carried high. The straight legs are heavy in bone and strong feet. The neck is long.

Bloodhounds have excellent scenting ability

HEAD

Bloodhounds have a long, narrow head, which appears to be of equal width throughout when viewed from above. The head shows an abundance of loose skin. The occipital protuberance is very pronounced. In profile the upper outline of the skull is almost in the same plane as that of the muzzle. The foreface is long and deep and should be at least equal in length to the skull. In front the lips fall squarely, making a right angle with the upper line of the foreface, while further back they form deep hanging flews that run into the loose dewlap. The thin ears are soft to the touch, very long, set low and hang in graceful folds, with the lower parts curling inward and backward. The medium-sized eyes are not too deeply set. The eyelids are oval in shape and should not obstruct the eyes.

SHOULDER HEIGHT

Dogs have a shoulder height ranging from $25^{1}/_{2}$ –$27^{1}/_{2}$ in (64–69 cm) and bitches from 23–25 in (59–64 cm).

WEIGHT

Bitches have an average weight of $79^{1}/_{2}$ –$99^{1}/_{4}$ lb (36–45 kg) and dogs usually weigh from $88^{1}/_{4}$–$110^{1}/_{4}$ lb (40–50 kg). Hounds of the maximum height and weight are preferred, provided the overall impression is well balanced.

COAT

The Bloodhound has a fairly short, close-lying coat that is slightly longer underneath the tail. On the head and ears the coat is soft and silky.

COLORS

Black and tan, liver and tan, and fallow. The latter color may be interspersed with lighter or badger-colored hair. A small amount of white on the chest, feet, and tip of the tail is permissible.

TEMPERAMENT

CHARACTER

Bloodhounds are good-natured, friendly, stable and affectionate in character, can be fairly boisterous when young, but calm down in adulthood. Universally known for their outstanding scenting nose, they make excellent trackers who enjoy the company of other dogs and people, but who are independent and stubborn as well. Although their voice is pleasant and deep, they do not bark excessively. Once their interest is aroused, it is difficult to distract them and they will carry on tenaciously.

SOCIAL BEHAVIOR

These remarkable dogs usually get on well with children. Make sure they do not pester the dog because these dogs are so good-natured that they will lie there and meekly let children clamber all over them. Both wanted and unwanted visitors will be greeted as if the Bloodhound thinks "the more, the merrier", and they are certainly not guard dogs. Bloodhounds can live in harmony with other dogs and rarely cause problems with other household pets.

Bloodhound

GENERAL CARE

GROOMING

The Bloodhound's coat is easy to groom. Brush the dog from time to time to remove loose and dead hair, and pay particular attention to the long, floppy ears. Regularly check the ear passages for dirt and excessive earwax, and clean the ears with a suitable lotion if necessary. The long ears sometimes end up in the feeding bowl and it does no harm to wash them occasionally. Most specimens have more or less drooping eyelids that can cause irritation. Regularly administer eyedrops with a suitable agent containing vitamin A. By providing the Bloodhound with a soft and comfortable bed you will largely prevent unsightly calluses developing on pressure points.

Bloodhound

TRAINING

Bloodhounds are intelligent but fairly willful and not born to obey orders. But with plenty of patience, tact and insight they can still be trained successfully. These dogs know full well how easily they can get around you with a pathetic look and make use of it to get their own way. The most important consideration is to be consistent, but offering your dog tasty snacks will no doubt help during the training. Once the dog realizes it will benefit from being obedient, it will be more prepared to obey you.

EXERCISE

This breed has tremendous stamina and can walk for many hours on end. If you want to keep this dog as a pet, you will have to take it for hikes quite regularly. Bloodhounds are primarily tracking dogs that want to investigate whenever they encounter an "interesting" scent. Make sure that your yard is well fenced. Bloodhounds are resistant to cold and can be kept in a kennel provided they get sufficient exercise and attention, although a soft bed is recommended. It is not advisable to overtire them with walks or overexercise them until fully-grown.

This dog grows rapidly and needs all its energy for developing strong bones, joints and muscles.

USES

Bloodhounds are bred specifically for tracking and excel at this skill. You could consider a tracking class for your dog. Bloodhounds are also frequently used for cleanboot and scenting.

Black and Tan Coonhound

BLACK AND TAN COONHOUND

COUNTRY OF ORIGIN	USA
ORIGINAL AND TODAY'S FUNCTION	DOGS OF THIS BREED ARE SPECIALIZED IN HUNTING RACCOON. THEY TREE RACCOONS AND HOLD THEIR QUARRY UNTIL THE HUNTER ARRIVES. THIS BREED CAN BARK IMPRESSIVELY THROUGHOUT THE HUNT SO THE HUNTER KNOWS WHERE TO FIND THE DOG – AND THE GAME.

APPEARANCE

BODY

The Black and Tan Coonhound has a straight, muscular back that slopes gently down from withers to croup. The tail is set on directly below the backline and curves slightly downward but is raised above the topline when the dog is alert in action. The deep, wide chest should ideally be round. The legs are straight and solid, and must not be too short and well angulated. The hind legs are normally a little behind the body in stance. The feet

Bloodhound

are round and well closed. The hind feet are in stance behind the body. The muscular neck is slightly arched and of medium length.

HEAD

The head of the Black and Tan Coonhound is a little narrow in relation to its body and is oval shaped when viewed from the front. The skull is slightly domed and has a medium stop midway. In profile the skull and nose bridge run parallel and the skull and muzzle are of equal length. The lips are fairly thick. The ears are low, set well back on the head and must reach beyond the tip of the nose, hanging in graceful folds. The eyes are almost round in shape. Black and Tan Coonhounds have a scissors bite.

SHOULDER HEIGHT

Dogs have a shoulder height ranging from $24^3/_4$–$27^1/_2$ in (63–69 cm). Bitches measure $22^3/_4$–$24^3/_4$ in (58–63 cm).

WEIGHT

Adult dogs weigh approx. 75 lb (34 kg) while bitches weigh slightly less.

COAT

Short and very dense.

COLORS

The name of this dog is derived partly from the color of its coat, which is always black with tan markings on the muzzle, cheeks, legs, chest, above the eyes and inside the ears (black and tan). Some white markings on the chest are permissible, but too much white will lead to disqualification. The eyes are hazel to dark brown.

TEMPERAMENT

Black and Tan Coonhound

CHARACTER

Black and Tan Coonhounds possess an excellent nose and an above average hunting instinct. When they catch wind of an interesting scent they tend to run off after it. They are reasonably independent and tough, and are moderately keen to please. That does not mean that the dogs are not interested in their owners, because they are

Black and Tan Coonhound

in fact very loyal and devoted to their family. These dogs are highly intelligent and like to be kept busy. Indoors they are relatively inactive and fairly affectionate, while outdoors they are a bundle of energy. But they are attentive to what goes on around them and are also quite vigilant. When they scent danger they will use their deep and imposing voice, and if their owners are threatened these dogs will not hesitate to come to their rescue.

SOCIAL BEHAVIOR

This breed generally gets on well with other dogs. Mixing with cats and other pets may present difficulties because of its hunting instinct, but if properly socialized while still young this dog will get on fine with other animals. Coonhounds are generally very friendly with children. Strangers will be announced but with welcome visitors that is usually all.

GENERAL CARE

GROOMING

This breed needs relatively little grooming. During the molt a rubber mitt can be used to remove dead and loose hair. Regularly check the ear passages for debris and clean them if necessary. The long ears will collect some dirt during walks and can end up in the feeding bowl. Occasionally it is necessary to clean the tips of the ears with a wet washcloth.

Black and Tan Coonhound

TRAINING

This breed is very intelligent and has the ability to learn a lot, but are also independent by nature, and will never be servile. A relaxed owner with natural authority who trains in a consistent but gentle manner will achieve best results.

EXERCISE

Black and Tan Coonhounds need a fair amount of exercise. Three walks a day is certainly not enough. If the dog can release its energy outdoors every day for about an hour then it will be very calm in the house. Make sure your yard is well fenced. The dog should only be allowed to run free off its leash in a safe area and when you can be sure that it will come back when called.

USES

Rarely kept as a household or family dog, this breed is uncommon outside its country of origin. As a raccoon hunter it has certainly proved its worth. You could consider using this dog for scenting and cleanboot.

OTTERHOUND	
COUNTRY OF ORIGIN	GREAT BRITAIN
ORIGINAL FUNCTION	PACK HOUND FOR OTTER HUNTING

APPEARANCE

BODY

Otterhounds have a square build. The back is straight and the chest deep, as is the oval-shaped ribcage. The tail, which reaches to the hock, is carried low at rest and either straight or in a slight curve in movement. The legs are strong and straight. The hind legs are moderately angulated. Otterhounds have large, round and straight feet, which are web-toed. The neck is long and powerful.

HEAD

The imposing head is narrow rather than wide. It has a well-domed skull, which curves slightly upward from the stop to the moderately developed occipital protuberance. The nose is large with wide nostrils. Otterhounds have long, low set, pendulous ears reaching easily to the nose and with a characteristic fold. The eyes are moderately deeply set. The scissors bite in this breed is complete and regular.

Otterhound

Otterhound

SHOULDER HEIGHT

Dogs have a shoulder height of approx. 26½ in (67 cm); bitches are slightly smaller, measuring approx. 24¾ in (63 cm) at the shoulder.

COAT

Approx. 1¾–3¼ in (4–8 cm) long, rough, hard and dense with a thick undercoat. The coat has an oily structure and is weather-resistant. The hair has a softer structure on the head and legs. The ears and the head (apart from the nose bridge) should be well covered with hair. Otterhounds must not be trimmed for exhibition. They are supposed to look natural.

COLORS

All recognized hound colors are allowed, including slate, blue, red, wheaten, sandy, black and tan, and blue and tan.

TEMPERAMENT

CHARACTER

Otterhounds are friendly, even-tempered, affectionate but also rather boisterous. They have a cheerful and amiable disposition, and in line with their original function they are companionable; they are not solitary animals. They are also fairly independent and have a mind of their own. Otterhounds can be kept either in the house or in a kennel. They are tough and able to withstand all weathers.

Otterhound

SOCIAL BEHAVIOR

Otterhounds get on very well both with other dogs and with children. However, in their friendliness and exuberance they can easily knock over a small child. Although they like to make their powerful voice heard when visitors arrive, they usually greet everyone enthusiastically and are therefore not natural guard dogs. Mixing with family pets such as cats should not be a problem, provided the dog is introduced to them when young.

GENERAL CARE

GROOMING

Otterhound should look as natural as possible and therefore not trimmed. Brush the coat as little as possible. Keep the ear passages free from dirt, keep the claws short and occasionally check the eyes for hair or dirt.

Otterhound

TRAINING

Otterhounds were not traditionally kept as a family pet and are therefore not the most obedient of dogs, but they can still be trained successfully. The best results are achieved with a soft but consistent hand, using the classic "Iron fist in a velvet glove" approach.

EXERCISE

These dogs need plenty of exercise, but bear in

Otterhound

mind that they have a tendency to forget everything in the chase after they discover an interesting scent. Therefore they should only be allowed to run free off the leash where they can be controlled and kept safe. Make sure that your yard is well fenced.

USES

The Otterhound has an excellent nose and is ideally suited to clean-boot and scenting.

LONG-LEGGED, LARGE, AND MEDIUM-SIZED FRENCH BASSETS

Grand Anglo Français Tricolore

Short-legged hounds such as the Basset Bleu de Gascogne, the Basset Fauve de Bretagne and the short-legged Griffons are regarded as ideally suitable for life as household pets and are indeed kept as such in many countries. In contrast, the long-legged French bassets from this group are kept almost exclusively in kennels in packs for hunting. This category includes:

Anglo Français de Petit Venerie
Beagle Harrier
Billy
Briquet Griffon Vendéen
(Grand-) Anglo Français Blanc et Noir
(Grand-) Anglo Français Blanc et Orange
(Grand-) Anglo Français Tricolore
Grand Bleu de Gascogne
Griffon Bleu de Gascogne
Petit Bleu de Gascogne
Poitevin
Porcelaine

Otterhound

Griffon Bleu
de Gascogne

All these breeds hunt (large) game in packs which they track or drive whilst giving tongue to let the hunters know where the quarry is. Such dogs obviously have a deeply rooted hunting instinct and a good nose. They get on well with other dogs but are also friendly to people and children, although they can be a little boisterous. Because these dogs hunt together without orders from their owners, they are highly independent

Billy

Poitevins

in character. These breeds are rarely seen outside France. As a rule, they are less suitable as a family pet than the short-legged French bassets. Due to the stringent placement policy of hunters, who place their puppies almost exclusively with fellow hunters, and the relative obscurity of the dogs outside their country of origin, these dogs have never been able to prove whether they can cope in a family setting. There are some examples of individual dogs of these breeds that live as a family pet to the satisfaction of both family and

Poitevins

Porcelaine

Grand Anglo Français Tricolore

dog, but it is not possible to draw any conclusions for the entire breed on the basis of a few cases.

Tyroler Bracke

TYROLER BRACKE

COUNTRY OF ORIGIN	AUSTRIA
ORIGINAL AND TODAY'S FUNCTION	THIS BREED SPECIALIZES IN TRACKING AND TRAILING BIG GAME (RED DEER, WILD BOAR) WHILST GIVING TONGUE, AND IS USED AS A SCENTHOUND, OFTEN ON DIFFICULT TERRAIN. THEY ARE ALSO EXPECTED TO RETRIEVE SMALL GAME (HARE, FOX).

APPEARANCE

BODY

This medium-sized dog is longer than it is tall. The back is of moderate length, the long and pronounced withers forming the highest point of the topline. The chest is long and very deep, and narrow rather than wide. The legs are well angulated both at the front and back, and the feet are tightly closed. The tail is set fairly high and is carried high when the dog is working. Tyroler Brackes have a moderately long, slightly sloping neck that should have no dewlaps.

HEAD

The long head is dry, fairly narrow and finely built. The skull is slightly domed. The superciliary ridges and the stop are not pronounced. The nose

bridge is narrow and may be straight or bulge slightly. The lips are dry and close fitting. The eyes are triangular and fairly large. The medium-sized, soft and rounded ears are set high, far back and are pendulous. Tyroler Brackes have a scissors bite.

SHOULDER HEIGHT

Varies between 16–19 in (40–48 cm). The Niederbracke is a short-legged Tyroler Bracke, with a shoulder height of 12–15$\frac{1}{2}$ in (30–39 cm).

COAT

Wiry, close lying with a soft undercoat. The tail is often more bristly.

COLORS

Tyroler Brackes are bred in black and in red to sedge. White markings on the chest, muzzle, neck and legs are allowed. There are also tricolor Tyroler Brackes with a black saddle or mantle and yellow brown to red markings on the legs, chest, belly and head, with a few white markings. The eyes are chestnut to brown. The nose is always black.

TEMPERAMENT

CHARACTER

These sober and agile working dogs are tenacious, have great stamina and an excellent scenting nose, and are keen hunters. They are very brave and tough on themselves. Although very active, willful and somewhat prone to wander, these dogs are very affectionate towards their owners and family members.

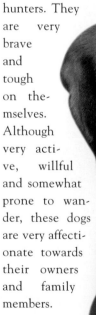

Tyroler Bracke

SOCIAL BEHAVIOR

Although they can be dominant at times, these dogs generally get on fairly well with other dogs. They mix reasonably well with children and are friendly to strangers. Socializing with pets such as cats can be a problem because this breed has a highly developed hunting instinct. Nevertheless, it is not impossible to get a Tyroler Bracke used to living with a domestic cat, provided the dog has been introduced to the cat as a puppy.

GENERAL CARE

GROOMING

The Tyroler Bracke needs very little grooming. Brushing may be necessary during the molt to remove loose hairs. The claws should be kept short.

Tyroler Bracke

TRAINING

The type of work for which this dog is often used comes natural; usually the dog only needs some guidance. This breed can also be taught other principles, such as basic obedience skills, but they require plenty of patience and insight from the owner.

EXERCISE

Tyroler Brackes need plenty of exercise. Provided their needs are met they are fairly calm in the home. They like to take off on their own which makes it necessary to fence off your yard and only take the dog out on a leash.

USES

This breed is seldom kept as a household pet and as a rule is not really suited for this purpose. It is mainly used by hunters who breed the dog for specific tasks. This dog comes into its own in remote areas; once it has found a track it will not give up, even if that means it will have to walk for a whole day or more. There is a strict selective breeding program in the country of origin; breeding is only allowed with dogs that have successfully completed the various working trials and that have also won the minimum qualification "very good" during field trials.

ERDELYI KOPO	
COUNTRY OF ORIGIN	HUNGARY
ORIGINAL AND TODAY'S FUNCTION	SCENTHOUND HUNTING FOR BIG AND SMALL GAME

Erdelyi Kopo

APPEARANCE

BODY

The Erdelyi Kopo has a rectangular build with a level topline and a slight curve at the loins. The tail, which is set low and reaches to the hock, is carried low at rest with the tip usually curving upwards. The belly is slightly tucked up. The legs are straight and vertical with moderate angulation. Erdelyi Kopos have cat's feet. The neck is of medium length and muscular.

HEAD

The skull is slightly domed and the stop fairly flat. The nose bridge is straight. The lips are tight and close fitting. The relatively short ears are set high and carried pendulously. The medium-sized eyes are oval in shape. The eyelids are close fitting. This breed has a scissors bite.

SHOULDER HEIGHT

There are two different types of this breed: long and short-legged. Long-legged dogs have a shoulder height ranging from $21^3/_4$–$25^1/_2$ in (55–65 cm)

Erdelyi Kopo

CHARACTER

This breed is independent, enterprising, intelligent and friendly. These dogs are keen hunters with an excellent nose and a lot of stamina. Outdoors they are active and agile, but in the house they tend to be placid and very affectionate. Usually they reach intellectual maturity at the age of 2 to 3 years. Erdelyi Kopos cope well with all weathers and can be kept in a kennel outside, provided they have enough contact with people and get plenty of exercise.

SOCIAL BEHAVIOR

Erdelyi Kopos are sociable dogs that mix extremely well with other dogs. As keen hunters they are not the most ideal companions for cats, livestock or rabbits, although proper socialization at an early age will certainly make a difference. These rare Hungarian dogs get on well with children, but they tend to be suspicious and aloof though not aggressive towards strangers. They will only use their teeth as a last resort, for instance when a family member is threatened.

GENERAL CARE

GROOMING

These dogs require very little grooming. Brushing the coat with a hard bristle brush once a week is sufficient. Use a rubber mitt to remove dead hair during the molt. The claws should be kept short.

and short-legged specimens measure 17³/₄–19¹/₂ in (45–50 cm) to the highest point of the withers. Conformation and type are usually considered to be more important than the exact height of the dog.

COAT

Short and glossy. The long-legged Kopo has a slightly coarser coat texture.

COLORS

Long-legged Erdelyi Kopos have a black background with tan and often also small white markings. The white markings must never cover more than one third of the total body area. Short-legged dogs have a brown-red coat with white markings.

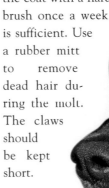

Erdelyi Kopo

Erdelyi Kopo

Erdelyi Kopo

TRAINING

Having been bred for this purpose for generations, they will soon learn the finer points of hunting. You can also teach them other commands, but this requires more patience and skill. An Erdelyi Kopo is intelligent enough to grasp what is expected of him but will often have a mind of its own. Do not pitch your expectations too high. Always be consistent and clear. A tough training is not recommended with this breed.

EXERCISE

These dogs need plenty of exercise and will not put up with three short walks a day. Allow at least one hour a day to take the dog for a walk, a run or a swim. Bear in mind that their urge to chase after game may be stronger than the bond with you; only let them run free in safe areas and keep your yard well fenced.

USES

In its country of origin this breed is used almost exclusively for hunting and its original function, trailing, has faded slightly into the background. Nowadays, these dogs are generally used as scenthounds. This breed can also be kept as a family pet, but only in very active families who can accommodate the dog's great need for exercise.

SABUESO ESPAÑOL	
COUNTRY OF ORIGIN	SPAIN
ORIGINAL AND TODAY'S FUNCTION	THESE GUNDOGS ARE USED FOR TRAILING GAME AND FOR WORKING AND TRACKING TRAILS. SABUESO ESPAÑOLS ARE USED FOR HUNTING FUR, SUCH AS HARE AND RABBIT, DEER, FOX AND WILD BOAR

APPEARANCE

BODY

The Sabueso Español has a rectangular build. The body is powerful, with a roomy chest and a well-defined forechest. The forehand is set somewhat lower than the hindquarters, which

Sabueso Español

gives the dog a slightly overbuilt impression. The tail forms a continuation of the topline and reaches slightly further than the hock joints. It is carried low at rest and above the topline during work.

HEAD
Elongated with a gently sloping stop and a small occipital protuberance. The muzzle and skull are equal in size. The ears are very long; they should reach beyond the forenose, and are rectangular in shape with rounded tips. The almond-shaped eyes have a friendly expression.

SHOULDER HEIGHT
In dogs $20^1/_2$ –$22^1/_2$ in (52–57 cm) and in bitches 19–$20^1/_2$ in (48–53 cm).

COAT
Short, thick and dense.

COLORS
Sabueso Españols are white with orange, or orange with white markings. The orange may be either very light or dark. The eyes are brown in color.

TEMPERAMENT

CHARACTER
These Spanish hounds are generally friendly and good-natured, though brave and tenacious during the hunt. They are also fairly hardy, not squeamish and tireless during walks. They tend to have an even-tempered but stubborn character. Sabueso Españols have a dark voice that may scare off intruders, but they are not suitable as a guard and defense dog.

SOCIAL BEHAVIOR
As can be expected from a hound, this Spanish dog usually behaves well towards other dogs and also gets on fine with children. Mixing with small and large pets should not cause any problems, provided the

Sabueso Español

dog is properly socialized with such animals as a puppy. Though somewhat aloof towards strangers at first, they are not unfriendly.

GENERAL CARE

GROOMING
Grooming the Sabueso Español is not labor-intensive. Weekly brushing is generally sufficient. During the molt you can remove dead and loose hairs from the coat quickly and efficiently using a rubber brush. The long leathers need to be cleaned when necessary. Check the ear passages for dirt every week.

Sabueso Español-
puppies

TRAINING

People who are looking for a dog that obeys them unconditionally should not consider this breed. Breeders have never aimed for unconditional obedience towards the owner. Character traits such as showing initiative and independence are very important for its original function. Training must be consistent and gentle. The owner must show some understanding of the dog's natural disposition. It is absolutely pointless to drill it or to put it under undue pressure, as this will only make the dog anxious. If properly trained, the Sabueso Español can grasp a surprising number of commands. The biggest shortcoming of this breed is that it has a tendency to take off when off-leash, particularly in areas where there is game. Owners should allow for this and emphasize the command "Come here" during the training, ideally supported by plenty of praise and snacks, thus making the "return to owner" a pleasant task.

EXERCISE

Sabueso Españols are not suitable for lazy people. They love walking and can carry on for hours without any sign of tiredness. By taking it for

Sabueso Español

Sabueso Español

a walk three times a day you would definitely do this dog an injustice. Despite a decent training you cannot expect this dog to keep close to you all the time during off-leash walks. In areas where there is a lot of traffic it is preferable to take the dog out on a long leash. These dogs are not yard-bound. A well-fenced yard is required to contain your dog. Indoors they tend to be placid but only if they get enough exercise.

USES

Aside from its original work, which is not allowed in every country, there are various other possibilities of doing something with your dog. Sabuesos have an excellent nose and love tracking. Tracking games as well as tracking dog training and disciplines such as cleanboot are ideally suited for this breed. They also do well as a house dog in a sporty family. Sabuesos that have been raised in a family behave well in the house and are fairly placid.

Hamiltonstövare

HAMILTONSTÖVARE	
COUNTRY OF ORIGIN	SWEDEN
ORIGINAL AND	HUNTING DOG (SCENTHOUND)
TODAY'S FUNCTION	FOR
	HARE AND FOX HUNTING

APPEARANCE

BODY
Medium lenght and with a powerful build, a wide, long croup that slopes slightly down. The chest is deep and reaches beyond the elbows. The ribs are moderately arched and the belly is slightly tucked up. The tail forms a continuation of the topline and reaches to the hock. It is straight or slightly curved and tapers towards the tip. The elbows are held close. The legs are well angulated, straight and muscular, with solid feet and tightly closed toes. The neck is long and muscular, with no loose dewlap.

HEAD
Long, rectangular in shape and dry. The skull is slightly domed. The stop and occipital protuberance are not well defined. Viewed from aside, the nose bridge runs parallel to the skull. The upper lip is full, but should not overhang too much. The ears are set on fairly high and are carried pendulously, reaching to almost half of the nose bridge. The eyes have a calm expression. Hamiltonstövares have a scissors bite.

SHOULDER HEIGHT
For dogs $20^1/_2$–$23^1/_2$ in (53–60 cm) and for bitches $19^1/_2$–$22^1/_2$ in (50–57 cm).

WEIGHT
These dogs weigh approx. 55–$66^1/_4$ lb (25–30 kg).

COAT
Hamiltonstövares have a dense, thick and close-lying upper coat with a short, dense and soft undercoat. The hair on the underside of the tail may be a little longer.

COLORS
The top of the neck, tail and back are black. White is shown on the tip of the tail, the legs and chest, the neck and muzzle. The other areas are brown. White patches on the top of the neck are allowed. Ideally the colors should be clearly separated. The eyes are light or dark brown.

TEMPERAMENT

CHARACTER
The Hamiltonstövare has a friendly and quiet character. It is a reasonably compliant and reliable worker. Its nose is excellent and it has a great hunting instinct. Although it barks when it senses danger, it is not a natural guard dog.

SOCIAL BEHAVIOR
These dogs tend to get on very well both with other dogs and with children, and they are friend-

Hamiltonstövare

Hamiltonstövare

ly towards strangers. Their hunting passion can lead them to chase cats and other pets, but proper and early socialization could make all the difference.

GENERAL CARE

GROOMING

This breed requires very little grooming. Brushing the coat with a soft brush once a week and keeping the claws short is sufficient. During the molt you could use a rubber brush or mitt to remove loose hairs. Occasionally check the ear passages.

TRAINING

Owners of a Hamiltonstövare must realize they are dealing with a highly independent working dog. Although affectionate to their owners, these dogs are also rather stubborn. Training can therefore be a lengthy procedure, which demands plenty of patience and understanding from the owner. Nevertheless, this dog can learn quite a bit if trained using a gentle and consistent approach, although owners should not expect absolute obedience. Most dogs of this breed like their food, and you can make use of this to support the training. Returning to the owner on command should be stressed during the training.

Hamiltonstövare

EXERCISE

Hamiltonstövares need plenty of exercise. Regularly take them for long walks on a leash. These dogs are not suited to ball games and the like. Do bear in mind that they will want to investigate if they smell an interesting scent. Only let your dog run free off-leash if you are sure it cannot endanger anyone or vice versa.

USES

In their country of origin these dogs are still employed in their original function, but they can also be used very well for scenting and scent trials. The stringent placement policy of hunters, who place their puppies almost exclusively with fellow hunters, makes it difficult for non-hunters to acquire a puppy.

Hamiltonstövare

SCHWEIZER LAUFHUND (SWISS HOUND)

THE SCHWEIZER LAUFHUND COMES IN 4 COLOR PATTERNS, EACH NAMED AFTER THEIR AREA OF ORIGIN:

- BERNER LAUFHUND (BERNESE HOUND)
- JURA LAUFHUND (JURA HOUND)
- LUZERNER LAUFHUND (LUCERNE HOUND)
- SCHWEIZER LAUFHUND (SWISS HOUND)

COUNTRY OF ORIGIN	SWITZERLAND
ORIGINAL AND TODAY'S FUNCTION	THESE SWISS HOUNDS WERE TRADITIONALLY BRED SPECIFICALLY FOR TRACKING GAME IN PACKS. HAVING FOUND A TRAIL, THE DOGS WILL TRACK IT WHILE LOUDLY INDICATING THEIR LOCATION TO THE HUNTER ("GIVING TONGUE"). NOWADAYS THESE DOGS ARE STILL USED FOR HUNTING, ALTHOUGH USUALLY SOLITARY RATHER THAN IN PACKS.

Jura Laufhund

APPEARANCE

BODY

Swiss Hounds are medium-sized, fairly elongated dogs built for strength and endurance. The back is rather long and straight, with strong loins. The tail reaches to the hock, is carried horizontally or with a slight curve, and should taper to the tip.

The chest is deep, must not be round or barrel-shaped, and reaches at least to the elbows. The legs are strong and straight, and the hindquarters are well muscled. Swiss Hounds have cat's feet. The neck is fairly long and powerful, with little dewlap.

HEAD

The dry head, with the long, twisted ears that are set on low and well back, give the Laufhund an aristocratic look. The stop is moderate and the nose bridge slightly curved. The eyes have a soft expression. Swiss Hounds have a level or scissors bite.

SHOULDER HEIGHT

Varies from $18\frac{1}{2}$–$22\frac{1}{2}$ in (47–57 cm).

COAT

The short, glossy coat is close lying. Most Laufhunds develop a thick undercoat in winter.

COLORS

The colors differ for each breed. The Berner Laufhund is white with a black saddle and tan markings; the Jura Laufhund is yellow or red brown either with or without a black saddle, or black and tan; the Luzerner

Luzerner Laufhund

Schweizer Laufhunds

Laufhund is blue roan with a black saddle and tan markings, and the Schweizer Laufhund is white with an orange to red saddle. An orange or red mantle is allowed with this breed, but is not preferred. The eyes are as dark as possible.

Schweizer Laufhund

TEMPERAMENT

CHARACTER

This is a gentle, intelligent and friendly breed of dog. They have a sociable attitude to life and an excellent scenting nose. They are sensitive to the atmosphere in the home. Although very affectionate and placid at home, they show a lot of initiative during the hunt and are capable of working independently. They are fond of the company of other dogs and of their handler.

Five-month old Schweizer
Laufhund bitch

SOCIAL BEHAVIOR

Laufhunds are very sociable animals, and you need not worry about problems with other dogs or with adults and children. But as a puppy they do need to be socialized well with cats and other pets. They will then live harmoniously alongside these animals.

GENERAL CARE

GROOMING

These dogs require relatively little grooming. Brushing the coat once a week with a grooming glove or a soft brush is sufficient. During the molt a rubber mitt can be used to remove dead hair from the coat. Rough and wire-haired dogs can be brushed with a slicker brush. These breeds have long pendulous ears that need to be regularly checked for dirt and excessive earwax. Use a good ear cleaner where necessary.

TRAINING

They will always be fairly independent hunting dogs that have to be trained gently but consistently with a lot of understanding for their character. Firm training is not recommended with these breeds. Most dogs are good eaters and a great deal can be achieved by offering them tidbits as a reward.

Jura Laufhund

Luzerner Laufhund

Schweizer Laufhunds

EXERCISE

Laufhunds need a fair amount of exercise. You can

Schweizer Laufhund

take your dog for off-leash walks if you have trained it from an early age to return promptly when called. There is always the chance that it will follow its sharp nose when it smells something interesting, although it cannot really be blamed for this. Make sure your yard is well fenced. Indoors these dogs are placid, sometimes to the point of laziness.

As a rule, these breeds make good companion dogs, provided they get to do "something" such as scent drags or the kind of hunting they were bred for. In Switzerland these dogs are also used for scenting.

NIEDERLAUFHUNDS

Schweizer Niederlaufhunds were created in a number of cantons in Switzerland early in the twentieth century. These dogs were developed when Laufhund lines were crossed with other breeds. The current Niederlaufhunds do not differ a great deal from the Schweizer Laufhunds, apart from the length of their legs; Niederlaufhunds have a shoulder height of 12–15 in (30–38 cm). They come in the same colors as the Laufhunds, but due to the influence of other breeds these dogs occasionally occur with rough-haired coats.

Jura Laufhund

German Brackes

GERMAN BRACKE

COUNTRY OF ORIGIN	GERMANY
ORIGINAL AND TODAY'S FUNCTION	THIS BREED IS USED FOR SCENTING GAME AND WORKING AND TRACKING TRAILS

APPEARANCE

BODY

The German Bracke is a finely made, elegant yet powerful dog that stands tall. The back is slightly arched and the croup slopes gently down. The long tail is thick, tapers to a point and is carried in a slight upward curve or level. The chest reaches to the elbows and is slightly arched with a long thorax. The shoulders are dry and the elbows are close fitting. The legs are dry, fine-boned and sinewy. The feet are round to oval and have tightly closed toes. The neck of this dog is moderately long and strong.

HEAD

The elongated head is light and dry, with a weakly defined stop and an almost imperceptible occipital protuberance. The nose bridge is slightly curved. The entire length of the head

is $8^1/_4$ in (21 cm) and the distance between the eyes is $3^1/_2$ in (9 cm). The ears are approx. $5^1/_2$ in (14 cm) long, carried pendulously and close to the head. The eyes are bright with a friendly expression. German Brackes should ideally have a scissors bite, but a level bite is allowed.

SHOULDER HEIGHT

Ranges from $16-20^1/_2$ in (40–53 cm).

COAT

German Brackes have a very dense, rough, short-haired coat, usually with an undercoat. The underside of the tail is generally covered with longer hair.

COLORS

The color is red to yellow, always with a black saddle and white markings. These markings are shaped like a continuous white blaze and muzzle, a white, preferably closed neck ring, white chest and white toes or feet and tip of the

German Bracke

German Brackes

tail. A flesh-colored line across the center of the nose is characteristic of the breed and should not be missing. The eyes are dark brown to hazel.

TEMPERAMENT

CHARACTER

This breed has a friendly, affectionate and sociable character. They often seem shy and are sensitive to the atmosphere in the home. They are reasonably obedient for a Bracke, but also independent. This dog will bark if it scents danger but is not suited as a defender of hearth and home. These dogs are curious about what goes on around them and prefer to live as part of the family. They have tremendous stamina, a great hunting instinct and an excellent nose.

SOCIAL BEHAVIOR

They rarely cause any problems with other dogs and also get on fine with children. If this breed is well socialized with cats and other pets, there will be no problems with these animals later on. With strangers they tend to be aloof at first, and prefer to make contact on their own initiative. Their attitude towards strangers is shy rather than proud.

GENERAL CARE

GROOMING

The German Bracke needs relatively little grooming. Run a rubber brush over the coat occasionally to remove dead and loose hair, and check the ear passages regularly for dirt or an excess of earwax.

TRAINING

Training this breed is not difficult to people who are familiar with the character of brackes. German Brackes are fairly docile and intelligent enough to grasp what is required of them. Firm training is counter-productive since this would ruin the dog's open and friendly nature. With patience, love, consistency and understanding the handler can achieve a lot.

EXERCISE

If you do not intend to hunt with this dog, make sure that you find some other means of fulfilling its exercise needs. They are keen on long walks through the woods and the countryside, but remember that this breed likes to follow its nose when it picks up an interesting scent trail. The dog will then follow its instincts and is oblivious to its owner's calls. Do not let this dog run free off-leash in places where this could be dangerous, such as near roads or in a wildlife area. A German Bracke that gets enough exercise outdoors is calm in the house, sometimes to the point of laziness, but when it gets too little exercise the opposite will be the case.

USES

German Brackes are ideally suited for scenting and for hunting hare, rabbit and wild boar. This breed lacks the right disposition for the various dog sports.

German Bracke

BEAGLE

COUNTRY OF ORIGIN	ENGLAND
ORIGINAL FUNCTION	PACK HOUND FOR TRACKING AND SCENTING GAME, MAINLY HARES AND RABBITS

Beagle

APPEARANCE

BODY

The Beagle is a sturdy dog of compact build with a straight, horizontal topline. The tail is set on high and carried gaily with a slight curve, but not over the back. It is hefty and should not be too long. The chest reaches to below the elbows and the arched ribs are carried well back. The loins are strong and short but not excessively tucked up.

Beagle puppy

The shoulders are fairly oblique. The solid elbows are not turned in or out, and are roughly halfway of the shoulder height. The forelegs are straight and round of bone across the entire length. The hocks are well arched. Beagles have close, strong feet with well-arched toes and short claws; hare-feet are not allowed. The neck is slightly curved and shows little dewlap.

HEAD

The head is fairly long and powerful without any coarseness, free from wrinkles and with a pronounced stop. The slightly domed skull is moderately broad with only a minor occipital protuberance. The muzzle is not snipey. The forenose is broad with wide nostrils. The rounded ears reach nearly to the forenose, are set low and hang gracefully alongside the cheeks. The eyes are fairly big, but not bulging or deep set and they are set well apart. Beagles have a scissors bite.

SHOULDER HEIGHT

The minimum height is $12^{1}/_{2}$ in (32 cm) with a maximum of $16^{1}/_{2}$ in (41 cm).

WEIGHT

Beagles weigh approx. $22–30^{3}/_{4}$ lb (10–14 kg).

COAT

The weather-resistant coat is short and dense.

COLORS

Any hound color, except liver, is allowed with this breed. The tip of the stern must be white. The tri-color beagle is the most common. The eyes are dark brown or hazel.

Beagles

dislike being left on their own. Rather sensitive, they are very good at sensing the mood in the house and their owners' feelings. They have an excellent scenting nose.

SOCIAL BEHAVIOR

The Basset Hound makes a terrific playmate for children, and also gets on well with dogs and other animals. Basset Hounds are friendly towards strangers, but they do start barking if they sense danger or if there are visitors. Although they are not natural guard dogs their deep voice is often enough to ward off any uninvited guests. These exceptional dogs do not usually like to be left on their own. If you need to leave the dog alone quite often, you would do well to consider having two Bassets.

Basset Hounds

Basset Hound bitch

GENERAL CARE

GROOMING

The coat of a Basset Hound is easy to care for. During the molt you can simply remove any dead and loose hairs using a rubber mitt. Outside this period weekly brushing with a soft bristle brush is adequate. The ears require a little more care. Regularly check the ear passages, and clean them with a special ear cleaner if necessary. Never use cotton swabs, but remove any dislodged debris from the surface with tissues. Because of the length of the ears the tips can become dirty. Wash them regularly with lukewarm water. The claws should be kept short. With some Basset Hounds, particularly specimens with very droopy eyelids, it is necessary to clean the eyes with an eye lotion or cream occasionally. This breed has a tendency to get fat and it is therefore important to watch its diet. Basset Hounds grow very quickly; do not skimp on high-quality food, especially during its growth period.

TRAINING

Basset Hounds have a mind of their own, which means that they are not very good at following your commands promptly. Though intelligent enough to grasp what you mean, they like to evade your authority, often in a comical fashion. However, with a consistent approach, a lot of patience and sympathy they can be taught quite a bit.

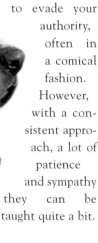

Male Basset Hound

Basset Hound

EXERCISE

Basset Hounds need an average amount of exercise. They are quite happy with three trots around the block each day and playing in the yard. The yard should be well fenced because most Basset Hounds cannot resist the temptation to explore the outside world on their own. A young Basset

Basset Hound

Hound should never be forced to go for exhausting walks, as it will need all its energy to develop a strong body.

USES

This breed is no longer used as a hunting dog as much as in the past, but they are clearly still up to this task. You could also consider doing cleanboot or scenting with your Basset Hound. However, these dogs also do extremely well purely as a family dog.

BASSET ARTÉSIEN NORMAND	
COUNTRY OF ORIGIN	FRANCE
ORIGINAL AND TODAY'S FUNCTION	THIS BREED IS USED AS A HUNTING DOG (HARRIER), MAINLY FOR HARES AND RABBITS, EITHER IN PACKS OR INDIVIDUALLY OR IN A BRACE, AND ALSO FOR WORKING TRAILS.

APPEARANCE

BODY

The Basset Artésien Normand is a short-legged, noble and comparatively long dog with a broad, powerful back. The croup slopes a little and the loins are slightly tucked up. The thighs are full and muscular. The tail is fairly long, thick at the root and tapers to the tip. It should not be carried over the back or gaily. The rounded chest is

Basset Artésian Normand

wide and moderately deep with a prominent breastbone. The ribs are rounded. The forelegs are short, thick and crooked or half-crooked. The feet are placed vertically, but the toes are turned out slightly. The fairly long neck has some dewlap, but not too much.

HEAD

The domed head is of medium width and looks dry. The stop is marked but not exaggerated. The black, wide nose has well opened nostrils and protrudes a little beyond the lips. The muzzle is slightly convex before the nose. The thin, supple ears are set as low as possible, but always below the line of the eye. They are narrow where attached to the skull, corkscrew-shaped and should reach at least as far as the muzzle. These dogs have large eyes. Basset Artésien Normands have a scissors bite.

Basset Artésian Normand

SHOULDER HEIGHT

Approx. 10¼–14¼ in (26–36 cm).

COAT

Short and very dense.

COLORS

Two colors are allowed with this breed: tricolor (red and white with a black hare or badger-colored mantle or back) and bicolor. The bicolor specimens are white with orange. The eyes are dark.

TEMPERAMENT

CHARACTER

This breed is known for its amiable, friendly and gentle character. They are affectionate and loyal to their owners, but can also be fairly headstrong and independent. Their sense of smell is excellent. The Basset Artésien Normand has a deep bark and will occasionally use its voice, although normally not excessively when the dog is kept in the house.

SOCIAL BEHAVIOR

In its country of origin this dog tends to live in packs and therefore gets on fine with other dogs. If socialized with cats and other pets early on, it will get along with them without any problems. Visitors are always announced, but can expect

Basset Artésian Normand

a warm and high-spirited welcome. These dogs generally get on well with children.

GENERAL CARE

GROOMING

The Basset Artésien Normand needs relatively little grooming. Brushing with a bristle brush once a week is usually sufficient. During the molt you can run a rubber brush through the coat to remove loose hair quickly and effectively. The ears have to be checked for dirt occasionally; use a good quality ear cleaner and a tissue to remove any dislodged dirt from the surface. Never use cotton swabs. Clean the tips of the ears with a washcloth and lukewarm water when necessary. Keep the claws short by filing them regularly.

TRAINING

Basset Artésien Normands are intelligent dogs, but not particularly eager to learn. Because of

Basset Artésian Normand

their willfulness the owner will need plenty of patience and understanding to complete the training successfully. However, they can be bribed with tidbits. It is pointless trying to force a dog with such an easy-going spirit or to treat it harshly; you would then experience its obstinate streak that will not allow it to give in.

EXERCISE

Regularly take this dog for longish walks, but be warned: when the Basset Artésien Normand discovers a scent, it can take off. Do not let your dog run off-leash or only where this can do little or no harm. For the same reason you should also make sure that your yard is well fenced. When they get plenty of exercise, Basset Artésien Normands are usually placid in the house.

Basset Artésian Normand

USES

In its country of origin – but also elsewhere – this breed is still used for hunting hares and rabbits, but it adapts very well to life as a family dog. You could consider doing scenting or cleanboot with a Basset Artésien Normand.

Bassets Bleu De Gascogne

BASSET BLEU DE GASCOGNE	
COUNTRY OF ORIGIN	FRANCE
ORIGINAL AND TODAY'S FUNCTION	PACK HOUND FOR HUNTING RABBIT AND HARE

APPEARANCE

BODY

Apart from the length of its legs, the Basset Bleu de Gascogne looks similar to the Grand Bleu de Gascogne. The back is long and solid. The loins are short and somewhat curved; the flanks are deep and the thighs muscular. The tail is rather long and is sometimes carried gaily. The fairly wide chest is rather deep and the ribs are arched. The shoulders are muscular, but not loaded. The forelegs should ideally be strong and straight, but half-crooked is allowed. The strong feet have a slightly elongated oval shape. The fairly long neck is slightly arched with some dewlap showing, but without excess.

HEAD

The head is long and wedge-shaped. The long muzzle is slightly convex but should not be snipey. The skull is domed, with a moderately pronounced occipital protuberance. The thin, curling ears are set below the line of the eye and should reach at least to the tip of the nose. Basset Bleu de Gascognes have eyes with a gentle and rather mournful expression. They have a scissors bite.

SHOULDER HEIGHT

Approx. 12–15 in (34–38 cm).

COAT

Short, not too fine and should be densely planted.

COLORS

Blue speckled with black, either with or without a mantle. Tan markings are found above the eyes, cheeks, lips, on the legs and the inside of the ears. In reality the coat is often white interspersed with black hairs, which confers a blue reflection. The palate, lips, nose, pads and genitals are always black in color. The eyes are always dark brown.

TEMPERAMENT

CHARACTER

These gentle, friendly and sociable dogs are fairly independent in character. Their sense of smell is

Bassets Bleu De Gascogne

Bassets Bleu De Gascogne

outstanding. The Basset Bleu de Gascogne has a loud bark, which will be music to a huntsman's ears. This tends to be rather less appreciated if the dog is kept as a household pet, although usually this does not become a problem.
This breed is even-tempered and seldom high-strung or nervous. It has a cheerful disposition and even appears to have a canine sense of humor.

SOCIAL BEHAVIOR

In its country of origin this breed lives primarily in packs and therefore gets on well with its own kind and with other dogs. Because of its even-tempered character and somewhat laid-back attitude this dog usually also gets on very well with children. If socialized well with cats and other pets as a puppy, then the dog will happily live alongside them. This Basset is somewhat aloof towards strangers and tends to bark whilst observing them from a distance. Although it has a dark voice that may scare off intruders, it is not suited as a defender of hearth and home. Family friends are generally greeted warmly.

GENERAL CARE

GROOMING

This breed needs very little grooming. Outside the molt you can brush the coat with a soft bristle brush once a week. A rubber brush or mitt can be used to remove dead and loose hair when the dog sheds. The ears require more attention, though. Regularly check the ear passages for excessive dirt or earwax, and clean them with an ear cleaner and a tissue.

Basset Bleu De Gascogne

The tips of the long leathers can get dirty; a wash-cloth and lukewarm water is generally sufficient to clean them. Keep the claws short by filing or clipping them regularly.

TRAINING

The Basset Bleu de Gascogne is fairly easy to train, although you may need a little more patience and understanding than with some other breeds. If you are not firm but always consistent and clear during the training, then this French dog will be a fine companion. In common with most hounds, this breed can be motivated with food; the use of tidbits can be particularly useful when training the "Come here" command.

EXERCISE

The Basset Bleu de Gascogne can walk for hours without tiring, but if you need to skip a day the dog usually adapts. It tends to be very placid in the house if exercised regularly. Bear in mind that these dogs have an outstanding sense of smell

Bassets Fauve De Bretagne

Bassets Bleu De Gascogne

which, together with their well-developed hunting instinct, can lead to a tendency to wander. A well-fenced yard is therefore essential. Never let the dog run free off-leash in places where this could be dangerous.

USES

In its country of origin this breed is kept almost exclusively in small packs (4 to 12 dogs) for hunting purposes. Elsewhere it is increasingly kept as a valued family dog. All sports and disciplines that require the use of its nose are suitable activities for this breed, such as tracking, cleanboot and scenting

BASSET FAUVE DE BRETAGNE	
COUNTRY OF ORIGIN	FRANCE
ORIGINAL AND TODAY'S FUNCTION	PACK HOUND FOR HUNTING SMALL GAME, MAINLY RABBIT. THIS BREED IS ALSO USED FOR SCENTING.

APPEARANCE

BODY

This breed is characterized by its short legged build, which makes the back seem long, although it is significantly shorter than other types of Basset. The tail is thick at the base, tapering to the tip. It should not be too long and is carried like a sickle. The shoulders are moderately oblique and the chest is wide and fairly deep. The ribs are long and slightly arched. The broad loins are strong and well muscled. The hips are well rounded and the thighs muscular. The powerful forelegs are straight or slightly crooked and the hocks are moderately bent. The neck is fairly short and should be well muscled.

HEAD

The skull is of medium length with a clearly defined occipital protuberance. The skull narrows

a little towards the poorly defined brow ridges. The fairly long muzzle has a straight or slightly ram-shaped nose bridge. The lips should not be too heavy. The ears are thin at the base and set on level with the corners of the eye, the pointed ends almost reaching to the tip of the nose. The eyes should have an alert expression and no apparent haw. Basset Fauve de Bretagnes have a scissors bite.

SHOULDER HEIGHT
Ranges between $12^1/_2$ –$14^1/_4$ in (32–36 cm). Some deviation is allowed, but a difference of $1^3/_4$ in (4 cm) during a show will lead to disqualification.

COAT
Very harsh and dense, should be flat and almost short. The hairs on the ears are finer than on the body, but never silky.

COLORS
This dog is bred in a red wheaten to fawn color. Sometimes (small) white markings are found on the forechest and neck. Although they are allowed, they are not desired during shows. The nose is black or very dark in color. The eyes should be dark.

TEMPERAMENT

CHARACTER
This breed has an even-tempered, cheerful and friendly disposition. Brave and, in common with most hounds, somewhat willful and quite intelligent, they have a well-developed hunting instinct and an outstanding scenting nose. Outdoors they tend to be fairly active.

Bassets Fauve De Bretagne

Bassets Fauve De Bretagne

SOCIAL BEHAVIOR
The Basset Fauve de Bretagne gets on well with children and can live harmoniously with other dogs. The breed needs to be properly socialized with cats and other pets, but then there will be no problems. These dogs bark when they hear anything out of the ordinary, although that does not make them guard dogs. The Basset Fauve de Bretagne is always friendly towards both welcome visitors and uninvited guests.

GENERAL CARE

GROOMING
This breed needs very little grooming, but annual to biannual plucking is required; the frequency depends on the coat quality. During

Bassets Fauve De Bretagne

plucking the old hair is hand plucked from the coat, giving the new coat the chance to emerge. A Basset Fauve de Bretagne that is treated at the right time will shed little in the house and can do with weekly combing. Any excess of hair growing in the ear passages should be regularly plucked by hand. The claws should be kept short.

TRAINING
This breed is a little willful, so the owner will need to rely on tricks and persistence. Always be consistent and clear, and reward good behavior. It is pointless to put undue pressure on a Basset Fauve de Bretagne or to treat it (too) harshly; it

will then show its very obstinate streak. But with the right approach this breed can still be obedience-trained reasonably well, provided the owner does not demand too much from his dog. Remember that these dogs were originally bred – and still are – for independently tracking and trailing wild game, and that character traits such as showing initiative and independence are important in fulfilling this function.

EXERCISE

Although the Basset Fauve de Bretagne can walk for hours without tiring, this breed does not need a great deal of exercise. Take the dog out regularly and take it on a long walk several times a week, but do allow for its hunting instinct. Once the dog has discovered an interesting scent, it is difficult to change its mind. Only let the dog run free on its own where this can do no harm and make sure your yard is well fenced.

USES

In France and in some other countries the Basset Fauve de Bretagne is mainly kept as a pack hound and primarily used for rabbit hunting. But this dog also does well as a family dog. Any disciplines that require the use of its nose, such as scenting, are suitable activities for this breed.

Grand Basset Griffon Vendéen

GRAND BASSET GRIFFON VENDÉEN	
COUNTRY OF ORIGIN	FRANCE
ORIGINAL AND TODAY'S FUNCTION	PACK HOUND, PARTICULARLY FOR HUNTING HARE AND DEER

APPEARANCE

BODY

The Grand Basset Griffon Vendéen has a very slightly elongated build. The back is long, wide and straight. The loins are slightly arched. The tail is set high and is carried fairly long in saber-fashion or slightly curved. The chest is wide, long and deep, and the ribs are rounded. The shoulders are dry, sloping, and close to the body. The legs are well developed with thick, close feet. The long, solid neck shows no loose dewlap.

HEAD

The head is elongated and not too broad, with a pronounced stop and occipital protuberance. The muzzle is long and square towards the end, with a very slightly curved nose bridge. The ears

Basset Fauve De Bretagne

Grand Basset Griffon Vendéen

are supple and narrow. They are set below the line of the eyes, reaching at least to the forenose. The large eyes have a friendly and intelligent expression. The eyelids are close fitting.

SHOULDER HEIGHT

For bitches this varies from $15^1/_2$ –$16^1/_2$ in (39–42 cm) and for dogs 16–$17^1/_4$ in (40–44 cm).

COAT

The coat is rough, not too long and should be sleek without any curls.

COLORS

These dogs come in three color patterns:
- single-color: dark fallow, hare-colored, white gray
- bicolor: white with gray, red, orange or black patches
- tricolor: white black red, white hare-colored and white gray and red.

The nose is always black and the eyes are dark.

TEMPERAMENT

CHARACTER

Grand Basset Griffon Vendéens are high-spirited, cheerful and uncomplicated dogs. They are agile and lively, but tend to be placid in the house. They are quite clever. This small breed has a sociable character and is sensitive to the atmosphere in the house. They are a little willful and very affectionate, but not dependent.

SOCIAL BEHAVIOR

This highly sociable breed gets on extremely well with other dogs and also with cats and other pets. They do well with children, but if these become too boisterous they will retreat. Unfamiliar visitors are announced but then greeted warmly.

GENERAL CARE

GROOMING

Grand Basset Griffon Vendéen

The Grand Basset Griffon Vendéen requires little grooming. Brush the dog thoroughly with a slicker brush once a week and comb or brush the beard more frequently. Any excess hair growing between the pads should be clipped because it could hinder the dog. Keep the ear passages clean and the claws short. Have the coat plucked in a good trimming parlor about once a year. This involves plucking any dead hair from the coat by hand allowing the new hair to emerge. For shows the length of the neck is accentuated by plucking it slightly shorter than the rest of the body.

Grand Bassets Griffon Vendéen

TRAINING

You can certainly teach the Grand Basset Griffon Vendéen quite a bit, but do not expect too much from this dog. To some extent it is and always will be an independent working dog and, although very fond of its owner, it is not cut out for hours of training sessions. By being consistent and always rewarding the correct response to a command

Grand Basset Griffon Vendéen

with something enjoyable – such as food treats – you can achieve a great deal. During the training extra attention could be paid to returning to the owner on command.

EXERCISE

In the field these dogs can walk for hours on end, and in a family situation they will happily go on long walks, come rain or shine. They are able to withstand all weathers. In spite of this, the dog will not protest if you need to skip a day, and they will also appreciate romping about in the yard. Make sure your yard is well fenced, though, because their scenting ability is outstanding and when they smell something interesting they have a tendency to investigate on their own. This can also happen off-leash in wooded areas, but a well-trained Grand Basset Griffon Vendéen will return to its owner without sulking when called.

USES

In its country of origin this breed is kept almost exclusively in packs for hunting. Elsewhere this breed is still relatively unknown, although it is gradually being discovered as a pleasant family dog. Nevertheless, it is advisable to do "something" with this dog, such as tracking or scenting.

Petit Basset Griffon Vendéen

PETIT BASSET GRIFFON VENDÉEN	
COUNTRY OF ORIGIN	FRANCE
ORIGINAL AND TODAY'S FUNCTION	PACK HOUND, PARTICULARLY FOR RABBIT HUNTING.

APPEARANCE

BODY

The Petit Basset Griffon Vendéen has a very slightly elongated body with straight, muscular and tucked-up loins. The tail is set on high, not too long and carried saber-fashion. The chest is deep, but not wide, and the ribs are moderately rounded. The shoulders are dry, sloping and held close to the body. The straight, powerful legs have medium-sized feet with closed toes.

HEAD

The skull is slightly domed, slightly elongated and not too wide. The occipital protuberance is fairly well developed and the stop is pronounced. The muzzle is much shorter than that of the Grand Basset Griffon Vendéen, although slightly elongated with a square end. The narrow, supple

Petit Basset Griffon Vendéen

expressive dogs. They have a stable and even-tempered disposition and are fairly self-confident. When they are working they display tremendous courage, tenacity and particularly stamina, but in the house they are rather placid and affectionate. They are often kept in outdoor kennels by hunters, but would really prefer to be in the home, close to their owners. In spite of this they are not submissive. They will always retain a high level of independence and can be willful at times. Their

Westphalian Dachsbracke

sense of smell and hunting instinct are highly developed.

SOCIAL BEHAVIOR

If socialized well with cats and other pets as a puppy, the dog is capable of living harmoniously with these animals. They generally mix extremely well with their own kind, and they get on well with children; their tolerance level is high and they are not easily offended. Westphalian Dachsbrackes are genuine people lovers. Although they will certainly bark to announce the arrival of visitors, they are greeted warmly. However, these dogs can act appropriately towards intruders and when their owner is away.

GENERAL CARE

GROOMING

Grooming this breed will not present any problems. Brushing the coat with a hard bristle brush once a week is sufficient. During the molt a rubber brush can be used to remove any dead hair from the coat efficiently. The claws should be kept short.

TRAINING

This breed is both fairly independent and devoted to its owner. Training is generally fairly easy, provided you bear in mind that these dogs are bred for tracking and trailing wild game independently which means they must be capable of moving away from their owners and making up their own minds. The "Come here" command should be emphasized during the training.

EXERCISE

This breed needs plenty of exercise. You cannot subject these dogs to spending their days in front of the fireplace. Allow about an hour a day – although ideally longer – for long walks with this dog, bearing in mind that its hunting instinct and excellent sense of smell can take it far away from its owner. The same scenting nose will eventually take it back to the place where it last saw you, but obviously this will cause problems in crowded areas. Therefore only allow your dog to run off-leash when you can be sure that you can call it back .

USES

These dogs can make very affectionate and amiable family dogs, but nearly always if they have plenty of other activities as well. In practice few people can give them the activity levels they need. If you enjoy hunting or scenting with your dog, then this will be a good choice.

DREVER

COUNTRY OF ORIGIN	SWEDEN
ORIGINAL AND TODAY'S FUNCTION	TRACKING AND STOPPING WILDGAME, PARTICULARLY FOX, HARE AND WILD BOAR, WHILST GIVING TONGUE.

APPEARANCE

BODY

Drevers have a straight and muscular back with a slightly sloping croup. The well-developed, long chest reaches beyond the elbow. The belly is slightly tucked up. The legs are relatively short, powerful, well angulated and strong of bone. The feet do not splay, and are strong with closed toes. The relatively long tail is carried hanging and can be carried a little higher in movement, although never above the topline. The neck is fairly long, strong and dry.

HEAD

The fairly large and elongated head is carried high on the neck. There is a lightly defined stop and a slightly domed skull. The skull tapers off toward the tip of the nose. The muzzle is well developed and the nose bridge is straight or slightly curved. The ears are set fairly low, relatively long and wide with a rounded tip, hanging against the cheeks on the inside. The eyes have close fitting eyelids and are full of expression.

Drever

SHOULDER HEIGHT

Ranging from 12–15 in (30–38 cm). For dogs 13³/₄ in (35 cm) is considered to be the ideal shoulder height and for bitches 13 in (33 cm).

COAT

Short, sleek, a little coarse in structure and densely planted. The hair underneath the tail may be a little longer.

COLORS

All colors and color combinations are allowed with this breed, with one restriction: the dog should always have white markings, which must be visible from all sides. In reality we mainly see red and white dogs and black dogs with tan markings and white. The eyes are (dark) brown in color.

Drever

345

TEMPERAMENT

CHARACTER

These brave and tenacious dogs are tireless in the field, but in the house tend to be placid to lazy. They are very affectionate and like to be close to their owners and family. They have an optimistic outlook and even show a sense of humor. Drevers can sometimes bark more than is desirable. They are fairly obedient and capable of learning quite a bit. However, this should be viewed in terms of their original function; they are fairly independent dogs and you cannot expect the same level of obedience that we know from dogs that are specifically bred for cooperation with their handlers. This breed has an excellent scenting nose. They are fairly unruffled, even-tempered and self-confident.

SOCIAL BEHAVIOR

These dogs generally get on well with other dogs. Mixing with cats and other pets should not present any problems, provided they are introduced to these animals when young. Drevers tend to be friendly and tolerant to children and kind to strangers.

Drever

GENERAL CARE

GROOMING

Grooming is very easy. During the molt dead hair can be removed from the coat simply and quickly with a rubber brush or mitt. Occasionally check the ear passages for debris and keep the claws short.

TRAINING

Drevers are reasonably easy to train, although the owner should bear in mind that he is dealing with an independent breed. Emphasize the "Come Here" command and practice keeping its barking habits under control during the training, although barking often appears to have an underlying reason, such as a lack of exercise or activity. Giving tongue (a continuous barking which is quite distinguishable to an expert) should not be confused with undesirable barking; this is a natural form of expression for a dog when trailing an interesting scent or when its hunting instinct is stimulated in other ways. Tidbits can be very helpful during the training, because these dogs love their food.

EXERCISE

Drevers need a fair amount of exercise. It is advisable to take this breed for walks only on a leash. A well-trained Drever that returns to its owner when called can also be taken for off-leash walks but only in areas where the dog cannot escape. Even so, vigilance remains necessary.

USES

This breed is not suited to life as an average family dog, but can thrive in a family setting if the dog is used for hunting or other work. You could consider doing cleanboot or scenting with this breed. Particularly the latter type of hunting will certainly appeal to these dogs. For its original work this breed is frequently used in Scandinavia, especially in Sweden.

DETAILS

The striking similarity between the Drever and the Westphalian Dachsbracke is no coincidence, as the Drever has fairly recently developed from Westphalian Dachsbrackes.

SECTION 2 Leash Hounds

BAYERISCHER GEBIRGSSCHWEISSHUND

COUNTRY OF ORIGIN	GERMANY
ORIGINAL AND	TRACKING AND POINTING
TODAY'S FUNCTION	WILD GAME, SUCH AS
	CHAMOIS, ROCK-GOAT AND
	DEER. IN ADDITION, THIS
	BREED IS ALSO FREQUENTLY
	USED FOR SCENTING ALL
	KINDS OF BIG GAME.

APPEARANCE

BODY

The Bayerischer Gebirgsschweisshund is a light, very agile dog of medium height. The body is slightly longer than high and the hindquarters are slightly overbuilt. The belly is slightly tucked up. The tail forms a continuation of the topline, reaches to the pasterns and is carried horizontally or sloping downward. The legs are well angulated and the oval feet are tightly closed. The supple neck is strong, dry and of medium length.

HEAD

Light with a slightly domed and fairly broad upper skull. The forehead is slightly wrinkled. The short muzzle tapers slightly. The lips must not droop. The wide, medium long ears are high set and carried pendulously. They are rounded at the tip. The eyes are of medium size with close fitting eyelids.

SHOULDER HEIGHT

Dogs measure $18^{1}/_{2}$–$20^{1}/_{2}$ in (47–52 cm) and bitches $17^{1}/_{4}$–19 in (44–48 cm).

Bayerischer Gebirgsschweisshund

COAT

Very short, rough and close lying.

COLORS

The Bayerischer Gebirgsschweisshund comes in various shades of yellow to deep red brown. The muzzle, ears, back and tail are usually darker in color; most dogs have a dark to almost black mask and ears. A small white patch on the chest is allowed. The eyes are dark or light brown.

TEMPERAMENT

CHARACTER

The Bayerischer Gebirgsschweisshund is quiet, fairly obedient and alert. Outdoors these dogs are active, while they are usually placid and

Bayerischer Gebirgsschweisshund

affectionate around the house. Their stamina is tremendous and their supple, light build enables them to be nimble even on fairly difficult terrain. They tend to become devoted to their owners, and are not suited to living in a kennel.

SOCIAL BEHAVIOR

Although this dog is traditionally used for solitary hunting, the average representative of the breed generally gets on well with other dogs. Mixing with a family cat does not need to present any problems, provided good socialization has taken place. These dogs can be rather shy toward strangers in adulthood, but friends of its owner are usually greeted warmly and openly. The Bayerischer Gebirgsschweisshund generally dislikes the noise produced by small children.

GENERAL CARE

GROOMING

These dogs need very little grooming. Brushing the coat once a week using a soft brush is adequate. During the molt a rubber grooming brush can be used to remove dead and loose hair from the coat efficiently. Occasionally check the ear passages for debris and keep the claws short.

Bayerischer Gebirgsschweisshund

Bayerischer Gebirgsschweisshund

EXERCISE

This dog has tremendous stamina and loves going on long walks. In contrast to many other hounds the Bayerischer Gebirgsschweisshund has less of a tendency to take off on its own. However, bear in mind that its hunting instinct remains intact, which means that when the dog smells the blood of wild game, it will find it hard to ignore its instinct and will want to follow the trail. But if the dog is trained as a puppy to return to his owner on command, then it can also be left to run off-leash in certain places. In the house a Bayerischer Gebirgsschweisshund tends to be placid to the point of laziness.

USES

This supple and tough dog is a real worker, a specialist par excellence for instance for scenting on inaccessible, mountainous terrain. This dog should on no account be condemned to the life of an average family dog or a dog that is only occasionally used for working. It is and always will be a passionate hunting dog that will not lend itself to this. In reality this will rarely happen in view of the stringent placement policy of breeders, which makes it virtually impossible for non-hunters to acquire a puppy of this rather uncommon breed.

DALMATIAN

COUNTRY OF ORIGIN	CROATIA
ORIGINAL FUNCTION	DALMATIANS WERE ORIGINALLY USED AS CARRIAGE DOGS (TO BE DECORATIVE WHEN RUNNING ALONGSIDE COACHES) AND AS WATCHDOGS IN THE STABLES.

APPEARANCE

BODY

The Dalmatian has a powerful, level back with well-defined withers. The loins are strong, slightly arched and the hindquarters are muscular and well rounded. The tail is wide at the root, tapering to a point. It reaches almost to the hock and is carried with a slight upward curve. The chest is not too wide, but deep and capacious, and the ribs are well sprung. The dry, muscular shoulders are moderately oblique and the elbows are close to the body. The legs are straight with round bone and the stifles are well bent. Dalmatians have cat's feet, which means they are round and tightly closed, with sturdy, arched toes. The fairly long, dry neck is nicely arched.

HEAD

Fairly long with a flat skull which is reasonably broad between the ears. The head is free from wrinkle. The stop is moderate. The muzzle is powerful and long – never snipey – and the tight lips are close fitting. The fine, thin ears are moderate in size and set on high. They are car-

Dalmatian

ried close to the head. The eyes are set moderately well apart. They are medium-sized and round with a bright and lively expression. The eye rims are close fitting. Dalmatians have a scissors bite.

SHOULDER HEIGHT

The ideal shoulder height for dogs is 22–24 in (56–61 cm), and for bitches 21^1/$_2$–23^1/$_2$ in (54–59 cm), but overall balance is regarded as more important.

WEIGHT

Approx. 53–70^1/$_2$ lb (24–32 kg).

COAT

Short, hard, dense, sleek and glossy.

COLORS

Dalmatians come in two color patterns: liver and black. The ground color is always pure white, with round and clearly defined spots that are ^{1}/$_2$–1^1/$_2$ in (2–3 cm) in diameter. Ideally, the spots should not overlap and be nicely distributed. Spots on the limbs should be smaller than those on the body. The nose color and eye rims should be brown in liver-colored dogs and black in black spotted dogs. Dalmatians are born white and acquire their spots later.

Dalmatian

Dalmatian dog

TEMPERAMENT

CHARACTER

Dalmatians are high-spirited, friendly and intelligent dogs. They are sociable and even-tempered in character, very affectionate to their owners and always curious about what goes on around them. Because of this they are not suited to kennel life.

This breed is vigilant and will let you know if

anything is wrong. Do not expect any defensive traits from this dog, because they are not aggressive.

SOCIAL BEHAVIOR

These dogs are generally very sociable and get on well with other canine members of the family and with other dogs they meet outdoors. They also do well with children. Mixing with pets such as cats does not usually cause any problems, provided the dog has been properly socialized. With visitors it depends on the character of the individual dog whether it acts either vigilantly or halfheartedly.

GENERAL CARE

GROOMING

One disadvantage of this breed is that it sheds almost constantly. You will find white hairs around the house and on your clothes, even outside the molt. Loose hairs can be easily removed using a rubber mitt. The claws should be kept short.

TRAINING

The Dalmatian is not difficult to train, but does have its stubborn side which emerges when too much is expected of it or when the dog loses interest in the training exercises. Praise it abundantly for desirable behavior – perhaps supported by tidbits – and vary the exercises. Firm training is inappropriate, as is an indulgent approach. Try to find the happy medum.

Dalmatian puppy

EXERCISE

This breed was traditionally used to run alongside coaches for miles. Although they have great stamina, this does not mean you need to take the dog

Dalmatian puppy

for long walks every day. The average Dalmatian will adapt very well to family life, although the dog will certainly lose some zest for life if it has to make do with three short walks a day. Swimming, playing and running free through the woods or in open countryside will all be good for this dog.

Dalmatian

USES

These dogs are appreciated all over the world as a family dog, preferably in a sports-minded family. You could consider taking part in dog sports, provided mutual enjoyment rather than competitiveness comes first.

RHODESIAN RIDGEBACK	
COUNTRY OF ORIGIN	AFRICA
ORIGINAL FUNCTION	USED IN GROUPS AS A HUNTING DOG FOR DRIVING BIG CATS AND BIG GAME TOWARDS THE HUNTERS, AND AS A GUARD DOG.

APPEARANCE

BODY

A muscular dog with a symmetrical build and a chest that is roomy and deep but not too wide. The back is powerful and the loins are strong and slightly arched. The distinctive characteristic peculiar to the Rhodesian Ridgeback is a strip of hair on the back that grows in an opposite direction from the rest of the coat. This strip, called a "ridge", begins immediately between the shoulders and ends between the hips. It should ideally be 2 in (5 cm) in diameter. The heavily boned, strong forelegs are straight and the elbows are close to the body. The hindquarters are well angulated and the hock joints are well let down. The feet are compact with well-arched toes. The tail is wide at the root, tapers to a point and is carried with a slight curve.

HEAD

Rhodesian Ridgebacks have a fairly elongated head with a flat, wide skull and a fairly pronounced stop. The ears are set on rather high, wide at the base and tapering to a rounded point. They are pendulous and are carried close to the head The eyes are round in shape, with an intelligent expression.

Rhodesian Ridgebacks

Rhodesian Ridgeback

SHOULDER HEIGHT
Ranges from $25^1/_2$ –$27^1/_2$ in (64–69 cm) for dogs and from 24–26 in (61–66 cm) for bitches.

WEIGHT
Bitches approx. $70^1/_2$ lb (32 kg), dogs $81^1/_2$ lb (37 kg).

COAT
Rhodesian Ridgebacks have a sleek, dense and short-haired coat with a characteristic "ridge" on the back, which looks darker in color than the rest of the coat because of the different pile implant.

COLORS
The coat is light to reddish wheaten. Some white on the chest is permitted. The eye color is in harmony with that of the coat.

TEMPERAMENT

CHARACTER
Rhodesian Ridgebacks are full of character, intelligent, clever and somewhat willful. Although aloof to strangers, they are honest and very loyal to their family. They are confident and even-tempered, brave and vigilant, and possess great stamina. They also have an excellent sense of smell and a well-developed hunting instinct. In the house these dogs are generally very quiet and will only bark when they sense there are real problems.

SOCIAL BEHAVIOR
Provided this dog is introduced to cats and other pets when young there will be few problems. Rhodesian Ridgebacks are usually tolerant and friendly to children if they do not pester the dog. They mix reasonably well with other dogs, although some can be dominant towards other males. Family friends are treated kindly. This dog will guard the house when you are away. They tend to be reserved with strangers but not aggressive.

GENERAL CARE

GROOMING
Grooming is easy. Brush regularly using a soft brush. During the molt remove dead hair with a rubber mitt or brush.

TRAINING
Should be even-handed and extremely consistent. Rhodesian Ridgebacks are a little stubborn which requires a confident approach from the owner. When a Ridgeback realizes that it will benefit from obeying commands, then it is capable and willing to learn new commands fairly quickly.

EXERCISE
Traditionally a hunting dog with tremendous stamina, the Rhodesian Ridgeback needs a great deal of exercise. Take it for a run or a long walk regularly but do bear in mind that this dog has a well-developed hunting instinct and an excellent sense of smell; off-leash walks are therefore only advisable for dogs that are well-trained. A Rhodesian Ridgeback who gets plenty of exercise will be placid in the house.

Rhodesian Ridgeback

USES
Rhodesian Ridgebacks are nowadays kept almost exclusively as a valued family pet and this breed is rarely seen in various branches of dog sports. However, you could consider tracking with this dog, because this is something it will certainly enjoy and do well.

Pointers

Vizsla dog

VIZSLA, SHORT-HAIRED

COUNTRY OF ORIGIN	HUNGARY
ORIGINAL FUNCTION	GUNDOG AND POINTER, ALSO USED FOR SCENTING AND RETRIEVING.

APPEARANCE

BODY

The Short-haired Vizsla has an elegant, yet strong and muscular build. The trunk is longer than its shoulder height. The back is short and straight, and the loins are slightly rounded. The tail is low set. In countries where this is permitted the last quarter section is usually docked. The ribs are moderately rounded. The chest reaches at least to the elbows. The forelegs are straight, with elbows close to the body. The hind legs are moderately angulated. The feet are somewhat oval-shaped, with closed toes. The moderately long neck is slightly arched and devoid of dewlap.

HEAD

Dry and noble, with a slightly domed skull and a median line that runs from the moderate occipital protuberance to the forehead. Vizslas have a moderate stop and a straight nose bridge. The lips are not pendulous. The medium-sized ears are low set and moderately back, hanging close to the cheeks. The eyes are slightly oval in shape, with a lively and intelligent expression. Vizslas have a scissors bite.

Vizsla bitch

Vizsla pointing

SHOULDER HEIGHT

The ideal height for dogs is 22–24 in (56–61cm) and for bitches $20^1/_2$–$22^1/_2$ in (52–57 cm). Deviations of $1^3/_4$ in (4 cm) up or down are allowed, provided the dog remains well balanced.

WEIGHT

Vizslas weigh approx. $41^3/_4$–53 lb (19–24 kg).

COAT

The straight and very short coat lies close to the skin. The hair is longer on the tail and softer in texture on the head and ears.

COLORS

The Short-haired Vizsla comes in various dark shades of plain dark wheaten or russet brown. (Very) small white markings on chest or toes are not a fault. It has a dudley nose and the rims of the lips and eyes are brown. The eyes are preferably dark in color.

TEMPERAMENT

CHARACTER

Vizslas are intelligent, friendly, even-tempered and sporty. They are keen to learn, compliant and as a rule very obedient as well. Extremely loyal and affectionate to their owners, they enjoy retrieving and swimming, have an excellent scent-

Vizsla

ing nose and great stamina. This breed loves being at home with their owners.

SOCIAL BEHAVIOR

The Vizsla rarely causes problems in terms of social behavior and gets on well with its own kind. If socialized well these dogs will also get on fine with other household pets and usually with children. Unfamiliar visitors will be announced, but that tends to be all.

Vizslas

GENERAL CARE

GROOMING

The Short-haired Vizsla needs very little grooming. During the molt a rubber groom brush can be used to remove dead and loose hair from the coat, but outside this period a Short-haired Vizsla will shed little. Keep the claws short.

TRAINING

The average Short-haired Vizsla is fairly easy to

train. The dog is smart enough to grasp what you are expecting it to do and is eager to please. Although it will seldom be necessary to discipline the dog with anything other than your voice, clear and consistent handling of this – or any other – breed is advisable.

Vizslas

EXERCISE

Vizslas are first and foremost hunting dogs that need plenty of exercise to feel happy. They should certainly not be denied the opportunity to romp about regularly. Vizslas that are able to exert themselves outdoors will be placid indoors.

USES

You could consider going hunting with this dog. Vizslas are famed for their retrieving skills, good nose and many other qualities that make them eminently suitable for hunting. If this does not appeal to you, then do allow your Vizsla to run and play off-leash regularly. Most Vizslas love retrieving and are fond of water. Although not bred for this purpose Vizslas can also do well in obedience trials.

VIZSLA, WIRE-HAIRED	
COUNTRY OF ORIGIN	HUNGARY
ORIGINAL FUNCTION	GUNDOG AND POINTER, ALSO USED FOR SCENTING AND RETRIEVING, MAINLY ON ROUGH TERRAIN.

APPEARANCE

BODY

The Wire-haired Vizsla is considerably more powerful and heavier than the Short-haired. The trunk is longer than the shoulder height. The back is short and straight and the loins are slightly rounded. The ribs are moderately arched and the chest reaches at least to the elbows. The forelegs are straight, with the elbows close to the body. The hind legs are moderately angulated. The feet are slightly oval in shape, with closed toes. The moderately long neck is slightly arched and fairly dry. The tail is set low, with the last third section usually docked in countries where this is permitted.

HEAD

Vizslas have a moderate stop and strong supraorbital ridges. The hair makes the head look somewhat angular. The muzzle is a little shorter than the slightly domed skull. The nose bridge is straight and the lips are not pendulous. The ears are set moderately high and are carried pendulously. The eyes are oval in shape, with a lively and intelligent expression. Vizslas have a scissors bite.

Vizslas

SHOULDER HEIGHT

For dogs the ideal shoulder height is $22^3/_4$–$24^1/_2$in (58–62 cm), for bitches $21^1/_4$–$22^3/_4$in (54–58 cm). Deviations of $1^1/_2$in up or down are allowed, provided overall balance is retained.

WEIGHT

Ranges from $46^1/_4$–$59^1/_2$lb (21–27 kg).

COAT

This Vizsla has a wire-haired coat, with a small beard on the chin and tough, harsh eyebrows. In contrast to their short-haired namesakes they have a dense woolly undercoat underneath the topcoat.

COLORS

The coat may be various shades of sandy yellow. (Very) small white patches on the chest or toes are not a fault. The eyes are preferably dark in color.

TEMPERAMENT

CHARACTER

Wire-haired Vizslas are even-tempered, confident, intelligent and sporty dogs. They are fairly vigilant, very affectionate and loyal. Like their short-haired relatives they love retrieving and water. They have an excellent nose and are eminently suited for working on more inaccessible terrain. Although they come across as somewhat more circumspect than the short-haired specimens, they have great stamina and are reliable workers.

Vizsla with practice dummy

SOCIAL BEHAVIOR

Wire-haired Vizslas tend to get on fine with other dogs and household pets, although this will depend upon the degree of their socialization. They generally get on well with children. They will bark when strangers arrive.

GENERAL CARE

GROOMING

The Wire-haired Vizsla needs to be plucked from

Two Vizsla pups

time to time. This involves removing the old and dead hair by hand. Outside these trims the coat can be brushed about once a week. Keep the claws short.

TRAINING

Training the Wire-haired Vizsla should not present any problems. This dog generally learns quickly and is smart enough to grasp what its owner expects it to do.

EXERCISE

Vizslas are real working dogs that will not settle for three short walks round the block each day. Let them rollick outdoors regularly. Nearly all kinds of exercise are suitable for this breed, from running to swimming and retrieving.

USES

This breed does extremely well as a companion dog in a sporty family. Since hunting is the Vizsla's original as well as its current function, you could consider attending a hunting class with this dog, which would certainly make your dog very happy.

DETAILS

In the 1930s the Wire-haired German Pointer was responsible for the Wire-haired Vizsla's rough coat.

GERMAN POINTER, SHORT-HAIRED

COUNTRY OF ORIGIN	GERMANY
ORIGINAL FUNCTION	ALL-ROUND GUNDOG

A somewhat older Short-hair German Pointer

APPEARANCE

BODY

The Short-haired German Pointer is an aristocratic, well-balanced dog, whose skin is taut against the body without showing any folds. The chest reaches to the elbows. The ribs are well sprung and carried well back. The wide loins are not too long and may be straight or slightly arched. The croup is wide and sufficiently long, and the belly has a slight tuck-up. The high set tail is docked to half its length in countries where docking is permitted. It should never be held too high over the back or be too curved. The legs show normal angulation with round or spoon-shaped, close-knit feet. The muscular throat is dry and the neck is slightly arched.

HEAD

The head is dry and striking, and must not be too light or too heavy. The skull is slightly domed and in profile the nose bridge also shows a slight arch. The lips must not overhang too much. The medium-sized ears are set on high and wide, carried close to the head, pendulous and without folds, the blunt rounded tips reaching almost to the corner of the mouth. The eyes are medium-sized with close fitting eyelids. Short-haired German Pointers have a powerful scissors bite.

SHOULDER HEIGHT

For dogs between 24^1/$_2$–26 in (62–66 cm); for bitches between 22^3/$_4$–24^3/$_4$ in (58–63 cm).

COAT

The short, dense coat feels firm and harsh to the touch. The hair is shorter and thinner on the ears and head.

COLORS

The Short-haired German Pointer comes in brown, both with and without small white markings on the chest and legs; brown roan; pale brown roan; and in white with brown markings on the head, and brown markings or spots. These markings also come in black instead of brown, but are relatively rare. Yellow markings are permitted. The eyes are dark brown.

TEMPERAMENT

CHARACTER

This breed of dog is intelligent and keen to learn. They have an excellent nose. Short-haired German Pointers are active, spontaneous, playful and friendly, and most love swimming. Loyal and biddable towards their owners and family, they do have a tendency to become particularly attached to one person. They display great courage and endurance in the field, and are virtually impervious to the weather. A Short-haired German Pointer will bark when it senses danger and will come to its owner's rescue in an emergency.

SOCIAL BEHAVIOR

These dogs generally get on well both with their own kind and with children. Provided the dog has had positive experiences and has been properly socialized when young, mixing with household pets such as cats can be trouble-free. They are friendly towards both familiar faces and strangers, but will defend their house and yard in the absence of the owners.

Short-hair German Pointer

GENERAL CARE

GROOMING

The Short-haired German Pointer needs relatively little grooming. Outside the molt occasional brushing with a soft bristle brush is sufficient. In the spring and fall loose hairs can be easily removed from the coat with a rubber mitt or a soft rubber brush.

Short-hair German Pointer

TRAINING

Short-haired German Pointers are intelligent and zealous dogs that are generally easy to train. This breed responds best to a very consistent, loving and fair approach, and really appreciates variety and activity.

EXERCISE

Indoors this dog will be exemplary and quiet, but only if it gets the chance to release its energy outdoors. The Short-haired German Pointer is therefore best suited to a sports-minded family or a hunter. It is primarily a hunting dog that loves to be active and will certainly not be willing to adapt to a sedate life. The majority love swimming and retrieving. If you are unable to go hunting with this dog, you will need to take it for long walks and allow it to run and play off-leash.

Short-hair German Pointer

USES

Short-haired German Pointers are excellent all-round gundogs that can point, track game as well as retrieve. They are frequently used for hunting waterfowl, but also for rabbit and hare. Provided their exercise needs are met, they can also do well as a family dog.

Short-hair German Pointer

GERMAN POINTER, WIRE-HAIRED

COUNTRY OF ORIGIN	**GERMANY**
ORIGINAL FUNCTION	**ALL-ROUND GUNDOG**

Wire-haired German Pointer

APPEARANCE

BODY

The German Wire-haired Pointer is a muscular dog with a taut skin showing no folds anywhere. The length of the trunk is equal to the shoulder height or slightly longer. The high withers are well defined, long and well muscled. The chest is deep and wide, showing an obvious brisket. The ribs are well sprung and the elbows are held close. The back is short and the loins are muscular. The hips are sufficiently wide. The groin is long, wide, and slopes slightly. The (docked) tail is set in line with the topline and carried horizontally or slightly upward. The belly is slightly tucked up towards the back. The forequarters are light and the hindquarters well angulated. The feet are oval-shaped, with closed toes. The very muscular neck is moderately long and curved.

HEAD

The head is in proportion to the dog's body size and sex, with long, wide and strong jaws and without pendulous lips. The high set ears are wide and carried pendulously, close to the head. The eyes are not deep set and the eyelids are close fitting. German Wire-haired Pointers have a complete scissors bite.

SHOULDER HEIGHT

For dogs between $23^{1}/_{2}$–$26^{1}/_{2}$ in (60–67 cm) and for bitches 22–$24^{1}/_{2}$ in (56–62 cm).

COAT

German Wire-haired Pointers have a harsh, wire-haired upper coat with a dense undercoat. The upper coat is $^{1}/_{2}$–$1^{3}/_{4}$ in (2–4 cm) long, should be densely planted and lie close to the skin. The hair is shorter on the legs and lower chest, belly, ears and head. The longer hair on the muzzle and above the eyes creates the characteristic eyebrows and beard.

COLORS

This breed comes in dark to medium brown and black, always speckled with or without blankets. A dark eye color is preferred.

TEMPERAMENT

CHARACTER

These active, intelligent and hardworking dogs have an excellent nose, are tireless when they work, and able to withstand all weathers. They have a stable temperament, are highly devoted to their owners and fairly vigilant. Dogs, in particular, can be slightly dominant.

The alert look of a Wire-haired German Pointer.

Short-haired German Pointer

Wire-haired German Pointer

SOCIAL BEHAVIOR

Provided the dog is well socialized and supervised, it will get on fine with children as well as with household pets such as cats. Mixing with other dogs does not need to be a problem, although some dogs will display dominant behavior towards other dogs. Friends of the family are greeted warmly, while strangers normally also receive a friendly welcome. However, the Wire-haired is a highly convincing guard dog when required.

Wire-haired German Pointer

GENERAL CARE

GROOMING

The coat should be as harsh as possible but must not look untidy. Depending on the coat quality you may need to hand pluck it either rarely or from time to time. The coat must be brushed about once a week between pluckings. Keep the beard clean, and trim any excess hair between the pads.

TRAINING

These dogs are intelligent and possess all the requirements to learn new commands quickly. Usually a bit more dominant in character than their short-haired cousins, Wire-haired dogs need consistent and very explicit training.

EXERCISE

The German Wire-haired Pointer is best suited to a sports-minded family or a hunter. This breed will certainly not take kindly to three short strolls a day, but needs lots of activity and exercise to feel happy. If the dog is allowed to release its energy regularly, ideally in a natural environment and with swimming and retrieving as its favorite activities, then it will be placid in the house.

USES

Wire-haired dogs are excellent all-round gundogs that can point, track game as well as retrieve. Because of their rough, close-lying coat they are frequently used on more inaccessible terrain. Provided their exercise needs are met, a Wire-haired can also do well as a family dog.

Wire-haired German Pointers

Wire-haired German Pointer

WEIMARANER

COUNTRY OF ORIGIN	**GERMANY**
ORIGINAL FUNCTION	**VERSATILE POINTER**

Long-haired Weimaraner

Weimaraner

APPEARANCE

BODY

The Weimaraner is a strongly built, well-muscled dog, with a body that is slightly longer than tall (ratio approx. 12:11). There is a marked difference between the sexes. The chest is strong, but not too wide and reaches almost to the elbows. The back is long, solid and straight. The tail, set rather low and curving downward, is usually docked in countries where this is permitted. However, the tail is kept significantly longer with the long-haired variety. The legs are straight, parallel and well angulated. The feet are strong, with closed and arched toes. The neck is fairly round and dry.

HEAD

The head is moderately long and dry, with the muzzle slightly longer than the skull. The occipital protuberance is only slightly pronounced, while the stop is hardly noticeable. The muzzle is angular with the lips drooping very slightly and a straight or slightly curved nose bridge. When viewed in profile the nose reaches beyond the chin. The high set ears are wide and reach almost to the corner of the mouth. The eyes are round, set slightly obliquely in the head and the eyelids are close fitting.

SHOULDER HEIGHT

Dogs have a shoulder height between $23^{1}/_{2}$–$27^{1}/_{2}$ in (59–70 cm). For bitches this ranges from $22^{1}/_{2}$–$25^{1}/_{2}$ in (57–65 cm).

WEIGHT

Weimaraners weigh approx. 53–$77^{1}/_{4}$ lb (24–35 kg).

COAT

There are two types of coat: short-haired and

Weimaraner

long-haired. The short-haired is by far the most popular. Short-haired dogs have very short, dense hair, without any or with very little undercoat. The longhaired variety may be with or without undercoat. Its hair is long, soft and can either lie flat or be slightly wavy. The Weimaraner has longer hair on the ears, tail, chest, belly, culottes and the back of the forelegs.

COLORS

The coat is silver grizzle, deer grizzle or mouse grizzle, with the head usually a slightly lighter shade. Small white markings on the chest and feet are permitted. Puppies have blue eyes, while adult dogs have light to dark amber-colored eyes.

Weimaraner puppies have blue eyes

TEMPERAMENT

CHARACTER

Weimaraners are friendly, energetic and keen to work, with great stamina. They are intelligent, smart and usually relatively easy to train. Apart from that they are undoubtedly vigilant. In an emergency they will convincingly protect the family against intruders. Their sense of smell is outstanding.

SOCIAL BEHAVIOR

Weimaraners are usually friendly with children. When properly socialized with cats and other household pets they will also get on fine with them. They also get on equally well with their own kind. This breed is reasonably vigilant but not particularly unfriendly or reserved towards strangers.

GENERAL CARE

GROOMING

The Short-haired Weimaraner needs very little grooming. Occasional grooming with a rubber brush to remove loose and dead hair is sufficient. The Longhaired needs equally little care. It should be groomed with a grooming brush, possibly followed by combing through any patches of longer hair. The ears should be checked regularly.

TRAINING

These dogs are relatively quick learners. They are eager to please their handler and intelligent enough to grasp what is expected of them.

EXERCISE

Weimaraners are popular hunting dogs, although they do not need to be used as such to feel happy.

Weimaraner

Longhaired Weimaraners

COUNTRY OF ORIGIN	SLOVAKIA
ORIGINAL FUNCTION	VERSATILE HUNTING DOG

APPEARANCE

BODY

The body of the Slovak Rough-haired Pointer is slightly longer than its shoulder height. This breed has a strong, level back of medium length, sloping gently downward towards the back. The withers are moderately high and the wide, sufficiently long groin must not slope down. The tail is set high and is carried horizontally or hanging. In countries where this is permitted the tail is normally docked to half its length. The chest is oval in shape and reaches to the elbows. The ribs are well sprung. The belly is slightly tucked up. The shoulder blades are set obliquely and the straight legs are moderately angulated. The feet are closed, with well-arched toes. The moderately long, dry neck is set high on the withers.

HEAD

The head is rectangular in shape, with clearly defined eyebrows and superciliary ridges. The muzzle and skull are roughly equal in length, divided by a moderate stop. The nose bridge is straight. The

Slovak Rough-haired Pointer

However, they do need lots of exercise and activity. They need to spend at least one hour each day on activities such as running and playing off-leash, swimming or retrieving. If a Weimaraner can release its energy outdoors, then it will be placid in the house. This breed is therefore well suited to people who like to do something with their dog and who are sporty.

USES

You could consider taking this breed hunting for both feather and fur. They are not only able to point and retrieve; their excellent nose also allows them to track (scent) trails.

Slovak Rough-haired Pointer has moderately long ears, which are set above the line of the eye and are carried pendulously. The tips are rounded. The eyes are almond-shaped. These dogs have a scissors bite.

SHOULDER HEIGHT

Dogs have a shoulder height of $24^1/_2$–$26^1/_2$ in (62–68 cm) and bitches $22^1/_2$–$25^1/_2$ in (57–64 cm).

WEIGHT

Between $55^1/_4$–$70^1/_2$ lb (25–32 kg), depending upon the sex and build.

Slovak Rough-haired Pointer

COAT

The coat is coarse and rough, approx. $1^3/_4$ in (4 cm) long, with a fine, dense undercoat. The hair is longer and softer on the head, its typical trademark. The ears are short and covered in fine hairs.

COLORS

These dogs come in silver gray, either with or without dark patches or speckles. The eyes of mature animals are amber-colored; puppies have blue eyes.

TEMPERAMENT

CHARACTER

This breed consists of intelligent, zealous and fairly obedient animals. They are alert to what goes on around them and will certainly bark when something is amiss. This breed will not keep quiet when uninvited guests arrive. They are devoted to their owners and families, and have a friendly, open character. These Rough-haireds are alert, active and agile. Their sense of smell is outstanding, as is their stamina. They are fairly hardy and can withstand all weathers.

SOCIAL BEHAVIOR

These dogs generally get on well with their own kind. Socialization with cats and other household pets should be adequately supervised at an early age, but the dog will then live in harmony with other animals. They usually get on fine with children. Slovak Rough-haired Pointers are friendly towards people, but in an emergency they will stand by the people they love.

GENERAL CARE

GROOMING

The coat needs to be groomed about once a week, ideally with a coarse slicker brush. During the molt when the undercoat sheds the dog requires a little more attention. Depending upon its quality the coat has to be hand-plucked about once to twice a year. Any hair that grows between the pads should be trimmed regularly, because pieces of gravel and the like can easily get stuck which could bother the dog. Keep the claws short.

Slovak Rough-haired Pointer

Slovak Rough-haired Pointer

TRAINING

This breed is very intelligent, keen to learn and eager to please its owner. Obviously, consistency is vital. These dogs respond very well to the voice. Punishments other than verbal rebukes are usually not necessary. If you vary the exercises so they remain fun for the dog to do, it will be able to learn rapidly and love obeying your commands.

EXERCISE

These dogs are real hunters with a great exercise

Slovak Rough-haired Pointer

need and lots of stamina. They lack the disposition required to lounge in front of the fire all day long. If left to its own devices this dog will start to look for its own activities, usually on the other side of the fence. Therefore you should take the dog out every day and give it an opportunity to release its energy off-leash. You can teach the dog to run alongside you if you go jogging, but most dogs will also love swimming and retrieving.

USES

This breed is traditionally used primarily as a hunter, both for pointing and for tracking and retrieving game. The dog does not mind whether it needs to retrieve from the water or from dense shrubs. Taking it to a hunting class is certainly worth your while. These dogs can also do well as a companion dog, provided the family is sporty and prepared to spend time with the dog. Sports such as advanced obedience classes are also worth considering, and this breed would certainly do well as a tracking dog.

DETAILS

In its country of origin the Slovak Rough-haired Pointer is better known as Slovensky Hruborsty Ohar. This breed originates from the Weimaraner and the Korthals Griffon.

Slovak Rough-haired Pointer

The influence of the Weimaraner is readily apparent with this Slovak Rough-haired Pointer.

Bracco Italiano

BRACCO ITALIANO

COUNTRY OF ORIGIN	ITALY
ORIGINAL FUNCTION	THE BRACCO ITALIANO IS USED AS AN ALL-ROUND GUNDOG FOR HUNTING FEATHERED GAME

APPEARANCE

BODY

The Bracco Italiano is a visually well-muscled dog with smooth movement. The long, muscular back shows a slight dip behind the high withers. The groin slopes slightly. The tail is carried level in movement and is usually docked to 6–10in (15–25cm) in countries where this is permitted. The chest is broad and deep. The belly is not tucked up, but nearly level. The legs are straight and well angulated, with

Fully-grown Bracco Italiano with puppy

big, round feet, preferably with (double) dew claws. The neck is strong and fairly short, with slight dewlap.

HEAD

The head is long and slightly angular, with a pronounced occiput and a slight stop. The nose bridge may be straight or slightly arched. The skull and muzzle are of equal length, with a slightly overhanging upper lip. The ears are set far back and level with the eye. They are carried folding forward, close to the cheeks. The tips of the

Bracco Italiano bitch

ear should reach to the tip of the nose. The eyes are oval in shape with close fitting eyelids and a gentle, intelligent expression. Bracco Italianos should preferably have a scissors bite, but a level bite is also allowed.

SHOULDER HEIGHT

Dogs have a shoulder height between $22^3/_4$–$26^1/_2$ in (58–67 cm) and bitches between $21^3/_4$–$24^1/_2$ in (55–62 cm).

COAT

The coat is short, thick and glossy.

COLORS

Permitted colors are white, white with more or less large orange, amber or chestnut brown patches, or white with light orange or chestnut brown speckles. A symmetrical mask is preferred, but is not compulsory. The eyes are (ochre) yellow.

TEMPERAMENT

CHARACTER

This breed is even-tempered, gentle-natured, thoughtful and compliant in character.

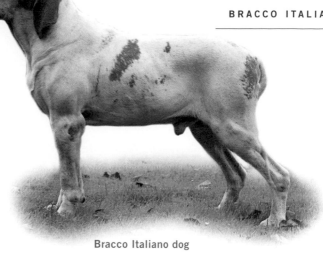

Bracco Italiano dog

They are sensitive and intelligent dogs, calm in the house, very affectionate and devoted to their owners and family members. This breed is generally obedient. It can take up to 2½ to 3 years for a Bracco Italiano to mature.

SOCIAL BEHAVIOR

Bracco Italianos are extremely sociable by nature and will get on well with other dogs and household pets irrespective of their sex. As a rule they also get on fine with children. Towards people they do not know they can be a bit aloof, but this is a sign of shyness rather than of arrogance or suspicion. The Bracco Italiano will bark when it senses danger, but it is not a defense dog.

GENERAL CARE

GROOMING

The Bracco Italiano needs relatively little grooming. During the molt dead and loose hair can be easily removed using a rubber brush. The ear passages require a little extra attention and need to be checked weekly for excessive earwax or dirt.

Young Bracco Italiano

TRAINING

Gentle but consistent training achieves best results. If a close bond exists its owner, the dog will respond well to voice inflection and further punishments will be unnecessary. Remember to praise the dog abundantly when it has done something well. These dogs are very sensitive. A firm approach and corporal punishment are counter-productive, as they lose their trust in their owner. If trained correctly, this dog grasps things quickly and is one of the most obedient breeds. Because they can be aloof towards strangers, socialization is very important; this will largely prevent shyness in adulthood.

EXERCISE

Although the Bracco Italiano needs a fair amount of free exercise, it does not become bad-tempered if denied the opportunity for a short while. Owners with access to a spacious yard are ideal. These dogs love retrieving. When mature (at the age of about 1½ years), they can be introduced gradually to running alongside you when jog. Do not let a growing dog climb stairs or overtax its constitution.

USES

The Bracco Italiano is an all-round hunting dog, specializing in hunting wildfowl. It can point and retrieve, and is frequently used for this purpose. During the hunt this dog is a steadfast worker, with an excellent nose. With the right approach a Bracco Italiano will score highly at obedience trials, but only if speed is not an issue. Although very obedient, a Bracco Italiano responds to every command at a leisurely pace and will also do so in the field. This breed also does extremely well as a family dog.

FRENCH BRAQUES (POINTERS)

The group of French Pointers or Braques includes the following breeds:

- Braque d'Auvergne
- Braque du Bourbonnais
- Braque Français
- Braque Saint-Germain
- Braque de Toulouse et de l'Ariàge

In terms of size these are medium to large dogs. Depending upon the breed the shoulder height varies from 19–26$^{1}/_{2}$ in (48–68 cm). In France

Braque d'Auvergne

these short-haired breeds are primarily used for hunting. The fact that they also make wonderful companion dogs is virtually unknown. Their character is described as friendly, compliant, affectionate, intelligent and obedient. They are relatively quick to learn new commands and do not require a firm hand. A consistent and loving training will get the best out of these breeds. As a rule they get on well with their own kind and are friendly with children. When properly socialized, they do not cause any pro-

Braques de Bourbonnais

blems with cats and other household pets either. These breeds need plenty of exercise and activity; attending a hunting class would be advisable with these dogs, although there are also other ways to meet their exercise needs. Outside their country of origin these breeds are extremely rare.

Braques d'Auvergne

Male Stabyhoun with pup

STABYHOUN

COUNTRY OF ORIGIN	THE NETHERLANDS
ORIGINAL FUNCTION	VERSATILE HUNTING DOG, PARTICULARLY WATERFOWL

APPEARANCE

BODY

The Stabyhoun has a straight, fairly long back, strong loins and a nearly level croup. The long tail reaches to the heel and is carried low, with the last third curving upward. The chest is wider than it is deep, reaching no further than the elbows. The ribs are well rounded and the belly has a moderate tuck-up. The legs are well angulated and have round feet with well-arched toes. The neck is short and round, and merges into the topline at an obtuse angle so that

Stabyhoun

the head is often carried low. The slightly arched throat shows no dewlap.

HEAD

The dry head has a slightly domed skull that is neither too wide nor too narrow. The muzzle and skull are of equal length, divided by a moderate stop. The muzzle tapers slightly toward the nose without being snipey. The nose bridge is wide and straight. The trowel-shaped ears are set fairly low and hang close to the head without twisting. The medium-sized eyes are set horizontally in the head, have close fitting eyelids and are round in shape. Stabyhouns have a scissors bite.

SHOULDER HEIGHT

The ideal height for dogs is $20^1/_2$ in (53 cm), and for bitches $19^1/_2$ in (50 cm).

COAT

The coat is long and lank all over the trunk, although a very slight wave on the croup is permitted. The feathering on the backs of the legs is thick and the tail is also well covered with long hair. The tops of the ears are covered with long feathering, but it is always short on the tips.

COLORS

The most common color is piebald. To a lesser degree we also see brown and white, black roan and brown roan coats. The nose and eyelids are black in black dogs and brown in brown dogs. The eyes are dark brown in black dogs and a little lighter in brown dogs. Yellowish eyes are not permitted.

TEMPERAMENT

CHARACTER

Stabyhouns are affectionate, compliant, intelligent and inquisitive dogs. They are fairly calm, stable and confident. They are alert to what goes on around them and make excellent watchdogs without being boisterous or excited; they do not bark unnecessarily. Dogs of this breed are high-spirited and have great stamina.

SOCIAL BEHAVIOR

These dogs get on fine with other dogs and will

Stabyhouns

TRAINING

A Stabyhoun is an intelligent dog that loves to please its owner, and it is therefore generally easy to train. These dogs respond well to voice inflection. Consistent, stable training, which emphasizes rewarding good behavior, will get the best out of this dog.

EXERCISE

Stabyhouns are originally hunting dogs and therefore need a fair amount of exercise. All Stabyhouns are keen on long walks in the countryside, and should be given the opportunity to run and play freely off-leash. These dogs are rarely inclined to wander very far away from their owners. Stabyhouns love retrieving and swimming. They are virtually impervious to the weather. A Stabyhoun will be placid indoors provided it gets adequate exercise.

hardly ever look for a fight. Mixing with other household pets is no problem either, provided they are socialized with such animals when young. Their socialization with children is usually excellent. The Stabyhoun will bark when it senses danger, but strangers can expect a friendly welcome.

GENERAL CARE

GROOMING

Stabyhouns require very little grooming. The coat is such that dirt and dried mud can be easily brushed off. In normal circumstances weekly brushing is sufficient to keep the coat of this breed in good condition. Brush and comb primarily those areas where tangles can occur, such as on the chest, the tail and between the legs. Trim any excess hair between the pads, as this can bother the dog. Keep the claws short and occasionally check the ear passages for excessive earwax and dirt.

Stabyhoun

Stabyhouns

USES

This breed of dog performs extremely well as a hunting dog, but also takes part in agility and flyball trials in which it can excel with the right guidance. This breed is also well suited as a companion dog in a sports-minded family.

DRENTSE PATRIJSHOND OR DUTCH PARTRIDGE DOG	
COUNTRY OF ORIGIN	THE NETHERLANDS
ORIGINAL FUNCTION	ALL-ROUND GUNDOG THAT POINTS, FINDS AND RETRIEVES SHOT GAME, ALSO USED AS A YARD DOG AND COMPANION DOG

Dutch Partridge Dogs

Dutch Partridge Dogs

APPEARANCE

BODY

The Drentse Patrijshond is a powerful dog of proportionate build. The strong back is moderately long. The slightly sloping croup is wide and long, and the loins are very muscular. The belly shows little tuck-up. The tail, which is set fairly high and reaches almost to the hocks, is carried pendulous, with the bottom half curving upward in a slight arch or curl. The spacious chest reaches to the elbows. This breed has long, well-sprung ribs with shoulders that are set obliquely. The legs are straight and well muscled, with tightly closed elbows. Both the forequarters and the hindquarters are well angulated. The feet are round to oval in shape, with close-knit and well-arched toes. The powerful neck is short rather than long and should merge smoothly into the trunk.

HEAD

The skull is fairly wide and slightly domed, with a shallow, gradual stop and a moderately developed occipital protuberance. The eyebrows are clearly visible. The muzzle is wedge-shaped with a blunt edge. The wide nose bridge should be neither concave nor convex, although a slight upward curve is allowed. The lips are thin and dry. The ears are set high and are carried close to the cheeks without any folds or wrinkles. The eyes are oval in shape, with close fitting eyelids. They are set fairly wide apart and have a good-natured and intelligent expression. Dutch Partridge Dogs have a scissors bite.

SHOULDER HEIGHT

Ranges from $21^3/_4$–$24^3/_4$ in (55–63 cm). These measurements may vary half an inch (1 cm) up or down if the dog is well proportioned and symmetrical.

WEIGHT

For bitches approx. 55–$66^1/_4$ lb (25–30 kg) and for dogs $66^1/_4$–$77^1/_4$ lb (30–35 kg).

COAT

The Drentse Patrijshond has a dense, medium long coat that should not curl. The coat is longer and more copious on the neck, the brisket, the backs of the legs, the ears and the tail.

Dutch Partridge Dog

COLORS

Permitted colors are white with brown or orange blankets, possibly with tan markings and either with or without flecks. A mantle, i.e. an area where such brown or orange patches are positioned all over the body like a mantle, is permitted.

TEMPERAMENT

CHARACTER

These dogs are intelligent, keen to work, alert and inquisitive. They commonly are even-tempered in character and are obedient and compliant. They bark when anything is amiss, and they are mild-mannered and affectionate towards their owners and house mates. Long-term kennel life does not suit them very well, and for their character building it is far better to take this breed into the house. Most specimens love swimming, but in many cases they will have to be taught first.

SOCIAL BEHAVIOR

The average representative of this breed gets on extremely well with children and, once it

Dutch Partridge Dog

is properly socialized, also bonds well with its own kind and other pets. Though vigilant, this breed is certainly not unfriendly towards strangers.

GENERAL CARE

GROOMING

The Drentse Patrijshond requires little grooming.

Dutch Partridge Dog working

Regularly brush areas of the coat covered in longer hair with a metal pin brush with plastic caps. The ear passages need to be checked for dirt and excessive earwax now and then, and may need to be cleaned using a suitable lotion. Trim any excess hair between the pads and keep the claws short. In the brown sections on the body you may come across some longer and lighter colored tufts of hair. This is old hair that can be plucked out by hand.

TRAINING

Dutch Partridge Dogs require consistent and gentle training. These intelligent dogs are keen to work for their owners and are quick to grasp what is expected of them. They are usually quick learners, but need to be kept entertained. Variety is therefore essential.

EXERCISE

The Drentse Patrijshond needs a fair amount of exercise. Nearly all types of exercise, such as swimming, running, long off-leash walks, retrieving and ball games, appeal to this dog. Provided it can be part of family life it will not start to misbehave if occasionally you have less time to take the dog out.

Dutch Partridge Dog

USES

Since this breed is highly rated as a hunting dog, particularly in its country of origin, a hunting dog class

Dutch Partridge Dog with practice dummy

is certainly worth considering. However, this does not mean that you will be expected to go on a real hunt with the dog. These dogs can also do well at agility and obedience trials, although field sports and swimming would no doubt appeal more to them.

Dutch Partridge Dog

EPAGNEUL FRANÇAIS	
COUNTRY OF ORIGIN	FRANCE
ORIGINAL FUNCTION	HUNT, POINT AND RETRIEVE DOG, PARTICULARLY USED FOR HUNTING WILDFOWL

Epagneul Français

APPEARANCE

BODY

The body of the Epagneul Français is approx. $\frac{1}{2}$–$1\frac{1}{2}$ in (2–3 cm) longer than its shoulder height. The back is moderately long. The loins are short and straight and the groin is slightly oblique. The long tail is set fairly low and carried in a slight curve. The fairly broad, deep and long chest reaches to the elbows. The ribs are not flat, but not too round either. The well-muscled shoulders are long and laid back. The legs are vertical and the hocks are slightly angular. The Epagneul Français has strong, compact feet with closed toes and hard pads. The feet are oval in shape. The round neck is not too heavy.

HEAD

The head is fairly long and strong, but not coarse.

375

The skull is slightly domed, with a slightly pronounced occipital protuberance. The muzzle is fairly long and broad, with moderately thick lips that are slightly curved. The long ears are set at eye level or slightly lower. The tips of the ears are rounded. The eyes are medium-sized and the eyelids are close fitting.

SHOULDER HEIGHT
Dogs have a shoulder height between 21³/₄–24 in (55–61 cm) and bitches 21¹/₄–23¹/₂ in (54–59 cm). Deviations of half an inch (2 cm) are acceptable for working dogs.

COAT
The coat is long, flat or slightly wavy, with thick, short hair on the head and longer hair on the ears, the backs of the legs and the tail.

COLORS
Epagneuls Français have a white base color with brown patches, either with or without brown spots, although too many spots are not appreciated. The eyes are dark amber. The nose should be solid brown and free from pigmentation.

TEMPERAMENT

CHARACTER
These dogs are intelligent, mild-mannered, keen

Epagneul Français

to learn and obedient. They are energetic and alert, with an excellent nose. Indoors they are affectionate and calm, but outdoors and when working they display plenty of action and stamina. They rarely bark.

Epagneul Français pointing

SOCIAL BEHAVIOR
The Epagneul Français usually gets on well with dogs and other household pets and is fine with children. Although very friendly with people, this dog will bark when it senses danger.

GENERAL CARE

GROOMING
The Epagneul Français is easy to groom. The coat, particularly any areas covered in denser hair, should be carefully combed and brushed about once a week. Regularly check the ear passages for dirt or excessive earwax and trim any hair growing between the pads.

TRAINING
Because of its intelligence, amiability and kindheartedness this breed needs to be trained with a soft hand and in a harmonious atmosphere. The dogs are very sensitive to voice inflection. Allow plenty of time for socialization and always be explicit towards the dog, as this will make it more balanced. This breed needs clear guidance.

EXERCISE
This archetypal hunting dog should clearly not lie in front of the fire all day long. If you are unable or lack the ambition to go hunting, then do make sure that the dog gets its exercise in some other way. Most dogs of this breed love retrieving and swimming, even in the foulest weather.

USES
This breed is eminently suited to be a hunting dog, and before buying such a dog you should at least seriously consider attending a hunting class. These mild-mannered dogs will also feel at home as a companion dog in a sports-minded family, but they would prefer to be taken to the countryside for their daily walk. A dog sport such as agility will no doubt appeal to most specimens.

EPAGNEUL BLEU DE PICARDIE

COUNTRY OF ORIGIN	FRANCE
ORIGINAL AND TODAY'S FUNCTION	ALL-ROUND GUNDOG

APPEARANCE

BODY

The moderately long back of the Epagneul Bleu de Picardie is slightly depressed behind the withers. The loins are straight, not too long and fairly wide and full. The rounded croup slopes slightly. The tail reaches almost to the hocks and is carried pendulously. The chest is fairly wide and deep. The ribs are well arched, but not too powerful. The belly is well tucked up. The fairly long shoulders are rather straight and well muscled. Epagneuls Bleu de Picardie have straight and slightly angular legs, with round, wide feet. The muscular, well-positioned neck may show a slight dewlap.

HEAD

The head has an oval skull with a slight occipital protuberance. The stop is oblique. The nose bridge should be neither too short nor too curved. The moderately thick lips droop slightly. The ears are set sufficiently low and the tips should reach to the nose. The eyes are fairly big. These dogs have a level bite.

SHOULDER HEIGHT

For dogs $22^1/_2$–$23^1/_2$ in (57–60 cm) with bitches being slightly smaller.

COAT

The flat or slightly wavy coat

Epagneul Bleu de Picardie

is moderately long, and should not curl or be silky in texture. The ears, tail, chest and legs are covered with longer hair.

COLORS

Black with white intermingled in such a way that the coat appears to be blue. Puppies are born with a black and white coat. The "blue" shade only develops after some time.

TEMPERAMENT

CHARACTER

Epagneuls Bleu de Picardie are very mild-mannered, compliant and affectionate dogs. They are friendly, fairly quiet and calm, as well as vigilant, although they bark relatively little. They are fairly intelligent and as a rule obedient. Nevertheless, these dogs are spaniels, which tend to have a mind of their own. Their sense of smell is outstanding and they possess great stamina. They are fairly weatherproof and love being outdoors but do not thrive as kennel dogs.

SOCIAL BEHAVIOR

This breed gets on very well with their own kind, and dogs generally also with other male dogs. Contact with cats and other household pets is no problem, provided the dog has been properly

Male Epagneul Bleu de Picardie

Epagneul Bleu de Picardie

Young Epagneul Bleu de Picardie bitch

socialized. They live in harmony with children. Strangers will be announced, but that is usually all. In an emergency the majority of these dogs will, however, jump to the family's rescue.

GENERAL CARE

GROOMING
This breed needs relatively little grooming. Brush the coat once a week with a pin brush, particularly where the coat is thickest. Regularly check ear passages for dirt and excessive earwax. Some dogs will grow a lot of hair around the ear passages, underneath the leathers. It is advisable to trim this, because it will block the ear passages and may cause an inflammation. Any wisps of hair sticking out between the pads should also be trimmed.

Epagneul Bleu de Picardie

TRAINING
The Epagneul Bleu de Picardie is a relatively quick and effortless learner. It responds well to its owner's voice and usually needs no harsh words or corrections. In view of its mild-mannered temperament such treatment is not advisable, as it would only make the dog uneasy. It will learn quickest if the training is presented in a fun way. Proper socialization is essential to ensure that the dog has every opportunity to grow into a stable and reliable house mate.

EXERCISE
The Epagneul Bleu de Picardie is primarily a hunting dog that can also be happy as a family dog. However, this breed does have above-average exercise needs. Regularly take the dog out and also allow it to run and play off-leash. Most of these dogs love swimming and retrieving.

USES
Unfortunately, this breed is not very common. People who own such dogs tend to be hunters who find them reliable workers. As a companion dog in a sports-minded family they will also do extremely well.

Epagneuls Bleu de Picardie

Epagneul Picard

EPAGNEUL PICARD	
COUNTRY OF ORIGIN	FRANCE
ORIGINAL FUNCTION	ALL-ROUND GUNDOG

APPEARANCE

BODY

The Epagneul Picard has a moderately long, powerful back. The fairly wide chest reaches below the elbows and the belly is tucked up. The

Epagneul Picard

tail is not too long and is carried hanging. The shoulders are rather long, fairly straight and well muscled. The legs are straight, with slightly arched hocks. The feet are round, wide and close-knit. The neck is muscular

HEAD

The head sits on a muscular, well positioned neck. The skull is round and wide, with a long and fairly broad forehead. The occipital protuberance is well pronounced and the stop is oblique. The nose bridge should be neither too short nor too curved. The moderately thick lips droop slightly. The ears are set sufficiently low and frame the head. They should not be too short. The eyes are well opened and very expressive. Dogs of this breed have a level bite.

SHOULDER HEIGHT

Varies from $21^3/_4$–$23^1/_2$ in (55–60 cm) although a deviation of half an inch (2 cm) up is permitted.

COAT

The coat is heavy and slightly wavy, and should not be too silky except on the ears.

COLORS

This breed of dog comes in a gray mixture with brown and tan-colored markings. The nose is always brown in color.

TEMPERAMENT

CHARACTER

Epagneuls Picards are friendly, affectionate and compliant dogs. They are fairly quiet, confident and stable in temperament. Their adaptability is excellent, as is their sense of smell and stamina. They will certainly bark when they sense danger, although they will not defend you. They are intelligent and to some extent obedient as well, although they can also be willful at times.

SOCIAL BEHAVIOR

Picards get on extremely well with other dogs. Mixing with pets such as cats is usually no problem either, provided the dog has been well socialized. These dogs are not timid and your visitors, whether they are welcome or unwelcome, will always be greeted warmly. These dogs generally live in harmony with children.

GENERAL CARE

GROOMING

The coat needs to be thoroughly brushed about once a week, particularly in places where the hair is longer and thicker. A pin brush is ideal for this. Check the ear passages regularly and clean them with a suitable ear cleaner if necessary. Any excess hair growing underneath the leathers, around the ear passages, could lead to

Epagneul Picard

Epagneul Picard

inflammation of the ear and should be trimmed. Any hair growing between the pads will also need to be clipped occasionally, because thorns, stones and spikes could easily get stuck in them.

TRAINING

Although this breed also has its more stubborn specimens, Epagneuls Picard are usually easy to train. A loving, consistent training brings out the best in this dog.

EXERCISE

The Epagneul Picard needs a fair amount of exercise. Daily walks around the block are not enough to offer this dog what it needs in terms of exercise. Regularly take the dog on long, off-leash walks in the countryside and occasionally let it do a few training exercises such as retrieving. Most Epagneuls Picards love swimming.

USES

The Epagneul Picard is relatively uncommon both in France and abroad, and is primarily kept by hunters. However, it also does very well as a family dog, provided it gets plenty of exercise.

GERMAN POINTER, LONG-HAIRED	
COUNTRY OF ORIGIN	GERMANY
ORIGINAL FUNCTION	ALL-ROUND GUNDOG, PARTICULARLY FOR HUNTING FEATHER

APPEARANCE

BODY

This breed of dog should ideally have a square build with a solid, level and a close-coupled back. The withers are slightly higher than the back, the loins are strong and the long croup slopes gently. The tail is carried with a slight upward curve or level. The chest reaches to the elbows, its width is in proportion to the build and there is a well-defined brisket. The belly is slightly tucked up. The legs are straight and well angulated, with closed and moderately long feet. The muscular neck is moderately long and slightly arched.

Long-haired German Pointer

HEAD

The elongated head is dry and sufficiently wide. The skull and muzzle are of equal length, separated by a stop that slopes upward. The nose bridge is slightly curved and the lower jaw is strong. The wide ears are set high, carried pendulously and close to the head. Long-haired German Pointers have close fitting eyelids.

Long-haired German Pointer

SHOULDER HEIGHT

For dogs this ranges from $24^3/_4$–26 in (63–66 cm) and for bitches from $23^1/_2$–$24^3/_4$ in (60–63 cm).

COAT

The coat is long-haired. On the back and flanks the hair should be $1^1/_2$–2 in (3–5 cm) long, though longer on the neck, brisket and belly. The legs, ears and tail should be well feathered.

COLORS

This breed comes in solid brown; brown with white flecks or ticking; light or dark roan with brown blankets and a brown head; dapple gray (white with small brown patches all over the body and a brown head) and in brown with white. The head including the ears should always be brown, with possibly a white marking, such as a star or a blaze. The eyes should ideally be as dark as possible.

Long-haired German Pointer puppy

TEMPERAMENT

CHARACTER

This breed of dog is lively, compliant, intelligent, keen to learn and mild-mannered. They are very affectionate and devoted to their families. They are lively, even-tempered and stable in character; nervousness and aggressiveness are alien to them. Their sense of smell is excellent.

Long-haired German Pointer

SOCIAL BEHAVIOR

Long-haired German Pointers are sociable with other dogs and most are gentle and patient with children. Mixing with pets such as cats is seldom a problem, although the puppy should obviously be socialized with such animals. They do tend to bark when there is something amiss, but generally are friendly towards unfamiliar faces.

GENERAL CARE

GROOMING

The Long-haired German Pointer needs very little grooming. Brushing the coat once a week is sufficient, particularly the areas with longer hair where tangles can occur. Outside these grooming sessions you can shape the coat from time to time by plucking the old hairs. Such hairs are easy to spot because they are lighter (brown) in color and often a little fluffy. Although you can do the plucking yourself, it might be better to leave this to a qualified trimming expert for the longer-haired dogs. Excessively long hair growing between the pads can be clipped with rounded scissors.

TRAINING

The Long-haired German Pointer is an intelligent dog that is quick and eager to learn from its owner. This makes training usually quite easy. They are very gentle-natured and a firm approach is not necessary. Do make ample use of voice inflection and remember to praise the dog abundantly when

Long-haired German Pointer

Long-haired German
Pointer bitch

Male Long-haired German Pointer

Puppy

ever it does something well.

EXERCISE

This dog is primarily a hunting dog that likes to swim, retrieve and track. You could do it no bigger favor than by taking it for regular treks into the countryside. The German Pointer belongs with sports-minded folks who love being active outdoors. When the Long-haired gets plenty of exercise and activity it will be calm in the house.

USES

This dog is appreciated most by hunters, who regard it as a very reliable worker. The Long-haired will also do well as a pleasant family dog, provided it gets plenty of exercise and activity.

Long-haired German Pointer

LARGE MÜNSTERLANDER

COUNTRY OF ORIGIN	GERMANY
ORIGINAL AND TODAY'S FUNCTION	ALL-ROUND GUNDOG, MAINLY USED FOR POINTING AND RETRIEVING WILDFOWL, BUT ALSO OTHER GAME.

Large Münsterlander

APPEARANCE

BODY

The Large Münsterlander has a body that is square or slightly longer than it is tall. The chest is wide and deep, with a pronounced brisket. The back is straight and short. The long, broad croup has a moderate slope. The withers are long and muscled, and the belly is slightly tucked up. The tail is straight and carried in line with the back or slightly higher. Large Münsterlanders have well-angulated and straight fore and hind legs with closed, moderately long feet. The powerful, dry neck is carried nobly.

Large Münsterlanders

HEAD

The head is fairly long and noble, with a moderate stop. The nose bridge is straight and the lips should not droop. The high-set ears are wide, with rounded tips and are carried pendulously and close to the head. The eyes have close fitting eyelids. Large Münsterlanders have a complete scissors bite.

SHOULDER HEIGHT

Dogs have a shoulder height between $23^1/_2$–$25^1/_2$ in (60–65 cm) and bitches are a little smaller, measuring $22^3/_4$–$24^3/_4$ in (58–63 cm).

COAT

The coat is longhaired, dense and lank. The coat should not curl or stand out. The hair is longer on the ears, the backs of the legs and the tail.

COLORS

Large Münsterlanders come predominantly in white with black blankets and spots, but black roan is also permitted. The head should always be black, with possibly a white patch around the nose or a blaze. The eyes are completely dark in color. The nose should be solid black.

TEMPERAMENT

CHARACTER

Large Münsterlanders are intelligent and eager to work. They have great stamina, an excellent nose, and are fairly hardy and brave. Some can be a little dominant. These dogs are extremely vigilant and bark when they sense anything amiss. They are devoted to their owners and very affectionate. When the family is threatened or uninvited guests appear while the owners are away, this breed will act convincingly as a watchdog.

SOCIAL BEHAVIOR

Large Münsterlanders generally get on reasonably well with dogs and other household pets, and most specimens are patient and tolerant towards children. They are normally friendly with people.

GENERAL CARE

GROOMING

This dog needs relatively little grooming. Regularly brush and comb the dog and check the ear passages for dirt from time to time. Keep the claws short.

TRAINING

The Large Münsterlander is not hard to train. It is intelligent, keen to learn and loves working. Some Münsterlanders, especially dogs, are a little more dominant in character and demand a handler who is confident and bold.

EXERCISE

These hunting dogs need a fair amount of exercise and you cannot limit them to three short walks a day. Apart from regular walks you should also allow the dog to romp about off-leash. Running is also excellent for this dog. They love retrieving and most enjoy swimming. They are able to withstand all weathers.

USES

The Large Münsterlander is primarily used as a hunting dog and can be taught both to point and to retrieve. Provided it gets enough exercise, it can also be a pleasant family dog.

Small Münsterlander.

HEIDEWACHTEL OR SMALL MÜNSTERLANDER	
COUNTRY OF ORIGIN	GERMANY
ORIGINAL AND TODAY'S FUNCTION	ALL-ROUND GUNDOG, MAINLY USED FOR POINTING AND RETRIEVING WILDFOWL, BUT ALSO OTHER GAME

APPEARANCE

BODY

The Small Münsterlander is a medium-sized hunting dog combining strength with elegance. The body has a deep chest and a short or moderately long back. The loins are wide and strong. The belly is slightly tucked up. The tail is of moderate length and is carried level, although the final third section may curve slightly upward. The legs are straight and well angulated, with round, close feet.

HEAD

The head is slightly domed and dry. The skull should not be too wide. The stop is not too pronounced. The powerful muzzle is straight and long and the lips are close fitting. The high set ears are wide, tapering to a point and are carried pendulously, close to the head. They should not reach very far beyond the corners of the mouth. The eyes have close fitting eyelids.

Small Münsterlander

SHOULDER HEIGHT

Bitches have a shoulder height of $19^{1}/_{2}$–$21^{1}/_{4}$ in (50–54 cm) and dogs $20^{1}/_{2}$–22 in (52–56 cm). A deviation of half an inch (2 cm) up or down is acceptable.

COAT

The Heidewachtel has a moderately long, smooth, full and close lying coat that is not very wavy. The tail, backs of the legs and ears are covered in longer hair.

COLORS

The coat color is brown with white, or brown roan. A few tan-colored markings around the muzzle and eyes are permitted, but these are very rare. The nose is solid brown in color and the eyes should preferably be dark brown.

Small Münsterlanders

Small Münsterlander

TEMPERAMENT

CHARACTER

Heidewachtels are biddable, intelligent and mild-mannered dogs with a positive disposition and an uncomplicated, high-spirited temperament. They are generally obedient. Tireless and rather tough on themselves in the field, they are largely quiet in the house. The weather does not affect them much. They usually love swimming, and tend to get very attached to their owners and families.

SOCIAL BEHAVIOR

Most Heidewachtels get on very well with children, and will also live in harmony with their own kind and other household pets. Strangers are greeted openly. Although they do bark when there are signs of danger, that is usually all.

GENERAL CARE

GROOMING

This breed needs an average amount of grooming. The coat may be brushed and combed about twice a week. From time to time light brown hairs will appear on brown-colored areas of the coat. These are old hairs that can be plucked by hand. Occasionally check the ear passages for dirt and trim any excess hair if necessary. Also trim the excess hair between the pads, because this can bother the dog. Heidewachtels reach maturity around the age of three.

TRAINING

Heidewachtels love to please their owners and are intelligent enough to grasp commands quickly. Dogs such as these need to be trained with a soft and consistent hand.

EXERCISE

The Heidewachtel is primarily a hunting dog, with the physique and mentality to work all day long. It would be unfair to limit a dog with such abilities to the sedate life of a family dog, although it would be unlikely to protest. Regularly take the dog out on long walks, let it retrieve and also give it the chance to go swimming from time to time. The dog does not mind the weather, and will love swimming in the rain just as much as when the sun is shining.

USES

Hunting training classes are obviously the most suitable types of training for this breed. If you are unable or lack the ambition to go hunting, then it is advisable to offer this dog a challenging alternative such as agility or flyball.

Small Münsterlander pup

CESKY FOUSEK

COUNTRY OF ORIGIN	CZECH REPUBLIC
ORIGINAL FUNCTION	ALL-ROUND GUNDOG SPECIALIZING IN POINTING

APPEARANCE

BODY

The topline gradually slopes down from withers to croup. The back is short and stocky, and the loins are fairly wide and slightly arched. The belly is slightly tucked up. The chest is oval in shape and reaches at least to the elbow joints. The sternum protrudes noticeably. The tail is planted in line with the back and is docked to three fifths in countries where this is permitted. The muscular, dry legs are straight, well angulated and free from dew claws. The feet are spoon-shaped and close-knit, with arched toes. The dry, normally curved and moderately long neck is set fairly high.

Cesky Fousek

HEAD

The head is dry, rather long and narrow, and is carried high. The nose bridge is slightly arched and the muzzle slightly longer than the skull. There is a pronounced stop. The well-defined supraorbital ridges make the head seem slightly angular. The upper lip droop slightly over the bottom lip. The fairly short-haired ears are set high, hang close to the head and have rounded tips. The deep-set eyes are almond-shaped. Cesky Fouseks have a scissors bite.

SHOULDER HEIGHT

Dogs have a shoulder height ranging from $23^1/_2$–26 in (60–66 cm) while bitches measure $22^3/_4$–$24^1/_2$ in (58–62 cm).

WEIGHT

Dogs weigh $61^3/_4$–75 lb (28–34 kg) and bitches approx. $48^1/_2$–$61^3/_4$ lb (22–28 kg).

COAT

The coat consists of three types of hair: a dense undercoat approx. half an inch (2cm) long, a harsh, rough upper coat approx. $1^1/_2$–$1^3/_4$ in (3–4 cm) long and 2–$2^3/_4$ in (5–7 cm) long, hard, bristly hair on the (fore)chest, back, groin and shoulders. Cesky Fouseks have a prominent beard, mustache and eyebrows.

COLORS

This breed of dog comes in off-gray either with or without any brown markings, solid brown, and brown with honey-colored markings on the chest and the bottom of the forelegs. The eyes are dark amber to brown. The nose is always brown in color.

TEMPERAMENT

CHARACTER

Cesky Fouseks are friendly, intelligent, gentle,

Cesky Fousek

biddable and obedient. Indoors they are fairly placid and affectionate, but at work they are active and fairly hard on themselves. They will bark when they sense danger.

SOCIAL BEHAVIOR

Cesky Fouseks get on extremely well with dogs. Contact with other household pets is generally fine, provided the dog has been properly socialized. These mild-mannered dogs generally live in harmony with children. Strangers will be announced, but that tends to be all.

GENERAL CARE

GROOMING

The condition of the coat determines how often the Cesky Fousek needs to be plucked: never or several times a year. The beard, mustache and eyebrows are left alone during this process. Brush the dog occasionally between plucking sessions and clip any excess hair between the pads of the feet. Check the ear passages for dirt and excessive hair growth from time to time.

TRAINING

This breed is not hard to train. They are keen to learn from their owners and are relatively quick at grasping new commands. Cesky Fouseks are devoted to their owners and sensitive to moods and voices. A soft,

explicit and consistent approach will achieve best results. The training should be varied. This is not the type of dog that derives pleasure from following the same command ten times in a row.

Cesky Fouseks

EXERCISE

These dogs are primarily hunting dogs. They need plenty of exercise to release their energy. If you are unable to go hunting with the dog then it is essential that you regularly take it running and let it play off-leash. Ball games, swimming and retrieving are favorite pastimes.

USES

Cesky Fouseks are all-round gundogs that are used for hunting both fur and feather. Their specialization is pointing, but they also excel at retrieving. They are nimble both in the water and on the field or in the woods. They will also adapt very well to being a companion dog, but only in a sports-minded family.

Cesky Fousek

KORTHALS GRIFFON

COUNTRY OF ORIGIN	FRANCE
ORIGINAL FUNCTION	VERSATILE HUNTING DOG, PARTICULARLY ON WATERFOWL

APPEARANCE

BODY

Korthals Griffons are well-built, strong and aristo-cratic dogs with a level back and well-developed loins. The chest is deep and slightly arched. The ribs are slightly rounded. The tail is carried hori-zontally or slightly up. In countries where docking is permitted the tail is usually docked to one third or nearly half its length. The shoulders are fairly long and laid back. The legs are straight and strong, with well-arched hock joints and round, solid feet with closed toes. The neck is fairly long and shows no dewlap.

Korthals Griffon

HEAD

The head is large and long, with a skull that is not too wide and a long, square muzzle. The stop is weak. The nose bridge is slightly convex. The ears are of medium size and carried pendu-lously, close to the head. They are not set on too low. The eyes are big. Korthals Griffons have a scissors bite.

SHOULDER HEIGHT

Dogs have a shoulder height between $21^3/_4$–$23^1/_2$ in (55–60cm) and bitches between $19^1/_2$–$21^3/_4$ in (50–55cm).

COAT

The hair is rough and harsh, feeling like fine thread or pigs' hair. A woolly or curly coat is not allowed. The undercoat is soft and dense. The head is rough, but not too covered with long hair, and with a distinct mustache and eyebrows. The eyebrows should not cover the eyes.

Korthals Griffon

COLORS

These dogs come in blue gray, gray with brown blankets or in solid brown, often intermingled with gray hairs. White with brown is also permitted. The forenose and eyes are always brown in color.

TEMPERAMENT

CHARACTER

This breed of dog is very intelligent, keen to learn and obedient. They have a friendly, affectionate and sociable temperament, and are brave and tough on themselves. If the need arises they will act as guards and defenders of the family and its possessions. They are extremely loyal and fond of their families. They have an excellent sense of smell and great stamina. They reach intellectual maturity fairly late. Their coat protects them from the cold, so they can also be kept in an outdoor kennel. However, in that case regular contact with the owner is a must.

Korthals Griffon

SOCIAL BEHAVIOR

The Griffon Korthals generally gets on well with children and mixing with its own kind does not cause many problems either. Provided they are well socialized and trained you do not need to expect any problems in their contact with cats and other household pets. Friends of the family are greeted enthusiastically but uninvited guests are stopped in their tracks.

GENERAL CARE

GROOMING

The Korthals should be brushed and combed thoroughly and regularly. The longer hair around the muzzle in particular requires extra attention. Check the ear passages for dirt and excessive earwax from time to time and clean them with a suitable ear cleaner when necessary. Sometimes excessive hair will grow between the pads, in which twigs, stones and other debris can get stuck. It is advisable to trim these long hairs regularly. Keep the claws short.

TRAINING

This breed of dog is generally not difficult to train. The Korthals is intelligent enough to grasp quickly what is expected. A consistent, clear and anything but firm training will get the best out of this dog. These dogs often reach intellectual maturity a little later than most other hunting dogs, which means that you should not demand too much from a young dog in terms of obedience.

Korthals Griffon

EXERCISE

The Griffon Korthals is every inch a hunter, and needs plenty of exercise and activity to feel physically and mentally well. If you do not intend to go hunting with this dog, you will have to meet the dog's exercise requirements in other ways. These dogs love being outdoors and can withstand all weathers. Regularly take the dog for long off-leash walks in the countryside. Swimming and retrieving are favorite activities of nearly all these dogs. Provided it is sufficiently mature, the Griffon Korthals can also happily accompany you if you go jogging.

It's good to rest after work (Korthals Griffon)

USES

This breed is mainly used as an all-round hunting dog, a task to which these dogs are eminently suited. They will also adapt to family life, provided they get enough attention, action and exercise.

The Korthals is named after Edward Korthals, who created this breed in the second half of the nineteenth century. Korthals was a Dutchman who lived in France.

Epagneul Breton

EPAGNEUL BRETON

COUNTRY OF ORIGIN	FRANCE
ORIGINAL FUNCTION	ALL-ROUND GUNDOG FOR WILDFOWLING

APPEARANCE

BODY

The Epagneul Breton has a stocky, compact build.
The back is short and has well-defined withers.
The loins are short, wide and strong, and the
groin slopes gently. If the dog is not born
tail-less, the tail is docked up to a length
of 4 in (10 cm) in countries where this
is permitted. It is carried level or
down. The chest reaches to the
elbows and the ribs are wide and
well arched. The flanks are well
tucked up, but not excessively so.
The shoulders are sloping and muscular. The legs are straight and moderately
angular, with tightly closed toes. The neck is of
average length with no dewlap.

HEAD

The head is of average length and slightly rounded. The stop is pronounced but sloping, and the
nose bridge is straight or very slightly arched. The
lips are thin. The upper lips hang slightly over the
bottom lips. The ears are preferably short and
rounded, set high and carried pendulously.

SHOULDER HEIGHT

The ideal height for dogs ranges between

19–19$\frac{1}{2}$ in (48–50 cm) and for bitches between
18$\frac{1}{2}$–19$\frac{1}{4}$ in (47–49 cm). A deviation of half an
inch (1cm) up or down is allowed.

WEIGHT

Epagneuls Breton weigh roughly 33 lb (15 kg).

COAT

The coat is flat or slightly wavy, has a fine texture
with feathering. The coat should not curl or be
silky in texture.

COLORS

The Epagneul Breton comes in white and orange,
white and chestnut brown, white and black, tricolor or one of these colors in brindle. By far the
most common color is white and orange. The eyes
are dark amber and the nose should be dark, without any pigmentation.

TEMPERAMENT

CHARACTER

These dogs are alert, lively, intelligent, good-
natured and affectionate. They are generally compliant, but can sometimes have a mind of their
own. They are sensitive to harsh words and moods
in the house, and get very attached to their
owners. Their sense of smell is
extremely well developed. They
have great stamina and love
retrieving. In times of

Epagneul Breton

danger the Epagneul Breton will bark, but that is usually all. They tend to bark little.

SOCIAL BEHAVIOR

A well-trained Epagneul Breton gets on really well with children and also with their own kind. After proper socialization there need not be any problems with cats and other household pets. Visitors will be announced but will then be greeted warmly.

GENERAL CARE

GROOMING

The Epagneul Breton's coat is fairly easy to groom. Weekly brushing, paying particular attention to the body parts covered in longer hair, is sufficient to keep the coat in good condition. Regularly check the ear passages for dirt, and keep the claws short.

TRAINING

The Epagneul Breton is not hard to train, provided the owner is consistent. This breed is intelligent and keen to learn and to work. However, there are also a few less compliant representatives of the breed who require rather more patience and understanding from their owners. In view of their sensitive nature firm training is not recommended. The owner should be consistent, unambiguous and loving.

EXERCISE

Despite the fact that it has adapted extremely well to its role as a family dog, the Epagneul Breton is every inch the hunter. This dog will certainly not put up with three short walks around the block, and it would not be fair to expect this either. Regularly take the dog out, giving it the chance to romp and run about off-leash. The majority of these dogs possess a fairly well developed hunting instinct which, combined with an inexperienced or indulgent owner, can lead to a dog that chases after game of its own accord. However, this can quite easily be prevented with proper training.

USES

This breed is primarily a hunting dog. In its country of origin this dog is tremendously popular with hunters, but elsewhere it is rare. You could consider attending a hunting class with this dog, which would meet both its need to work and its exercise needs. Sports such as agility and flyball are recommended as substitute activities, al-

though advanced obedience is another option. Epagneuls Breton are also kept as a family dog and are excellent for this purpose provided their exercise needs are not overlooked.

Epagneul Breton

DETAILS

The Epagneul Breton has an American counterpart known by the breed name Brittany. This breed developed from Epagneul Bretons. Basically, there are few differences between both breeds; there are some deviations in shoulder height and permissible colors. The Epagneul Breton has been recognized by the FCI, whereas the Brittany has been recognized by the American and English Kennel Clubs where a breed standard applies that differs slightly from the Breton's.

British and Irish Pointers

POINTER

COUNTRY OF ORIGIN	ENGLAND
ORIGINAL FUNCTION	HUNTING DOG, SPECIALIZED IN POINTING FOWL (PARTICULARLY PARTRIDGE)

APPEARANCE

BODY

The Pointer is a well-built, symmetrical dog. The chest reaches to the elbows and the well-arched ribs become gradually shorter towards the back. The distance between the back ribs and the groin is short. The tail is moderately long and is carried in line with the back. It is wide at the root and tapers to a point. The legs are long and straight, with oval bones. The oval feet have tightly closed toes. The neck is muscular and round.

The Pointer's nose is pointing at something

HEAD

The skull is moderately wide and has a pronounced stop and occipital protuberance. The nose bridge is slightly concave (dish-faced) and the soft lips are well developed. The medium long ears are set fairly high and carried pendulously, close to the head. The leathers are slightly pointy. The eyes have a friendly expression. Pointers have a scissors bite.

SHOULDER HEIGHT

Dogs have a shoulder height from $24^3/_4$–$27^1/_2$ in (63–69 cm), but bitches are a little smaller, measuring 24–26 in (61–66 cm).

WEIGHT

Pointers weigh between 44–55 lb (20–25 kg).

COAT

The glossy short-haired coat has a hard, fine texture and is perfectly close lying and straight.

COLORS

Pointers come in white with yellow or orange, white with liver or white with black. Tricolors and solid colored coats are also permitted.

TEMPERAMENT

CHARACTER

Pointers are typically intelligent, sporty, friendly, affectionate, good-natured and even-tempered.

Pointer

They are general-
ly obedient dogs with an
excellent nose and an above-
average hunting instinct.

SOCIAL BEHAVIOR

This breed of dog gets on
well with their own kind.
Most are friendly and pa-
tient towards children.
Pointers are usually friendly towards both familiar
faces and strangers. Following
proper socialization mixing with cats and other
household pets will cause no problems.

Pointer pointing

GENERAL CARE

GROOMING

The Pointer needs very little grooming. During
the molt you can simply remove any dead and
loose hairs from the coat with a rubber brush.
Check the ear passages from time to time and
keep the claws short.

TRAINING

The Pointer is a reasonably quick learner. It is
intelligent enough to grasp quickly what you want
and loves to work for its owner. This dog needs to
be trained using a consistent, but gentle approach.
Harsh words and a firm approach will ruin the
open, gentle temperament of this dog.

EXERCISE

Pointers need plenty of exercise. In addition to

Pointer

Pointer

short daily walks the owner should allow at least
one hour each day to let the dog run and romp
about off-leash. Pointers can also be taught to
accompany you on your daily runs, and are virtually indefatigable and despite their short coats
fairly impervious to the cold and wet.

USES

This breed specializes in pointing feather, especially partridges, although the hunter can also train
them to point other types of game. While this
breed has been exclusively bred as a specialist
pointer, it is intelligent and compliant enough to
be able to learn other skills and do reasonably well
at those.

Irish Setter

<table>
<tr><td colspan="2">IRISH SETTER</td></tr>
<tr><td>COUNTRY OF ORIGIN</td><td>IRELAND</td></tr>
<tr><td>ORIGINAL FUNCTION</td><td>HUNTING DOG, SPECIALIZED IN TRACKING AND INDICATING GAME ("POINTING")</td></tr>
</table>

APPEARANCE

BODY

The Irish Setter should look "racy", with a well-proportioned build, refined looks and a friendly expression. The topline is solid, muscular and level, gradually sloping down from shoulders to withers. The fairly low set tail of moderate length is thick at the root and tapers to a point. It is carried as near as possible on a level with the back or lower. The chest is as deep as possible and rather narrow when viewed from the front. The ribs are well arched. The shoulders are set well back. The forelegs are straight and sinewy. The elbows are free, but are not turned either in or out. The hindquarters are wide and strong, and the stifle and hock joints are well arched. The feet are small and solid, with strong, arched and closed toes. The very muscular, dry neck is slightly arched, moderately long and must not be too thick.

Irish Setter

HEAD

The head is long and dry, and should not be narrow or snipey or coarse near the ears. The oval skull displays a well-defined occipital protuberance. The nose bridge and occiput run in parallel, with a pronounced stop in the center. The eyebrows protru-de. The muzzle is fairly deep and practically square at the end. The lips are not pendulous. The nostrils are wide. The ears are low and set well back. They are delicate, moderate in size, hanging in elegant folds close to the head. The eyes are not too large and preferably almond-shaped. They are set level in the head and have a friendly, intelligent expression. Irish Setters have a scissors bite.

SHOULDER HEIGHT

The shoulder height has not yet been described in the breed standard, but the Irish breed society has suggested aiming for the following measurements in the long term: a shoulder height of $22^1/_2$–26in (58–66 cm) for dogs and $21^1/_4$–24 in (54–61 cm) for bitches.

COAT

The coat is fairly long and flat, as free from curl or wave as possible. The feathering is long and silky on the tips of the ears and long and fine on the backs of the legs. There is also fairly long hair on the belly, which may extend to the chest and neck. The tail should have a fringe, which decreases in length towards the tip of the tail. The coat is short and fine on the head, the front of the legs and the tips of the ears.

COLORS

Irish Setters have a deep chestnut brown coat, without any trace of black. Small white markings on the chest, chin or toes, a small star on the forehead or a narrow white blaze do not lead to disqualification, but are not desirable. The nose is dark mahogany, brown or black. The eyes are dark hazel to dark brown.

TEMPERAMENT

CHARACTER

The Irish Setter is a good-natured, intelligent, high-spirited and affectionate breed. These dogs become very attached to their owners and families. They love being part of their daily lives and do not do well as kennel dogs. They are sensitive to moods in the house and harsh words, but equally they can be rather willful and persistent once they have made up their minds. As a rule, these dogs are gentle and patient. Aggressiveness is alien to them. In the house they tend to be placid – provided they get plenty of exercise – but once they get outside their lively, active and playful nature will emerge. Irish Setters generally bark little and have an excellent nose.

SOCIAL BEHAVIOR

Irish Setters are usually friendly with people. Your visitors, both welcome and unwelcome, will be announced and then greeted boisterously. To children this breed is friendly and patient, and will also live in harmony with its own kind. Contact with other household pets should not be a problem if the dog has been properly socialized.

Irish Setter puppy.

Irish Setter dog

ear passages "to breathe" thus preventing inflammation. In addition, an Irish Setter is brushed with a pin brush about once a week. Show dogs require more grooming. They are normally clipped in such a way that their streamlined profile looks well chiseled.

TRAINING

Irish Setters are generally not difficult to train, but the owner should still allow for the rather willful streak of this breed. They are intelligent enough to grasp quickly what is expected of them, but if coercion is involved or the training is disproportionately firm they will strongly resist. They can then be fairly stubborn and will become uncontrollable. Do not allow this to happen by teaching your dog some basic principles in a loving, but definitely consistent and explicit manner. Do not expect your Setter to derive pleasure from repeating the same exercises over and over again either. It will soon lose interest.

EXERCISE

The Irish Setter needs a fair amount of exercise. Take it out on long walks

GENERAL CARE

GROOMING

This breed needs an occasional trim to remove excess – and any dead – hair from the coat. Pets can be kept neat between trimmings by clipping any excess hair between the pads and underneath the leathers. This is necessary to allow the

Irish Setter

Irish Setters

or let it run alongside you regularly once the dog has grown sufficiently. But do bear in mind that some Irish Setters follow their noses when they feel they are picking up an interesting scent. Most specimens will then play deaf when their owners call them. This breed should be taught at an early age to return to their owners on command.

USES

Most modern Irish Setters are kept as companion dogs and we also see them relatively frequently at dog shows. If you are considering attending a hunting class with this dog, then it is advisable to select a puppy from hunting lines.

IRISH RED AND WHITE SETTER	
COUNTRY OF ORIGIN	IRELAND
ORIGINAL FUNCTION	POINTING HUNTING DOG, SPECIALIZED IN TRACKING AND POINTING, PRIMARILY WILDFOWL

APPEARANCE

BODY

The Irish Red and White Setter is a strong and well-balanced dog. The back should be very strong and muscular. The tail is of medium length, strong at the root, tapering to a point and carried level with the back or slightly lower. Irish Red and White Setters have a deep chest with well-arched ribs. The shoulders are sloping and the elbows are not turned either in or out. The legs are vertical and strong. The stifle and hock joints are well angulated. The feet have closed toes. The fairly dry, muscular neck is slightly arched.

HEAD

This Setter has an elongated and fairly strong head, which is proportionally broad, with a pronounced stop. The skull is domed, with an indistinct occipital protuberance. The muzzle is rectangular in shape. The ears are set far back, level with the eyes and carried pendulous and close to the head. The eyes are round and the eyelids are close fitting. The Irish Red and White Setter has a scissors bite, although a pincer bite is allowed.

SHOULDER HEIGHT

Dogs have a shoulder height of 24$^1/_2$–26 in (62–66 cm) while bitches measure approx. 22$^1/_2$–24 in (57–61 cm) at the withers.

Irish Red and White Setter

Irish Red and White Setter

COAT

The coat is long and silky. Both the tail and the backs of the legs should be well feathered. The flanks and ears are well covered with hair. The feathering should preferably be flat but may also be slightly wavy.

COLORS

Irish Red and White Setters have a brilliant white base color with sharply defined, deep red patches. Small red spots are only allowed on the bottom halves of the legs and the muzzle. The eyes are dark hazel to dark brown in color.

TEMPERAMENT

CHARACTER

Irish Red and White Setters are very friendly, gentle-natured and intelligent dogs. They are stable, lively and active, and they have an excellent nose. They become very attached to their owners and families and are affectionate and compliant. They bark little, but do make themselves heard when something is amiss.

SOCIAL BEHAVIOR

This breed usually gets on fine with its own kind.

Young Irish Setter

When proper socialization has taken place mixing with cats and other household pets should not cause any problems either. They are naturally friendly with children. Irish Red and White Setters are friendly with people. They will bark when something is amiss but expect their owners to take action.

GENERAL CARE

GROOMING

The Irish Red and White Setter needs very little grooming, and normally weekly brushing with a pin brush will suffice. From time to time you could trim any excess hair that grows underneath the leathers. This will prevent the ear passages from getting blocked and causing an inflamma-

Irish Red and White Setter

countryside, then it will be really grateful. But do bear in mind that this dog possesses a discerning nose and will be keen to investigate any game scents. You should therefore teach the dog at an early age to return to you immediately when you call its name.

USES

Most Irish Red and White Setters are kept by hunters, but also by people who want to work with the dog for fun. That is not to say that they would not make a suitable family dog. They certainly would, provided the dog gets plenty of exercise. This breed tends to do best in a sports-minded family.

Irish Red and White Setter

Irish Red and White Setter

tion. Cut the claws short and also keep short any hair growing between the pads. From time to time you could have the dog trimmed to remove the old and protruding hairs from the coat. After such a treatment the dog will look well groomed again.

TRAINING

This breed is usually fairly easy to train. These dogs are intelligent, compliant, and love to please their owners. Punishment is usually not necessary, although this does not mean that you should not be firm and clear towards the dog. A cheerful, consistent and explicit training is essential. These are not dogs that lend themselves to endless training sessions; they enjoy variety.

EXERCISE

Irish Red and White Setters are real workers who are able and eager to work in the field for many hours if necessary. They love being in natural surroundings and are impervious to the weather. If you take your dog for off-leash walks in the

Irish Red and White Setter

ENGLISH SETTER

COUNTRY OF ORIGIN	ENGLAND
ORIGINAL FUNCTION	HUNTING DOG, SPECIALIZED IN TRACKING AND POINTING WILDFOWL

APPEARANCE

BODY

The English Setter is a medium-sized dog with a clean outline and an elegant appearance. The body is moderately long, with a close-coupled, level back and slightly arched, strong and wide loins. The tail is straight, does not reach below the hocks and is carried level with the topline or lower. The chest is deep and wide between the shoulder blades. The ribs are well sprung and widely arched, with deep back ribs. The shoulders are set well back and oblique. The low set elbows are held close to the body. The vertical legs have rounded bone. The stifles are well angulated. English Setters have tightly closed, arched toes with thick, sturdy pads with hair growing between them. The dry is fairly long and muscular, and gradually widens towards the shoulders. The neck is slightly arched. The transition to the head is sharply defined.

HEAD

The head is long and fairly dry, with a well-defined stop.

English Setters

The skull is oval in shape, with a pronounced occipital protuber-ance. The moderately deep muzzle is rather square and about equal in length to the skull. The lips must not droop too much. The moderately long ears are set low, and lie in nice folds against the cheeks. The eyes are oval in shape and must not protrude. English Setters have a complete scissors bite.

SHOULDER HEIGHT

Dogs have a shoulder height between 25½–26½ in (65–68 cm) while bitches measure 24–25½ in (61–65 cm).

COAT

The coat is long, silky and slightly wavy. The legs and tail are well feathered.

COLORS

English Setters come in the following color patterns: blue belton (white with black flecks), orange belton (white with orange flecks), lemon belton (white and lemon-colored flecks), liver belton (white with liver-colored flecks) and tricolor; liver belton and tan (white with liver and tan flecks) and blue belton and tan (white with black and tan flecks). The eyes are dark brown to hazel.

TEMPERAMENT

CHARACTER

English Setters are friendly, very mild-mannered, affectionate and sensitive.

English Setters

Intelligent and sociable, they become strongly attached to the members of their family. They are lively and agile, but not impetuous. They sense atmospheres in the house with an unerring instinct. They prefer to live in peaceful, harmonious surroundings. English Setters have a strong will and can therefore be rather obstinate. They bark very little.

SOCIAL BEHAVIOR

These dogs are very sociable by nature and aggressiveness is alien to them. They get on extremely well with their own kind, including with their own sex. Mixing with cats and other household pets does not need to present any problems so long as proper socialization has taken place. They are compliant and patient towards children. It is up to the owners to ensure children do not abuse their gentle nature. English Setters are real people lovers; your visitors may be announced but can also expect a friendly welcome.

English Setters

GENERAL CARE

GROOMING

This breed needs regular grooming. From time to time an English Setter needs to have old, spiky or excessive hair trimmed. In addition, the dog should also be thoroughly brushed once or twice a week, and any excess hair growing around the ear passages, underneath the leathers, will also have to be clipped regularly. This is necessary to allow the ear passages "to breathe" thus preventing inflammation. Show dogs require more grooming and are normally clipped.

English Setter puppy

TRAINING

The English Setter is easy to train, so long as its owner realizes that this gentle-mannered dog can also show quite a willful streak. This breed needs a consistent, explicit and very loving training: the classic "Iron fist in a velvet glove" approach. The owner should try to encourage desirable behavior. Firm training is counter-productive. This will only serve to blunt these dogs to the extent that they will stubbornly ignore or refuse to obey any commands, and it can take a long time before they are prepared to open up towards their owners again.

EXERCISE

The English Setter needs a fair amount of exercise. Regularly take the dog for long walks or, when it has become sufficiently mature, let it run alongside you when you go jogging. An English Setter is usually not terribly yard-bound, so make sure that your yard is well fenced and only let it run free in areas where this is absolutely safe.

USES

Although traditionally bred for hunting, this dog is no longer a common sight in the field. In contrast, this breed can frequently be seen at dog shows where they often steal the show with their graceful gait and elegant appearance. The various dog sports are generally wasted on the average English Setter.

English Setter puppy

GORDON SETTER

COUNTRY OF ORIGIN	SCOTLAND
ORIGINAL FUNCTION	HUNTING DOG, SPECIALIZED IN TRACKING AND POINTING WILDFOWL

Young Gordon Setter

APPEARANCE

BODY

The Gordon Setter is a stylish dog built for the gallop. His build is similar to that of a hefty hunter. The body is of moderate length. The loins are wide and slightly arched. The tail is straight or slightly saber-like, carried horizontally or just below the topline, and should not reach below the hocks. The brisket is deep but not too broad, and the well-sprung ribs are carried well back. The long shoulder blades are sloping well back and the shoulders are not loaded. The elbows are well let down and held close. The stifles and hocks are well angulated. The hocks are fairly low set. The feet are oval in shape with well-arched toes with plenty of hair growing between the pads. The slightly arched neck is long and dry.

HEAD

The well chiseled head is deep rather than wide. The slightly domed skull is widest between the ears and is longer than the muzzle. There is a pronounced stop. The muzzle is fairly long and does not taper to a point. The upper lips are well defined but should not hang over the bottom lips. The ears are set low and are carried pendulously, close to the head. They are of moderate length and thin. The eyes are set well below the supra-orbital ridges and should not be too deep set or protrude. Gordon Setters have a scissors bite.

SHOULDER HEIGHT

Dogs have a shoulder height of 26 in (approx. 66 cm) and bitches stand 24$^1/_2$ in (approx. 62 cm) tall.

COAT

The Gordon Setter has a moderately long, smooth coat, which should ideally be free from curl or wave. The feathering should be as flat and straight as possible.

COLORS

Gordon Setters are exclusively bred in black and tan. The black should be deep and shiny, and the tan a warm mahogany red. A tiny white spot on the chest is permissible. The eyes are always dark brown in color.

TEMPERAMENT

CHARACTER

These intelligent dogs are very confident and even-tempered by nature. They are friendly, sociable and gentle as well as a little stubborn, and often have a mind of their own.

They are sensitive to harsh words and moods in the house. Gordons generally behave dignified and restrained, but can be quite energetic and active outdoors. They dislike being left

Young Gordon Setter

on their own and become strongly attached to their owners. Gordon Setters mature (very) late. As their adolescence lasts long, they demand great tolerance from their owners during their puppyhood. Gordons are not really vigilant. They do tend to bark when they sense danger, but that is all.

Gordon Setters

SOCIAL BEHAVIOR

As a puppy the Gordon Setter should become exposed to lots of different situations, people, animals and objects in a positive way in order to grow up even-tempered. Gordon Setters generally get on well with their own kind and will cause no problems with children either. Contact with cats and other household pets will not be a problem if the dog has been sufficiently socialized as a puppy. Towards strangers they can initially be somewhat aloof, although they are certainly not unfriendly – aggressiveness is usually alien to them.

GENERAL CARE

GROOMING

This breed of dog needs to be well groomed regularly with a pin brush, particularly in places where the hair is long. Check the ear passages regularly for dirt or excessive earwax. Any excess of hair that sometimes grows underneath the leathers, around ear passages, is best trimmed to allow the ear passages to "breathe" freely and to prevent an inflammation of the ear. In contrast with other setters, the hair on the outside of the ear should never be trimmed. The long feathering on the ears is one of the characteristics that distinguish the Gordon from other setter breeds. The Gordon Setter is groomed for shows.

TRAINING

Gordons are fairly willful but sensitive as well; a combination which requires a degree of understanding from the trainer. However, to the right owner, who knows or is prepared to study the character of the Gordon Setter, this breed is not difficult to train. The Gordon Setter demands a loving and understanding owner, who can praise the dog

abundantly for desirable behavior but also display iron consistency. Firm training is counter-productive with this breed; their stubborn streak will prevail in such cases. These dogs mature slowly, which means that you can expect adolescent antics until well beyond the age of two. After that the dogs slow down considerably and become much calmer.

Gordon Setter

EXERCISE

The Gordon Setter needs a fair amount of exercise. Letting it run alongside you when you go jogging is an excellent way to meet its exercise needs, but you should only start with this once the dog has grown sufficiently. A Gordon Setter that gets plenty of exercise will be calm in the house. Dogs of this breed are not terribly yard-bound; keep your yard well fenced, and teach the dog to come to you promptly when called, so you can let it romp around off-leash.

USES

This breed can sometimes be seen with hunters in the field, but is more common as a valued companion dog in sports-minded families.

Six-month old Gordon Setter dog

Retrievers, Flushing Dogs and Water Dogs

SECTION 1 Retrievers

GOLDEN RETRIEVER

COUNTRY OF ORIGIN	ENGLAND
ORIGINAL AND TODAY'S FUNCTION	THIS BREED HAS TRADITIONALLY BEEN BRED FOR RETRIEVING (MAINLY) SHOT WATERFOWL. ALTHOUGH STILL USED FOR THIS PURPOSE TODAY, THESE DOGS HAVE ALSO WON THEIR SPURS IN COUNTLESS OTHER AREAS (SEE USES)

Golden Retriever

APPEARANCE

BODY

The Golden Retriever is a well-proportioned dog of sturdy build. The topline is level and the muscular loins are short. The tail is carried level with the back, reaching to the hocks with no curl at the tip. The ribs are deep and well sprung. The shoulders are long and well laid back.

The elbows are held close to the body. The forelegs are straight with good bone. The stifles are well bent and the hocks are well let down, neither turning in nor out. The metatarsals are perpendicular when viewed from behind. Golden Retrievers have round cat's feet. The dry, muscular neck has a good length.

Golden Retriever

HEAD

The Golden Retriever's head is balanced, well chiseled and well set in the neck. The skull is broad without being coarse. The muzzle is powerful, wide and deep. The length of the nose bridge approximately equals the length of the skull. Golden Retrievers have a pronounced stop and occipital protuberance. The ears are of moderate size and set on almost level with the eyes. The eyes are set well apart. Golden Retrievers have a scissors bite.

SHOULDER HEIGHT

For dogs ranging from 22–24 in (56–61 cm) while bitches stand 20–22 in (51–56 cm) tall.

WEIGHT

Adult Golden Retrievers weigh between 59$^1/_2$–72$^3/_4$ lb (27–33 kg).

COAT

The coat is flat or wavy, with good feathering. The dense undercoat is water-repellent.

COLORS

The coat may be any shade of gold or cream, but never red or mahogany. A few white hairs are permissible, but only on the brisket. The nose is preferably black, but may fade to a lighter shade under the influence of hormones or ambient

Start them young (Golden Retriever puppy)

temperature. The eye rims are dark in color and the eyes are brown.

Golden Retriever

TEMPERAMENT

CHARACTER

Golden Retrievers are extremely sociable, friendly, even-tempered and confident dogs. Kindly and compliant by nature, they are fairly laid-back and completely docile. They bark very little, are very adaptable and have an excellent sense of smell. Golden Retrievers are extremely intelligent and like to work for their owners. They are sensitive to harsh words and moods in the house, and dislike being left on their own. Most specimens love jumping in the water and are fairly sporty.

SOCIAL BEHAVIOR

Dogs of this breed get on fine with their own kind and even male specimens will happily tolerate each other. Mixing with other household pets is generally no problem, although a thorough socialization period is required. Golden Retrievers get on very well with children. They are too soft to protest, so parents will need to make sure the dog is not pestered. Some Golden Retrievers are vigilant with unknown visitors, although they are exceptions; most are fond of people and will give both welcome and unwanted visitors a friendly reception.

GENERAL CARE

GROOMING

These dogs should be combed and brushed regularly, particularly any areas that are prone to matting, such as the culottes. Any excess hair growing between the pads should be clipped regularly, because twigs, stones and the like can get stuck in it. The ears should be checked regularly. If necessary, trim any excess hair growing underneath the leathers, around the ear passages. This will prevent blocking of the ear passages, which could cause inflammation. A visit to a good trimming parlor once a year is recommended. Show dogs require more grooming, as these are usually clipped for exhibition.

TRAINING

The Golden Retriever is a fast learner and remembers what it has learned for the rest of its life. Never treat these dogs harshly, because that would harm their sensitive nature. The training should be varied and consistent with emphasis on rewarding good behavior.

EXERCISE

A Golden Retriever will adapt itself to circumstances, but needs to be taken outdoors regularly for walks or to play. Golden Retrievers have great stamina and love being outdoors. Most specimens love swimming, retrieving and, of course, long, varied off-leash walks through the countryside. Once fully grown the dog can accompany you on your daily runs.

USES

This breed is very popular in nearly all types of dog sports such as flyball, obedience and agility. It is also widely used all over the world as a working dog, for instance as a hearing dog, guide dog for the blind and rescue dog. Because of their excel-

Golden Retriever with her pup

lent sense of smell they can also do well at tracking. Most dogs are very skillful at their original job, retrieving waterfowl, although the majority of the current population is kept as a family dog.

Golden Retriever

Golden Retriever

CHESAPEAKE BAY RETRIEVER	
COUNTRY OF ORIGIN	USA
ORIGINAL FUNCTION	RETRIEVER OF (WATER) FOWL, GUARD DOG

APPEARANCE

BODY

The Chesapeake Bay Retriever has a trunk of moderate length with well-sprung ribs and a deep, broad chest. The well-coupled, powerful back is more concave than convex, with well tucked-up flanks. The very powerful hindquarters should be as high as or slightly higher than the shoulders. The tail is of medium length and should not curl over back or kink to the side. The shoulders are well laid back. The legs are straight, with well-webbed hare feet and rounded, close toes. The muscular neck is of medium length.

HEAD

Chesapeake Bay Retrievers have a broad, round skull with a medium stop. The muzzle is fairly short and tapers toward the nose but should not be snipey. The lips should not be pendulous. The small ears are well set up on the head and are hanging loosely. The eyes are medium size, with the corners approximately $3^1/_4$ in (8 cm) apart. Chesapeake Bay Retrievers have a scissors bite.

SHOULDER HEIGHT

Dogs range from 23–26 in (59–66 cm) and bitches should stand $20^1/_2$–24 in (53–61 cm) tall.

WEIGHT

Dogs weigh between $66^1/_4$–75 lb (30–34 kg) and bitches approx. $55^1/_4$–$66^1/_4$ lb (25–30 kg).

COAT

The Chesapeake's coat is its trademark: thick and short with a dense, fine woolly undercoat. Its length varies from 1–$1^1/_2$ in (3–4 cm), but the hair is shorter on the head and legs. The coat may be wavy in some places but never curly, is slightly oily and completely water-repellent. It may be

Chesapeake Bay Retriever

longer on the tail and culottes, but never more than $1^3/_4$ in (5 cm).

COLORS

Any shade of brown from dark to pale, as well as "dead grass", is permissible. A white spot on the chest and/or toes is allowed, but specimens without are preferred.

TEMPERAMENT

CHARACTER

Chesapeake Bay Retrievers are full of charac- ter, intelligent and even-tempe- red dogs. They do possess a certain degree of willfulness and males,

Chesapeake Bay Retriever

Young Chesapeake Bay Retriever

in particular, can be rather dominant. They show tremendous courage, persistence and toughness at work. During their puppyhood, which lasts for quite some time with this breed, these energetic dogs can be rather boisterous. Both sexes are vigilant and will also convincingly defend their owners, home and yard from prowlers.

SOCIAL BEHAVIOR

Mixing with a cat that is already present in the house will generally be no problem, but a Chesapeake will often find it hard not to chase after a fleeing cat outdoors. The dogs, in particular, can be rather dominant toward other dogs, although this depends largely upon their social training. Chesapeake Bay Retrievers tend to get on extremely well with children. Toward strangers they are somewhat aloof, yet not excessively so.

GENERAL CARE

GROOMING

The coat of this breed has a unique texture: it is slightly oily and completely water-repellent. Washing a Chesapeake Bay Retriever is not recommended, because this would (partly) remove the protective oily layer. Brushing and combing is usually not necessary and is not advisable because it can make coat look fluffy. Regular grooming will only be welcome during the molt to keep the amount of loose hairs in the house acceptable. Keep the claws short.

Chesapeake Bay Retriever

TRAINING

The Chesapeake Bay Retriever is a little tougher in temperament than other retrievers. This dog tends to mature slowly, and the owner will therefore have to put up with any "wild oats" until the dog is fully grown around the age of two or later. They are generally slow learners, partly due to their long period of adolescence. This breed is less suitable for the impatient hunter who wants his efforts to be rewarded quickly. But once they are fully grown and well trained they are often more reliable and obedient than many other breeds – perseverance pays off. A novice Chesapeake Bay Retriever owner must be able to train the dog consistently and lovingly. Its character building will benefit from proper socialization.

EXERCISE

This breed needs a fair amount of exercise. The Chesapeake is a real working dog and will soon get bored if forced to spend its days in front of the fire. It is virtually impervious to the weather. Chesapeake Bay Retrievers love swimming and retrieving.

USES

Traditionally a hunting dog specializing in tracking and retrieving shot game, the Chesapeake Bay Retriever has proved its worth especially on inaccessible terrain and in marshland. You could do your dog no bigger favor than by taking it to a hunting class. The dog is intelligent and eager enough to do well in dog sports such as obedience and agility, but it is first and foremost a hunting dog.

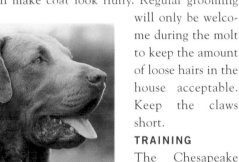

Male Chesapeake Bay Retriever

Curly Coated Retriever

CURLY COATED RETRIEVER

COUNTRY OF ORIGIN	ENGLAND
ORIGINAL FUNCTION	HUNTING DOG, SPECIALIZING IN TRACKING AND RETRIEVING WATERFOWL

APPEARANCE

BODY

The Curly Coated Retriever is not too long in the loins and has powerful, muscular hindquarters. The tail is straight, tapers to a point and is carried low. The brisket has a good depth and the ribs are well sprung. The shoulders are deep, muscular and well laid-back. The muscular legs are well bent with round, compact feet. The moderately long neck is dry and should not be coarse.

HEAD

This dog has a long skull of good proportions. The long, strong jaws are neither snipey nor coarse. The fairly small ears are set on low, lying close to the head. The eyes are rather large, but not prominent. Curly Coated Retrievers have a scissors bite.

SHOULDER HEIGHT

The ideal size for dogs is approx. 27 in (68$^1/_2$ cm)

and bitches should preferably stand 25 in (63$^1/_2$ cm) tall.

COAT

The Curly Coated Retriever has a virtually water-resistant coat of tight, crisp curls. The hair is short and free from curl on the head and the legs.

COLORS

This breed comes in solid liver and solid black.

TEMPERAMENT

CHARACTER

Dogs of this breed are intelligent, active, friendly and sometimes rather boisterous. The males in particular can be dominant as well as a little more independent than the females. Most specimens are fairly vigilant and will bark when something is amiss. They will also stand by their families in an emergency. Curly Coated Retrievers have an excellent nose.

SOCIAL BEHAVIOR

As a rule, Curly Coated Retrievers get on well with dogs and other household pets, although dogs can show a dominant streak toward other male specimens. Provided children do not pester them, they are usually very patient with them. When strangers visit they tend to keep their distance at first. They are not everybody's friend.

Curly Coated Retriever

Curly Coated Retriever

GENERAL CARE

Curly Coated Retriever

GROOMING

Curly Coated Retrievers need relatively little grooming. Regular brushing is not recommended because this will make the coat too fluffy and lose its curl. But during the molt even a Curly Coated Retriever cannot do without regular grooming. Soaking the coat after brushing – for instance by letting the dog swim – will make the curl reappear. If the coat becomes too long it needs to be trimmed with scissors. Follow the natural contours of the body during trimming; the dog is not clipped according to any particular style.

TRAINING

The Curly Coated Retriever is smart enough to grasp quickly what you mean. Nevertheless, this dog can be somewhat willful. Like the Chesapeake Bay Retriever this breed is slow to mature, which demands more patience from its owners than other Retrievers. This dog will learn rapidly if it enjoys the tasks it is given. Make sure that the training is varied and challenging. Monotonous exercises will only lead to loss of interest and demotivation. Be consistent at all times.

EXERCISE

This Retriever is first and foremost a sturdy working dog that enjoys retrieving, loves swimming and is tireless in the field. Although plenty of Curly Coated Retrievers are kept – and are equally suitable – as a family dog, they do like to be kept busy. A Curly Coated Retriever that is restricted in its freedom of movement and is too inactive can become extremely badly behaved, although ultimately the dog is not to blame.

USES

The most obvious type of exercise for this breed is a hunting class. Do not expect any immediate results, though, because it can take a few years for the dog and yourself to become attuned to each other. An average Curly Coated Retriever will then be a reliable, hard worker who works closely with its owner. If a hunting class is not your style, then you could consider taking part in a fun and varied type of dog sport, such as agility or advanced obedience. A Curly Coated Retriever can also be taught to track and will certainly enjoy it.

Curly Coated Retriever

Flat Coated Retriever

USES

These intelligent dogs were traditionally bred for tracking and retrieving game, particularly waterfowl such as ducks, a task for which they are still eminently suited. Attending a gundog trial with this dog would therefore be ideal. Other options would be training as a rescue dog, avalanche search dog or a tracker dog, as well as sports like advanced obedience and agility. Yet in practice, most Flat Coated Retrievers are kept as a family dog. They are well suited to this task, provided all their needs are met. A sports-minded family that loves doing activities with their dog would be preferable.

LABRADOR RETRIEVER	
COUNTRY OF ORIGIN	ENGLAND
ORIGINAL FUNCTION	GUNDOG, PARTICULARLY FOR RETRIEVING WATERFOWL

APPEARANCE

BODY

The Labrador Retriever is a strongly built dog with a level topline and broad, short and powerful loins. The hindquarters are strong and do not taper toward the tail. The tail is very thick at the base and of medium length. The short, dense coat gives the tail its rounded appearance. The shape of the tail is a distinctive feature of the breed and has been described as "otter tail." Labrador Retrievers have a wide, deep chest and well-sprung ribs. The long shoulders are sloping. The legs are powerful and straight, with well-turned stifles and with the hocks well let down. Labrador Retrievers have round, compact feet with well-arched toes. The neck is dry, strong and powerful.

HEAD

The skull is wide and clean-cut without fleshy cheeks. The foreface is of medium length and is not snipey. Labradors have a pronounced stop. The ears should not be too large or too heavy. They are set rather far back and hang close to the head. The eyes are of medium size, with an intelligent expression. These dogs have a strong, complete and regular scissors bite.

SHOULDER HEIGHT

Dogs range from $22-22^1/_2$ in (56–57 cm) and bitches from $21^1/_4-22$ in (54–56 cm).

WEIGHT

Labrador bitches weigh between $55^1/_4-66^1/_4$ lb (25–30 kg) and dogs between $66^1/_4-77^1/_4$ lb (30–35 kg).

COAT

The coat is short, dense without wave or

Pair of yellow Labrador Retrievers

Labrador Retriever

feathering, and is fairly hard to the touch. The undercoat is weather-resistant.

COLORS

This breed comes in three colors: solid black, liver (also called chocolate), and yellow. The yellow color may range from light cream to red fox. The nose color, rims of the lips and eyes are black in black and yellow dogs and liver in chocolate dogs. The eyes are brown or hazel. A small white spot on the chest is permissible.

TEMPERAMENT

CHARACTER

Labrador Retrievers are stable, friendly, good-natured, affectionate and extremely active. Dogs tend to be more boisterous (and stronger) than bitches. Both sexes have a sociable disposition. Aggressiveness or shyness is alien to them. They are also highly intelligent, keen to work with and for their owners and are generally obedient and compliant. Labradors are mentally and physically late to mature, which means that they will often remain playful and boisterous until they are two. Their sense of smell is outstanding and they are soft in the mouth. Because of their sociable disposition they flourish in a family setting, and they will not appreciate a lonely kennel existence.

Labrador Retriever puppies get up to everything

SOCIAL BEHAVIOR

This sociable breed usually gets on fine with other dogs. Once they have been properly socialized they will also get along well with cats and other household pets and they tend to be patient and good-natured with children. Labradors love people and are not particularly vigilant; your visitors can expect a warm and enthusiastic welcome.

Labrador Retriever

GENERAL CARE

GROOMING

The coat of the Labrador Retriever is fairly easy to care for. It needs to be thoroughly groomed with a pin brush about once a week and requires a little more attention during the molt. The coat texture is such that dirt and mud will dry quickly and can be easily brushed off. Keep the claws short. This breed has a tendency to become overweight, so make sure you never overfeed the dog and give it plenty of exercise.

Nova Scotia Duck Tolling Retriever

ful dog. It is fairly intelligent and generally very obedient. Tollers are lively and active, although not excessively so. Indoors they are usually quiet. Most Tollers love swimming and retrieving. They tend to bark little. Its sociable and peaceful character is also a hallmark of this breed.

SOCIAL BEHAVIOR

Nova Scotia Duck Tolling Retrievers are excellent family dogs that get on well with their own kind and other household pets and are patient toward children. They are always in for a ball game. They bark when they sense danger, but that is all. These remarkable dogs are friendly towards strangers.

GENERAL CARE

GROOMING

The Toller requires little grooming. Brush the coat about once a week, although more attention is required during the molt. Keep the claws short.

TRAINING

This breed is easy to train. They learn new commands relatively quickly and are keen to work for their master. The owner can achieve quite a lot using his voice.

Nova Scotia Duck Tolling Retriever

EXERCISE

Tollers need a fair amount of exercise. Apart from the usual daily walks you will need to take this dog out regularly. Most specimens love retrieving and swimming, even on colder and rainy days. If you need to skip a day, then these dogs will usually adapt to circumstances.

USES

With the right supervision this odd-ball among the Retrievers can do extremely well in dog sports such as flyball, agility and obedience. They are equally well suited as a companion dog in a sports-minded family.

Nova Scotia Duck Tolling Retrievers in their element

Flushing Dogs

ENGLISH COCKER SPANIEL

COUNTRY OF ORIGIN	ENGLAND
ORIGINAL FUNCTION	HUNTING DOG, SPECIALIZING IN DRIVING WOODCOCKS

APPEARANCE

BODY

The English Cocker Spaniel is a sturdy, well-balanced and compact hunting dog. The distance from the top of the shoulders to the root of the tail is approximately the same as the shoulder height. These dogs have short, wide loins. The firm, level topline slopes gently downward toward the set-on of the tail. The muscular hindquarters are wide and well rounded.

The tail set slightly below the topline and is carried in line with the topline in action. Cocked-up tails are a fault. With this breed the tail is customarily docked in countries where this is permitted. The chest is well developed and the brisket is deep, though neither too wide nor too narrow. The ribs are well sprung and the shoulders are sloping.

The legs are well boned and sufficiently short, but not so as to interfere with work. The stifles are well bent and the hocks are fairly low. Cocker Spaniels have cat's feet with firm, thick pads. The neck is muscular and moderate in length. It should be free from dewlap and blends neatly into the shoulders.

English Cocker Spaniel pup

English Cocker Spaniel

HEAD

The head is well developed, well chiseled and should be neither too fine nor too coarse. The cheek bones should not be prominent. The skull and the square foreface are of equal length, sepa-

English Cocker Spaniel

rated by a clearly defined stop. The lobular ears are set level with the eyes, with the leathers reaching to the nose. The eyes should be full but must not bulge and the lids are tight. English Cocker Spaniels have a complete and regular scissors bite.

SHOULDER HEIGHT

Dogs range from $15^1/_2$–16 in (39–41 cm) and bitches measure 15–$15^1/_2$ in (38–39 cm).

WEIGHT

Approx. $27^1/_2$–32 lb (13–15 kg).

COAT

The coat is flat and silky. It should not be stiff, wavy, curly or overabundant. The hair is longer on the ears, the backs of the legs, the trousers and the chest.

COLORS

English Cocker Spaniels come in solid red, black, liver and black and tan, with some white only allowed on the chest. Clearly marked Cockers with a white ground color and black, red or liver markings are more popular. These multi-color Cockers may also have tan markings. Blue, orange and liver roan specimens are also common and like the multi-colors may have tan markings. The eye color is preferably dark brown to brown, but may be hazel in liver dogs.

English Cocker Spaniel

TEMPERAMENT

CHARACTER

These dogs are renowned for their perpetual cheerfulness. Their short tail appears to be wagging all the time. They are gentle and friendly, lively and affectionate. Their intelligence must not be underestimated. Although to some extent fairly tractable and obedient, they can also show a headstrong streak. Cocker Spaniels have an excellent nose and generally love water. These dogs will become blunted if kept in a kennel; their cheerful, sociable nature will only thrive if they can live in the house and with the family.

SOCIAL BEHAVIOR

Cockers usually get along fine with other dogs and contact with cats and other pets also rarely causes problems. They can live in harmony with children, but will not let themselves be used as a toy. Although an English Cocker Spaniel will certainly use its voice when something is amiss or when visitors arrive, it is not a real watchdog or defense dog. All visitors will be sniffed and greeted enthusiastically.

GENERAL CARE

GROOMING

The coat of a Cocker Spaniel will soon tangle unless it is combed and brushed very regularly. Particularly the hair between the legs, on the trousers and on the ears needs a little extra attention. The ears should be checked regularly. Trim any excess hair that grows underneath the leathers, around the ear passages. This will prevent blocking of the ears which could lead to inflammation. Occasionally long hair grows between the pads, which may bother the dog. You can trim off these tufts of hair yourself. Cocker Spaniels need to visit a trimming parlor about 2 to 4 times a year, depending upon the thickness and quality of the coat. A proper trimming expert will pluck the old hair from the coat and will also thin out any excess hair sticking out on top of the head, underneath the ears and in the neck. After a thorough trim a Cocker Spaniel will look neat and tidy again. Some dogs develop tear marks, which you can reduce by dabbing them regularly with a special lotion.

TRAINING

Compliant by nature, a Cocker Spaniel is keen to please its owner, but also has a mind of its own that tends to dominate now and then – a typical Spaniel trait. If you train the dog in a consistent manner, with lots of variety and ensuring

English Cocker Spaniel

English Cocker Spaniels

that the training remains fun and challenging, then it will soon learn what is expected. English Cocker Spaniels – especially puppies – have a very expressive look in their eyes and know full well that they can use this to fool their owners. If you will put up with anything then the dog will soon fail to take you seriously and will do as it pleases.

EXERCISE

These dogs are traditionally bred for hunting on difficult terrain covered with undergrowth. They should be capable of walking for many hours without tiring. In spite of this an English Cocker does not need a great deal of exercise. If you take the dog for a walk three times a day as well as on longer treks a few times a week and occasionally play with it in the yard, then it will be perfectly happy. Most Cockers love swimming and do not shrink from a walk in the rain.

USES

This breed used to be immensely popular as a hunting dog, but is now no longer such a common sight in the field. However, we see them all the more in the show-ring and of course as family dogs. If you want to do something with your dog you could consider a hunting class, although an active sport such as agility is also likely to appeal to the Cocker.

AMERICAN COCKER SPANIEL	
COUNTRY OF ORIGIN	USA
ORIGINAL FUNCTION	ORIGINALLY A HUNTING DOG, BUT A SOON BECAME A COMPANION DOG

APPEARANCE

BODY

American Cockers have a sturdy, compact and muscular build. The level, strong back gradually slopes down to the croup. They have wide hips and well muscled and rounded hindquarters. The deep ribs are well sprung and the chest reaches to the elbows. The tail is customarily docked in countries where this is allowed. It is carried in line with the topline or slightly higher. The legs are straight and strong, well angulated, with straight and compact, yet large, round and solid feet. The muscular neck displays some dewlap.

HEAD

The head has a domed skull with a deep stop and well defined supraorbital ridges. The skull and foreface are of equal length. The deep, broad muzzle has full upper lips that cover the lower jaw. The nose is large with well-developed nostrils. The ears are set in line with the lower eyelid or lower. They are lobular, fine, thin and long. The eyes are round and full. They look slightly almond-shaped and are very expressive. The eyelids are close fitting.

SHOULDER HEIGHT

Dogs stand approx. 15 in (38 cm) tall and bitches are approx. 14 in (35^1/$_2$ cm). Any departure from these measurements should be no more than half an inch (1 cm).

American Cocker Spaniel

American Cocker Spaniels

COAT

The coat is short and fine on the head and medium length on the body. The ears, chest, belly and legs are well feathered, silky and flat or slightly wavy in texture. The coat should not be fluffy or curly.

COLORS

American Cocker Spaniels come in solid black and other solid colors (such as deer red, brown and light cream). But we also see black and tan coats, as well as liver and tan. The tan markings should be located in the usual areas (except the chest) and should not cover more than ten per cent of the coat. In solid and black and tan coats a small white spot on the chest or throat is permissible but white in any other location will lead to disqualification. Also popular are bi and tricolored dogs and roans of which one color should always be white. The colored areas should be clearly defined and evenly distributed across the dog.

TEMPERAMENT

CHARACTER

American Cocker Spaniels are cheerful, uncomplicated and sociable

American Cocker Spaniel

dogs. Gentle in nature and devoid of any aggressiveness, they are lively and playful, even-tempered and very affectionate. They are also of above-average intelligence and reasonably biddable, although a certain degree of – comical – willfulness is characteristic of this breed.

SOCIAL BEHAVIOR

Dogs of this breed get along fine with other dogs and household pets, as well as with children. It is advisable to teach children to respect the dog because most specimens are more inclined to endure their rough games meekly rather than run away or defend themselves. Visitors will be announced before being welcomed enthusiastically with plenty of tail wagging.

GENERAL CARE

GROOMING

This is an important part of looking after an American Cocker Spaniel. The coat must be brushed and combed every day to prevent tangling. In addition, the coat should be expertly trimmed about every 4 to 6 weeks by a good trimming spe-

American Cocker Spaniel

cialist. This is important not only to maintain a beautiful coat and to ensure that the dog's appearance complies with the breed standard, but also for the dog's general health. Of course, the ears should be examined regularly and cleaned if necessary, while the hair under the ear, near the ear passages, should be trimmed. The same applies to any excess hair growing between the pads. It is vital that an American Cocker Spaniel is properly groomed and cared for. If you regard grooming as a necessary evil then you would be better off looking for a less labor-intensive breed.

American Cocker Spaniel

TRAINING

The American Cocker Spaniel is usually easy to obedience train, provided the owner allows for the fact that this dog can be a little willful at times. These dogs are sensitive to the tone of your voice and moods in the house, and should therefore be trained consistently and gently.

EXERCISE

American Cockers love to play and frolic. They are mad about retrieving and ball games, but also enjoy accompanying you on long walks either in the countryside or through the city. Although this breed was originally used as a hunting dog, the current American Cocker has very little hunting instinct left. Once the dog is well trained and obedient you can safely let it run free on a sizable playing field or in the country. An American Cocker that gets enough exercise and plenty of time to play will be placid in the house.

USES

American Cockers are used for hunting on a small scale, but the majority of specimens are kept as family dogs and show dogs. In view of its intelligence and nimbleness this breed should do extremely well in various dog sports such as flyball and agility.

SUSSEX SPANIEL	
COUNTRY OF ORIGIN	ENGLAND
ORIGINAL FUNCTION	HUNTING DOG, SPECIALIZING IN TRACKING, FLUSHING AND RETRIEVING PARTICULARLY WILDFOWL IN MARSHLANDS AND THICKETS

Sussex Spaniel

APPEARANCE

BODY

The back and loins of the Sussex Spaniel are long, wide and very muscular. The tail is set slightly lower than the back and should not be carried above the topline. In countries where this is allowed the tail is normally docked to a length ranging from 5–7 in (12$\frac{1}{2}$–18 cm). The deep and well-developed chest must not be too round or too wide. The shoulders are sloping and free. Sussex Spaniels have muscular, fairly short and heavily boned legs. The hindquarters are not too heavily angulated. The feet are round. The long, powerful neck is slightly arched and shows little throatiness.

HEAD

The head is usually carried not much higher than the back. The skull is moderately long and wide,

Sussex Spaniel dog

with fairly heavy eyebrows and a pronounced stop. The muzzle is fairly long and square and the lips are slightly pendulous. The ears are fairly large, thick and lobular. They are set low, hanging close to the head. The eyes are fairly large with a soft expression. The lower eyelid should not sag too much. Sussex Spaniels have a scissors bite.

SHOULDER HEIGHT
Approx. 15–16 in (38–41 cm).

WEIGHT
Varies between 39$^1/_2$–46$^1/_4$ lb (18–21 kg). The Sussex Spaniel is a heavy dog for its weight.

COAT
The Sussex Spaniel has medium-length hair with a good undercoat, which should not curl. The tail and ears are covered with longer hair and the legs are well feathered.

COLORS
Sussex Spaniels come exclusively in rich golden liver, with gold-colored tips. The eyes should be deep amber to hazel.

TEMPERAMENT

CHARACTER
These dogs are lovable, affectionate, cheerful and gentle. They are intelligent, clever and headstrong in a very appealing, almost comical fashi-

on. They like to bark but are generally pleasant and fairly quiet house mates.

SOCIAL BEHAVIOR
Sussex Spaniels have a sociable disposition and get on well with other dogs, cats and other household pets. They are also fine with children; make sure that the children do not annoy the dog, because it is usually too gentle to take action itself. They bark when visitors are at the door, but will subsequently react cheerfully and enthusiastically. They are not shy.

GENERAL CARE

GROOMING
The coat of this breed needs regular combing and brushing, particularly where tangles are likely to occur. Keep the ears clean and trim excess hair underneath the ears, around the ear passages, to allow the ear to breathe better and prevent inflammation. Excess hair between the pads of the feet may bother the dog and should be trimmed. Tufts of hair between the toes on top of the feet should be left; these are characteristic of the Sussex. When new teeth emerge check they do not push the existing ones aside, resulting in crooked teeth. If necessary, have the lighter older hairs plucked by a good trimming expert.

TRAINING
The Sussex Spaniel is intelligent and therefore a quick learner of commands. These dogs know how to use (or rather misuse)

Sussex Spaniel

their funny and cute appearance which makes it hard for their owners to remain consistent. Nevertheless, a consistent training is essential if you do not wish to end up with a high-spirited loafer that only does as it pleases. Because they like to use their voices it would be sensible to teach the dog at a young age that you do not tolerate excessive barking.

Sussex Spaniel Bitch

EXERCISE

These dogs generally adapt to circumstances, but a Sussex Spaniel will quickly put on weight if it does not get enough exercise. They are always keen on walks through fields or woods but beware their tendency to follow their noses whenever they smell an interesting scent. They usually love swimming and retrieving.

USES

Sussex Spaniels are excellent family dogs. You could consider gundog trials with your dog.

KOOIKERHONDJE OR DUTCH DECOY SPANIEL	
COUNTRY OF ORIGIN	THE NETHERLANDS
ORIGINAL FUNCTION	THIS BREED WAS ORIGINALLY BRED TO HELP LURE AND CATCH DUCKS USING DUCK DECOYS.

APPEARANCE

BODY

The Kooiker's body is slightly longer than it is tall, with a powerful back, a deep chest and well-sprung ribs. The tail reaches to the hocks and is carried level to gaily, but not curled over. The forelegs are straight and the hocks are sufficiently angulated. The neck is straight, strong and muscular.

HEAD

The skull is sufficiently broad and moderately domed. The muzzle and the skull are of equal length, separated by a stop that is pronounced but not too deep. The muzzle is also not too deep in profile and the lips should not overhang. The ears are medium-sized and carried hanging, close to

Kooikerhondje

Kooikerhondje

the cheeks. The almond-shaped eyes have a friendly and alert expression. Kooikerhondjes usually have a scissors bite, but a pincer bite is allowed.

SHOULDER HEIGHT

Ranges between $13^3/_4$–$15^3/_4$ in (35–40 cm).

WEIGHT

Kooikerhondjes weigh approx. 22 lb (10 kg).

COAT

These dogs have a medium-length coat with slightly wavy to straight hair, which should be close fitting and must not curl. The undercoat should be well developed. The forelegs are feathered, but not too heavily. The ears and tail are well feathered, as are the breeches, but the hair should be short below the hock.

COLORS

This dog is bred in a white coat with distinct orange red patches. The color should always dominate. White hairs on the ears are allowed but not preferred. The tips of the ears should preferably be black. These black tips are called "earrings" and are a distinguishing feature of this breed. In the show-ring dogs with colored cheeks and a white blaze are preferred. The nose is always black and the eyes are dark brown.

TEMPERAMENT

CHARACTER

These intelligent dogs are lively, sporty, alert, brave and eager to learn. They are also fairly sen-

Kooikerhondjes

sitive and can be rather inscrutable. They seldom bark, but do like to be vocal when visitors arrive or when something is amiss. They become devoted to their owners.

SOCIAL BEHAVIOR

The Kooikerhondje generally gets on well with other dogs. Mixing with cats and other animals will not be a problem, provided the dog has been socialized with them from an early age. The Kooikerhondje is reserved and slightly vigilant toward strangers, although family friends will be greeted enthusiastically. They will not put up with any mischief from children and, as a rule, this breed is therefore not recommended as a playmate for young or unruly children.

Kooikerhondje

GENERAL CARE

GROOMING

The Kooikerhondje needs fairly little grooming. Brush the coat regularly with a pin brush and check the ears regularly for debris and excessive earwax. Sometimes excessive hair will grow between the pads, which can interfere with the dog's movements. If necessary, trim any hair growing between the pads using rounded scissors.

TRAINING

In common with all dogs, the Kooikerhondje should be trained consistently. Kooikers are

Kooikerhondje

intelligent and eager to learn – qualities which combine to create a dog that is easy to train. They are sensitive to the intonation of the voice and do not require a tough approach. In spite of this, the Kooiker's owners must be fairly firm, because over-leniency will bring out the breed's dominant traits.

EXERCISE

The Kooikerhondje is a real working dog that is not suited to spend its days lying on the sofa or in its basket. It likes to run around and to frolic, and will not be restricted to a sedate life. Most Kooikers like swimming and retrieving, and they love playing.

USES

With an owner who understands and can handle the peculiar characteristics of this dog, this breed can do pretty well in obedience trials, flyball and agility.

CLUMBER SPANIEL	
COUNTRY OF ORIGIN	ENGLAND
ORIGINAL FUNCTION	TRACKING AND RETRIEVING GAME, PARTICULARLY FUR FROM THICKETS

APPEARANCE

BODY

A Clumber Spaniel has a long, heavy body that is near to the ground. The broad back is long, with muscular loins and deep flanks. The chest is deep and the ribs are well sprung. Clumber Spaniels have well-developed, powerful hindquarters. The low-set tail is carried in line with the topline. The shoulders are sloping, strong and well muscled. The forelegs are short and straight, with heavy bones. The hocks are low and the stifles are well bent. The feet are large and round. The neck is fairly long, thick and powerful.

HEAD

The massive, square head has a pronounced occiput, heavy brows and a deep stop. The square muzzle is heavy, with well-developed jaws. The ears are fairly large and are hanging slightly forward. The eyes should not be too deep set. Clumber Spaniels have a scissors bite.

SHOULDER HEIGHT AND WEIGHT

The breed standard provides no guidelines regarding weight or shoulder height. As a rule, these dogs weigh approx. $66\frac{1}{4}$–$79\frac{1}{2}$ lb (30–36 kg), with a shoulder height of approx. $17\frac{3}{4}$ in (45 cm), so they are fairly heavy for their size.

COAT

The Clumber Spaniel's coat is abundant, dense, silky and straight. The chest and legs are well feathered, as is the tail. The feathering of the ears should not extend beyond the fleshy part.

Clumber Spaniel

Clumber Spaniel bitch

COLORS

The preferred color is white with lemon markings on the head and freckles on the muzzle. Orange markings are also permitted. The eyes are dark amber.

TEMPERAMENT

CHARACTER

Clumber Spaniels are extremely even-tempered, calm and confident. They have a positive disposition and are good-natured, gentle and friendly. They are usually dignified and very fond of their owners and members of the family. They are fairly

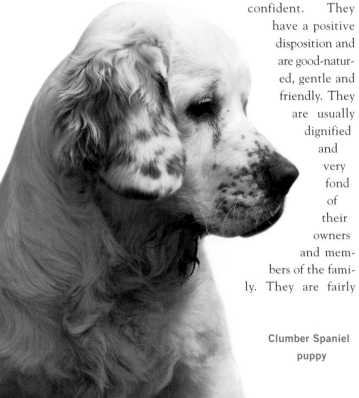

Clumber Spaniel puppy

obedient. They bark little and have an excellent nose.

SOCIAL BEHAVIOR

These spaniels have an amiable disposition and get along fine with other dogs. Their contact with cats and other pets should not present any problems either. Good-natured and tolerant towards children, they will often avoid strangers. Though not friends with everybody, they will always remain friendly.

GENERAL CARE

GROOMING

The coat should be brushed and combed regularly. Depending on the thickness and quality of the coat the dog needs to be trimmed at least twice a year or more frequently. This involves plucking any unruly hairs that stick out and trimming the coat neatly. After such trimming sessions the Clumber Spaniel will look neat and tidy again. Between trimmings you can clip any excess hair growing underneath the ear, around the ear passages. This will allow the ear to "breathe" better and prevent inflammation. Regularly check the ear passages and use a good ear lotion to remove excessive earwax and dirt. Many Clumbers have drooping eyelids that can cause irritation now and then. Flushing the eyes with a special lotion every so often will prevent this problem.

Clumber Spaniel

TRAINING

These dogs are eager to please their owners and they are intelligent enough to grasp what is expected of them. This makes a Clumber Spaniel generally a quick learner. By not demanding too much, rewarding the dog with a bit of fun (or a tasty snack!) when it follows a command and by remaining consistent at all times you will get the best out of this dog. Firm training is not recommended.

EXERCISE

Clumber Spaniels may be traditional gun dogs, yet

Clumber Spaniel

they still have the unique ability to adapt seamlessly to their owners when it comes to exercise. If dogs of this breed get little exercise, then you do need to watch their diet as Clumbers have a tendency to become fat. A Clumber Spaniel is usually very placid indoors, sometimes to the point of laziness.

USES

Although this breed is now seldom used for its original function, its retrieving instinct is undiminished in most specimens and you could certainly consider doing a gundog trial with this dog.

WELSH SPRINGER SPANIEL	
COUNTRY OF ORIGIN	WALES
ORIGINAL FUNCTION	FLUSHING DOG AND RETRIEVER, PARTICULARLY FOR WILDFOWL

APPEARANCE

BODY

Muscular, with a deep chest and sloping shoulders. The tail is never carried above the topline and is customarily docked in countries where this is permitted. The straight legs are well boned and well bent both at the front and the back. The stifles are moderately angled. Welsh Springer Spaniels have round, closed feet (known as cat's feet), which should not be too large. The head is set on a long, muscular, dry neck.

HEAD

The skull is slightly domed, with a well-defined stop and a straight, fairly square muzzle of medium length. The comparatively small, moderately low-set ears hang close to the cheeks and are lightly feathered. The eyes are of medium size. Welsh Springer Spaniels have a scissors bite.

SHOULDER HEIGHT

For dogs approx. 19 in (48 cm) and for bitches approx. 18 in (46 cm).

COAT

Welsh Springer Spaniels have silky, lank medium-length hair which must not be tough in texture, wavy or even curly. The coat is longer on the backs of the forelegs, the culottes, and on the ears and tail.

Welsh Springer Spaniel

Welsh Springer Spaniels

COLORS

This breed comes exclusively in white with rich red. The eyes are dark or hazel.

TEMPERAMENT

CHARACTER

Welsh Springer Spaniels are gentle, highly intelligent, cheerful and lively. A well-trained Welsh Springer is generally obedient and pliable, although, like all spaniels, this breed also has a stubborn streak. They are even-tempered, very affectionate and very fond of human company. They are less suitable as kennel dogs and much prefer to be indoors with the family. Their fondness of water is innate to most specimens and their sense of smell is usually excellent. These dogs will bark when strangers visit or when something is amiss but no further action is to be expected from them.

SOCIAL BEHAVIOR

Welsh Springer Spaniels tend to be sociable towards other dogs and patient and friendly with children. Mixing with cats and other pets should not be a problem, provided the dog has been properly socialized. As a rule, Welsh Springer Spaniels are friendly to everybody. They are not shy.

GENERAL CARE

GROOMING

The coat of this breed needs regular attention. Regularly clip excess hair from the ears to prevent infection. For the same reason you also need to clip excess hair underneath the leathers around the ear passages as well as any excess hair growing between the pads. The coat should be combed and brushed regularly. Depending on the quality of the coat and whether the dog will be put on show, the Welsh Springer's coat needs to be trimmed two to four times a year by a professional dog trimmer. This involves removing the lighter (dead) red hairs from the coat, clipping the hair on the ears and generally tidying the dog's hair. If you have an aptitude for it, then it is a good idea to learn how to barber a Welsh Springer Spaniel from an experienced breeder or trimmer.

Welsh Springer Spaniel

TRAINING

Although they display a certain amount of willfulness (playing deaf) this breed is generally easy to train. They are intelligent enough to grasp what is expected and will soon obey your commands when they realize they will benefit from it. The training should therefore concentrate on rewarding desired behavior, but above all should be consistent. Punishments other than through rebukes will seldom be necessary with

Welsh Springer Spaniels

this breed and firm punishments are definitely not recommended. The Welsh Springer Spaniel has a great working instinct, which makes it essential to teach the dog from an early age to return quickly and without hesitation on command.

EXERCISE

Welsh Springer Spaniels are active and lively dogs that need a reasonable amount of exercise. Out-

Young Welsh Springer Spaniel bitch

side the usual daily walks you should regularly take this dog out to let it release its energy. Nearly all specimens love both swimming and retrieving. If a Welsh gets plenty of exercise outdoors, then it will be peaceful in the house.

USES

The Welsh Springer Spaniel can be used as a gundog. It specializes in flushing and retrieving birds. But working is not strictly necessary with this dog, as the Welsh Springer Spaniel also does well as a companion dog in a sports-minded family. You could also consider agility sports.

ENGLISH SPRINGER SPANIEL	
COUNTRY OF ORIGIN	ENGLAND
ORIGINAL AND TODAY'S FUNCTION	VERSATILE GUNDOG, MAINLY USED FOR TRACKING, FLUSHING AND RETRIEVING PARTICULARLY WILDFOWL

APPEARANCE

BODY

The English Springer Spaniel is well balanced, compact and strong with a body that is strong and not too long. The loins are short, muscular and moderately arched. The tail, which is normally docked in countries where this is permitted, is set low and is never carried above the topline. The well-developed chest is deep and the ribs are well sprung. The elbows lie close to the body. The legs are straight with strong, nimble pasterns. The stifles and hocks moderately bent. English Springer Spaniels have compact, tight, round feet with strong pads. The slightly arched, dry neck is strong and muscular.

HEAD

The slightly rounded skull is fairly broad and of medium length, with a slight groove that starts between the eyes and ends at the occipital peak. The cheeks are flat. The muzzle is fairly deep and broad, with square lips. The lobular ears are set level with the eyes and fairly close to the head. The almond-shaped eyes are medium sized. They should neither protrude nor be deep set. The eyelids should fit tightly. English Springer Spaniels have a scissors bite.

SHOULDER HEIGHT

Approx. 20 in (51 cm).

COAT

The coat is dense, smooth and weather-resistant. The legs, ears and some parts of the body are moderately feathered. The tail is well feathered.

COLORS

Permitted colors are liver with white and black with white, which may include tan markings. The eyes are dark hazel.

English Springer Spaniel

FIELD SPANIEL

COUNTRY OF ORIGIN	ENGLAND
ORIGINAL FUNCTION	GUNDOG, SPECIALIZING IN TRACKING, FLUSHING AND PARTICULARLY RETRIEVING BIRDS

Field Spaniel

APPEARANCE

BODY

The Field Spaniel is a well-built sporting spaniel, with a strong, muscular back and loins. The tail is set slightly below the back and is never carried above the topline. In countries where this is permitted it is customarily docked. The chest is deep and well developed. The ribs are moderately arched. The hindquarters are solid and muscular. The long, sloping shoulders are set well back.

The straight forelegs are of moderate length. The hind legs are moderately bent and the hocks well let down. The feet are tight and round, with sturdy pads. They should not be too small. The neck is long, strong and muscular.

Young Field Spaniel dog

HEAD

The head should convey an impression of high breeding and nobility. The well-developed skull displays a clear occipital protuberance, slightly raised eyebrows and a moderate stop. The long, dry muzzle should be neither snipey nor square and the forenose is well developed. The wide ears are set on low and moderately long. The eyes are wide open and almond-shaped. The eyelids should close tightly. Field Spaniels have a scissors bite.

SHOULDER HEIGHT

The size for this breed is approx. 18 in (46 cm).

WEIGHT

These dogs weigh approx. $39^{1}/_{2}$–$50^{3}/_{4}$ lb (18–23 kg).

COAT

The long, sleek coat should lie close to the body. It is very glossy and silky in texture. The coat should not be curly, wiry or short. The dog should have feathering on the chest, the ears, under the body and on the backs of the legs.

Field Spaniel

COLORS

The Field Spaniel comes in solid black and solid liver, either with or without roan or tan markings. The eyes are dark hazel.

TEMPERAMENT

CHARACTER

This breed is very gentle and affectionate, intelligent and a little temperamental. Outdoors Field Spaniels are fairly high-spirited and playful, but indoors they tend to be calm. They have an excellent nose and a deeply rooted hunting instinct. It is claimed that Field Spaniels are inclined to become especially attached to one particular person within the family, and often this will be true. The Field Spaniel certainly has a great need to be with people and will become neurotic if it has to live in a kennel. Although most specimens will bark when something is amiss, you

Field Spaniel

Field Spaniel

should not demand or expect too much from these dogs in this respect.

SOCIAL BEHAVIOR

Field Spaniels are very sociable and cheerful dogs that tend to get along fine with virtually everybody. As a rule, they are very patient with children. If the kids get too rough for them they will withdraw, and adults should always ensure that they can. Make sure that children do not pester the dog. If properly socialized with cats and other household pets from an early age, there will be no problems with a Field Spaniel later on. They can live in harmony with other dogs.

GENERAL CARE

GROOMING

These dogs are normally trimmed four times a year. This involves removing any excess and old hairs from the coat and thinning the hair on the neck, ears and legs. In addition to these trimmings the coat should also be groomed weekly using a pin brush, particularly in areas covered with denser and longer hair. As with virtually all dogs with long, well-feathered hanging ears, the ears of these dogs also need a little extra attention. Regularly clip any excess hair around the ears, underneath the leathers. This will prevent the ear passages from blocking which could cause infection.

Field Spaniel

You will obviously need to keep the claws short and clip any excess hair that grows between the pads.

TRAINING

The Field Spaniel is a quick learner who responds easily to the voice. It needs a loving, cheerful and very consistent training. Harsh words and an overly firm approach will damage its sensitive nature and bring out the dog's stubborn traits.

EXERCISE

The Field Spaniel will adapt very well to a family setting but will always primarily be a working dog. It needs plenty of exercise and will therefore do best in a sports-minded family. The yard should be well fenced, because the dog's excellent nose will lead it away from the yard now and then.

USES

Although the Field Spaniel is a real working dog, it can adapt very well to a family situation. Even so, you could consider doing a field class with this dog, as the dog will certainly enjoy this.

GERMAN QUAIL DOG	
COUNTRY OF ORIGIN	GERMANY
ORIGINAL AND TODAY'S FUNCTION	VERSATILE HUNTING DOG, PARTICULARLY IN WATER AND IN THICKETS

APPEARANCE

BODY

The German Quail Dog is longer than it is high, heavily built and well boned. The body as a whole is very muscular. The chest is oval in shape and reaches to the elbows. The long, high withers flow smoothly into a level and reasonably short back. The croup is long and flat. The belly is moderately tucked up. Both the front and the hind legs are straight and well angulated, with spoon-shaped feet and close-knit toes. The tail is set high and is always carried below the topline. In countries where this is permitted, a third of the tail is usually docked.

HEAD

The head is dry and long. The skull and muzzle are roughly equal in length. The top of the skull is flat without a discernible occiput. German Quail Dogs have virtually no stop or median line. The nose bridge is wide and a ram's nose is preferred. The lips are tight. The ears are set high and are carried pendant, close to the skull. They should reach roughly to the tip of the nose. The almond-shaped eyes are medium-sized and the eyelids are close fitting. A scissors bite is essential.

SHOULDER HEIGHT

Dogs range from 19–21$\frac{1}{4}$ in (48–54 cm) and bitches stand 17$\frac{3}{4}$–20 in (45–51 cm) tall. Deviations up to $\frac{3}{4}$ in (2 cm) up or down are permitted in exceptional dogs.

German Quail Dog

434

COAT

The coat consists of tough, dense, long hair, which is slightly wavy or flat. German Quail Dogs are well feathered on the ears, the tail and the chest. The backs of the forelegs and the trousers are also covered in longer hair.

German Quail Dog

COLORS

The German Quail Dog may be solid dark brown, with or without white spots on the chest and white toes, and roan brown or spotted brown, either with or without tan markings. Red and orange specimens are also recognized, although these are rare. The eyes are dark brown.

TEMPERAMENT

CHARACTER

German Quail Dogs are real hunting dogs with an excellent nose and a deeply rooted hunting instinct. They are tireless, tough, cheerful and obedient with a strong will to please. A fondness of water is a distinctive feature of the breed.

SOCIAL BEHAVIOR

This dog tends to get on very well with other dogs and with children. It is not shy and is friendly with everyone. Mixing with (small) livestock and other household pets can be more problematic. Their hunting instinct is strong.

GENERAL CARE

GROOMING

This dog needs very little grooming. A good brush and combing the long hair once a week is sufficient. The ears should be checked regularly and cleaned if necessary. German Quail Dogs have hair growing between the toes, which is one of the characteristics of the breed. However, in certain circumstances it may be better to clip this to ensure their freedom of movement.

TRAINING

German Quail Dogs are highly intelligent and love to please their owners. The training should therefore not present any major problems.

EXERCISE

It would certainly be unfair to deny the dog the opportunity to work. German Quail Dogs have a tremendous amount of energy and need a lot of exercise. The breed's innate hunting instinct should not be underestimated. With untrained specimens it can result in the dog spontaneously chasing after game whilst giving tongue.

USES

This breed is eminently suitable as a hunter's dog. Although the name "German Quail Dog" implies that it is used exclusively for hunting quail – or at least feather – this is not the case. German Quail Dogs are also successfully employed hunting fur and pests (fox). They are excellent trackers, give tongue on the trail, and are well suited to scenting. But they are also used to flush and retrieve game, particularly in marshlands and woodland. They can even be taught to point. Although the average German Quail Dog is devoted to its owner and family it is primarily a true hunting dog, which will feel cheated if kept purely as a companion dog. If hunting does not appeal to you, you should really look for a different breed.

German Quail Dog

435

SECTION 3   Water Dogs

WETTERHOUN

COUNTRY OF ORIGIN	THE NETHERLANDS
ORIGINAL FUNCTION	HUNTING DOG, USED MAINLY ON OTTERS, BUT ALSO GUARD AND FARM DOG

Wetterhoun

APPEARANCE

BODY
The Wetterhoun is solidly built but in no way lumbering. Its chest is broader than deep, so the forelegs are fairly wide apart. The chest should not be deeper than the elbows. Dogs of this breed have well-sprung ribs and a short, straight back. The loins are powerful and the croup slopes slightly. The long tail is carried moderately high above the croup in a curl. The belly is moderately tucked up. The legs are straight, powerful and moderately angulated, with round, powerful feet. The neck is strong, round and slightly arched, without dewlap.

HEAD
The usually low-set head is sturdy, dry and powerful. The slightly domed, broad skull is equal in length to the strong muzzle. The nose bridge is straight and the close-fitting lips should not be pendulous. The stop is not very pronounced. The ears are carried close to the head and are set on fairly low. The eyes are oval, medium-sized and slightly slanted in the head.

SHOULDER HEIGHT
The ideal size for dogs is 23 in (59 cm) and for bitches $21^3/_4$ in (55 cm).

COAT
The Wetterhoun has harsh, oily curls that cover the entire body except for the short-haired head. The ears are also covered with curly hair except for the last section of the ears. These dogs should on no account have a woolly coat.

COLORS
This breed comes in black or brown, either with or without white patches. Specimens with roan coats are also allowed. The eyes are dark brown or brown, depending on coat color.

TEMPERAMENT

CHARACTER
Dogs of this breed are physically tough on themselves and sober. Despite their devotion to their owners they are fairly independent and can be rather stubborn when given commands they feel are pointless. They are doubtless intelligent, sometimes a bit sensitive, and have an excellent nose. Wetterhouns

Wetterhoun

can be a little reserved towards strangers. They are outstanding watchdogs that will not shrink from defending their property and their family from intruders. Most specimens like swimming. They

Wetterhoun

Wetterhoun

lack the temperament to wander off very far on their own, and the average Wetterhoun is reasonably yard-bound. Dogs of this breed can live happily in a kennel or outdoors, provided they get regular contact with their owners and are taken on daily walks.

SOCIAL BEHAVIOR

The Wetterhoun will be a gentle-natured, reliable and friendly dog for its own people. This is also the case with the children of the family and any other children, provided they treat the dog properly. Towards unknown visitors – who will invariably be announced – they tend to be reserved, although family friends are greeted boisterously. In general they get on well with other dogs and pets.

GENERAL CARE

GROOMING

The Wetterhoun generally requires little grooming. It is sufficient to run a coarse metal comb through the coat now and then and to check the ears for debris.

TRAINING

The Wetterhoun is not a dog for people with little experience in training dogs. This breed is intelligent and can learn quickly, but is also strong-willed enough to ignore your commands completely if it fails to see the point of them. A consistent yet loving training with a patient owner will get the best out of this breed.

EXERCISE

These dogs love being outdoors and are less suited to an apartment life. They need a reasonable amount of exercise. Swimming and off-leash walks through the woods will certainly appeal to them, but they are not keen on ball games and similar activities. These dogs are calm indoors.

USES

This breed will do very well as a yard dog on a farm. It will automatically take on certain tasks, such as guarding the home and destroying vermin. But the Wetterhoun can also be used for hunting, and is particularly useful on tough terrain and in marshlands. However, because it is not one of the most pliable pupils in the field, this dog is only used for hunting by true enthusiasts and determined hunters.

PORTUGUESE WATER DOG

COUNTRY OF ORIGIN	**PORTUGAL**
ORIGINAL FUNCTION	**FISHERMAN'S DOG**

APPEARANCE

BODY

This muscular dog has a short, solid back, a slightly sloping croup and a tucked-up abdomen. The chest is broad and reaches down to the elbows. The ribs are long and well sprung. The tail is thick at the root and tapers to a point. When the dog is attentive it is carried in a ring above the back. The tail should not reach below the hocks. Both the front and the hindquarters are well angulated. The straight legs have fairly flat, round feet with well-feathered webbing and thick pads. The neck is straight and strongly muscled, without dewlap.

HEAD

The massive head has a skull that is slightly longer than the muzzle. The occiput is well defined. Portuguese Water Dogs have a central furrow, a pronounced stop and brow ridges. The thin ears are set above eye level and held close to the head. They should not be too long. The eyes are slightly oblique and set well apart. They are round and the eyelids fit closely. A scissors bite is essential.

SHOULDER HEIGHT

The size for dogs can range from $19^1/_2$–$22^1/_2$ in (50–57 cm), but dogs with a shoulder height of

Portuguese Water Dog

$21^1/_4$ in (54 cm) are preferred. Bitches have a shoulder height of 17–$20^1/_2$ in (43–52 cm), with a preference for bitches measuring approx. 18 in (46cm).

WEIGHT

Dogs weigh $41^3/_4$–$55^1/_4$ lb (19–25 kg) and bitches weigh on average $35^1/_4$–$48^1/_2$ lb (16–22 kg).

COAT

There are two types of coat: wavy, which is long, wavy, and with a slight sheen; and curly, which is very similar in texture to the frizzy hair of a poodle. This coat is very curly, very dense and hardly shines at all. Portuguese Water Dogs have no undercoat.

COLORS

The Portuguese Water Dog comes in black and brown, with or without white markings on the chest, the head and the legs. Very rarely solid white specimens are also seen. Spotted and white animals should have obvious dark pigmentation on the rims of the lips, the eyelids and the nose.

TEMPERAMENT

CHARACTER

Portuguese Water Dogs are sociable, cheerful, happy, friendly, highly intelligent and keen to work. They are quick-witted and smart, and generally

Portuguese Water Dog

Two young Portuguese Water Dogs. The right-hand dog has too much white for Portuguese standards

obedient. They have an excellent nose, are fairly tough on themselves and have an uncomplicated and optimistic outlook on life.

SOCIAL BEHAVIOR

The Portuguese Water Dog gets on extremely well with its own kind and can live in harmony with other pets, provided it has been socialized with them at an early age. Although it will use its voice when something is amiss, this dog is friendly towards everyone and gets on fine with children.

GENERAL CARE

GROOMING

The wavy coat is easier to groom than the curly type. This coat is customarily clipped short on the hindquarters (from the last rib). The same applies to a large part of the tail, leaving a plume of hair at the end of the tail. The face is also clipped short. This model, which shows some resemblance to the Lion Clip in poodles, is also sometimes used on the curly coat. However, with this type of coat the "Retriever Clip" is becoming more common. This involves close-clipping the tail only and clipping the rest of the hair at the same length following the outline of the dog. This model is not allowed in the show-ring in most FCI member countries. Apart from these regular trimmings, both coat varieties need to be brushed and combed regularly, particularly in areas that are prone to tangling. Clip any excess hair from the ear passages. The Portuguese Water Dog sheds very little.

Curly coat Portuguese Water Dog puppy

TRAINING

Training this breed is not difficult because it is extremely intelligent and loves to learn from and work for its owner. The dog is very sensitive to the intonation in your voice and punishments will rarely be necessary. Alternate training exercises frequently with play, and always be consistent and fair. But do bear in mind that this dog is very smart and in its own comical way will take

Full-grown curly coat Portuguese Water Dog

liberties with your authority when it gets the chance.

EXERCISE

As its name implies, the Portuguese Water Dog loves swimming. It will be more than delighted if you throw sticks or balls into the water and let it retrieve them. Apart from this, nearly all types of exercise are suitable for this breed, from romping off-leash to accompanying you on your daily runs. If the dog gets plenty of exercise it will be placid indoors.

USES

Portuguese Water Dogs are eminently suited for various dog sports, particularly flyball and agility. Obedience as a sport is a less obvious choice, because it does not offer enough action and challenges. This still rather uncommon breed will also do well as a companion dog in a sports-minded family.

Various types of coat exist for Barbets

BARBET

BARBET	
COUNTRY OF ORIGIN	FRANCE
ORIGINAL FUNCTION	HUNTING DOG, SPECIFICALLY FOR TRACKING AND RETRIEVING WATERFOWL

APPEARANCE

BODY

The Barbet has a slightly convex topline with short, strong, arched loins and a rounded croup. The low-set tail has a slight hook at the tip and is held somewhat raised but not level. The broad chest is well developed and fairly high. The ribs are round. The shoulders are sloping. The legs are straight, with heavy bones, and the feet are round and wide. The neck is short and strong.

HEAD

The Barbet has a round, broad skull, a broad forehead, a pronounced stop and a square muzzle. The ears are set on level with the eyes or lower. When pulled forward the skin should reach at least 2 in (5 cm) beyond the forenose. The eyes are round.
Shoulder height
The minimum size for dogs is $21^{1}/_{4}$ in (54 cm) and for bitches $19^{1}/_{2}$ in (50 cm).

COAT

There are two types of coat with this breed: wavy or curly. The coat should be dense, abundant, long and woolly. The hair on the head should cover the eyes and form a clear beard and mustache around the muzzle (the breed name "Barbet" is derived from the French for beard, "barbe").

COLORS

The most common color in this breed is black, although solid gray, various shades of brown and (off-)white coats are also recognized. The coat should always be a solid color, without any minor variations or markings. Chestnut eyes are preferred.

TEMPERAMENT

CHARACTER

Barbets are uncomplicated, even-tempered, friendly, pliable and cheerful dogs. They are lively, fairly intelligent, eager to learn and usually obedient. Straightforward by nature and fairly tough on themselves, Barbets are delightful family dogs that love to be involved in the everyday life around the house. This dog is generally not considered suitable kennel dog material.

SOCIAL BEHAVIOR

These dogs have a sociable disposition and generally get on very well with other dogs. If the puppy has been well socialized then there should be no problems with other household pets, such as cattle and cats. These dogs get along fine with children. The Barbet will bark if it senses danger or if strangers visit, but that tends to be all. It is not cut out to be a defender of house and home.

Barbet

GENERAL CARE

GROOMING

The coat is such that it has a tendency to felt with

Barbet

a lack of care and regular grooming is therefore essential. Wash the mustache and beard when dirty and pluck any excess hair from the ear passages. The hair between the pads can grow quite long so that thorns, twigs and stones and in winter even lumps of ice could get stuck in it. Therefore, any long hairs sticking out between the pads should be trimmed.

Although not clipped for shows, Barbets are presented well groomed.

TRAINING

Barbets are intelligent and eager to learn. A consistent training which relies a great deal on the tone of voice achieves best results. But do bear in mind that an owner who is over-indulgent and exudes little authority will not be taken seriously by any dog, including a Barbet.

EXERCISE

This dog needs plenty of exercise and loves water and retrieving. Regularly take it for long walks and give it the opportunity to romp about off-leash. But if you need to skip a day then this dog will certainly adapt.

USES

In its country of origin this relatively rare breed is still used as a water retriever, although it is also very suitable as a family dog. Sadly, this breed is extremely rare outside its country of origin. This breed can also excel in various dog sports such as obedience, agility, flyball, but is equally suited to "real work", such as rescue dog and avalanche search dog.

Irish Water Spaniel puppy

IRISH WATER SPANIEL	
COUNTRY OF ORIGIN	IRELAND
ORIGINAL FUNCTION	HUNTING DOG, USED MAINLY FOR RETRIEVING WATERFOWL

APPEARANCE

BODY

The Irish Water Spaniel is a strongly built dog that is not too leggy. The body is a fair size and looks rather square. The close-coupled back is broad and level and the loins are deep and wide. The tail is fairly short, thick at the root and tapering to point. The tail should not reach to the hock joint and should be held nearly level with the back. The chest is deep, but not too wide or too round. The ribs are well sprung and carried well back. The shoulders are very powerful, but not over-loaded. The legs are straight and well angulated. The feet are large and the toes somewhat spreading. The neck is powerful, fairly long and arching.

Irish Water Spaniel

HEAD

The head is carried considerably above the top-line. The domed skull is fairly broad and of a good length. The muzzle is long, strong and somewhat square. The nose is well developed. Irish Water Spaniels have very long, lobular ears that are set low and carried hanging. The eyes are comparatively small with an intelligent expression.

close-fitting lids. They should never be deep set. Maltese Terriers have a scissors bite.

SHOULDER HEIGHT

For dogs $8\frac{1}{2}$–$10\frac{1}{4}$ in (21–26 cm) and for bitches $7\frac{1}{2}$–$9\frac{1}{2}$ in (20–24 cm). Dogs that are exceptionally beautiful may be half an inch (1 cm) taller.

WEIGHT

Maltese Terriers weigh approx. $6\frac{1}{2}$–$8\frac{1}{2}$ lb (3–4 kg).

COAT

The Maltese has a thick, shiny, heavy and very long coat that is silky in texture. The average length of hair on the body is $8\frac{1}{2}$ in (22 cm). In practice, this means that the coat of an adult Maltese reaches down to the ground. The coat hangs with a parting on the back and there is no undercoat.

COLORS

The coat should be pure white, although a light shade of ivory white is also allowed. Lemon shades are considered a fault. The eyes are dark ochre. The nose, pads, lips and eye rims are black, the claws should be dark in color, although black claws are preferred, and the skin should be well pigmented.

Maltese

TEMPERAMENT

CHARACTER

Dogs of this breed are cheerful, gentle, pliable and amiable animals. They are friendly, lovable and playful and sensitive by nature. Harsh words affect them deeply. They are fairly intelligent and eager to learn. They are even-tempered, rarely nervous and aggressiveness is alien to them. They become devoted to their owners and the family and do not like to be left alone. In fact, this is not really necess-

ary either because their diminutive size means they can be taken everywhere. Partly due to their great adaptability these dogs are no bother to anyone. They are totally unsuitable as kennel dogs. They will bark when something is amiss, but are not excessive barkers.

Two Maltese puppies

SOCIAL BEHAVIOR

These dogs are very sociable and get along fine with other dogs, household pets and children, although the owner does need to make sure the dog is not pestered by children. Visitors are usually greeted boisterously.

GENERAL CARE

GROOMING

The Maltese requires extremely intensive grooming. The coat should be long, down to the ground, with a clear parting on the back. The long hairs are kept away from the face with a hair band. The coat should be thoroughly combed daily and washed regularly. Keeping the coat in show condition is very hard. Owners of show dogs oil the coat and wind the hair in curling papers to prevent it from breaking. The coat of Maltese Terriers that are kept as house dogs can be clipped a little shorter now and then to simplify the grooming. Sometimes hairs can grow in the corners of the eyes which can irritate the eye. It is a good idea to remove such hairs. Some Maltese Terriers may get unsightly tear stains which can be prevented using a special lotion. Although the grooming requirements of the Maltese should not be underestimated, one great advantage

Maltese

of its coat is that it does not shed; dead hairs simply stick to the brush during grooming.

TRAINING

This breed is fairly easy to train. If you are consistent and clear, give cheerful commands and reward the dog for desirable behavior then a Maltese will learn very quickly. But because it is very sensitive to harsh words and negative vibes in the house it should not be trained with a firm approach.

EXERCISE

A Maltese does not need to be taken for long walks, but if you are a keen walker this dog will love to accompany you. You need not fear that your Maltese might run off, because it does not like to lose

Maltese pup

sight of you. Indoors a Maltese tends to be very quiet.

USES

The Maltese is a genuine companion dog in the true sense of the word. This breed does not cope very well in a very chaotic household and does best in a harmonious environment.

HAVANESE	
COUNTRY OF ORIGIN	**CUBA**
ORIGINAL AND TODAY'S FUNCTION	**COMPANION DOG**

Havanese puppy

APPEARANCE

BODY

The body is longer than it is tall. The topline ends in a sloping croup. The tail is carried curled upwards. The ribs are arched and the belly is well tucked up. The legs are straight and fairly dry. The feet are moderately long with closed toes.

HEAD

Havanese dogs have a flat, broad skull, a fairly snipey muzzle and flat cheeks. The pointed ears are folded slightly and are pendulous. The eyes are fairly large and almond-shaped. Havanese dogs have a scissors bite.

SHOULDER HEIGHT

Ranges from $9^{1}/_{2}$ –$13^{3}/_{4}$ in (25–35 cm). Deviations of $^{3}/_{4}$ in (2 cm) up or down are permissible.

WEIGHT

Havanese dogs should weigh no more than $13^{1}/_{2}$ lb (6 kg).

COAT

This breed has a soft, wavy, silky coat. The hair on the muzzle may be trimmed. There is no undercoat.

COLORS

This breed comes in the following solid colors: white, cream, fawn to Havana brown, black and gray. The animals may also be white with spotting in the above colors.

Havanese

TEMPERAMENT

CHARACTER

These dogs are happy, playful, gentle, affectionate and sociable. Highly intelligent and eager to learn, they are sensitive to harsh words and moods in the house. They will certainly bark when there is something wrong.

SOCIAL BEHAVIOR

Havanese dogs are trouble-free and pleasant companions. They get on well with other dogs, even if these are of their own sex, and are friendly to children. It is up to the owners to make sure that children do not pester the dog; it is too gentle to defend itself. A Havanese will live in harmony with cats and other pets. They can be a little timid towards strangers.

GENERAL CARE

GROOMING

The Havanese needs considerable grooming. The coat must be thoroughly brushed and then combed through twice a week. This is best done with a coarse comb. A special lotion can be applied to the coat before grooming, which can help to protect the hair from splitting. Any excess hair growing between the pads should be clipped. The feet themselves may be clipped to look round so that the dogs do not walk around with "floss" on their feet. Although rather labor-intensive, the coat of a Havanese does not shed. Dead hairs stick to the

brush rather than fall out. The eyes should also be checked regularly.

TRAINING

The Havanese learns quickly and enjoys performing tasks for people. This is why this breed used to be very common as a circus dog. Havanese dogs are sensitive to the tone of your voice. Harsh words and punishment will only upset the dog unnecessarily. You will achieve best results by addressing the dog in a cheerful manner, by always being as clear as possible and praising it abundantly when it has done something well. Some specimens are prone to barking more than is necessary. They should be cured of this as early as possible, so that it does not become a habit that could irritate you or the neighbors.

EXERCISE

The Havanese has an average need to exercise and is quite happy with three walks a day. This breed is devoted to its owner and is not inclined to wander off during off-leash walks.

USES

This breed is suitable as a companion dog for peo-

Havanese

ple with or without children. If you fancy doing obedience or agility classes with your Havanese then this neat little dog will not disappoint.

Bichon Frisé

BICHON FRISÉ

COUNTRY OF ORIGIN	BELGIUM/FRANCE
ORIGINAL AND TODAY'S FUNCTION	COMPANION DOG

APPEARANCE

BODY

The Bichon Frisé has a well-developed chest with a clearly defined brisket and tucked-up flanks. The loins are broad, muscular and slightly arched, and the pelvis is broad with a slightly rounded croup. The tail is carried curved over the back, but never curled up. The elbows are held close to the body. The legs are finely boned. They are straight and spaced well apart with good angulation. The feet are tight. The neck is fairly long and carries the head proudly.

HEAD

The flat skull is longer than the muzzle, with a slightly accentuated stop and a barely visible superciliary ridge. The lips are fine and fairly tight. The jaws are flat and not too heavily muscled. The ears are carried hanging, with the leathers reaching midway to the muzzle. Bichon Frisés have large eyes, which are round rather than almond-shaped and show no white.

SHOULDER HEIGHT

The maximum size is $11^1/_2$ in (30 cm), but smaller dogs are preferred.

WEIGHT

Bichon Frisés weigh approx. $8^1/_2$ lb (4 kg), but heavier dogs up to approx. $15^1/_2$ lb (7 kg) are no exception.

COAT

The fine, silky coat hangs down loosely in small spiral curls. The coat should be at least 3–4in (7–10cm) in length. Dogs of this breed have no undercoat.

COLORS

Bichon Frisés are always white, with sometimes shadings of cream. The nose, lip rims and eyelids must be black and pigmentation is also preferred elsewhere on the skin. A typical feature of all types of Bichons is the "halo", the wide, pigmented rim around the eyes. The eyes are always dark in color.

TEMPERAMENT

CHARACTER

Bichon Frisés are sensitive, affectionate, sociable playful and intelligent. They are pliable and stable by nature, with a cheerful attitude. Aggressiveness is alien to them. They are fairly lively, but not boisterous. Bichon Frisés generally bond very closely with their owners and the family, and may find it hard to be left on their own at times. Often, this will not be necessary because their diminutive size and great adaptability mean they can be taken virtually anywhere. They tend to bark little.

Bichon Frisé bitch

SOCIAL BEHAVIOR

Bichons are naturally sociable dogs, which are happiest in a family that takes them everywhere. Their sociable trait also means that they get on fine with other dogs, pets and children. Visitors will be announced, but then greeted boisterously.

GENERAL CARE

GROOMING

The coat of a Bichon Frisé is labor-intensive. It has to be combed through right down to the skin each day, but may also need to be trimmed if it becomes too long. Like many other dogs with similar coats, the Bichon Frisé is trimmed in a particular clip, which is best done at a good trimming parlor. Two to three trimmings a month will be sufficient on average, but show dogs require considerably more grooming. The clips for show dogs differ for each country: in the USA the coat is shaped and blown dry with a hairdryer after bathing and made completely white for a show. But in countries like France and Belgium Bichon Frisés should present a very natural impression. In these countries the coat must not be trimmed and clipping is only allowed on the feet and face. To keep the coat white, washing the Bichon Frisé with a good dog shampoo is recommended. Regularly check whether the hairs around the eyes are causing irritation and use a good lotion to prevent any ugly "tear" stains. Clip any excess hair between the pads, keep the claws short and the ears free from loose hair and dirt. The Bichon Frisé does not shed, which is regarded as a great advantage by many owners. Any dead and loose hairs stick to the brush. People who dislike seeing an unkempt appearance or who know in advance that they lack the time or the inclination to care properly for such a coat are advised to consider a different breed; the grooming requirements of this breed are considerable.

Bichon Frisé dog

TRAINING

This breed is very easy to obedience train. These dogs are very intelligent and love to please their owners. Giving commands cheerfully, being consistent and rewarding good behavior will achieve the best results with this dog.

EXERCISE

This Bichon will adapt to circumstances in terms of exercise. They love to play and frolic, but if you need to skip a day then they will just entertain themselves with a ball or other toy without becoming a nuisance. Indoors a Bichon Frisé is usually placid.

Bichon Frisé

USES

Dogs of this breed have traditionally always been popular as companion dogs, but also used to perform regularly as circus dogs or on fairgrounds. You could consider sports such as agility (with equipment adapted to the dog's size) and obedience with this dog. It is clever, obedient and agile enough to do well at this.

Bichon Frisé

BOLOGNESE

COUNTRY OF ORIGIN	**ITALY**
ORIGINAL AND TODAY'S FUNCTION	**COMPANION DOG**

APPEARANCE

BODY

The Bolognese has a square build. The chest reaches to the elbows and the ribcage is ample, with well-sprung ribs. The back is straight. The withers lie above the topline and are fairly broad. The loins are slightly arched. The croup is wide and slightly sloping. The tail is set on in line with the croup and is carried curved over the back. The feet are oval, although the hind feet are often more round in shape.

HEAD

The dry neck is equal in length to that of the moderately long and slightly domed head. The skull is broad, especially at the eyes. The stop and occipital protuberance are clearly defined. The short, strong muzzle must not taper to a point and the nose bridge is straight. The ears are high-set and long. The round eyes are full and large.

SHOULDER HEIGHT

The size for dogs is approx. $10^1/_2–11^1/_2$ in (27–30 cm) while bitches stand $9^1/_2–11$ in (25–28 cm) tall.

WEIGHT

Bolognese dogs weigh from $6^1/_2–8^1/_2$ lb (3–4 kg).

COAT

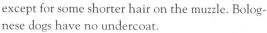

Bolognese

The coat consists of long, very dense hair that stands out a little. The hair is the same length across the entire body, except for some shorter hair on the muzzle. Bolognese dogs have no undercoat.

COLORS

The coat of the Bolognese is always pure white, but pale yellow patches or shades are allowed. The nose, lips, eyelids, claws and pads must be black.

Bolognese

TEMPERAMENT

CHARACTER

Bolognese dogs are good-natured, very even-tempered and friendly. Intelligent and usually obedient and compliant, they are very affectionate, reasonably calm, loyal and amiable, which makes them well suited as a companion dog in the true sense of the word. A well-trained Bolognese can be taken virtually anywhere and adapts itself to its owner. Although a Bolognese will bark when something is amiss or when it hears anything out of the ordinary, it is not a barker.

SOCIAL BEHAVIOR

The Bolognese gets on well with other dogs, and generally lives in harmony with other pets and children. It enjoys the company of its owner and

Coton de Tuléar

Tuléar does not shed; loose hairs tend to stick to the coat. These can be brushed and combed off to prevent tangling. Remove excess hair between the pads of the feet and from the ears. The Coton de Tuléar does not need to be washed more than twice a year, which is ample to keep the coat clean. Keep the claws short.

TRAINING

Although the Coton de Tuléar is fairly intelligent and learns quickly, consistent training is still required. Some specimens do have a mind of their own, but when they learn that desirable behavior has certain advantages – perhaps in the form of tidbits – they will be better motivated.

EXERCISE

The Coton de Tuléar will adapt itself to the lifestyle of the family in this respect, but this should not mean that this playful dog gets insufficient exercise. These dogs usually like swimming, are crazy about ball games and can play in the yard or romp around in the woods for hours.

USES

If you like to do an activity with your dog you could consider flyball or agility classes. Most Coton de Tuléars do reasonably well in these areas. Of course, they are also well suited to being companion dogs.

LÖWCHEN (LITTLE LION DOG)	
COUNTRY OF ORIGIN	FRANCE
ORIGINAL AND TODAY'S FUNCTION	COMPANION DOG

APPEARANCE

BODY

The Löwchen has a short, well proportioned, elegant body. The legs are straight and fine of bone. The feet are small and round. The tail is of medium length.

HEAD

The short head is rather wide in the skull. The pendant ears are fairly long. The eyes are round and large, with an intelligent expression.

SHOULDER HEIGHT

Ranges from $9^1/_2 - 12^1/_2$ in (25–32 cm).

WEIGHT

The weight is $8^1/_2 - 17^1/_2$ lb (4–8 kg).

COAT

Fairly long and wavy but must not be curly or twisted. The feathering on the ears should be long. Löwchen have no undercoat.

COLORS

All colors are allowed, except for chocolate brown. White, black and lemon coats are preferred.

TEMPERAMENT

CHARACTER

Löwchen are highly intelligent, eager to learn and lively. They are cheerful, playful, agile and sociable with a gentle, affectionate and sensitive disposition. They love company and get extremely attach-

Löwchen

ed to their owners and the family. Because of their light weight, diminutive stature and great adaptability they can be taken along virtually anywhere. They will use their voice when something is amiss, but are not amongst the most yappy of dogs. As a rule they are fairly quiet.

SOCIAL BEHAVIOR

These are very sociable animals that will get on fine with their own kind. Contact with other pets should not present any problems either and they are gentle with children. It is up to the owners to make sure that children treat the dog with respect. They are friendly to people, but their own family will come first. They will do best when they are part of the family.

Löwchen

GENERAL CARE

GROOMING

This breed has the advantage that it does not shed; any dead hairs will usually stick to the brush. Nevertheless, regular grooming is essential to keep the often rather silky coat free from tangles and presentable. Regularly clip the longer hair growing between the pads. The breed name "Little Lion Dog" refers to the lion clip in which the dog is trimmed. The lion clip is compulsory at shows, but nobody will stop you if you prefer to leave the coat long. If you have a certain flair for it and if you own a pair of good quality clippers then trimming the Löwchen is fairly easy. But otherwise it should be left to a qualified trimmer.

TRAINING

Löwchen are generally quick learners. If you treat the dog consistently and clearly, with frequent use of the tone of your voice, then the dog will soon learn what is expected. A firm approach is not recommended with gentle-natured dogs such as these; it is better to emphasize rewarding good behavior.

EXERCISE

The Löwchen has average exercise needs and will usually adapt to circumstances. If you like going for long walks then this little dog will happily accompany you without getting tired. This dog is quiet in the house.

USES

This dog was traditionally bred as a companion dog and possesses all the qualities that make it ideal for this task. In spite of this, these dogs are highly intelligent, eager to learn and agile. If both you and your dog would enjoy this, then taking part in one of the dog sports is recommended.

Löwchen

SECTION 3 · Small Belgian dogs

GRIFFON BRUXELLOIS, BELGIAN GRIFFON AND PETIT BRABANÇON

COUNTRY OF ORIGIN	BELGIAN
ORIGINAL AND TODAY'S FUNCTION	COMPANION DOG

APPEARANCE

BODY

These dogs have a sturdy, thickset build with a fairly broad, deep chest. The tail is carried high and is customarily docked to one third of its length in countries where this is allowed. The straight legs are of medium length with a good stance. The feet are short, round and closed (these are known as cat's feet).

HEAD

The head is wide and round, with a domed skull and a well-defined stop. The nose is extremely short and the tip is wide. The chin is broad and extends beyond the upper jaw. The ears are carried semi-erect. The eyes are large and round, but do not bulge and are set well apart. These dogs have an undershot bite, which means that the incisors of the lower jaw extend beyond the upper incisors. The tongue should not show when the mouth is closed.

SHOULDER HEIGHT

The breed standard does not mention size, but the shoulder height of most dogs is approx. 11 in (28 cm).

WEIGHT

The weight is approx. 11 lb (5 kg).

COAT

Griffon Bruxellois

The Griffon Bruxellois and Belgian Griffon are rough-haired; the coat

Belgian Griffons

should be shaggy, hard, medium length and dense. The hair around the eyes, on the muzzle, the cheeks and the chin is longer, which is a characteristic feature of this breed. The Petit Brabançon has a short-haired coat.

COLORS

The two roughs can be distinguished by their coat color. The Griffon Bruxellois is always reddish brown in color, with possibly some black on the mustache and the chin. The coat colors of the Belgian Griffon are black, black and tan and black mixed with brown. The Petit Brabançon comes in the same colors. The claws and the pads are always black, as are the eyes and eye rims.

Petit Brabançon

TEMPERAMENT

CHARACTER

Dogs of these breeds are very inquisitive and always alert to what goes on around them. They become strongly attached to their owners and the family and are very affectionate. They like to stay close to their people and sometimes follow them around the entire house. They also hate being left on their own. This is usually not necessary. Because of their handy size and great adaptability they can be taken everywhere. They are active and playful, and will certainly bark when they notice anything out of

Belgian Griffon

the ordinary. They are also fairly intelligent, eager to learn and obedient. Being very adaptable, they can be kept either on a farm or in a city apartment.

SOCIAL BEHAVIOR

These highly sociable dogs are very fond of human company and usually get on fine with children. Mixing with cats and other pets should not cause any problems and the same applies to contact with other dogs. They will always announce strangers, but that is all – aggressiveness is totally alien to them.

GENERAL CARE

GROOMING

The coat of the Petit Brabançon is easy to care for. weekly brushing or combing is sufficient. In some Petit Brabançons it may be necessary to regularly clean the folds below the eyes using a special lotion. Long tufts of hair on the tip of the tail may be trimmed. Griffons require a little more attention. Their coats can be brushed twice a week using a small slicker brush. The facial hair features should be thoroughly brushed regularly. The hairs in the corners of the eyes should be removed if necessary to prevent them pricking the eyeball and causing irritation. The coats of Griffons kept as companion dogs should be plucked about twice a year, but the coats of show dogs need rather more attention. Keep the claws short.

Griffon Bruxellois

TRAINING

These dogs are usually no problem to train. These intelligent and obedient dogs love to please their owners. They are sensitive to the tone of your voice.

Petit Brabançon

Chinese Crested

TEMPERAMENT

CHARACTER

Chinese Crested Dogs are high-spirited, smart and playful. They are very active and lively, also in the house. They are sensitive to a bad atmosphere in the home and very alert to noises. They will certainly use their voices if they sense there is anything amiss. This breed becomes fairly strongly attached to its owners; they are not friendly to all comers.

SOCIAL BEHAVIOR

Dogs of this breed generally get along fine with other dogs and pets. They are somewhat reserved and vigilant toward people they do not know. The Chinese Crested gets along reasonably well with children, but should not be kept with very young or boisterous children.

GENERAL CARE

GROOMING

The skin of the Chinese Crested requires careful attention. Show dog handlers regularly scrub the skin (using a skin exfoliating cream made for humans) to remove dead skin cells and to soften the skin. The main point is that the skin stays supple and smooth and is protected from becoming dry. There are excellent lotions and creams for this purpose. The unpigmented areas of the skin are especially sensitive to sunlight and it is advisable not to expose the dog to the sun for prolonged periods and to use a quality suntan lotion as protection. The Powder Puff should be brushed now and then and may be washed occasionally. In show dogs the hair on the face down to the neck is usually shorn downwards into a point. Regularly check the teeth for tartar and keep a close eye on the eruption of new teeth.

TRAINING

Chinese Crested Dogs are not difficult to train. Although they are intelligent and will quickly grasp what is expected of them it is still important to be consistent at all times. Pay a lot of attention to socialization; this will benefit the character building.

EXERCISE

The Chinese Crested adapts to the family in terms of its exercise needs. It will happily accompany you on long walks but does not protest when you need to skip the odd day. Bear in mind that skin wounds will often leave behind

Chinese Crested

visible scars on the Crested's skin; protect the dog from playing rough games with other dogs and from walks through rough terrain.

USES

This small, unusual dog is generally kept as a companion dog but is also seen relatively frequently in the show-ring.

SECTION 5   Tibetan breeds

SHIH TZU

COUNTRY OF ORIGIN	TIBET
ORIGINAL AND TODAY'S FUNCTION	COMPANION DOG

Shih Tzus

APPEARANCE

BODY

The Shih Tzu has a rectangular build and short, straight, solid legs. The feet are round and firm. The chest is broad and deep, the back is level and the loins are short and powerful. The tail is set high and carried over the back. When viewed from the side, the height of the tail is equal to that of the skull. The nicely arched neck is sufficiently long to carry the head proudly.

HEAD

The head is round and wide between the eyes. The muzzle is of ample width, square, flat and not wrinkled. The distance from the nose to the pronounced stop is one inch ($2^{1}/_{2}$ cm). The top of the forenose should be level with the lower eyelids, or slightly below. Shih Tzus should have large nostrils and a slightly tip-tilted nose. The hair on the nose grows upwards, giving the dog its distinctive "chrysanthemum-like" face. The large eyes are dark in color, not prominent and should show no white. The ears are set slightly below the crown of the skull, carried hanging and with large leathers. Dogs of this breed may have either a pincer bite or a slightly undershot bite.

SHOULDER HEIGHT

The maximum size is $10^{1}/_{2}$ in ($26^{1}/_{2}$ cm).

WEIGHT

The ideal weight is between 10–16 lb ($4^{1}/_{2}$–$7^{1}/_{2}$ kg), although the total breed characteristics of the dog are regarded as more important than size alone.

COAT

Shih Tzus have a long, dense coat with a good undercoat. The hair should not curl, but a slight wave is permitted.

COLORS

All colors are permitted. Parti-colored dogs are relatively common. In these markings a white blaze on the forehead and a white tip to the tail are highly desirable in the show-ring.

TEMPERAMENT

CHARACTER

Shih Tzus are intelligent, even-tempered, friendly and fairly sociable with an outgoing disposition. In spite of their somewhat artificial appearance they are remarkably tough on themselves and not squeamish. They are devoted to their owners and the family and show them great affection, while always retaining a certain degree of independence. This is not the type of dog that slavishly does what it is told and it is not clingy. The Shih Tzu rarely barks, but will certainly use its voice when something is amiss. This dog is very adaptable.

SOCIAL BEHAVIOR

Dogs of this breed usually get on well with other household pets, such as cats and rabbits. Their contact with other dogs is generally excellent and they also do well with children. They can be reserved towards strangers and are not friends to all.

Shih Tzu

Young Lhasa Apso

at least once a week. This should be done with great care, making sure that not just the (visible) topcoat is disentangled but the undercoat as well. Do not pull too hard during brushing to prevent breaking the hairs. There is a special lotion which you could use to stop them becoming too brittle. The coat of show dogs requires considerably more attention than that of house dogs. In the show-ring a long, well groomed coat is very important, but it is not easy to get a coat into show condition. In pet dogs the coat is sometimes clipped short, which is better than having a dog with a coat full of tangles. Regularly check the eyes for dirt and for any irritating hairs, clip excess hairs between the pads and keep the ears clean.

TRAINING

In common with all Eastern breeds, the Lhasa Apso is somewhat obstinate with a mind of its own. It is intelligent enough to understand your rules, but if it cannot see the point or has other ideas it will prefer to follow its own mind. Do not expect this dog to perform tricks just to please you; it will do them but only if it enjoys doing them. Guide its character in the right direction by rewarding the dog when it does well and always be clear and consistent. Harsh words can hurt it deeply; the dog will withdraw feeling offended and very upset.

EXERCISE

The Lhasa Apso has an average need to exercise. It is fairly homey by nature and happily cope without long walks. This breed is therefore particularly suited as a city dog for people living in an apartment.

not be a good choice, although the average Lhasa will get along fine with older or quiet children who will not pester the dog. In their contact both with children and with dogs and cats this breed will not allow itself to be bullied. The Lhasa can be wary of strangers.

GENERAL CARE

GROOMING
This breed requires very intensive grooming. The coat should be brushed and combed

Lhasa Apso bitch

USES

The Lhasa Apso is a great dog for people who can

Lhasa Apsos

appreciate its sometimes inscrutable character and who do not regard grooming as a job that can be done in between. In view of its independent disposition this breed is unsuitable for the various dog sports.

Lhasa Apso

TIBETAN TERRIER	
COUNTRY OF ORIGIN	TIBET
ORIGINAL FUNCTION	SHEEPDOG AND COMPANION DOG

APPEARANCE

BODY

This medium-sized dog has a powerful, well-proportioned and square build with a level topline and slightly arched loins. The legs are straight with large, round feet. The tail is set fairly high and is carried in a gay curl over the back.

HEAD

The head is of moderate length with a marked stop that is not exaggerated. The ears are V-shaped and pendant. The eyes are large and set fairly wide apart.

SHOULDER HEIGHT

Dogs stand approx. 14–16 in (35½–41 cm) tall. Bitches are a little smaller.

COAT

This Tibetan fellow has a double coat. The long topcoat is luxuriant and fine, and may be straight or wavy. The undercoat is dense and woolly. The ears are well feathered and the hair hangs over the eyes. One of the characteristics of this breed is the dense feathering between the toes.

Tibetan Terrier

COLORS

Tibetan Terriers come in all colors and color combinations, except liver and chocolate. The eyes should be dark in color and the eye rims black.

TEMPERAMENT

CHARACTER

Tibetan Terriers are lively, alert, cheerful, intelligent, even-tempered and vigilant and will bark when they hear anything out of the ordinary. They are also brave and not easily intimidated. They are devoted to their owners and the family but somewhat cautious with strangers. Beneath their cuddly appearance these are fairly tough and sober dogs. Tibetans do not always cope well with being left alone and are dedicated to their handlers.

TEMPERAMENT

CHARACTER

Tibetan Spaniels are full of temperament, confident, cheerful and alert little fellows with a strong constitution. Even-tempered and brave, they are not easily intimidated. They are vigilant, but not particularly yappy. These dogs are usually very quiet and affectionate indoors, although they can also be extremely playful and active at times. They are devoted to their own people.

SOCIAL BEHAVIOR

These even-tempered dogs tend to get on well with children. If properly socialized, they will also live in harmony with other dogs, cats and other pets. Strangers usually get a cool reception; these dogs will initially be wary with unfamiliar visitors.

GENERAL CARE

GROOMING

Though longhaired, the coat of this dog is not dense or heavy and grooming is fairly easy. It is generally sufficient to brush and comb the coat once a week. Check the ears for dirt now and then, but do not trim the hair between the pads, because that is one of the characteristics of this breed.

TRAINING

Tibetan Spaniels are intelligent and fairly easy to train. They will

Tibetan Spaniels

quickly grasp your intentions and are eager to please. In spite of this they are not the type of dog that will blindly obey your commands, because they do have a mind of their own.

EXERCISE

Tibetan Spaniels have average exercise needs and generally adapt to the family. Three short walks around the block and running and playing off-leash in the yard is sufficient to keep these dogs in good condition.

USES

This small Tibetan does best as a small family dog that warns its owners when something is amiss. You could consider taking this dog to agility classes. Although many Tibetan Spaniels do enjoy this sport, you should not expect too much at trial level.

Young Tibetan Spaniel

SECTION 6   Chihuahuas

CHIHUAHUA

COUNTRY OF ORIGIN	**MEXICO**
ORIGINAL AND TODAY'S FUNCTION	**COMPANION DOG**

APPEARANCE

BODY

Chihuahuas have a very compact body that is slightly longer than it is tall. The back is level and flat and the ribcage is well arched. The high-set tail is flat in shape, broader in the center than at the base and tapering to a point. The tail may be carried either up, in a loop or over the back with the tip touching the back. The tail should not curl. The chest reaches roughly to the elbows. The distance from the lower chest to the ground is equal to that from the lower chest to the highest point of the withers. The belly is moderately tucked up. The shoulders are well laid and the elbows are held close to the body. The legs are sturdy and straight, with good angulation. The feet are oval and the toes are placed well apart, but not spread. The neck is slightly arched.

Chihuahua

HEAD

The head is large but in proportion to the body. The cheeks and jaws are lean. The skull is apple-domed. The forehead is wide and very round. The stop is well pronounced. The short muzzle is straight and tapers slightly. The lips fit tightly. The large, flaring ears are fairly low set. The large eyes are set well apart, and are round, full and very expressive. They should not be prominent. The ear set, the stop and the middle between the eyes are all in the same horizontal plane. Chihuahuas have a pincer or scissor bite.

Longhaired Chihuahua

WEIGHT

The Chihuahua is the smallest dog breed in the world, weighing 1–5$\frac{1}{2}$ lb (500–2500 g). Any weight above 5$\frac{1}{2}$ lb (2500 g) is a fault. Any dogs weighing over 6lb (3000 g) in the show-ring are disqualified.

COAT

There are two varieties of coat: the Short Coat and the Long Coat. The short-haired Chihuahua has smooth, soft and glossy hair that lies close to the body, with an undercoat preferred. The hair is slightly longer on the neck and on the tail, and a little shorter on the head and the ears. The coat of the longhaired Chihuahua is softer and finer in texture than that of the Short Coat. The hair may be flat or slightly wavy, again with an undercoat preferred. The hair is longer on the culottes, the tail, around the collar, on the ears, the feet and on the backs of the forelegs. On the face, (fore)head and on the front of the legs it is short.

COLORS

All colors and color combinations are allowed with this breed. The eyes may also be any color. Ruby eyes are seen as a particular feature of this breed.

TEMPERAMENT

CHARACTER

These tiny Mexican fellows are intelligent, alert, playful and a little stubborn. They are generally confident but sometimes a bit reckless. Chihua-

English Toy Spaniel

pets such as cats, insofar as these live under the same roof. However, they do possess some hunting instinct and will occasionally view cats outside as hunting targets. There should be no problems with other dogs, although there are some specimens that are less tolerant towards their canine house mates. This may be due to the fact that these dogs prefer not to share their owners with other dogs. They get on fine with children, provided they approach the dog calmly and do not pester it. The English Toy Spaniel shows little interest in strangers, but is not shy or wary.

GENERAL CARE

GROOMING

The coat should be brushed thoroughly about twice a week, with particular attention to the hair on the ears, the culottes, the chest and the legs. The facial folds can be treated with a special lotion to prevent tear stains, which can be rather unsightly especially in light-colored dogs. Clip any excess hair growing between the pads, regularly check the

English Toy Spaniel

teeth for tartar and clean the ears with a suitable ear cleaner and a tissue. The claws should be kept short. Some English Toy Spaniels have two fused toes on one or more feet. This is a typical breed characteristic, which can occur from time to time and which does not bother the dog. But the claws of such dogs do need to be checked regularly because they tend to grow crooked.

English Toy Spaniel

TRAINING

The English Toy is intelligent enough to quickly grasp what is expected, but like any other spaniel can also be rather willful. A certain degree of assertiveness and consistency is therefore required. Obedience training is recommended.

EXERCISE

Dogs of this breed have an average need to exercise. This dog will not mind if you are not very sporty yourself. English Toy Spaniels are perfectly happy with three walks around the block with their owners each day if they are also allowed to play in the house and the yard now and then. When it is not too hot the dog will love to accompany you on long walks, but at the height of summer it will prefer to find itself a quiet spot in the shade. Because of their small size and great adaptability they will adjust to all kinds of circumstances; this dog can therefore also get used to an apartment life.

USES

This breed is exclusively seen as a companion dog, a task for which these dogs are eminently suited. Very occasionally, they will take part in agility trials and will then do surprisingly well.

CAVALIER KING CHARLES SPANIEL

COUNTRY OF ORIGIN	ENGLAND
ORIGINAL AND TODAY'S FUNCTION	COMPANION DOG

APPEARANCE

BODY

The Cavalier is a lively, graceful and well-balanced dog with a gentle expression. The length of the tail is in proportion to the body and is optionally docked (in countries where this is permitted) up to a third of its length. The tail is carried gaily, but never much above the topline. The body is of normal build, carried by straight legs and compact, well-feathered feet. The neck is of moderate length and slightly arched.

HEAD

The head of the Cavalier is almost flat between the ears and has a shallow stop. The lips are well developed, but not pendulous. The ears are set high with plenty of feathering. The muzzle is approx. 1½ in (3½ cm) long and tapers towards the tip of the nose. Any tendency to snipiness is undesirable. The face is well filled below the eyes. The eyes are large and round but not prominent, and placed well apart. The jaws are strong with a complete scissors bite.

SHOULDER HEIGHT

The breed standard provides no guidelines, but these dogs are approx. 13¼ in (35 cm).

WEIGHT

Varies from 12–18 lb (5½–8 kg).

COAT

The coat is long, silky and profuse, without curls although a slight wave is allowed. The rich feathering on the ears, chest, legs, tail and feet is typical of the breed. The coat must not be trimmed.

COLORS

This breed comes in four different color patterns. Solid red dogs are called "ruby." In the black and

Cavalier King Charles Spaniel

tans the ground color is raven black with bright tan-colored markings above the eyes, on the cheeks, inside the ears, on the chest, the legs and on the underside of the tail. White markings are undesirable both in the ruby and in the black and tan. The "tricolor" is black and white with bright tan-colored markings in the same places as the black and tan. The most common color in this breed is the "Blenheim", a pearly white dog with chestnut markings. These markings must be well broken up on the body and symmetrical on the head, with plenty of room between the ears for the highly desirable "beauty spot." This is a lozenge-shaped mark. The nose should be black in all colors. The eyes are dark.

Cavalier King
Charles
Spaniel

Cavalier King Charles Spaniel

TEMPERAMENT

CHARACTER

These dogs are known for their gay, gentle and friendly temperament. Stable and not nervous by nature, they are quite charming, affectionate and intelligent. Cavalier King Charles Spaniels are generally obedient and pliable, but can also be willful at times and like chasing after game. They are very adaptable. Although they do like the constant attention and presence of their owners, they can certainly be left on their own now and then, provided they have been trained to get used to this from an early age.

SOCIAL BEHAVIOR

These uncomplicated dogs are sociable animals and there should be no problems either with other dogs or with other household pets. Their contact with children is also okay, provided they are supervised. Although, in common with nearly all dogs,

they do bark to announce the arrival of visitors, they are friendly to everyone and not vigilant.

GENERAL CARE

GROOMING

The coat should be combed regularly, particularly on the chest, on and behind the ears and between the legs. Keep the ears and the feathering on the feet free from dirt and the claws short.

TRAINING

This breed is usually fairly easy to train, as these dogs are eager to learn and intelligent enough to grasp what you want – but also smart enough to fool you! They are very gentle and should therefore never be treated harshly. A firm approach would only make the dog timid and anxious. You will achieve best results by cheerfully rewarding desirable behavior, being consistent and using the tone of your voice a lot.

EXERCISE

These little dogs are not demanding when it comes to exercise. They are lively and playful, and certainly capable of accompanying you on your walks for hours. If you need to skip a day then they will adapt. Every Cavalier King Charles Spaniel loves ball games, retrieving and romping around off-leash in the yard or in the countryside.

USES

Dogs of this breed are lovely companion dogs that can be happy both with sports-minded and with less active people. With the right supervision a Cavalier King Charles Spaniel can do well at sports such as agility, obedience and flyball.

Cavalier King Charles
Spaniel puppy

| SECTION 8 | Pekinese and Japanese Spaniel |

Pekinese

PEKINESE

COUNTRY OF ORIGIN	CHINA
ORIGINAL AND	COMPANION DOG
TODAY'S FUNCTION	

APPEARANCE

BODY

The Pekinese has a thickset, powerful and sturdy build with heavy bones. The breed is characterized by a lion-like appearance. The chest is broad and the back level. There is a distinct waist and the ribs are well sprung. The tail is set high, is carried slightly curved over the back and falls to the side. The heavy bones of the forelegs are slightly bowed and the large, flat front feet are slightly turned out. The feet must not be round. Because of the broad chest the forelegs are wider apart than the hind legs. The neck is very short and thick.

HEAD

The head is broader than it is deep, with a wide, flat skull. The stop is deep and the short, broad nose with large, open nostrils lies between the eyes. In profile, the Pekinese has a flat face. The muzzle is wide and the lower jaw is very strong and powerful. The large eyes have a clear expression and are set well apart. The ears are heart-shaped and carried close to the head. The leathers must not reach below the muzzle line.

SHOULDER HEIGHT

Approx. $7^1/_2$ in (20 cm).

WEIGHT

Approx. $8^1/_2$–12 lb (4–$5^1/_2$ kg). Bitches are generally a bit heavier than dogs.

COAT

The long, straight coat has profuse manes. The topcoat is fairly hard and the undercoat is soft and luxuriant. The long feathering on the ears, tail, feet and culottes are characteristic of the breed.

COLORS

Nearly all colors are permitted in this breed, except liver or albino. In parti-colored specimens symmetrical markings are preferred. Common colors are various shades of yellow, gray and red with black fringes and a black mask. The pigment of the lips, nose and eyelids must be black in all colors. The eyes are dark in color.

TEMPERAMENT

CHARACTER

Pekinese dogs are affectionate and devoted to their owners, without being dependent. Dignified in a charming manner and fairly headstrong, they are very brave, self-confident and even-tempered by nature. Pekinese are one of the quietest dog breeds. You will rarely hear them bark. They are not particularly fond of strangers. They will decide who will be their "master."

SOCIAL BEHAVIOR

Pekinese dogs get on reasonably well with other dogs, in the sense that they do their own thing and are not bothered by other dogs. Pekinese generally have no problems mixing with other animals either, but this depends largely on how well the dogs have been socialized. Since they do not usually like being disturbed, they are less suitable for a family with young kids. They keep aloof from people they do not know.

Pekinese

GENERAL CARE

GROOMING

Pekinese

The coat of a Pekinese requires fairly intensive grooming. The puppy should be taught to be brushed and combed regularly from an early age to prevent trouble later on. Pay particular attention to the hair under the leg joints, the belly and the legs, where most tangles occur. A coarse comb with wide teeth is best for this purpose. Before, during and after grooming you can sprinkle the coat with talcum powder or dry shampoo. The face requires particular care and attention, otherwise infections can occur in the facial creases. In some specimens the eyes need a little extra care. Any hair growing between the pads should be clipped and the claws should be clipped short at regular intervals using a suitable claw clipper. If you regard the grooming requirements of a dog such as this one as a necessary evil then you would be wise to consider a less demanding breed.

TRAINING

Although a Pekinese will not be told what to do, you will still have to teach it some basic principles if you do not want to end up with a bad-tempered dog that wants to have everything its own way. The fastest way to teach it is by praising it abundantly for desirable behavior. The average Pekinese will withdraw feeling terribly upset and offended if it is punished.

EXERCISE

Most Pekinese are not too keen on long walks. This is partly due to their build and the shape of their skull, but also to their disposition. The dog will be perfectly happy if you take it for a short walk a few times a day. In warm weather they prefer to lie down in a cool spot rather than going out for a walk with you.

USES

The Pekinese is an ideal city dog and very suitable for people who are not very sporty.

JAPANESE CHIN (JAPANESE SPANIEL)

COUNTRY OF ORIGIN	CHINA
ORIGINAL AND TODAY'S FUNCTION	COMPANION DOG

APPEARANCE

BODY

The Japanese Chin has a square build, which means that the trunk is about as long as it is tall. The withers are placed high and the back is level. The tail is carried over the back. The loins are wide and rounded. The moderately wide chest is deep and the ribs are well sprung. The belly is tucked up. The legs are straight and fine boned. The hind legs are moderately angulated. Japanese Spaniels have slender hare feet, with springy pads. The thick, short neck carries the head high.

HEAD

The head is comparatively large. The skull is round and broad, and the deep stop is well defined. The nose is wide with very wide open nostrils. The jaws are wide and short, with the mandible curving upwards. The long ears are triangular in shape, set on the sides of the head and carried pendulously. The eyes are large, round and forward facing. Japanese Spaniels should preferably have a scissors bite, but a pincer bite or a slightly undershot bite is also permitted. The teeth must not show when the dog's mouth is closed.

SHOULDER HEIGHT

Approx. $7^1/_2$–$9^1/_2$ in (20–25 cm), but dogs may be a little taller.

WEIGHT

Ranges from approx. $5^1/_2$–$6^1/_2$ lb ($2^1/_2$–3 kg).

Japanese Spaniel

COAT

The coat is long, soft, silky and straight. It does not lie flat against the body but has a tendency to stand out. The hair on the face, the forehead and the front of the legs is short, but considerably longer on the culottes, the upper part of the backs of the legs, the collar, the ears and the tail.

COLORS

By far the most common color in this breed is black and white, but white and red is also allowed and may vary from lemon to dark red. Sable and white and tricolored coats also occur but these are not widely recognized. In the showring white on the muzzle and a sufficiently large white blaze are highly desirable. Markings that are evenly distributed on the trunk, the sides of the head and the ears are also very desirable.

Japanese Spaniel

Young Japanese Spaniel puppy

Pug

company and attention of their people. They are sensitive by nature and will pick up on any bad atmosphere in the house. They are playful but not noisy, clownish and friendly. Dogs of this breed are fairly intelligent and compliant. They do bark when something is amiss, but that tends to be all. They are physically very hard on themselves. Most Pugs snore.

SOCIAL BEHAVIOR

These dogs generally get on well with their own kind and contact with other household pets is also rarely a problem. They get on extremely well with children. Any visitors – both wanted and unwanted – are usually given a friendly welcome, but their own people will always come first.

GENERAL CARE

GROOMING

This breed needs very little grooming. Loose hair can simply be removed from the coat using a rubber brush. Treat the facial creases with a special

lotion and administer eye drops to the eyes when necessary. Keep the claws short.

TRAINING

This breed can be trained with a gentle hand. Pugs are sensitive to the tone of your voice and because they love to please their owners harsh punishments are usually not necessary.

EXERCISE

Dogs of this breed have average to low exercise

Pug

needs and are therefore suitable as city dwellers or for apartment life. In fine weather the Pug loves to romp and play outdoors, but if it is too hot the dog prefers to withdraw to a cool, shady spot. Pugs have no hunting instinct and are territorial, which means they are not prone to wander off on their own. Indoors Pugs tend to be quiet.

USES

This breed has traditionally been popular as a companion dog, a task for which it still used today. You can easily teach these dogs to do tricks and it is surprising how many Pugs love doing agility. People who are serious about taking their Pug to obedience classes will be amazed about their dog's achievements.

Pugs

French Bulldog

FRENCH BULLDOG

COUNTRY OF ORIGIN	FRANCE
ORIGINAL AND TODAY'S FUNCTION	COMPANION DOG

APPEARANCE

BODY

The French Bulldog has a cobby build with a broad, muscular back. The wide loins are short and sturdy. The topline gradually slopes up from the withers to the loins from where it curves down toward the set of the tail. The croup is sloping. The short tail is carried low against the buttocks. The belly and flanks are tucked up. The brisket is wide, deep and barrel-shaped. The ribs are well sprung. The shoulders are short and rather stiff. The forelegs are set wide apart and are a little shorter than the hind legs. The hocks are well let down and may not be too steep. French Bulldogs have small, round feet, which are turned out slightly. The neck is short and slightly arched, without dewlap.

French Bulldog puppies

HEAD

The head is powerful, broad and square. The skin on the head should form nearly symmetrical wrinkles. The skull is broad, but nearly flat and the forehead is domed. The brows are pronounced and separated by a well defined superciliary ridge that should not run on to the forehead. The stop is well pronounced. French Bulldogs have a short, wide tip-tilted nose. The lips are thick and somewhat loose, the upper lip completely covering the teeth. The jaws are broad, square and powerful. The well-developed cheek muscles do not protrude. The medium-sized ears are wide at the base and rounded at the top ("bat ears"). They are set high on the head and are carried erect but not too close together. The eyes are set low down and far away from the nose and the ears. They are round, fairly large and slightly bulging. The white of the eye must not be visible from the front. French Bulldogs have a slightly undershot bite, which means that the incisors of the lower jaw extend beyond the upper incisors. The teeth and/or tongue must not show when the dog's mouth is closed.

SHOULDER HEIGHT

The breed standard gives no guidelines regarding shoulder height.

WEIGHT

At least $17\frac{1}{2}$ lb (8 kg) and at most $28\frac{1}{2}$ lb (13 kg).

COAT

The short coat consists of soft, shiny, close-lying hair.

COLORS

French Bulldogs come in three different color patterns: brindle with white, white with brindle patches (pied) and fawn. Brindles may have white markings on the chest and forehead, but not too many. There are also (almost) completely white Bulldogs. These are classified as pieds.

TEMPERAMENT

CHARACTER

French Bulldogs are individual, clown-like, outgoing, cheerful and playful animals. Fairly intelligent and smart, they can be extremely stubborn when they have made up their minds. Although they are brave, spirited and physically tough, they can be rather sensitive as well; they will pick up on any bad atmosphere in the house and harsh words affect them deeply. They are very affectionate and

Borzois

The large, almond-shaped eyes are set fairly close together. Borzois have a complete and regular scissors bite.

SHOULDER HEIGHT

Dogs are generally approx. $27^1/_2$–$32^1/_4$ in (70–82 cm), sometimes more. Bitches are often approx. 2 in (5 cm) smaller. Larger specimens are preferred, as long as this is not at the expense of overall balance and conformation.

COAT

The long coat of the Borzoi is silky in texture and may be wavy or curly. The coat is longer on the neck and tail, the back of the chest, the culottes and the back of the forelegs.

COLORS

Borzois are bred in nearly all common colors, including solid white, golden either with or without dark hair tips, black, red, gray, patched and brindle. The eyes are dark chestnut.

TEMPERAMENT

CHARACTER

These impressive aristocrats are even-tempered, proud and dignified, calm, slightly aloof and very self-confident. Though extremely loyal to their owners and their family, they are not overbearing. They are very fond of their home comforts and like being close to their family. They are not suited to kennel life. Indoors they are quiet to the point of laziness, but outside they can be very active and capable of developing a tremendous turn of speed. They have a highly developed hunting instinct.

SOCIAL BEHAVIOR

Borzois will often get along fine with similar dogs such as other sighthounds, but are usually not keen on intrusive, playful or dominant dogs. It is possible to teach a Borzoi to get along with one or more pet cats, but this requires a thorough period of socialization and an owner with plenty of insight. Borzois will get on reasonably well with older children, but will certainly not feel happy in a busy, young family and they are not suited as playmates for young children. They are aloof towards people they do not know – they dislike intrusive strangers and prefer to take the initiative in getting to know the visitors better.

GENERAL CARE

GROOMING

The Borzoi's coat requires regular brushing, preferably using a brush with the pins covered in plastic. Trim any excess hair between the pads when necessary.

TRAINING

The training of this dog should be based on mutual respect. Borzois are self-confident dogs that derive no pleasure from following unnecessary commands. However, they will obey their owners when they can see the sense of it. So, teach the dog the basic requirements and do not expect it to perform for you or to repeatedly obey unnecessary commands. Mainly use the tone of your voice and do not shout, hit or worse – such treatment will certainly be counter-productive with these dignified dogs.

Young Borzoi bitch

EXERCISE

Although quiet and almost inconspicuous indoors, the Borzoi needs plenty of space outside to

Borzoi dog

AFGHAN HOUND	
COUNTRY OF ORIGIN	AFGHANISTAN
ORIGINAL FUNCTION	SIGHTHOUND USED FOR LARGE AND SMALL GAME, WATCHDOG

APPEARANCE

BODY

Afghan Hounds have a level back of moderate length, which falls away slightly toward the hip. The hipbones are wide apart and very prominent. The loins are short and broad. The tail has a ring at the end and is raised in movement. The chest is deep and the ribs are well sprung. Afghans have straight, solid legs, with the elbows close to the body. The feet are large and strong, with well-arched toes. The hind feet are not as broad as the forefeet. The neck is long and powerful, and placed in such a way that the head is carried high and proudly.

HEAD

The skull is long, with a slight stop and a long muzzle. The occipital protuberance is very prominent. The eyes are nearly triangular and are placed slightly obliquely in the head. The ears are set well back and low. They are carried close to the head.

walk and run around. Only take them outside on the leash and make sure your yard is well fenced. Most Borzois love running, but with this breed its owners need to react very quickly when their Borzoi catches sight of a prey. These majestic dogs will do best with an owner who has a well-fenced piece of land where the dog is able to run and play for a few hours during the day. The rest of day they would prefer to spend indoors in the company of their people.

USES

The two main dog sports where Borzois are often seen are coursing and dog racing. Apart from that, this breed is kept mainly as a companion dog.

In some countries it is forbidden to allow sight-hounds, such as Borzois, Greyhounds and similar breeds, off the leash.

Borzois

Afghan Hound

SHOULDER HEIGHT

The size for dogs is $26^1/_2$–$29^1/_2$ in (68–74 cm) and for bitches $24^1/_2$–$27^1/_2$ in (63–69 cm).

COAT

Afghans have a long coat of silky texture that covers the entire body, except for the back and the face, which are furnished with dense, short hair. The tail is lightly feathered and the ears are covered with long, silky hair.

Afghan Hound

COLORS

All colors are permitted in this breed. The most common colors are red, often with a dark mask, and black and tan. Dark eyes are preferred.

TEMPERAMENT

CHARACTER

Afghan Hounds are independent, aristocratic, proud and dignified animals. These intelligent sighthounds are placid indoors, but alert and active outside. They have a well-developed hunting instinct and will instinctively chase after fast-moving objects or animals. Although they are eager to please their owners, compliance or subservience is not part of their character. The average Afghan barks very little, but will stand its ground when the need arises and will then display great courage. These dogs are therefore pretty vigilant. Dogs may sometimes be dominant, but this is not true of all specimens. Afghan Hounds are dogs for devotees of the breed who will appreciate its independent and occasionally inscrutable character.

SOCIAL BEHAVIOR

Afghan Hounds are usually aloof with people they do not know and dislike being treated overly familiar by them. Afghans will choose their own time to make your acquaintance. Males can be a little dominant toward other males. Provided children do not pester the dog, they can live happily side-by-side. Afghans are better suited to a family with slightly older children because very young kids cannot be expected to leave the dog alone. Any cats living in the household will be accepted by these dogs but if an Afghan catches sight of a fleeing cat outside then the dog's deeply rooted hunting instinct will be aroused.

GENERAL CARE

GROOMING

This is an important part of keeping an Afghan Hound. The long coat is very soft and silky, and is prone to tangling. How much time you need to spend on grooming will depend on the length of

Afghan Hound

the coat and on whether you are showing the dog. To groom a long-coated Afghan you should allow on average one hour or longer twice a week. If the dog often walks in areas where it will get dirty, such as in parks and woods, then grooming

Afghan Hound

will inevitably be an almost daily ritual. The same applies to show dogs. To prevent the coat from breaking off it must be combed very carefully tuft

Afghan Hound

by tuft. An Afghan should be bathed about once every two months using a good dog shampoo. Check the ear passages for dirt now and then, and clean them if necessary. A well-groomed Afghan is a feast for the eye and seems to be well aware of this. If you regard grooming as a necessary evil, then you would be better off to look for a less labor-intensive breed.

TRAINING

Afghan Hounds are not suitable for inexperienced owners. They are not easy to train because of their independent temperament. Perfect obedience cannot (and should not) be expected from this breed. It is completely pointless to force a dog such as this one to respect you by using violence or shouting. Afghans can be taught quite a bit if trained in a firm but gentle manner.

EXERCISE

The Afghan Hound needs plenty of exercise to keep fit and be happy. It needs regular opportunities to release its tremendous energy, and it is

Afghan Hound

a good idea to train the dog to accompany you if you go jogging. Most Afghan owners keep their dogs on a leash outside, because there is always a risk that the dog sees something interesting and takes off. Only allow an Afghan to run off-leash in areas that are enclosed or where it is safe.

USES

These graceful and distinguished-looking dogs are now rarely used for their original function. A sport such as coursing is a very suitable alternative for this breed, but you could also let your Afghan compete on the racecourse.

Afghan Hound

SALUKI	
COUNTRY OF ORIGIN	IRAN
ORIGINAL FUNCTION	SIGHTHOUND, HUNTING FOR GAZELLE AND OTHER GAME

APPEARANCE

BODY

This graceful dog with its fleet-footed gait is longer than it is tall. The back shows a slight dip behind the withers. The hindquarters are strong with the hipbones wide apart. The chest is deep and fairly narrow. The belly is tucked up. The long tail is set low and flat and is carried in a curve. The elbows are held close and the straight forelegs are long from elbow to wrist. The hind legs have moderately bent stifles and hocks that are low to the ground. The supple feet are of moderate length and the toes are long and well arched. The middle toes are longer than the outer ones. The neck is long, supple and well muscled.

Saluki

HEAD

The long, narrow and aristocratic head has a moderately wide skull that is not domed. The stop is not pronounced. The muzzle runs parallel to the skull and is roughly the same length. The mobile ears hang close to the skull

Saluki

and should reach at least to the corner of the mouth. The eyes are oval and large. They have a dignified, gentle expression, and appear to see far into the distance.

SHOULDER HEIGHT

Dogs range from $22^{1}/_{2}$–28 in (58–71cm). Bitches are slightly smaller.

COAT

The coat is smooth, soft and silky. The hair on the underside of the tail, the ears and backs of the legs and thighs should be longer (feathering).

COLORS

Salukis come in white, cream, fawn, golden, red, grizzle, tricolor (black, brown and white), black with brown, and variations of these colors. The eyes are dark hazel.

TEMPERAMENT

CHARACTER

Salukis are full of contrasts. While quiet and dignified in their daily routine, they can

Saluki

also be very active and playful at times. They enjoy the company of their owners and dislike being excluded, but they are also independent, headstrong and reserved. Salukis rarely bark, which is an extra reason to investigate when the dog does use its voice. They have a keen hunting instinct and find it hard to resist chasing after fast-moving objects or fleeing animals. They can reach incredibly high speeds.

SOCIAL BEHAVIOR

Salukis can live very well alongside similar dogs. Salukis and children also mix well, provided the dog has been socialized with the kids from an early age and provided the kids are taught to respect the dog. Mixing with other household pets, whether these are cats, rabbits or chickens, is very difficult in view of the Saluki's strong hunting instinct. This breed is slightly reserved towards strangers.

GENERAL CARE

GROOMING

The coat is kept in top condition with occasional thorough brushing, particularly the areas covered with longer hair. Check the ear passages for dirt now and then and keep the claws short.

Saluki

TRAINING

The Saluki needs to be reared with a certain degree of care, and the training should emphasize rewarding desirable behavior and should respect the dog's dignified and Oriental temperament. You will never be able to turn a Saluki into a perfectly behaved dog; so do not set your sights too high. With a great deal of patience and insight it will certainly be possible to get a dog that is fond of you and will not want to fail you.

EXERCISE

Salukis are very calm indoors, but outside they are lively and agile, displaying great stamina. When exercising this dog you need to be aware of their strong hunting instincts; you can let the dog run off-leash in an area where there is no traffic for

Saluki

miles around, but do remember that the dog will be deaf to your calls if it catches sight of any prey. In some countries, sighthounds such as these are not allowed to walk off-leash. You can teach the dog to run alongside you when you go jogging, to make sure it can release its energy.

USES

Salukis are eminently suitable for coursing, but are also seen on the dog track.

Greyhound

GREYHOUND	
COUNTRY OF ORIGIN	ENGLAND
ORIGINAL FUNCTION	SIGHTHOUND USED FOR LARGE AND SMALL GAME, RACING DOG

APPEARANCE

BODY

A Greyhound is a strongly built, muscular, proud dog of generous proportions. The sturdy back is fairly long and the powerful loins are slightly arched. The thighs are broad and muscular. The long tail is set on rather low and tapers to a point. It is carried hanging in a slight curve. The chest is deep and spacious. The ribs are long, well sprung and carried well back. The flanks are well cut up. The sloping, well-positioned shoulders are well muscled, but not loaded. The forelegs are long and straight, with the elbows free and well set under the shoulders. The moderately long pasterns are slightly sprung. The stifles are well bent and the hocks are straight. Greyhounds have moderately long feet with compact and well-arched toes. The long, muscular neck is elegantly arched.

HEAD

The head has a long, flat skull of moderate width, a slight stop and powerful, well-chiseled jaws. The ears are small and very thin. They are carried folded back (rose ears), except when the dog is alert. The oval eyes are set obliquely in the head. Greyhounds have a strong scissors bite.

SHOULDER HEIGHT

Dogs range from 28–30 in (71–76 cm). Bitches stand $26^1/_2$–28 in (68–71 cm) tall.

COAT

Greyhounds have a fine, close-lying short-haired coat.

COLORS

This breed comes in black, (pale) red, fawn, blue and brindle, either with or without some white. The white can vary from a small patch on the chest to an almost entirely white dog with a number of colored patches. Solid white Greyhounds also exist. The eyes are preferably dark.

TEMPERAMENT

CHARACTER

Greyhounds are intelligent, affectionate and sensitive dogs that bond strongly with their own people. They rarely bark and are not particularly vigilant. They are calm and sociable indoors. Their owners will hardly notice they are there. Outside they are active and alert to what goes on around them. Their hunting instinct is well developed and they possess great stamina. Greyhounds are very gentle and create a sensible impression.

SOCIAL BEHAVIOR

As a rule, these dogs can be trusted with children and are always friendly to people, whatever the situation. They can come across as shy with people they do not know. They rarely cause problems with other dogs, except when hunting or racing; they can be a little snappish in the heat of the moment. It is in their blood to chase after fast-moving objects; their hunting instinct is very strongly developed. They can learn to socialize with a calm pet cat but only if they have been supervised from an early age. Outside, this breed will continue to regard a fleeing animal as a prey.

GENERAL CARE

GROOMING

This breed needs little grooming. It is sufficient to brush the coat with a soft bristle brush and then polish it with a hound glove. Keep the claws short and regularly check the teeth for tartar. In spite of their short coat Greyhounds are fairly resistant to the weather and can be kept in an outdoor kennel. However, the place where they sleep should not be too hard and must be well-insulated.

TRAINING

Compared with most other sighthound breeds, the Greyhound is reasonably easy to train. They can learn almost all commands and are fairly obedient, except when they have caught site of a prey. At such moments they will ignore your commands. They respond best to a gentle, loving and consistent approach.

EXERCISE

This breed can run incredibly fast and likes to demonstrate this. Nevertheless, a Greyhound needs less exercise than people might think. It is difficult to let a Greyhound romp about off-

Greyhound

leash. There is a risk that the dog could run off and endanger not just itself but also present a danger to wild animals and road users. Accompanying you as you go jogging is a good alternative for working off the dog's energy, but you could also let the dog run about in a well-enclosed area. Indoors Greyhounds are calm to the point of laziness.

USES

This breed is eminently suited to racing. Do bear in mind though that Greyhounds that are normally used for racing differ from their cousins from show lines. Show dogs are usually (considerably) bigger. To prevent injury as much as possible there should be a thorough training program before a race. These dogs also do well as companion dogs.

Greyhound

GALGO ESPAÑOL	
COUNTRY OF ORIGIN	SPAIN
ORIGINAL FUNCTION	SIGHTHOUND, MAINLY USED
	FOR SMALL GAME, BUT ALSO
	FOR FOX AND WILD BOAR

APPEARANCE

BODY

The Galgo Español exudes ruggedness, agility and stamina. The body is rectangular (long rather than high) with an ample chest; the chest size is bigger than the shoulder height. The ribs are flat. The back is level and long and the loins are slightly higher than the withers. The long croup is powerful and well-arched. The long, low-set tail is carried downward, between the hind legs, and ends in a hook that almost reaches the ground. The tail is thick at the root but tapers to a thin point. The belly has a pronounced tuck-up. The legs are vertical and straight. Galgo Españols have hare feet with well-arched toes. The long neck is flattened, strong and supple.

Galgo Español

HEAD

The head is narrow, long and dry. The muzzle is slightly longer than the skull, which displays a marked median line. The stop and occipital protuberance are faintly perceptible. The narrow nose bridge is slightly arched. The lips are tight, dry and fine. The corner of the mouth must not be visible. The ears are wide and high-set, ending in a rounded, fine tip. At rest they are rose-shaped and semi-erect when the dog is alert. The eyes are small and almond-shaped. Galgo Españols have a scissors bite with well-developed canines.

SHOULDER HEIGHT

The size for dogs is $25^1/_2$–$27^1/_2$ in (65–70 cm) and for bitches $23^1/_2$–$26^1/_2$ in (60–68 cm). A deviation of $^3/_4$ in (2 cm) is permissible for otherwise outstanding specimens.

COAT

The Galgo Español has a short-haired and a wire-haired variety. The short-haired has very fine, dense and smooth hair, which is slightly longer on the backs of the thighs. The wire-haired has slightly rougher hair, which is of medium length.

COLORS

This breed may be bred in any color but the most typical shades are chestnut (dark brindle), black, spotted black, cinnamon, yellow, red, white and spotted white.

TEMPERAMENT

CHARACTER

These dogs are intelligent and affectionate. They are alert to what goes on around them and also fairly inquisitive. The Galgo Español is very loyal to its owner and its family.

SOCIAL BEHAVIOR

These dogs will rarely cause any problems with children because they are still very close to nature and know instinctively that small persons should be treated with consideration. They like to play with other dogs and show off their speed. The Galgo Español is not an ideal choice if you have cats or other small pets because their strong hunting instinct makes them chase anything that moves quickly – and they will not be able to leave it at that. A Galgo tends to be a little reserved towards strangers, but is not suspicious although it will come to your rescue when the need arises.

GENERAL CARE

GROOMING

The Galgo Español needs relatively little grooming; weekly brushing is usually sufficient, which also app-

Galgo Español

Smooth-hair Galgo
Español

lies to wire-haired dogs. Regularly check the ears for dirt or excessive earwax and keep the claws short.

TRAINING

With a consistent approach, much patience and insight these relatively untamed dogs can certainly be taught the basics. Direct its character in the desired direction, but do not try to transform it into a perfectly obedient dog, because the Galgo Español is simply not the type for that. It is extremely important that young dogs of this breed are properly socialized.

Galgo Español

EXERCISE

A Galgo Español possesses a strong hunting instinct, so it is advisable not to take it out off the leash. It needs a lot of exercise. If it has the freedom of a large piece of ground that is well fenced, then it will be sufficient to take the dog for a run twice a week to give it a change of scenery. If this is not an option, then the owner will have to take his Galgo out for daily runs to prevent it becoming frustrated.

USES

This breed is well suited to the racing track but performs even better at coursing. This is a sport which requires not just speed but also agility and intelligence.

AZAWAKH	
COUNTRY OF ORIGIN	MALI
ORIGINAL FUNCTION	SIGHTHOUND USED FOR SMALL AND LARGE GAME

APPEARANCE

BODY

The body of the Azawakh is always taller than it is long. The hips are level with or slightly higher than the withers. The topline is straight and the pelvis slopes up. The croup is slightly inclined. The tail is long, thin and dry, tapering to a point. The tail hangs down at rest, with the tip curving slightly upwards. When the dog is alert the tail may be carried above the topline. The chest is ample and deep. The rounded ribs should be visible through the fine skin. The legs are long, straight and dry, and the feet are round and close-knit. The dry, muscular neck is long and fine, and slightly arched.

HEAD

The long, dry head is well chiseled. The elongated skull is nearly flat, but the occipital protuberance is prominent. The stop is very slight. The ears are fine and triangular in shape, carried pendulously. The almond-shaped eyes are fairly large. Azawakhs have a scissors bite.

Azawakh

Azawakh

SHOULDER HEIGHT
For dogs from 25–29¹/₂ in (64–74 cm) and for bitches from 23¹/₂–27¹/₂ in (60–70 cm).

COAT
The Azawakh has a short, soft coat. A striking feature is the hair covering the abdomen which is much sparser and may even be absent.

COLORS
The color may vary from sandy to brown. A white chest, tip of the tail and some white on all four legs is required. White stockings are highly desirable. A black mask is possible and a not very pronounced blaze is permitted. Dark pigmented eyelids are preferred.

TEMPERAMENT

CHARACTER
Azawakhs have retained much of their original natural behavior. They are high-spirited, dignified, very proud and highly independent. They are also rather vigilant and will fiercely defend their owner and their home when necessary. An Azawakh only shows its affection and its gentle side to people it genuinely likes. These dogs act as if they are equal to their owners and do not display any subservient or dependent traits. Their sense of self-esteem is fairly well developed and they possess a keen hunting instinct. They like their creature comforts and enjoy lying down in a soft, warm spot. They do not make good kennel dogs.

SOCIAL BEHAVIOR
The Azawakh will present few problems in the company of other similar dogs and they also tend to get on well with the family's children, provided they treat the dog with due respect. They may be better off in a family with slightly older children. In view of their strong hunting instinct these dogs cannot be trusted with cats and other pets. Azawakhs are generally distrustful of strangers. They dislike being approached enthusiastically or in an intrusive manner by strangers and can then be rather snappy.

GENERAL CARE

Azawakh bitch

GROOMING
The Azawakh needs little grooming. Brushing the coat with a soft brush once a week is sufficient. Keep the claws short and check the teeth for tartar now and then.

TRAINING

A successful training can only be achieved with insight into the original, independent character of this dog and by someone who can appreciate and respect such a character. This breed cannot be forced to respect you by means of corporal punishment, because that will certainly be counter-productive. In spite of this, you must not allow the dog to take liberties with you. This dog is not suitable for obedience trials, but it can be taught the basics. Allow plenty of time for socialization.

Azawakh

This has a positive influence on character building.

EXERCISE

This breed needs a considerable amount of exercise. An Azawakh is an ideal dog for keen runners; it can accompany you over long distances without tiring. These dogs are not suitable for off-leash runs. There is a high risk that their hunting instinct will emerge and they take off. Make sure your yard is well-fenced. High temperatures do not affect this dog, which is hardly surprising in view of its origins.

USES

This is a companion dog for people who are attracted to its natural behavior and its majestic looks. This breed is very suitable for coursing.

SLOUGHI	
COUNTRY OF ORIGIN	MOROCCO
ORIGINAL FUNCTION	SIGHTHOUND USED FOR SMALL AND LARGE GAME

Sloughis

APPEARANCE

BODY

Sloughis have a square build; the shoulder height is usually equal to the length of the trunk, although the length of the trunk may also exceed the shoulder height by a few inches. They have short, dry, broad and slightly arched loins and a bony, oblique croup. The topline is almost level. The thin, lean tail is set in line with the croup and reaches at least to the hocks. The chest is not too broad and reaches barely to the elbows. The ribs are fairly flat. The belly is well tucked up. The legs are slender and long, with long feet. The dry neck is long and very slender, with a slightly arched neck.

HEAD

The head is elongated, elegant and finely chiseled. When viewed from above, the head has the shape of an elongated wedge, which is broadest between the ears. The skull is flat and the stop is barely visible. The muzzle and skull are equal in length. The lips are thin and supple. The corners of the mouth are barely visible. Sloughis have high-set ears that are rounded and triangular in shape. They are carried hanging, close to the head. The large eyes have a soft and somewhat wistful expression.

SHOULDER HEIGHT

Dogs range from 26–28$^{1}/_{4}$ in (66–72 cm), but the ideal height is 27$^{1}/_{2}$ in (70 cm). Bitches stand

24–26$\frac{1}{2}$ in (61–68 cm) tall, with an ideal height of 25$\frac{1}{2}$ in (65 cm).

Ten-week old Sloughi

COAT
The Sloughi has a very short, soft and dense coat.

COLORS
This breed comes in various shades of sandy and to a lesser extent brindle, either with or without a black mask or black points. Solid black and sandy with a black coat also occurs, but is fairly rare. The eyes are dark in color.

TEMPERAMENT

CHARACTER
Dogs of this breed are proud and dignified. Indoors they are calm to lazy but they are high-spirited outside. They have a strong hunting instinct and tremendous stamina. A Sloughi only shows affection to people it really likes, but is never dependent or subservient. This breed is very vigilant and will ferociously defend its owners and the house against intruders. Sloughis are not suited to kennel life; they value their creature comforts. Most also hate being left on their own. They are sensitive to the atmosphere in the house.

SOCIAL BEHAVIOR
This breed is reserved and aloof towards strangers. They will make the first move when they like someone and dislike being approached with great enthusiasm by strangers. When the dog has got used to one or more domestic cats from puppyhood, it can live alongside them in harmony. But bear in mind that this is a dog with a highly developed hunting instinct; it will find it hard to resist chasing after a fleeing animal. Normally, these dogs will get along fine with other similar dogs, although some specimens may react a little fiery towards other dogs they meet in the street. Most are friendly to children but will not tolerate being teased.

Sloughis

GENERAL CARE

GROOMING
Sloughis require very little grooming. It is sufficient to brush the coat with a rubber mitt or a rubber brush once a week. The coat can then be polished with a hound glove. Keep the claws short and check the teeth regularly for tartar. Sloughis will do best with a soft place to sleep.

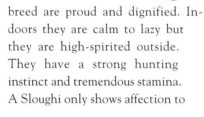

Sloughi

Sloughi dog

TRAINING

This independent dog is not easy to train, although it is not impossible to teach it a few basic commands. A patient handler who treats the dog with respect, consistency and insight into its sighthound character will bring out the best in this breed. A Sloughi obeys out of respect, not out of fear or subservience. It is therefore pointless to train it with a firm hand and usually this achieves the opposite. This breed is not suited for prolonged training sessions and they need to see the point of a command.

EXERCISE

Sloughis have tremendous stamina and need a great deal of exercise. You can let them run on a regular basis. Only let the dog run off-leash in areas where this is absolutely safe; when gripped by its hunting passion a Sloughi can take off, endangering wild animals, road users and itself.

USES

This breed is eminently suited for greyhound racing and coursing. Obviously, this dog also does well as a companion dog.

CHART POLSKI

CHART POLSKI	
COUNTRY OF ORIGIN	POLAND
ORIGINAL FUNCTION	SIGHTHOUND USED FOR SMALL AND BIG GAME, INCLUDING DEER, WOLF, FOX AND HARE

APPEARANCE

BODY

The Chart Polski is the largest and most powerful of the short-haired sighthounds. The body is a little longer than high. The backline shows a slight "dip" behind the withers, is then almost level and has slightly arched loins, particularly in the males. The chest is deep and very spacious, with a long breastbone. The chest should ideally reach to the elbows. The frontal view is narrow. The belly is tucked up. The tail is long and strong. It is sickle-shaped with the end curved upwards, possibly in the shape of a closed ring, but never carried above the topline. The legs are straight and long. The hindquarters are well angulated. The feet are oval in shape, with arched and close-knit toes. The hind feet are longer than the forefeet. Chart Polskis have long, powerful necks.

Chart Polskis

HEAD

The head is powerful, dry and long, with a moderate stop and a slightly arched nose bridge. The powerful muzzle is somewhat blunt and equal in length to the skull or a little longer. The skull is flat. The relatively large, slanting, almond-shaped eyes have an expressive, piercing look. The fleshy ears are medium sized and should reach to the inner corner of the eye. They are usually carried folded back, but erect with tilted tips when the dog is alert. Chart Polskis may have a scissors or a pincer bite.

SHOULDER HEIGHT

Chart Polski

The ideal size for bitches is 26¹/₂–29¹/₂ in (68–75 cm) and for dogs 27¹/₂–31¹/₂ in (70–80 cm). When this is not detrimental to the overall balance, the dog may also be slightly bigger or smaller.

COAT

The coat is short and supple, feeling neither rough nor soft. The hair is slightly longer underneath and at the end of the tail.

COLORS

All coat colors and color combinations are permitted. The eyes are dark brown or amber.

TEMPERAMENT

CHARACTER

This breed has the character of a true sighthound, with a touch of "Oriental aloofness and dignity." These dogs are extremely self-confident, even-tempered, brave and poised. They are also vigilant and you can rely on the dog to defend you and your property ferociously if necessary. Indoors they tend to be calm to the point of laziness, but in the field they are single-minded, incredibly fast and tireless.

SOCIAL BEHAVIOR

The Chart Polski is generally reserved towards people it does not know. Visitors are always announced. Unfamiliar faces are accepted, provided their behavior towards the dog is not too genial. The dog will come over to meet them on its own accord after a little while. Mixing with quiet or older children should not present any difficulties, provided the children treat the dog with respect and the dog has been properly socialized.

Contact with other dogs, particularly similar dogs from this breed category, will not normally be a problem. A Chart Polski can be trained to live in harmony with one or more domestic cats, but proper socialization is again required. Do bear in mind, however, that the cat with which the dog shares its basket indoors is sometimes seen as prey outside.

GENERAL CARE

GROOMING

The Chart Polski requires very little grooming. A rubber mitt can be used during the molt to remove loose and dead hair from the coat.

TRAINING

It is fairly easy to teach a Chart Polski the basic commands, although the owner should make allowances for its dignified temperament. An owner with respect and appreciation for the sighthound character will bring out the best in this breed.

Chart Polskis

EXERCISE

The Chart Polski needs a fair amount of (off-leash) exercise, but will usually adapt if it gets a little less now and then. You can confidently take this dog for a walk on the leash without being pulled along. They usually walk peacefully alongside their owners.

USES

You could consider coursing, but the Chart Polski will also feel at home on the race track. To prevent injury there should be a thorough training program before coursing or a race. This breed also does extremely well as a companion dog.

DETAILS

This breed is probably one of the oldest breeds of sighthound, which originates in the East and is not related to the Greyhound.

Chart Polski

Chart Polski

Breeds that are not recognized

MARKIESJE

COUNTRY OF ORIGIN	THE NETHERLANDS
ORIGINAL AND	COMPANION DOG
TODAY'S FUNCTION	

APPEARANCE

BODY

The Markiesje is an elegant and well-proportioned, finely built dog that should show no signs of dwarfism. The body is slightly longer than tall. The well-developed chest is oval shaped and the back is straight. The fairly long tail hangs down slightly arched at rest. The body is light-boned, yet muscular. The belly is slightly tucked up. The shoulders are sloping and held close to the body. The legs are straight with good angulation and strong pasterns.

Markiesjes have hare feet with close-knit toes. The long, muscular neck supports the head proudly.

HEAD

The head is in proportion to the body. The skull seems almost flat, is not as wide as it is long and has a noticeable occipital protuberance. The stop is pronounced, but in no way abrupt. The muzzle tapers slightly towards the nose which is not pointed and slightly shorter than the skull. The lips are close-fitting. The ears are set high, hang down from the head and do not stand out from the skull. The eyes are oval shaped, but do

Markiesje

Markiesje

Markiesje

COAT

The coat is fine, soft and medium length. It is smooth and close lying. The coat may be slightly wavy. The ears, tail and legs, particularly the culottes, are well feathered.

COLORS

Breeders try to breed a dog with a beautiful, deep black coat color. Nevertheless, we do occasionally see differently colored pups. White markings on the feet, tip of the tail, chest and a white blaze are acceptable.

TEMPERAMENT

Markiesje

CHARACTER

Markiesjes are sensitive, intelligent, lively and playful dogs that love to please their owners. They are alert to danger and will therefore guard well. Outdoors they can be fairly active and spirited, but indoors they tend to be quiet. They get very attached to their owner and the family, and love to be involved in the daily household routine. They are real companion dogs; they do not like to be on their own. Usually, that isn't necessary; their handy size and great adaptability ensures that they can be taken along practically anywhere.

SOCIAL BEHAVIOR

By temperament this dog gets on well with other dogs and contact with cats and other pets seldom causes problems. They usually get on fine with children and are friendly towards strangers. But to these dogs their own people come first.

not protrude. They have a soft and calm expression. Markiesjes have a scissors bite.

SHOULDER HEIGHT

Approx. $13^3/_4$ in (35 cm).

Markiesje

GENERAL CARE

GROOMING

This breed requires regular grooming, which takes very little time. Regular brushing of the coat is sufficient to prevent tangles and remove loose hairs. Keep the ear passages clean and the claws short.

TRAINING

These dogs should not be difficult to train. They are intelligent and keen to learn and love to please their owner. A cheerful, consistent and varied training will achieve best results.

EXERCISE

Markiesjes have an average need to exercise. This breed will love to accompany you on your walks, either through the town on a lead or off-leash through the countryside. Ball games in the garden also meet with their approval. Indoors they tend to be quiet.

USES

Markiesjes are almost exclusively kept as a companion dog, a task to which this breed is eminently well suited. With the right supervision this breed can achieve great results in areas of dog sports, including flyball and agility.

DETAILS

This breed is rarely seen outside its country of origin, because the breeding association does not like to see dogs go abroad when they are so badly needed to further enhance the breed. But within the Netherlands this breed is not very common either. Markiesje-type dogs, which we still find everywhere, may be used for breeding purposes after approval by the breeding association. In 1999 the breed was recognized as a national breed in the Netherlands.

Markiesje

WHITE SHEPHERD (FORMERLY: AMERICAN-CANADIAN WHITE SHEPHERD)

COUNTRY OF ORIGIN	ALTHOUGH THIS BREED IS A DIRECT DESCENDANT OF THE GERMAN SHEPHERD, THE WHITE SHEPHERD WAS DEVELOPED IN THE USA AND CANADA.
ORIGINAL FUNCTION	COMPANION DOG

APPEARANCE

BODY

The White Shepherd is a powerful, well-muscled shepherd of moderately heavy build and with a well-balanced, smooth outline. The trunk is slightly longer than tall (in a ratio of 12:10). The chest reaches to the elbows and is not too broad. The brisket is pronounced. The legs are powerful and moderately heavy. The elbows are close to the body. The withers blend smoothly into the neck and back. The back itself is level (horizontal) and well-muscled. The croup is long and slopes down gently. The belly is slightly drawn up. The tail is set low and reaches at least to the hocks. At rest it hangs down like a saber but in movement it is raised, although the tail should not be held above the topline. There is a marked gender difference between dogs and bitches.

White Shepherd

HEAD

The wedge-shaped head is powerful and dry, narrowing to the nose. The skull is nearly flat and the stop is visible, but not prominent. The muzzle and skull run parallel to each other when viewed from the side. The lips are tight and close-fitting. White Shepherds have a complete scissors bite.

White Shepherds

SHOULDER HEIGHT

The size for dogs is $23^1/_2$–$25^1/_2$ in (60–65 cm) and for bitches $21^3/_4$–$23^1/_2$ in (55–60 cm). Dogs that conform to the breed standard should not be disqualified for a slight deviation up or down.

COAT

There are White Shepherd with stiff-haired and long stiff-haired coats. The coat should be close-lying and have a rich, woolly undercoat. The dog is furnished with longer hair around the neck, on the backs of the legs and on the tail. The hair on the ears, the head and the legs is shorter.

White Shepherds generally learn very quickly

White Shepherd

COLORS

The coat is always white. A light fawn color, i.e. shades of pale cream to brownish red on the tips of the ears, the back and on top of the tail, is judged as a minor fault. The skin is dark pigmented. A black nose is desirable, as are black claws.

TEMPERAMENT

CHARACTER

These are cheerful, alert, intelligent and vigilant, even-tempered and friendly dogs. They are eager to work for their owners and their family and are generally obedient. They are very affectionate and do not like to be excluded.

SOCIAL BEHAVIOR

This breed generally gets on well with children and there should be no problems with other dogs. When the dog has been properly socialized, they will also get along with cats and other pets. White Shepherds tend to be a little wary of unfamiliar people and situations.

GENERAL CARE

GROOMING

The White Shepherd needs a fair amount of grooming. Brush the dog thoroughly about once a week, but daily brushing and combing is recommended during the molt. A "teasel brush" is the most practical tool for this. Keep the claws short.

TRAINING

White Shepherds are intelligent and love to work for their owners; a combination which produces obedient dogs that are easy to train. It is vital that the young dog gets to meet all kinds of different animals, people, things and situations, so that it will get used to them and can grow up into a well-balanced animal.

EXERCISE

This breed has average exercise needs, but will soon become bored if it is restricted to a few short walks a day. Taking a White Shepherd out for a walk is relaxing; if the dog has a close bond with its handler, then it will stay close by. These are not usually the type of dogs that wander off on their own to explore the neighborhood or the woods nearby. Apart from taking it out for walks,

White Shepherd

White Shepherd

GERMAN SHEPHERD, WHITE
COUNTRY OF ORIGIN   **GERMANY**

APPEARANCE

The external features of the white-coated German Shepherd are identical to those of the German Shepherd, except for pigmentation and coat color. The White German Shepherd differs in its appearance from the White Shepherd discussed previously in the color of its coat: shades of yellow and wolf occur frequently in the White German Shepherd's coat, whereas these are classed as a (minor) fault in White Shepherds. There is also a difference in pigmentation: unlike White Shepherds, White German Shepherds have no black noses or lip and eye rims; these are usually more

you will also make the dog very happy by taking it swimming, taking it for a run, and with ball games and retrieving.

USES

This breed is very suitable for various types of dog sports, such as obedience, flyball or agility trials, but it also does extremely well as a companion dog.

White German Shepherds

pink to light brown in color. Finally, the backline in these dogs is similar to that in German Shepherds, while White Shepherds have a more horizontal backline.

White Shepherd

FEATURES

Essentially, the characteristics of this breed are similar to those of the German Shepherd. The grooming might perhaps be more demanding than with the German Shepherd, because white hairs are more conspicious indoors. White German Shepherds have not yet been officially recognized, although they are normal-

White German Shepherd

ly still issued with a pedigree. The pedigree will then list that this is a non-recognized color. This why these dogs have not (yet) featured at FCI shows.

Smooth-haired White German Shepherd

Long-haired White German Shepherd

Jack Russell Terrier

JACK RUSSELL TERRIER

COUNTRY OF ORIGIN	ENGLAND
ORIGINAL FUNCTION	THIS BREED HAS BEEN DEVELOPED TO BOLT UNDERGROUND FOXES AND BADGERS, WHICH CAN THEN BE HUNTED.

APPEARANCE

BODY

The Jack Russell Terrier is a short-legged dog with a muscular, dry body. The back is level. The short, high-set tail is carried gaily. The legs are straight and dry with good angulation. Jack Russell Terriers have cat's feet.

HEAD

The small ears are V-shaped and dropped, carried close to the head. The eyes are almond-shaped. Jack Russells have a scissors bite.

SHOULDER HEIGHT

Jack Russell Terriers are no taller than 11 in (28 cm).

COAT

Jack Russell Terriers have a double coat, which means that they have a top and an undercoat. They come in either smooth or rough coats. Both types of coat are stiff, closed and dense. Rough-haired Jack Russell Terriers should not have a woolly or curly coat.

Jack Russell Terrier

COLORS

White dogs and dogs with markings on the head and set of the tail are preferred. The markings may be black, brown, lemon or black and brown (black and tan). Brindle markings are undesirable.

TEMPERAMENT

CHARACTER

Jack Russell Terriers are very spontaneous and lively. They are extremely brave, hardy, active and enterprising, rather playful and confident. They ooze confidence. Some specimens, particularly males, can be a little dominant. Their sharp intelligence should not be underestimated and they are also fairly willful. Jack Russell Terriers are very alert to what goes around them and pretty vigilant. Consequently, some specimens may bark more than is desirable, but this can be largely remedied by a good training. They are quite capable of keeping themselves entertained, but do appreciate the company of their owners.

Jack Russell Terrier

SOCIAL BEHAVIOR

Provided the dog has been well socialized and trained, contact with other dogs will not be a problem, although dogs in particular may be a little reckless and pushy towards other male dogs. The Jack Russell Terrier can live in harmony with a domestic cat if it has grown up with it from puppyhood, but will often find it hard to ignore fleeing cats outside. These healthy dogs generally get along fine with children; the dogs are fairly sturdy and are not easily intimidated by them. Although this breed is vigilant towards strangers who visit, they usually leave it at that.

Jack Russell Terrier

Jack Russell Terrier

smooth-haired Jack Russell Terrier should be groomed daily with a rubber brush to remove any dead and loose hair. Outside the molt weekly brushing is sufficient. The rough-haired Jack Russell Terrier should be plucked three to four times a year. This involves hand-plucking the dead and

GENERAL CARE

GROOMING

These sober dogs are fairly easy to groom. During the molt the coat of the

Jack Russell
Terrier

old hairs from the coat, so that the new hair has room to grow. Keep the claws short.

TRAINING

For a consistent handler who will stand no nonsense this clever dog is not difficult to train. It is quite another matter if the handler is too lenient or allows himself to be fooled by the dog's extensive repertoire of tricks. In such cases the handler will end up with a rascal who will do as he pleases and will not be stopped by anyone. Therefore, always remain consistent. Introduce a policy of deterrent regarding excessive barking and teach the dog from an early age to come to you when called.

Jack Russell Terrier

EXERCISE

This breed has tremendous energy and likes to be busy. They are not happy with three short walks each day. They love to run and play, and are mad about digging and ball games. Keep your yard well fenced, because these terriers have a tendency to take off on their own. During off-leash walks in the countryside there are very few Jack Russells that can resist small game that might cross their paths! You should therefore teach your dog from an early age to return promptly when called.

USES

These little rascals can be frequently seen at stab-

Jack Russell Terrier

les and on ranches, where they make themselves extremely useful as vermin destroyers. They will also do well as a companion dog in a sports-minded family. If you are thinking of entering this dog in dog sports, then agility and flyball would be an excellent choice. The action and challenges involved in these sports will certainly appeal to this breed.

DETAILS

This popular breed has not been officially recognized by the FCI, although breed organizations in certain countries including the Netherlands, Ireland and Australia have. The normal-legged Parson Jack Russell Terrier has been officially recognized by the FCI. The Parson Jack Russell Terrier is classed in breed group 3.

Jack Russell Terrier

Young Boerboel dog

BOERBOEL

COUNTRY OF ORIGIN	SOUTH AFRICA
ORIGINAL FUNCTION	GUARD DOG ON FARMS

Boerboel

APPEARANCE

BODY

The Boerboel is a large, sturdily built and muscular dog. The back is level, wide and strong. In countries where this is permitted the tail is usually docked short. The chest is wide. The legs are firm and straight, with well-shaped feet. The thick, strong neck is of adequate length.

HEAD

The strong, large head is broad between the ears. The wide muzzle is approx. $3\frac{1}{4}$–4 in (8–10 cm)

long, tapering slightly towards the tip of the nose. The nose bridge is level. The lips are fleshy, but should not overhang too much. The ears are medium-sized and carried pendulously.

SHOULDER HEIGHT

The minimum height for dogs is 26 in (66 cm). Bitches should stand at least 24 in (61 cm) tall.

COAT

The coat is short and soft to the touch.

COLORS

The coat color varies from pale yellow to dark red, either with or without brindle and with a black mask. Animals without white markings are preferred. The eye color may vary from light to dark brown. The muzzle is always black.

TEMPERAMENT

CHARACTER

The Boerboel is a stable, confident and generally calm dog. It is very loyal and attached to its family and if necessary will guard them with its life. It is extremely courageous, sober and rather tough on itself. Obedient and compliant for its own people, the Boerboel can also show initiative. It is very territorial, vigilant and defensive, and any intruders will not stand a chance when they try to enter your property. A Boerboel is controlled in the way it guards, and usually only barks when something is wrong. Owners who keep their Boerboel as a kennel dog will neglect its need for company. In view of their devotion to their own people it is better to

Boerboel

let these dogs be part of the family. This will also benefit their character building.

SOCIAL BEHAVIOR

Young Boerboel

This breed gets along extremely well with all the people and animals that are part of its own family. Children will often get special attention in a positive sense. They are vigilant towards strangers, especially if they try to enter the home, but if the owner makes it clear that the visitors are welcome then the dog will accept them. The Boerboel usually gets on well with other dogs that are part of the family but can be dominant towards strange dogs, for instance in the street.

Boerboel

GENERAL CARE

GROOMING

This breed requires little grooming. During the molt a rubber brush or rubber mitt can be used to remove dead hair from the coat.

TRAINING

Boerboels are intelligent dogs that love to please their owners, which makes them easy to train. You can teach them nearly anything. But this is certainly not the right breed for everybody: the owner should be someone with a natural authority over dogs and who is able to train the dog with great consistency and in complete harmony. This breed is not suitable for indecisive, inexperienced or indulgent people.

EXERCISE

The Boerboel has average exercise needs. It is very nimble and can walk for many hours without tiring. Nearly all Boerboels love ball games and retrieving.

USES

The Boerboel is worshipped by the rural population in South Africa and Namibia, where it has certainly proved its worth as a guard dog and protector of vast farms and their families. This breed is rare in other countries where it is mainly kept as a vigilant companion dog by devotees. In view of its characteristics and origin this type of dog is best suited to people with plenty of space and with a sizable, well-fenced yard. A busy city district is not the ideal environment for the average Boerboel.

Boerboel

AMERICAN BULLDOG

COUNTRY OF ORIGIN	USA
ORIGINAL FUNCTION	THIS BREED USED TO ASSIST THE FARMER IN DRIVING WAYWARD CATTLE BUT WAS ALSO EMPLOYED AS A GUARD. IT WAS ALSO USED AS A HUNTING DOG, ESPECIALLY FOR BOAR AND FERAL DOGS.

American Bulldog

APPEARANCE

BODY

American Bulldog

The American Bulldog has a compact build with a fairly short, broad and powerful back. The loins show a slight curve. The tail is set low and is carried hanging down to the hocks. It is thick at the root and gradually tapers to a point. The tail may be raised but should not curl over the back. The chest is deep and of moderate width. The ribs are well sprung and the belly is slightly tucked up. The elbows are held close to the body. The legs are straight and heavy boned. The hindquarters are angulated. The medium-sized feet have well-arched and close-knit toes. The well-muscled neck is moderate in length and slightly arched, narrowing gradually towards the head.

HEAD

The head is comparatively large and broad, with the top of the skull flat and a pronounced superciliary ridge. The stop is deep and the cheeks are well-developed. The muzzle is broad and square, with well-muscled jaws. The lips are full. The ears are medium-sized and may be carried either hanging or folded back (rose ears). The medium-sized eyes are round to almond-shaped and well apart. The eyelids are close-fitting. American Bulldogs have an undershot bite.

SHOULDER HEIGHT

The size for dogs is $21^3/_4$–$27^1/_2$ in (55–70 cm). Bitches stand $19^1/_2$–$25^1/_2$ in (50–65 cm) tall.

WEIGHT

Bitches can weigh up to $99^1/_4$ lb (45 kg) and dogs up to $110^1/_4$ lb (50 kg). A greater weight is undesirable, because that would be detrimental to their nimbleness.

COAT

The coat is short-haired and soft in texture. The hair should be no longer than one inch ($2^1/_2$ cm).

American Bulldog

COLORS

The most common color is white with brindle, black or red patches. The brindle and red can vary from very light to dark. Solid white specimens also occur. Dark colored dogs are less desirable. Black to dark brown eyes, with black eye rims and a black nose are preferred.

TEMPERAMENT

CHARACTER

The American Bulldog is an extremely even-tempered, confident dog with a natural instinct to guard and defend its family, home and property. It does this in a calm and considered manner, but very convincingly. These dogs are highly intelligent and very loyal and devoted to their owners and their family. They are alert, very courageous and tough on themselves. A kennel is not the ideal place to keep a dog of this breed. They should live in the home, amongst their own people. Indoors they are fairly calm. They will only bark when something is wrong.

American Bulldog

SOCIAL BEHAVIOR

These dogs will defend the people of their own family, including the children, with their lives. They are very vigilant towards strangers who enter their property, but when their owner says it's okay they will accept them. Most specimens are pretty hostile towards other dogs that do not belong their own pack, particularly if they challenge the dog. But they usually get along fine with doggy house mates that act submissively towards them. Animals that belong to the family and that the dog has grown up with are accepted without any problems.

GENERAL CARE

American Bulldog

GROOMING

These dogs require little grooming. You can brush the coat with a hard bristle brush once a week. During the molt a rubber mitt is the ideal tool to remove dead hair from the coat.

TRAINING

This breed is not suitable for inexperienced people or for those who are insecure or indecisive. An aspiring American Bulldog owner should be both mentally and physically strong. A calm owner who has a natural authority over dogs will make a good team with this dog. These dogs are intelligent and can learn a great deal within a short space of time. A hard training is not recommended, but a clear, consistent and loving approach is essential. Teach them from an early age that you do not allow any pulling on the leash, because once they are fully grown they will be far too strong to correct them. American Bulldogs should be thoroughly socialized, so they get every chance of growing up into even-tempered dogs that react to all kinds of influences in a stable manner.

EXERCISE

These dogs are very nimble and can walk for many hours at a time, but when their owner has no time once in a while they will usually adapt. If you have a well-fenced yard, then this dog will partly see to its own exercise needs. Most are very fond of ball games. Indoors they are quiet.

USES

In some parts of the USA this breed is still used to help drive straying cattle. The majority of these dogs are kept as a vigilant companion.

Important addresses:

For all your questions regarding breeds in general you can contact your national cynological or dog institution.

In the USA this is:

The American Kennel Club
260 Madison Avenue
New York
NY 10016
Tel: 212-696-8200

In Great Britain this is:

The Kennel Club
1–5 Clarges Street
Piccadilly
London W1Y 8AB
Tel: 0870 606 6750
Fax: 020 7518 1058

And the international organization is:

Fédération Cynologique Internationale (FCI)
13 Albert Place
B-6530 Thuin
Belgium
Tel: +32.71.59.12.38
Fax: +32.71.59.22.29

Miniature Bull Terriers

Photograph acknowledgments and thanks

The photographer and publishers would like to thank the following dog owners for their kind co-operation with photography. The dogs pictured belong to the following owners (listed alphabetically):

Red and White Irish Setter

Black and Tan Coonhound

Sheepdogs and cattle herders

Denis Amoros (Fr); Bianca Avontuur; F.H.M. Backx; Mr & Mrs Beenen; Andrea van de Bergh (D); Barjo Blom; Maxime Boidin (Fr); Janny Bokkers; Mascha Bollen; Danielle Boshouwers; the Van Boven family; Charles-Louis Brands; Martine Drauden (Fr); Catherine Dufay-Jacobson (Fr); Marina Eggermond (B); Marita van Enckevort; B. and G. Enthoven; Marit van Ewijk; I. Folmer; P.B.T. Gerritsen; Mr & Mme Gibson (D); J. de Gids; D. Griffijn; H. ten Haaf; Ria van Haarlem; the De Haas family; T. van der Heijden; Jigal van Hemert; W.L. van der Hoek; Toos Huyskens; Eline Jagtenberg; P. Karacsony; C.A. Keizer; Hans and Ellen Kersten (D); L. Kilwinger;

Schwyzer Laufhunden

Pinscher, Schnauzer, Molossian, Mastiff and Swiss Sennenhunds breeds

Marja Alberts; Ricky Beekmans; Jacco Bom; W. Boogaard; J. Bouland-Planken; J.J. Bourret; Denise van Kleef; the Laberté family; A. de Liefde; Judith Lissenberg; Yvonne Maas; Jacky Marks; S. Meyboom-Turkic; Susan Meijer; Ellen van der Meyden; Maurice and Ellen van Mierlo; Arjan Monster; the Van de Nieuwenhof family; Laura van de Nieuwenhuijzen; A. van de Noorda; M. Olsthoorn; M. van Ooijen; R. Peschier; Bianca Pijpers; G. Post; the Reineke family (D); Sylvie Renaud (Fr); Josiane Richard (Fr); Emmy de Rijk (B); Karin van Rijn; Mr & Mrs van Rodijnen; Raphaëlle Ruiz; the Van Rumpt family; Diane Sari; P. Schmits; D. Schoenmakers; Marina and Jean Sels-Eggermont (B); Dominique Souttre (Fr); M.E. Spiering; H. van Steenes; Walter Stehmann; René and Annette Tetteroo; Jocelyne Thomas (Fr); Ciska Tuin; F. and D. van Veldhoven; H.P.P. Verbakel; E. Verhoef; Janine Vermeulen; J. Vermeulen; M. Verver-Woltjer; the Vifmans family (B); Mr & Mrs Welvering; M. and J. Wibier; Nancy Wijnhoven (B); Irene van Will; Annet Wouters.

Newfoundlander

Paulona Boven; Karin Brand; C. Brandt; Patricia Cruet (Fr); L. David (Fr); Allevamento Degli Olmi (I); M. van Deursen; A. van Dongen; W. van de Ende; Kees Faber; Mme. Ghislaine Facquez (Fr); P. Gest; Laurent Goullez (Fr); Anja Griekspoor; Els Groen; H. and I. Hartgers-Wagener; S. Hartjes; C. Heeren; P. Hendriks; Piet and Corry Hendriks; Mieke Hesen; Peter Hoevenaars; Karin Honselaar-

Chart Polski

Bull Terrier

Sheltie

Bearded Collie

René Polak; the Pranger family; Mme Prouvensier & Cagnac (Fr); the Reijnen-Labee family; Janet van Reijsen; Ella Roelfs-Rijzebot; J.P. Rossignol (Fr); Melle Magalie Royer (Fr); M. de Ruiter; J. Rutten; Karel and Beatrice van Sambeek; P.M. Schemstok; Esther and Robert Schmiesing; Linda Scholing; Bart Segers (B); Ad Smits; S. Suir; Christien and Willy van Uden; Joke and Jan Verberkt; B. Verhoef; J. Vermeulen; Mrs J. Verstappen; Joanne and Paul Verwey; Antoon and Wilma Vos, C. Wervenbos; Christa Westerhoven; A. van Wijk; F. and L. van Wijk; Annette Wijnsouw; Marijke Woudstra; Peter van de Zanden; Joop van Zon; C. Zuydeweg-Roxs.

Heuser; Francoise Ingebrand (Fr); Ineke van Jaarsveld-Kevelam; Dominique Janssens (B); J.C.G. van der Kant; the G. Kemps family; Mary Kerssen; V. Kling; J. and E. Kloosterhof; E. Kluijs; D.A. Kuyper-Schuller; Kees van der Laak; M.C. Langendoen; A. and T. Loos; Ria Mauriks; Emanuelle Napierala (Fr); the Nettenbreijer family; the Oudendijk family; J. van Pavert; Marjan Peters;

Grand Bassets Griffon Vendéen

Sealyham Terriers

Drever

Cesky Fousek

M. Scholten; T. Schotel; Mat Smeets; R. Snip; Marga Steenvoorden; Tico Steinhage; W. Tijsse Claase; J. Verstappen; Th. and W. van Vessem; Niels Visser; C. van Vliet; Teunis de Waal; the Van de Walle family; L. Weber; Marjan Weessies; Peter and Nicole Weyers; B. van Wijk; Ingrid Wildschut; the De Wolf family.

Terriers

J.H. Albers; Marjolein and Sander Amelsbeek; Marianne Baas Becking; Marjan Baks; Sandra Berendsen; Frans and Mandy Bommele; Mrs De Bondt-Fonteyn (B); Richard van de Bosch; Allan Brine (Fr); M. van de Broek; L. van Calsteren-Daems (B); J. Dekker; A. van Dijk; C. Froon; the Van Gothel family (D); Dominique Granier (Fr); A. Hartmann-Tibbe; T. Hoffman; A. van Hoorn; Jac Houben; D. Jacobs; Karin Jenniskens; Colette de Jong; Rianne Kamphuis; R. and I. Kelleter; Ingrid Knobbe; E. Lahaye; the Langmaat family; W. van Leeuwen; G. Leusink; J. van Lieshout; Daniel Lombard (Fr); G.H.J. Lugtigheid; K. Lust; Franck Marolleau (Fr); Jane Maurin (Fr); C. Meijer; Philippe Pereira (Fr); T. Posthuma; W. Pul; Diana Ramakers; Nadine Regard (Fr); the De Reus family; Jane-Michele Rodolfi (Fr); H.M. van de Roer (B); Irma de Roo-Strous; Henny and Rob van Schaik;

Schwyzer Laufhund, pup

Dachshunds

Ilonka Balvert; Mrs Blom; Jan Deetman; L. Donkersteeg; Jeanine van de Heuvel; P. van Leeuwen; the Van Oers family; Jacqueline Wagener.

Shiba Inu

White Shepherd

Shar Peis

Spitz and other primitive breeds

Mrs J.C. Asselbergs; J.A. van de Berkmortel; Noelle de Bie; J.C. Bijker; Mrs S.E. van Boetzelaer; A. W. Bruynzeel; Yvonne Buijs; Mme Rose-Marie Carlsen (DK); Michel Cayol (Fr); Melle Celine Conte (Fr); the Van Deursen family; R. Doedijns; Paul Ehrsam (Fr); Chris Eisenga; P.A.P. Evers; S. Fahrenkrog (D); R. and M. Fisher; Jennifer Gielisse; G. Glastra; Sandra van de Graaf; K. Hesseling; D. Honcoop; Th. Honcoop-den Hartog; Francoise Ingebrand (Fr); F. Kerkhof; Cornelis Koot; Lideke van Laake; B.J.M. Ledder; Renate Leijen; A. Meijer; Nicole Metz (Fr); Thea Niessen; M. van Oers-van Mimpen; Mr van de Pavert; the Van de Poel family; Michel Puyrenier (Fr); Helma & Theo van Rijswijk; Ivan Roberteau (Fr);

Long-haired German Pointe

Tibetan Mastiff

F.W. Schoppert; G. Schouten; the Stegehuis family; Esther Stigger; Mme Tanneur (Fr); Christine Varoqueax (Fr); Wil Verkuil; the Vunderink family; the De Wolf family; Mr & Mrs Wong-Pinto (USA); O. Zeypveld; D. and I. Zwier.

Hounds

Nel Adema; Ellen Bon; R. Bosman; W. van de Broek; Nelleke van Erp; O. de Fielliettaz; E. Gevers; Rianne Kamphuis; G.M. Koenraadt; Madeleine Hiemstra; H. and F. Huikeshoven; the Langmaat family; the Leunk family; K. van Lier; M. van Loon; M. Matveev; Ria Mauriks; R. Morgans; Andrea Nagy; the Noordenbos family; Marjon Ploeger; the Plomp family;

R. Rosenkrantz; the Rust family; P.M. Schemstok; Hester Seinen; R. Smits; W. Strikkers; J. Tresoor; the Tukkers family; Corien Verbeek; the Vlietstra family; Angelique van Voorst; Lilian Zurendonk.

Pointers

Hellen and Jeroen Assen; Luv Augis (Fr); Mrs Berendse; Ilonka Balvert; Esther Booker; Hans Braakhuis; J.F.A. Brocken; Peter de Bruin; A. Couwenbergh; Marianne van Dam; A. Dekker; the Dolmans family; J. van Dommelen; H. van Dronkelaar; Lianne Eekman-Lampio; Marjo Eras; H. and C. Franken; Margriet Gijsen-van den Bosch; Stijn van Gils (B); Josien de Haan; Jan van Haren; Marian and Nico Hermans; Dirk de Jong; Jolanda Kamsteeg; the G. Kemps family; R. Key; Marianne Krans; R.C.B. Kreuger; Judith Kroon; the Laberté family; Trudy van Lieshout; B.G.A.W. Maton; J. van Nierop; A. van Oirschot; R. Perfors; Thea Post; Arie and Marja Scherphof; A. and E. van de Schouw; P. and A. van der Sluis; Ankie Somers; Cor Streutjens; Margreet Swen; R. Tulen; Michel Vatin (Fr); Annette Wijnsouw.

Gundogs and retrievers

J. and D. Andringa; Gitte Ariëns; Gerard Beaumont (Fr); Bert van de Berg; Jan and Brigitte van de Berg; Esther Booker; Patrick Cazovlat (Fr); M. Cat; A. van Dijk; Michel Ducoin (Fr); Wilma Firet; Inge Fischer (Lux); Rainer T. Georgii (Lux); Jolanda van Gils; A. de Goede-van den Burg; Marie-Madeleine van Grinsven; U.R. Haccou; Ellen Hagendijk; the Hartog family; Sasha van Hekke; Hazel Huijbregts-Kingham; Mr Kaleghi; A.T. Kamer; G. and R. Kleynen; Anja Klinkenberg; the Knol family; H. Konings; Jaap Kraal; J. Kugel; Marion Kühn; R. Lochs-Romans; J. Luyks; Tonnie Oomen; Kees Oostenbrink; J.P. and V. Perennec (Fr); the Van de Poel family; A. Roefs; Toon and Sjannie Roefs-de Kok; M. Roeterdink; Rolf and Mieke Sorber; Mme. Sotteau (Fr); M. Ummelen; C.N. van Veen-van de Vos; Henk-Jan Wesselink; Marc Wynn; C. Zuydeweg-Roxs.

Toy and other miniature dogs

H. Beeks; Hans Bleeker; Anita van Boheemen; M.W.A.H. Cooijmans; Mrs van Deursen; Arie Dijkhuizen; A. van Dongen; Claudia van Dongen; A. Duin; C.E. Goesting-Meester; Ellen Hagendijk; Fernande Harnist (Fr); T. Hinten; A.P.M. van de Horst; Jetty van der Hulst; H.R. Jacobs; Reina Jansen; Wim and Ria Jansen; R. Janssen-Spits; M. Kavelaars; J. and E. Kloosterhof; T. Koster; D.A. Kuyper-Schuller; J. van Lieshout; H.M. van Luijken; Pierre Maisonneuve (Fr); Erwin Manders; Meta Meijer; Jan den Otter; Mr & Mme Pelletier (Fr); Bianca Pijpers; W. van de Zanden; J.J.M. van Rijn; M. de Ruiter; B. and Chr. Schiltman-van Ooijen; Yvonne Schultz; Mrs Tang; J. Tekelenburg; J. Timmers; C.N. van Veen-van de Vos; E. Verhoef;

Dandie Dinmont Terrier

Ans Verschuren; A. Vink-Dekker; Mrs de Wit-Peemen.

Sighthounds

J.M. Cornelisse; Mrs Devaux (Fr); Mrs Germain (Fr); Anita M.T.H. Gielisse; Jennifer Gielisse; Sandra van de Graaf; Helene Guelfi (Fr); Jean-Luc Guerlot (Fr); E. van der Have-van Dipten; K. Hesseling; A. and J. Hoffman; S. and G. Jipping; Henk Joffer; Monika Kessler (Switz); Josette Lalemend (Fr); Mr Lemouzy (Fr); Phil Morgan; Jean-Michel Pothet (Fr); the Oudendijk family; S. van Rij; Carla Thepen; C.N. van Veen-van de Vos; John Zoll.

Tibetan Mastiffs

White German Shepherd

Breeds that are not recognized

Elly van de Bruggen; Marita van Enckevort; S. Gademann; J.D. van Ginneke; Karin Jenniskens; A. Klerken; A. Monster; H.L. Noordhoek; Rob and Ingrid van Olderen; L. Toetenel; Niels Visser; the Wisse family.

Epagneul Nain Papillon

Dachshund

Thanks are also due to all the breed societies, judges, breeders and breed specialists who have made important contributions to ensure accurate descriptions of the breeds in question and who have provided additional information where necessary.

The author particularly wishes to thank Annet Wouters, Lilian Zurendonk and Ina Peters, who were able to mobilize many of the dogs pictured and their owners.

Finally, thanks are due to the Stichting Vrienden der Geldersche Kasteelen, Arnhem, for the use of the castle grounds of Kasteel Ammersoyen, where some of the photographs were taken.

Index